ENDANGERED SPECIES: PROTECTING BIODIVERSITY

ISSN 1930-3319

ENDANGERED SPECIES: PROTECTING BIODIVERSITY

Kim Masters Evans

INFORMATION PLUS® REFERENCE SERIES
Formerly Published by Information Plus, Wylie, Texas

GALE
CENGAGE Learning·

Farmington Hills, Mich • San Francisco • New York • Waterville, Maine
Meriden, Conn • Mason, Ohio • Chicago

GALE
CENGAGE Learning

Endangered Species: Protecting Biodiversity

Kim Masters Evans

Kepos Media, Inc.: Steven Long and
Janice Jorgensen, Series Editors

Project Editors: Laura Avery, Tracie Moy

Rights Acquisition and Management: Lynn Vagg

Composition: Evi Abou-El-Seoud, Mary Beth
Trimper

Manufacturing: Rita Wimberley

Gale
27500 Drake Rd.
Farmington Hills, MI 48331-3535

ISBN-13: 978-0-7876-5103-9 (set)
ISBN-13: 978-1-57302-697-0

ISSN 1930-3319

This title is also available as an e-book.
ISBN-13: 978-1-57302-674-1 (set)
Contact your Gale sales representative for ordering information.

Printed in the United States of America
1 2 3 4 5 6 7 18 17 16 15 14

TABLE OF CONTENTS

PREFACE

Endangered Species: Protecting Biodiversity is part of the *Information Plus Reference Series*. The purpose of each volume of the series is to present the latest facts on a topic of pressing concern in modern American life. These topics include the most controversial and studied social issues of the 21st century: abortion, capital punishment, care for the elderly, crime, health care, the environment, immigration, race and ethnicity, social welfare, women, youth, and many more. Although this series is written especially for high school and undergraduate students, it is an excellent resource for anyone in need of factual information on current affairs.

By presenting the facts, it is the intention of Gale, Cengage Learning to provide its readers with everything they need to reach an informed opinion on current issues. To that end, there is a particular emphasis in this series on the presentation of scientific studies, surveys, and statistics. These data are generally presented in the form of tables, charts, and other graphics placed within the text of each book. Every graphic is directly referred to and carefully explained in the text. The source of each graphic is presented within the graphic itself. The data used in these graphics are drawn from the most reputable and reliable sources, such as from the various branches of the U.S. government and from private organizations and associations. Every effort has been made to secure the most recent information available. Readers should bear in mind that many major studies take years to conduct and that additional years often pass before the data from these studies are made available to the public. Therefore, in many cases the most recent information available in 2014 is from 2011 or 2012. Older statistics are sometimes presented as well, if they are landmark studies or of particular interest and no more-recent information exists.

Although statistics are a major focus of the *Information Plus Reference Series*, they are by no means its only content. Each book also presents the widely held posi-

tions and important ideas that shape how the book's subject is discussed in the United States. These positions are explained in detail and, where possible, in the words of their proponents. Some of the other material to be found in these books includes historical background, descriptions of major events related to the subject, relevant laws and court cases, and examples of how these issues play out in American life. Some books also feature primary documents, or have pro and con debate sections that provide the words and opinions of prominent Americans on both sides of a controversial topic. All material is presented in an evenhanded and unbiased manner; readers will never be encouraged to accept one view of an issue over another.

HOW TO USE THIS BOOK

The status of endangered species is an issue of concern both for many Americans and for people around the world. In particular, balancing biodiversity with economics has led to much controversy. This book looks at what has been done to protect endangered species in the United States and around the world and examines the debate over what future actions are warranted.

Endangered Species: Protecting Biodiversity consists of 10 chapters and three appendixes. Each chapter is devoted to a particular aspect of endangered species. For a summary of the information that is covered in each chapter, please see the synopses that are provided in the Table of Contents. Chapters generally begin with an overview of the basic facts and background information on the chapter's topic, then proceed to examine subtopics of particular interest. For example, Chapter 1: Extinction and Endangered Species begins by describing how species are named by scientists. It then discusses historical mass extinctions and presents data regarding modern species loss. The importance and various realms of biodiversity are examined in terms of the consequences of extinction to ecosystems and humans. The numbers of imperiled species worldwide and in the United States are summarized based on data from the International Union for Conservation of Nature and U.S. government sources. The benefits and costs to humans of saving endangered species are reviewed with a focus on practical factors, such as commerce and other economic considerations. The chapter ends with brief descriptions of the U.S. entities—government and private—that work to conserve endangered species and the international programs and agreements that are in place to help prevent extinctions from happening. Readers can find their way through a chapter by looking for the section and subsection headings, which are clearly set off from the text. They can also refer to the book's extensive Index if they already know what they are looking for.

Statistical Information

The tables and figures featured throughout *Endangered Species: Protecting Biodiversity* will be of particular use to readers in learning about this issue. The tables and figures represent an extensive collection of the most recent and important statistics on endangered species, as well as related issues—for example, graphics cover the number of endangered species and the reasons for their endangerment, foreign endangered and threatened plant species, and the life cycle of Pacific salmon. The photographs illustrate some of the most threatened species on the earth, such as the red wolf. Gale, Cengage Learning believes that making this information available to readers is the most important way to fulfill the goal of this book: to help readers understand the issues and controversies surrounding endangered species and reach their own conclusions.

Each table or figure has a unique identifier appearing above it, for ease of identification and reference. Titles for the tables and figures explain their purpose. At the end of each table or figure, the original source of the data is provided.

To help readers understand these often complicated statistics, all tables and figures are explained in the text. References in the text direct readers to the relevant statistics. Furthermore, the contents of all tables and figures are fully indexed. Please see the opening section of the Index at the back of this volume for a description of how to find tables and figures within it.

Appendixes

Besides the main body text and images, *Endangered Species: Protecting Biodiversity* has three appendixes. The first is the Important Names and Addresses directory. Here, readers will find contact information for a number of government and private organizations that can provide further information on aspects of endangered species. The second appendix is the Resources section, which can also assist readers in conducting their own research. In this section, the author and editors of *Endangered Species: Protecting Biodiversity* describe some of the sources that were most useful during the compilation of this book. The final appendix is the detailed Index. It has been greatly expanded from previous editions and should make it even easier to find specific topics in this book.

COMMENTS AND SUGGESTIONS

The editors of the *Information Plus Reference Series* welcome your feedback on *Endangered Species: Protecting Biodiversity*. Please direct all correspondence to:

Editors
Information Plus Reference Series
27500 Drake Rd.
Farmington Hills, MI 48331-3535

CHAPTER 1
EXTINCTION AND ENDANGERED SPECIES

The earth is richly supplied with different types of living organisms that coexist in their environments, forming complex, interrelated communities. Living organisms depend on one another for nutrients, shelter, and other benefits. The extinction of any one species can set off a chain reaction that affects many other species, particularly if the loss occurs near the bottom of the food chain. For example, the extinction of a particular insect or plant might seem inconsequential. Small animals, however, may feed on that resource. The loss can threaten the survival of these creatures and the larger predators that prey on them. Extinction can have a ripple effect that spreads throughout nature.

Besides its biological consequences, extinction poses a moral dilemma for humans, which is the only species capable of saving other species. The presence of humans on the planet has affected all other life forms. Human lifestyles have proven incompatible with the survival of some other species. Purposeful efforts have eliminated animals that prey on people, livestock, and crops or pose any threat to human livelihoods. Some wild animals have been decimated by human desire for meat, hides, fur, and other body parts. Likewise, the demand for land, water, timber, and other natural resources has left many wild plants and animals with little to no suitable habitat. Humans have also affected nature by introducing nonnative species and producing pollutants that negatively impact the environment and climate. The combination of these anthropogenic (human-related) effects with natural obstacles that limit survival, such as disease or low birth rates, have proven to be too much for some species to overcome. They have no chance of survival without human help.

As a result, societies have difficult choices to make about the amount of effort and money they are willing to spend to keep imperiled species from becoming extinct. Will people accept limits on their property rights, recreational activities, and means of livelihood to save a plant or animal? Should saving popular species such as whales and dolphins take priority over saving annoying or feared species? Is it the responsibility of humans to save every life form from disappearing, or is extinction an inevitable part of nature, in which the strong survive and the weak perish? These are some of the difficult questions that people face as they ponder the fate of other species living on this planet.

DEFINING AND NAMING LIFE ON THE EARTH

Living organisms are named and categorized according to a taxonomy, a hierarchical system of order that is based on the natural relationships among life forms. Table 1.1 shows the taxonomic chart for blue whales, the largest creatures on the earth. They are described by eight taxonomic levels ending with "species." A species is a group of organisms that are capable of interbreeding with one another. A subspecies (abbreviated ssp.) ranks immediately below species and is a population of a particular geographical region that is genetically different from other populations of the same species, but can still interbreed with them.

Animals and plants are identified by their common names and by unique scientific names. Some organisms have more than one common name. For example, the mountain lion is also called a puma or cougar. To avoid confusion, scientific bodies have established a nomenclature (naming) system for life forms. This system is based on the example set by Carolus Linnaeus (1707–1778), a Swedish naturalist who published classifications for thousands of plants and animals. Linnaeus popularized a binary naming system in which the first word names an organism's genus (a group of closely related species). This is followed by a specific epithet (a descriptive word or phrase) that differentiates one species from another. Linnaeus used Latin words in his nomenclature because

TABLE 1.1

Taxonomic chart for blue whales

Classification	Blue whale example	Explanation
Kingdom	Animalia	Whales belong to the kingdom Animalia because whales have many cells, ingest food, and are formed from a "blastula" (from a fertilized egg).
Phylum	Chordata	An animal from the phylum Chordata has a spinal cord and gill pouches.
Class	Mammalia	Whales and other mammals are warm blooded, have glands to provide milk for their offspring, and have a four-chambered heart.
Order	Cetacea	Cetaceans are mammals that live completely in the water.
[Suborder]	Mysticeti	Whales that belong to the suborder Mysticeti have baleen plates (big filters in their mouths) rather than teeth.
Family	Balaenidae	The family Balaenidae, also called rorqual whales. They have pleats around their throat that allow them to hold lots of water (which contains their food).
Genus	*Balaenoptera*	A genus is a group of species that are more closely related to one another than any group in the family. *Balaenoptera* refers to the genus.
Species	*Musculus*	A species is a grouping of individuals that interbreed successfully. The blue whale species name is *musculus*.

SOURCE: "The Chart below Is a Sample Taxonomic Chart for Blue Whales," in *What Is Taxonomy?* National Oceanic and Atmospheric Administration, Alaska Fisheries Science Center, National Marine Mammal Laboratory, undated, http://www.afsc.noaa.gov/nmml/education/taxonomy.php (accessed November 1, 2013)

Latin was the preferred language for scientific publications during the 18th century.

Modern convention dictates that the scientist who first describes an organism in a scholarly publication chooses the organism's scientific name. The latter must be in Latin or contain words that have been rendered to appear Latin. Scientific names are either italicized or underlined in print. The first letter of the genus is capitalized; the specific epithet is in lower case.

Subspecies are indicated in scientific nomenclature with an additional term. For example, the scientific name of the blue whale is *Balaenoptera musculus*. A subspecies, the pygmy blue whale, is called *Balaenoptera musculus brevicauda*. Genus reassignments are indicated with the "=" sign in a scientific name. When the royal snail was discovered in 1977, it was assigned to the genus *Marstonia*. Ten years later biologists decided the snail was more properly a member of the genus *Pyrgulopsis*. Thus, the scientific name of the royal snail is written as *Pyrgulopsis (=Marstonia) ogmorhaphe*. When the species is not known for an organism of known genus, the scientific name is written with sp. (indicating a single species) or spp. (indicating multiple species) as the specific epithet. The latter format is also used when referring to all species in a genus. For example, *Pyrgulopsis* spp. refers to all species within the genus *Pyrgulopsis*.

The rules governing scientific names for animals are overseen by the International Commission on Zoological Nomenclature, which is headquartered in London, England. The International Code of Botanical Nomenclature for plants is managed by the International Botanical Congress (IBC), a meeting of botanists from around the world that is held every six years. The most recent IBC took place in Australia in 2011, and the next will be in China in 2017.

ASSESSING SPECIES

The question of how many different species exist on the earth is hotly debated by scientists. Estimates range from 3 million to more than 100 million. Based in Switzerland, the International Union for Conservation of Nature (IUCN) is the world's largest conservation organization. According to the IUCN (http://cms.iucn.org/about/union/members/index.cfm), in February 2014 it had more than 1,200 members and 11,000 scientific experts working in over 160 countries "to help the world find pragmatic solutions to our most pressing environment and development challenges."

Since 1960 the IUCN has compiled the *Red List of Threatened Species* (http://www.iucnredlist.org/), which examines the status of species worldwide. The IUCN indicates in *Red List of Threatened Species Version 2013.2* (http://www.iucnredlist.org/about/summary-statistics) that as of November 2013 more than 1.7 million species had been officially described. The largest groups were insects (1 million), flowering plants (268,000), arachnids (e.g., spiders; 102,000), and mollusks (e.g., clams; 85,000). Mammals, which are probably the best-studied group—and the one that includes humans—had 5,506 described organisms.

EXTINCTION

A species is described as extinct when no living members remain. Scientists know from the study of fossils that dinosaurs, mammoths, saber-toothed cats, and countless other animal and plant species that once lived on the earth no longer exist. These species have "died out," or become extinct.

Mass Extinctions

In the billions of years since life began on the earth, species have formed, existed, and then become extinct. Scientists call the natural extinction of a few species per million years a background, or normal, rate. When the extinction rate doubles for many different groups of plants and animals at the same time, this is described as a mass extinction. Mass extinctions have occurred infrequently and, in general, have been attributed to major cataclysmic geological or astronomical events. Five mass extinctions have occurred during the last 600 million years. These episodes, known as the Big Five, occurred at the end of five geologic periods:

- Ordovician (505 million to 440 million years ago)
- Devonian (410 million to 360 million years ago)
- Permian (286 million to 245 million years ago)
- Triassic (245 million to 208 million years ago)
- Cretaceous (146 million to 65 million years ago)

After each mass extinction the floral (plant) and faunal (animal) composition of the earth changed drastically. The largest mass extinction on record occurred at the end of the Permian, when an estimated 90% to 95% of all species became extinct. The Cretaceous extinction, which is hypothesized to have resulted from the collision of an asteroid with the earth, saw the demise of many species of dinosaurs.

The Sixth Mass Extinction?

Scientists estimate that hundreds, or even thousands, of species are being lost annually worldwide. This suggests that another mass extinction is taking place. However, the current extinction is not associated with a cataclysmic physical event. Rather, the heightened extinction rate has coincided with the success and spread of human beings. Researchers predict that as humans continue to destroy and alter natural habitats, create pollution, introduce nonnative species, and contribute to global climate change, the extinction rate will continue to rise. The United Nations (UN) concludes in *Global Biodiversity Outlook 3* (2010, http://www.cbd.int/doc/publications/gbo/gbo3-final-en.pdf), the most recent report on this topic as of February 2014, that "the news is not good. We continue to lose biodiversity at a rate never before seen in history—extinction rates may be up to 1,000 times higher than the historical background rate." The UN warns that continuing this trend could "catastrophically reduce the capacity of ecosystems" to provide humans with food, fresh water, and other essential services.

RECENT EXTINCTION STATISTICS. In *IUCN Red List Categories and Criteria, Version 3.1 Second Edition* (2012, http://jr.iucnredlist.org/documents/redlist_cats_crit_en.pdf), the IUCN notes that it considers a species extinct "when there is no reasonable doubt that the last individual has died." As of November 2013, the IUCN (http://www.iucnredlist.org/documents/summarystatistics/2013_1_RL_Stats_Table_3a.pdf) counted 709 animal species as extinct. Another 32 animal species were classified as extinct in the wild, meaning that no individuals were believed to exist in the wild, but some individuals were being cultivated, kept in

captivity, or otherwise maintained "well outside the past range." Of the extinct animal species, the largest numbers were gastropods, such as snails (281 species), birds (130 species), and mammals (77 species). The IUCN (November 2013, http://cmsdocs.s3.amazonaws.com/summarystats/2013_2_RL_Stats_Table3bc.pdf) also counted 90 plant species as extinct and 29 plant species as extinct in the wild.

One recent animal extinction noted by the IUCN is the Alaotra grebe (*Tachybaptus rufolavatus*), a bird that was found exclusively in and around Lake Alaotra in Madagascar. The organization (http://www.iucnredlist.org/details/22696558/0) states that surveys conducted since 2009 have found no individuals. Thus, the IUCN categorized the species as extinct in 2012.

Resurrecting Extinct Species?

In the 1993 film *Jurassic Park* scientists use ancient deoxyribonucleic acid (DNA) that was preserved in amber to clone dozens of prehistoric dinosaur species. With the advent of modern genetic science the possibility of resurrecting extinct species has left the realm of science fiction and is fast becoming a reality. According to Charles Q. Choi, in "First Extinct-Animal Clone Created" (*National Geographic News*, February 10, 2009), in 2003 scientists conducted the first-known cloning of an extinct subspecies: *Capra pyrenaica pyrenaica*—commonly called the Pyrenean ibex. Ibex are wild goats. The Pyrenean ibex went extinct in 2000. Choi indicates that hundreds of clone embryos were created using frozen skin cells that were taken from the last living Pyrenean ibex. They were implanted in Spanish ibex and ibex-goat hybrids. Only seven of the embryos developed into fetuses, and only one of the fetuses survived to full term, but it died "immediately after birth" because of lung abnormalities. Choi notes that "such abnormalities are common in cloning" due to irregularities that arise during DNA transfer.

Cloning as a means of resurrecting extinct species is fraught with challenges and is highly controversial. Scientists note that many nonclosely related members of a species would have to be reproduced for the species as a whole to survive. The resurrection of long-extinct species, such as the wooly mammoth, is even more daunting because of DNA deterioration over time and the lack of suitable surrogate mothers. Cloning also raises ethical questions, for example, the morality of treating animals as objects for scientific manipulation and experimentation.

U.S. HISTORY: SOME EXTINCTIONS AND SOME CLOSE CALLS

The colonization of the North American continent by European settlers severely depleted the ranks of some native wild species. The introduction of livestock brought new animal diseases that devastated some native animals.

FIGURE 1.1

Bison (or American buffaloes) are the largest terrestrial animals in North America. © *Steve Degenhardt/Shutterstock.*

Widespread hunting and trapping led to the demise of other species. During the early 1800s the United States was home to millions, perhaps billions, of passenger pigeons. These migratory birds traveled in enormous flocks and were extremely popular with hunters. By the beginning of the 20th century the species was virtually exterminated. The last known passenger pigeon died in the Cincinnati Zoo in 1914. The heath hen, a small wild fowl native to the United States and once very abundant, was wiped out of existence by 1932. Stocks of other animals—beaver, elk, and bison (American buffalo; see Figure 1.1)—were driven to the brink of extinction, but saved by conservation efforts.

The U.S. Fish and Wildlife Service (USFWS) tracks imperiled animal and plant species under mandates set out in the Endangered Species Act (ESA), which was passed in 1973 and is described in detail in Chapter 2. Through 2013, 10 U.S. species had officially been declared extinct under the act:

- Tecopa pupfish (*Cyprinodon nevadensis calidae*); a fish species—1982
- Blue pike (*Stizostedion vitreum glacum*); a fish species—1983
- Longjaw cisco (*Coregonus alpenae*); a fish species—1983
- Santa Barbara song sparrow (*Melospiza melodia graminea*); a bird species—1983
- Sampson's pearlymussel (*Epioblasma sampsoni*); a clam species—1984
- Amistad gambusia (*Gambusia amistadensis*); a fish species—1987

- Dusky seaside sparrow (*Ammodramus maritimus nigrescens*); a bird species—1990
- Guam broadbill (*Myiagra freycineti*); a bird species—2004
- Mariana mallard (*Anas oustaleti*); a bird species—2004
- Caribbean monk seal (*Monachus tropicalis*); a marine mammal species—2008

In addition, in March 2011 USFWS researchers recommended in *Eastern Puma (=Cougar) (*Puma concolor couguar*): 5-Year Review: Summary and Evaluation* (http://ecos.fws.gov/docs/five_year_review/doc3611.pdf) that the eastern puma (*Puma concolor couguar*), a terrestrial mammal, be officially declared extinct. However, as of February 2014 that designation had not yet become final.

CONSEQUENCES OF EXTINCTION: LOSS OF BIODIVERSITY

In general, the major consequence of extinction is the loss of biodiversity. The term *biodiversity* is short for biological diversity, and it refers to the variability among all living organisms. In 1992 representatives from dozens of nations around the world met in Rio de Janeiro, Brazil, at the UN Conference on Environment and Development. One of the outcomes was the Convention on Biological Diversity (CBD), an international agreement devoted to protecting the earth's biodiversity. The CBD (http://www.cbd.int/convention/articles/default.shtml?a=cbd-02) notes that biodiversity encompasses three interconnected realms: ecosystems, species, and genetics.

Biodiversity Realms

Ecosystems are natural areas that include communities of living organisms. The earth contains a wide variety of ecosystem types including forests, swamps, deserts, and oceans. Different ecosystems provide different habitats for different types of plants and animals that have evolved to thrive in their environments. Ecosystem variety is important to maintaining a rich array of species across the planet.

The organisms within an ecosystem are affected by the physical environment in which they live, such as the weather, the climate (weather conditions over the long term), and the air, water, and soil conditions. In addition, the organisms interact with each other. Scientists have shown that habitats with species diversity are more stable—that is, better able to adjust to and recover from disturbances. This is because different species may perform overlapping functions in a biologically diverse ecosystem. Ecosystems with a great variety of species tend to best support sustainable food sources. Dramatic declines in one or more species in the ecosystem can greatly stress the remaining species. This is true at multiple levels of the food chain. For example, the disappearance of prey species (e.g., deer) harms predator species (e.g., wolves) that depend on them for food. In contrast, a dramatic decline in predator populations can allow prey to overpopulate to the point that the available food is not sufficient to sustain them.

Biodiversity is also important at the genetic level. There are natural genetic differences between members of the same species that affect individual characteristics, such as coloring, resistance to disease, and behavioral traits. Genetic variation within a species is desirable because it increases the chances that at least some members will survive environmental changes or other stressors. For example, if all members of a species are equally susceptible to a disease, then the entire population can be decimated by the sickness. If the members have varying resistance levels, then some will succumb, but others will survive to perpetuate the species.

High genetic variation also lowers the chances that problems associated with inbreeding will occur. Inbreeding is mating between closely related individuals with extremely similar genetic material. It is almost certain that if one of these individuals has a gene disorder, the other individual will also have it. This disorder might not cause any notable problems in the parents, but it could become concentrated in the offspring and cause serious health problems for them. Many animal and plant species naturally avoid inbreeding. For example, studies show that humans and some other animal species appear to rely on genetic markers (such as the major histocompatibility complex—a group of molecules built into the immune system) to avoid mating with individuals that are genetically similar to themselves. In addition, humans have social and cultural taboos against inbreeding with their closest relatives. However, some animal species—particularly those in isolated and/or small populations—may engage in inbreeding when there are no other viable mating choices.

There is a certain lower limit to the population of some species, particularly those that are isolated in location. If the population falls too low, the remaining individuals will be so closely related that any inherent gene problems can kill off the resulting offspring and ultimately wipe out the entire species.

Extinction Consequences for Specific Species

It is difficult to quantify the consequences of the extinction of a particular species. Every species plays some kind of role in its particular ecosystem. In some cases, these roles are quite evident and easily identified as beneficial. For example, as described in Chapter 9, elephants dig water holes, keep forest growth in check, and open up grasslands that support other species. These activities are important to maintaining the savanna habitats. As such,

elephants are called a "keystone species" because other species in their ecosystems are highly dependent on them and would suffer major impacts if they disappeared. As explained in Chapter 7, the desert tortoise is another keystone species because the burrows it makes for itself provide habitat for multiple other desert animals. Some actions by one species indirectly benefit other species. Chapter 3 notes that sea otters prey on sea urchins, an aquatic creature that consumes seaweed such as kelp. Keeping the sea urchins from overpopulating allows kelp forests to spread, providing valuable habitat and sustenance to many other aquatic species.

In addition, there are a multitude of complex interactions between species of different types. For example, many plants depend on animals to propagate. Bees visit flowers for nourishment and in the process help flowers reproduce by transferring pollen from one location to another. Birds and other animals that consume berries and seeds and then expel them in their waste unwittingly help plants spread. Losing any of the species involved in these interactions harms the other species involved.

HOW MANY SPECIES ARE ENDANGERED?

As noted earlier, the IUCN compiles the annual *Red List of Threatened Species*, in which it examines the status of species worldwide. The so-called Red List categorizes species based on the level of risk of their extinction in the wild as follows:

• Critically endangered—extremely high risk

• Endangered—very high risk

• Vulnerable—high risk

The IUCN refers to species in all three of these categories as "threatened" species.

Determining how many species of plants and animals are imperiled is difficult. In fact, only a small fraction of the species in existence have even been identified and named, let alone studied in detail. In *Red List of Threatened Species Version 2013.2*, the IUCN designated 21,286 species as threatened in 2013. Nearly 72,000 species were examined out of the 1.7 million species that the IUCN considers "described species." Thus, only 4% of all known species were evaluated. Further study will likely result in many more species being added to the Red List.

In the United States imperiled species are identified and listed as either endangered or threatened in accordance with the ESA. Endangered species are at risk of extinction through all or a significant portion of their natural habitats. Threatened species are likely to become endangered in the future. Management at the federal level of listed species is handled by the USFWS and the National Marine Fisheries Service (NMFS). The USFWS is an agency of the U.S. Department of the Interior and oversees terrestrial (land-based) and freshwater species. The NMFS is an agency of the National Oceanic and Atmospheric Administration under the U.S. Department of Commerce and has jurisdiction for marine (ocean-dwelling) species and those that are anadromous (migrate between the ocean and freshwater).

Table 1.2 tabulates the number of ESA-listed species as of November 2013. Of the 1,266 animal species, 644 were found in the United States. Among these, 468 were endangered and 176 were threatened. Among animals, the greatest numbers of endangered and threatened species occurred among fish, birds, and mammals. Of the 875 plant species, 872 were found in the United States. Among these, 720 were endangered and 152

were threatened. Nearly all the endangered plants were flowering plants.

Figure 1.2 shows the number of U.S. species listed per calendar year between 1967 and November 2013. The peak year was 1994, when 127 species were listed. As of November 2013, 83 species had been added to the list during 2013.

Within the United States, endangered and threatened species are not evenly distributed but are clustered in specific geographical areas. Table 1.3 shows the number of listed species in each state as of November 2013. It should be noted that some species are found in multiple states. Four states (Hawaii, California, Alabama, and Florida) each had over 100 listed species. Despite its

TABLE 1.2

Count of endangered and threatened species and U.S. species with recovery plans, November 1, 2013

Group	United States* Endangered	Threatened	Total listings	Foreign Endangered	Threatened	Total listings	Total listings (U.S. and foreign)	U.S. listings with active recovery plans
Mammals	70	16	86	256	20	276	362	62
Birds	80	16	96	212	16	228	324	86
Reptiles	14	22	36	70	20	90	126	35
Amphibians	18	11	29	8	1	9	38	17
Fishes	85	71	156	11	1	12	168	102
Clams	75	13	88	2	0	2	90	71
Snails	33	12	45	1	0	1	46	29
Millipedes	0	0	0	0	0	0	0	0
Insects	60	10	70	4	0	4	74	41
Arachnids	12	0	12	0	0	0	12	12
Crustaceans	21	3	24	0	0	0	24	18
Annelid worms	0	0	0	0	0	0	0	0
Flatworms and roundworms	0	0	0	0	0	0	0	0
Hydroids	0	0	0	0	0	0	0	0
Sponges	0	0	0	0	0	0	0	0
Corals	0	2	2	0	0	0	2	0
Animal totals	**468**	**176**	**644**	**564**	**58**	**622**	**1,266**	**473**
Flowering plants	688	149	837	1	0	1	838	641
Conifers and cycads	2	1	3	0	2	2	5	3
Ferns and allies	28	2	30	0	0	0	30	26
Lichens	2	0	2	0	0	0	2	2
Plant totals	**720**	**152**	**872**	**1**	**2**	**3**	**875**	**672**
Grand totals	**1,188**	**328**	**1,516**	**565**	**60**	**625**	**2,141**	**1,145**

The U.S. species counted more than once are:

• Plover, piping (Charadriusmelodus)
• Salamander, California tiger (Ambystomacaliforniense)
• Salmon, chinook (Oncorhynchus (=Salmo) tshawytscha)
• Salmon, chum (Oncorhynchus (=Salmo) keta)
• Salmon, coho (Oncorhynchus (=Salmo) kisutch)
• Salmon, sockeye (Oncorhynchus (=Salmo) nerka)
• Sea-lion, Steller (Eumetopiasjubatus)
• Sea turtle, green (Cheloniamydas)
• Sea turtle, loggerhead (Carettacaretta)
• Steelhead (Oncorhynchus (=Salmo) mykiss)
• Tern, roseate (Sterna dougallii dougallii)

The foreign species counted more than once are:

• Argali (Ovisammon)
• Caiman, broad-snouted (Caiman latirostris)
• Chimpanzee (Pan troglodytes)
• Crocodile, saltwater (Crocodylusporosus)
• Dugong (Dugong dugon)
• Leopard (Pantherapardus)
• Sea turtle, loggerhead (Carettacaretta)

Notes: 18 animal species (11 in the United States* and 7 foreign) are counted more than once in the above table, primarily because these animals have distinct population segments (each with its own individual listing status).
There are a total of 593 distinct active (draft and final) recovery plans. Some recovery plans cover more than one species, and a few species have separate plans covering different parts of their ranges. This count includes only plans generated by the U.S. Fish and Wildlife Service (USFWS) (or jointly by the USFWS and National Marine Fisheries Service), and only listed species that occur in the United States.
*United States listings include those populations in which the United States shares jurisdiction with another nation.

SOURCE: "Summary of Listed Species Listed Populations and Recovery Plans as of Fri, 01 Nov 2013 16:05:31 GMT," in *Species Reports*, U.S. Department of the Interior, U.S. Fish and Wildlife Service, November 1, 2013, http://ecos.fws.gov/tess_public/pub/Boxscore.do (accessed November 1, 2013)

FIGURE 1.2

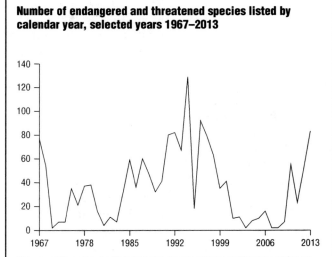

Number of endangered and threatened species listed by calendar year, selected years 1967–2013

Note: As of November 1, 2013. Experimental populations and foreign species are not included. Distinct population segments (DPS) are included, as are species listed due to similarity of appearance and joint U.S./foreign listings. Species listed by National Marine Fisheries Service (NMFS) are also included. The effective date (as given in the Federal Register notice) is used to determine in which calendar year a species is counted.

SOURCE: Adapted from "U.S. Federal Endangered and Threatened Species by Calendar Year," in *Species Reports*, U.S. Department of the Interior, U.S. Fish and Wildlife Service, November 1, 2013, http://ecos.fws.gov/tess_public/pub/speciesCountByYear.jsp (accessed November 1, 2013)

TABLE 1.3

Number of endangered and threatened species, by state or territory, November 1, 2013

Alabama	137 listings
Alaska	25 listings
Arizona	66 listings
Arkansas	35 listings
California	317 listings
Colorado	35 listings
Connecticut	20 listings
Delaware	23 listings
District of Columbia	7 listings
Florida	128 listings
Georgia	76 listings
Hawaii	431 listings
Idaho	21 listings
Illinois	44 listings
Indiana	37 listings
Iowa	23 listings
Kansas	21 listings
Kentucky	54 listings
Louisiana	31 listings
Maine	16 listings
Maryland	30 listings
Massachusetts	26 listings
Michigan	28 listings
Minnesota	20 listings
Mississippi	46 listings
Missouri	40 listings
Montana	15 listings
Nebraska	19 listings
Nevada	41 listings
New Hampshire	15 listings
New Jersey	25 listings
New Mexico	50 listings
New York	33 listings
North Carolina	64 listings
North Dakota	10 listings
Ohio	35 listings
Oklahoma	24 listings
Oregon	61 listings
Pennsylvania	27 listings
Rhode Island	17 listings
South Carolina	43 listings
South Dakota	12 listings
Tennessee	104 listings
Texas	102 listings
Utah	44 listings
Vermont	12 listings
Virginia	70 listings
Washington	50 listings
West Virginia	28 listings
Wisconsin	22 listings
Wyoming	18 listings
American Samoa	3 listings
Guam	13 listings
Northern Mariana Islands	10 listings
Puerto Rico	77 listings
Virgin Islands	16 listings
Outlying Caribbean Islands	0 listings
Outlying Pacific Islands	0 listings

SOURCE: "Species Listed in Each State Based on Published Historic Range and Population Data," in *Species Reports*, U.S. Department of the Interior, U.S. Fish and Wildlife Service, November 1, 2013, http://ecos.fws.gov/tess_public/pub/stateListing.jsp (accessed November 1, 2013)

small size, Hawaii harbored 431 listed species, more than any other state. This is because a significant proportion of Hawaiian plant and animal life is endemic (found nowhere else on the earth). Endemism is dangerous for imperiled species for a variety of reasons. A single calamitous event, such as a hurricane, earthquake, or disease epidemic, could wipe out the entire population at one time. The likelihood of inbreeding and resulting genetic problems is also higher for species that are geographically isolated.

SAVING ENDANGERED SPECIES: BENEFITS AND COSTS TO SOCIETY

As described earlier, saving endangered species and preventing their extinction has numerous benefits to the ecosystems in which they live. Extinction can also negatively affect human society both directly and indirectly in areas such as aesthetics (e.g., the beauty of nature), education, and scientific study. Wildlife also has practical value to society in terms of recreation and tourism.

This is evidenced by the popularity of hunting, fishing, and wildlife viewing. Later in this chapter, national programs will be described that have designated millions of acres across the country as national parks, wilderness areas, and wildlife refuges. They are visited by millions of people each year that help support local economies. Other wildlife ventures with economic value include zoos,

safaris, and bird-watching tours. Wild plants and animals have commercial uses in other industries as well. Plants provide the genetic diversity that is used to breed new strains of agricultural crops, and many plants have been used to develop pharmaceutical products. For example, during the 1960s scientists discovered a cancer-fighting chemical called taxol in Pacific yew trees in northwestern forests. At the time, the trees were considered a nuisance species and were destroyed as weeds. If the species had disappeared, then humans would likely not have discovered taxol, which became a major component of the chemotherapy treatments used against some types of cancer.

However, as will be explained in Chapter 2, saving endangered species does have costs. Taxpayer dollars are used to fund agencies that carry out the ESA and state-level laws devoted to imperiled species. In addition, the laws put certain restrictions on what property owners are allowed to do on their own land. Some people believe that humans have a moral obligation to attempt to preserve species in decline regardless of the costs or the potential benefits to humans. This might be called "saving nature for nature's sake." The lawmakers who crafted the ESA in 1973 seemed to have this idealistic viewpoint. The original law did not require economic analyses or consideration of the costs versus the benefits of saving endangered species. Over time, Congress has amended the law to add a few mechanisms for weighing costs against benefits in certain situations. Overall, however, the ESA as it exists in the 21st century continues to reflect the principle that nature should be saved for nature's sake. This makes the law extremely controversial and subject to harsh criticism that it is impractical and favors the welfare of plants and animals over the welfare of human beings. Throughout this book numerous battles are described in which conflicts have arisen over the well-being of an imperiled species versus the interests (chiefly economic) of humans.

Although the overall value of wildlife to society is well recognized, the relative value of specific species to humans is highly variable. In general, the public places high value on some species and not on others. For example, whales and seals are popular animals for which protection measures receive widespread support. By contrast, several species listed under the ESA are considered pests or predators because they pose a threat to human livelihoods or safety. For example, Utah prairie dogs are burrowing animals that produce networks of underground tunnels. The resulting holes and dirt mounds can ruin cropland and trip and injure livestock. The protection of Utah prairie dogs and other imperiled rodents is a source of contention for people who believe that the ESA puts animal interests above human interests. The same debate rages over predators such as wolves and mountain lions that may prey on livestock, pets, and even people.

Under the ESA species are listed for protection based on their biological status (e.g., population, health, and well-being) and the threats against them, not for their importance to humans or the potential costs of protecting them. This does not mean, however, that the ESA process is immune from economic influences. As will be explained in Chapter 2, financial considerations do come into play.

Although the number of species eligible for protection under the ESA skyrocketed from around 100 during the early 1970s to more than 2,000 in 2013, federal funding for the agencies responsible for administering the act has not increased sufficiently to allow them to handle the expansion in the workload. There is a lack of political and public will to fund the activities needed to pursue the very optimistic (and some say unrealistic) goals laid out in the ESA to save all endangered species.

Public Opinion

The Gallup Organization conducts an annual poll on environmental issues. Table 1.4 shows the results from March 2013, when participants were asked to express their level of worry about various environmental problems. Thirty-five percent of those asked expressed a "great deal" of concern and 29% expressed a "fair amount" of concern regarding the extinction of plant and animal species. This placed extinction sixth in terms of the amount of worry about the various environmental problems. As shown in Table 1.5, concern over extinction has generally declined since 2000, when Gallup first polled people about the issue. In 2000, 45% of respondents expressed a "great deal" of concern and 33% expressed a "fair amount" of concern.

U.S. ENTITIES CONSERVING IMPERILED SPECIES

A variety of government and private entities in the United States conduct activities that help conserve imperiled species.

TABLE 1.4

Poll respondents expressing their level of worry regarding environmental problems, March 2013

I'M GOING TO READ YOU A LIST OF ENVIRONMENTAL PROBLEMS. AS I READ EACH ONE, PLEASE TELL ME IF YOU PERSONALLY WORRY ABOUT THIS PROBLEM A GREAT DEAL, A FAIR AMOUNT, ONLY A LITTLE, OR NOT AT ALL. FIRST, HOW MUCH DO YOU PERSONALLY WORRY ABOUT—[ITEMS A–H READ IN RANDOM ORDER, ITEM I READ LAST]?

2013 Mar 7–10 (sorted by "a great deal")	Great deal	Fair amount	Only a little/ not at all
Pollution of drinking water	53	26	20
Contamination of soil and water by toxic waste	46	29	25
Pollution of rivers, lakes, and reservoirs	46	32	22
Air pollution	40	30	29
The loss of tropical rain forests	37	27	36
Extinction of plant and animal species	35	29	35
Climate change	33	24	43
Global warming	33	25	43
Urban sprawl and loss of open spaces	26	28	46

SOURCE: Jeff Jones and Lydia Saad, "I'm going to read you a list of environmental problems. As I read each one, please tell me if you personally worry about this problem a great deal, a fair amount, only a little, or not at all. First, how much do you personally worry about...?" in *Gallup Poll Social Series: Environment*, The Gallup Organization, March 2013, http://www.gallup.com/file/poll/161663/Global_Warming_130408.pdf (accessed November 1, 2013). Copyright © 2013 Gallup, Inc. All rights reserved. The content is used with permission; however, Gallup retains all rights of republication.

TABLE 1.5

Poll respondents expressing their level of worry regarding extinction of plant and animal species, various dates, selected years 2000–13

Extinction of plant and animal species	Great deal	Fair amount	Only a little	Not at all	No opinion
2013 Mar 7–10	35	29	22	13	*
2012 Mar 8–11	36	29	23	12	
2011 Mar 3–6	34	30	23	13	1
2010 Mar 4–7	31	30	24	15	1
2009 Mar 5–8	37	28	22	12	*
2008 Mar 6–9	37	31	20	11	*
2007 Mar 11–14	39	30	19	12	*
2006 Mar 13–16	34	29	23	14	*
2004 Mar 8–11	36	26	23	15	1
2003 Mar 3–5	34	32	21	12	*
2002 Mar 4–7	35	30	22	12	1
2001 Mar 5–7	43	30	19	7	1
2000 Apr 3–9	45	33	14	8	*
Urban sprawl and loss of open spaces					
2013 Mar 7–10	26	28	29	17	*
2011 Mar 3–6	27	30	27	15	1
2008 Mar 6–9	33	35	19	12	*
2001 Mar 5–7	35	34	19	10	2
2000 Apr 3–9	42	31	14	12	1
Climate change					
2013 Mar 7–10	33	24	23	20	*

*less than 0.5%.

Federal Government

As noted earlier, the USFWS and the NMFS conserve endangered and threatened species through the authority of the ESA, which allows them to issue rules and regulations that govern how imperiled species are managed. They also educate the public by maintaining websites and publishing fact sheets and other documents about the issue. Since 2006 Congress has annually declared an Endangered Species Day on which the agencies work with private partners to raise awareness about species conservation. In 2013 the day was celebrated on May 17 and included events around the country.

The USFWS, like many other agencies within the Interior Department, is also responsible for land conservation. Protecting natural ecosystems and habitats helps ensure that imperiled species (and other native plants and animals) have places to flourish. The USFWS manages the National Wildlife Refuge System (NWRS), the only network of federal lands and waters that is managed principally for the protection of fish and wildlife. In 2013 the NWRS (2013, http://www.fws.gov/refuges/refuge LocatorMaps/index.html) included 561 refuges and thousands of small natural wetlands and grasslands around the country.

Fifty-nine of the refuges were established specifically for endangered species. (See Table 1.6.) Protected species include a variety of plants and animals. Many other listed animal species use refuge lands on a temporary basis for breeding or migratory rest stops.

The USFWS, the U.S. Forest Service, the National Park Service (NPS), and the Bureau of Land Management oversee the National Wilderness Preservation System of undeveloped federal land. According to Wilderness.net, in "Creation and Growth of the National Wilderness Preservation System" (http://www.wilderness.net/NWPS/fast facts), as of 2013, 757 so-called wilderness areas had been designated across the country covering approximately 109.5 million acres (44.3 million hectares [ha]). Alaska, California, and other western states are home to most of the wilderness areas.

The NPS (January 30, 2014, http://www.nps.gov/faqs.htm) notes that in 2014 there were 401 units in the National Park System covering more than 84 million acres (34 million ha). The units include national parks, monuments, preserves, lakeshores, seashores, wild and scenic rivers, trails, historic sites, military parks, battlefields, historical parks, recreation areas, memorials, and parkways. Besides preserving habitats that range from Arctic tundra to tropical rain forest, the system protects many imperiled plant and animal species.

The national parks have played a significant role in the return of several species, including wolves and peregrine falcons. The national parks also contain designated

TABLE 1.6

National wildlife refuges (NWR) established for endangered species

State	Unit name	Species of concern	Unit acreage
Alabama	Sauta Cave NWR	Indiana bat, gray bat	264
	Fern Cave NWR	Indiana bat, gray bat	199
	Key Cave NWR	Alabama cavefish, gray bat	1,060
	Watercress Darter NWR	Watercress darter	7
Arkansas	Logan Cave NWR	Cave crayfish, gray bat, Indiana bat, Ozark cavefish	124
Arizona	Buenos Aires NWR	Masked bobwhite quail	116,585
	Leslie Canyon	Gila topminnow, Yaqui chub, Peregrine falcon	2,765
	San Bernardino NWR	Gila topminnow, Yaqui chub, Yaqui catfish, Beautiful shiner, Huachuca water umbel	2,369
California	Antioch Dunes NWR	Lange's metalmark butterfly, Antioch Dunes evening-primrose, Contra Costa wallflower	55
	Bitter Creek NWR	California condor	14,054
	Blue Ridge NWR	California condor	897
	Castle Rock NWR	Aleutian Canada goose	14
	Coachella Valley NWR	Coachello Valley fringe-toed lizard	3,592
	Don Edwards San Francisco Bay NWR	California clapper rail, California least tern, Salt marsh harvest mouse	21,524
	Ellicott Slough NWR	Santa Cruz long-toed salamander	139
	Hopper Mountain NWR	California condor	2,471
	Sacramento River NWR	Valley elderberry longhorn beetle, Bald eagle, Least Bell's vireo	7,884
	San Diego NWR	San Diego fairy shrimp, San Diego mesa mint, Otay mesa mint, California orcutt grass, San Diego button-celery	1,840
	San Joaquin River NWR	Aleutian Canada goose	1,638
	Seal Beach NWR	Light-footed clapper rail, California least tern	911
	Sweetwater Marsh NWR	Light-footed clapper rail	316
	Tijuana Slough NWR	Light-footed clapper rail	1,023
Florida	Archie Carr NWR	Loggerhead sea turtle, Green sea turtle	29
	Crocodile Lake NWR	American crocodile	6,686
	Crystal River NWR	West Indian manatee	80
	Florida Panther NWR	Florida panther	23,379
	Hobe Sound NWR	Loggerhead sea turtle, Green sea turtle	980
	Lake Wales Ridge NWR	Florida scrub jay, Snakeroot, Scrub blazing star, Carter's mustard, Papery whitlow-wort, Florida bonamia, Scrub lupine, Highlands scrub hypericum, Garett's mint, Scrub mint, Pygmy gringe-tree, Wireweed, Florida ziziphus, Scrub Plum, Eastern indigo snake, Bluetail mole skink, Sand skink	659
	National Key Deer Refuge	Key deer	8,542
	St. Johns NWR	Dusky seaside sparrow	6,255
Hawaii	Hakalau Forest NWR	Akepa, Akiapolaau, 'O'u, Hawaiian hawk, Hawaiian creeper	32,730
	Hanalei NWR	Hawaiian stilt, Hawaiian coot, Hawaiian moorhen, Hawaiian duck	917
	Huleia NWR	Hawaiian stilt, Hawaiian coot, Hawaiian moorhen, Hawaiian duck	241
	James C. Campbell NWR	Hawaiian stilt, Hawaiian coot, Hawaiian moorhen, Hawaiian duck	164
	Kakahaia NWR	Hawaiian stilt, Hawaiian coot	45
	Kealia Pond NWR	Hawaiian stilt, Hawaiian coot	691
	Pearl Harbor NWR	Hawaiian stilt	61
Iowa	Driftless Area NWR	Iowa Pleistocene snail	521
Massachusetts	Massasoit NWR	Plymouth red-bellied turtle	184
Michigan	Kirtland's Warbler WMA	Kirtland's warbler	6,535
Mississippi	Mississippi Sandhill Crane NWR	Mississippi sandhill crane	19,713
Missouri	Ozark Cavefish NWR	Ozark cavefish	42
	Pilot Knob NWR	Indiana bat	90
Nebraska	Karl E. Mundt NWR	Bald eagle	19
Nevada	Ash Meadows NWR	Devil's hole pupfish, Warm Springs pupfish, Ash Meadows amargosa pupfish, Ash Meadows speckled dace, Ash Meadows naucorid, Ash Meadows blazing star, Amargosa niterwort, Ash Meadows milk-vetch, Ash Meadows sunray, Spring-loving centaury, Ash Meadows gumplant, Ash Meadows invesia	13,268
	Moapa Valley NWR	Moapa dace	32
Oklahoma	Ozark Plateau NWR	Ozark big-eared bat, gray bat	2,208
Oregon	Bear Valley NWR	Bald eagle	4,200
	Julia Butler Hansen Refuge for Columbian White-tail deer	Columbian white-tailed deer	2,750
	Nestucca Bay NWR	Aleutian Canada goose	457
South Dakota	Karl E. Mundt NWR	Bald eagle	1,044
Texas	Attwater Prairie Chicken NWR	Attwater's greater prairie chicken	8,007
	Balcones Canyonlands NWR	Black-capped vireo, Golden-cheeked warbler	14,144
Virgin Islands	Green Cay NWR	St. Croix ground lizard	14
	Sandy Point NWR	Leatherback sea turtle	327

TABLE 1.6

National wildlife refuges (NWR) established for endangered species [CONTINUED]

State	Unit name	Species of concern	Unit acreage
Virginia	James River NWR	Bald eagle	4,147
	Mason Neck NWR	Bald eagle	2,276
Washington	Julia Butler Hansen Refuge for Columbian white-tail deer	Columbian white-tailed deer	2,777
Wyoming	Mortenson Lake NWR	Wyoming toad	1,776

SOURCE: "National Wildlife Refuges Established for Endangered Species," in *National Wildlife Refuge System*, U.S. Department of the Interior, U.S. Fish and Wildlife Service, November 7, 2012, http://www.fws.gov/Refuges/whm/EndSpRefuges.html (accessed November 1, 2013)

critical habitat for many listed species. However, not all of these are publicly disclosed, to protect rare species from collectors, vandals, or curiosity seekers.

In 2013 the U.S. Forest Service (March 23, 2013, http://www.fs.fed.us/aboutus/meetfs.shtml) managed nearly 193 million acres (78.1 million ha) of public lands in 155 national forests and 20 national grasslands. National Forest lands also include many lakes and ponds. National Forest lands are, in general, not conserved to the same degree as NPS lands. For example, much logging occurs within these forests. Endangered, threatened, and sensitive species on National Forest lands are subjected to biological evaluations to determine the effects of management activities on them. Conservation measures are also incorporated to preserve these species.

The Debate over Use of Federally Protected Lands

Ever since federal conservation lands were first set aside, a national debate has raged over how they should be used. Many of these lands contain natural resources of great value in commercial markets, including timber, oil, gas, and minerals. Political and business interests that wish to harvest these resources are pitted against environmentalists, who want to preserve the lands. During the 1990s such a battle raged over the issue of logging in old-growth forests of the Pacific Northwest—the same forests that provided habitat for endangered northern spotted owls. A similar controversy has been brewing for decades over the drilling of oil and gas in the Arctic National Wildlife Refuge.

OIL DRILLING IN THE ARCTIC NATIONAL WILDLIFE REFUGE. The Arctic National Wildlife Refuge (ANWR) is located in northern Alaska. (See Figure 1.3.) Covering 19 million acres (7.7 million ha), it is the largest national wildlife refuge in the United States. The ANWR was established in 1980 by passage of the Alaska National Interest Lands Conservation Act. In Section 1002 of the act, Congress deferred a decision on the future management of 1.5 million acres (607,000 ha) of the ANWR, because of conflicting interests between potential oil and gas resources thought to be located there and the area's

importance as a wildlife habitat. This disputed area of coastal plain came to be known as the 1002 area.

There has been interest in tapping the oil deposits in northern Alaska since the mid-1900s. In 2002 and 2010 the U.S. Geological Survey (USGS) estimated the volumes of oil and natural gas potentially available in the NPRA. In "2010 Updated Assessment of Undiscovered Oil and Gas Resources of the National Petroleum Reserve in Alaska (NPRA)" (October 2010, http://pubs.usgs.gov/fs/2010/3102/pdf/FS10-3102.pdf), the USGS estimates that 896 million barrels of oil and 52.8 trillion cubic feet (1.5 trillion cubic meters) of natural gas are available in "conventional undiscovered accumulations."

Environmentalists argue that USFWS studies suggest that oil drilling in the refuge will harm many Arctic species by taking over habitat, damaging habitats through pollution, interfering with species' activities directly, or increasing opportunities for invasive species. The ANWR harbors the greatest number of plant and animal species of any park or refuge in the Arctic, including unique species such as arctic foxes, caribou, musk oxen, polar bears, and snow geese.

The protected status of the ANWR has been challenged by large oil companies and their political supporters, particularly Republicans. However, bills seeking to lift the protections have failed to pass Congress. Thus, as of February 2014 federal legislation had not been passed that allowed drilling in the ANWR.

State Governments

Every state has its own agency that is charged with managing and overseeing land and wildlife conservation. The USFWS (July 10, 2013, http://www.fws.gov/offices/statelinks.html) maintains a database of website links to agencies in all 50 states, the District of Columbia, and U.S. territories, such as Guam and the Virgin Islands.

Most states maintain their own lists of endangered, threatened, or "special concern" species. For example, as of December 2013 the New York Department of Environmental Conservation (http://www.dec.ny.gov/animals/

FIGURE 1.3

Map of northern Alaska showing the National Petroleum Reserve—Alaska (NPRA) and Arctic National Wildlife Refuge (ANWR)

☐ *Federal lands* ■ *Known petroleum accumulations*

Northern Alaska
36 petroleum discoveries
~15 BBO[a] and 35 TCFG[b] recoverable
commercial production

Arctic Ocean

Point Barrow

Prudhoe Bay

1002 area

NPRA[c]

Mackenzie River delta

ANWR[d]

Mackenzie River delta
48 petroleum discoveries
~2 BBO[a] and 12 TCFG[b] recoverable
no commercial production

Northern margin
of Brooks Range

TAPS[e]

**Wilderness
area**

Canada
United States

ANWR[d] = 19 million acres
1002 area = 1.5 million acres
Wilderness area = 8 million acres
NPRA[c] = 23 million acres

0   100 miles

[a]BBO = Billion barrels of oil (includes cumulative production plus recoverable resources).
[b]TCFG = Trillion cubic feet of gas recoverable resources.
[c]NPRA = National Petroleum Reserve—Alaska.
[d]ANWR = Arctic National Wildlife Refuge.
[e]TAPS = Trans-Alaska Pipeline System.

SOURCE: "Figure 1. Map of Northern Alaska and Nearby Parts of Canada Showing Locations of the Arctic National Wildlife Refuge (ANWR), the 1002 Area, and the National Petroleum Reserve—Alaska (NPRA). Locations of Known Petroleum Accumulations and the Trans-Alaska Pipeline System (TAPS) Are Shown, as well as Summaries of Known Petroleum Volumes in Northern Alaska and the Mackenzie River Delta of Canada. BBO, Billion Barrels of Oil (Includes Cumulative Production Plus Recoverable Resources); TCFG, Trillion Cubic Feet of Gas Recoverable Resources," in *Arctic National Wildlife Refuge, 1002 Area, Petroleum Assessment, 1998, Including Economic Analysis*, U.S. Department of the Interior, U.S. Geological Survey, April 2001, http://pubs.usgs.gov/fs/fs-0028-01/fs-0028-01.pdf (accessed November 1, 2013)

7494.html) listed 53 animal and fish species as endangered, 35 as threatened, and 58 as special concern. It should be noted that state lists of imperiled species often include species that are not federally listed.

Private Organizations and Individuals

Federal and state governments are not the only entities involved in land conservation and conserving imperiled species. Increasingly, environment-minded private organizations and citizens are purchasing land with the intent of preserving it for wildlife. National environmental groups such as the Nature Conservancy participate in these endeavors. The Nature Conservancy (2014, http://www.nature.org/about-us/index.htm) notes that it helps protect more than 119 million acres (48.2 million ha) worldwide. Other major groups engaged in private land conservation include the Conservation Fund, the Land Trust Alliance, the Rocky Mountain Elk Foundation,

the Society for the Protection of New Hampshire Forests, and the Trust for Public Land.

Every five years the Land Trust Alliance conducts a census on lands that are held for private conservation. The alliance states in *2010 National Land Trust Census Report: A Look at Voluntary Land Conservation in America* (November 16, 2011, http://www.landtrustalliance.org/land-trusts/land-trust-census/national-land-trust-census-2010/2010-final-report) that approximately 47 million acres (19 million ha) of land were held in local, regional, or national land trusts in 2010. Land trusts either purchase land outright or develop private, voluntary agreements called conservation easements or restrictions that limit future development of the land.

As will be explained in Chapter 2, the ESA allows private organizations and individuals to participate directly in the federal listing of endangered and threatened species by petitioning the USFWS or the NMFS on behalf of particular species. In addition, private parties can file lawsuits against the government for alleged failures to abide by the ESA.

INTERNATIONAL EFFORTS AT CONSERVATION

The UN Environment Programme (UNEP) was established to address diverse environmental issues on an international level. Many of its conventions have been extremely valuable in protecting global biodiversity and natural resources. The UNEP has also helped regulate pollution and the use of toxic chemicals.

Convention on International Trade in Endangered Species of Wild Fauna and Flora

The Convention on International Trade in Endangered Species of Wild Fauna and Flora (CITES) is an international agreement administered under the UNEP that regulates international trade in wildlife. CITES is perhaps the single most important international agreement relating to endangered species and has contributed critically to the protection of many threatened species. The international wildlife trade is estimated to involve hundreds of millions of specimens annually.

CITES was first drafted in 1963 at a meeting of the IUCN and went into effect in 1975. Protected plant and animals are listed in three separate CITES appendixes, depending on the degree of endangerment. Appendix I includes species that are in immediate danger of extinction. CITES generally prohibits international trade of these species. Appendix II lists species that are likely to become in danger of extinction without strict protection from international trade. Permits may be obtained for the trade of Appendix II species only if trade will not harm the survival prospects of the species in the wild. Appendix III lists species whose trade is regulated in one or more nations. Any member nation can list a species in Appendix III to request international cooperation to prevent unsustainable levels of international trade. Nations agree to abide by CITES rules voluntarily. In 2013 there were 179 nations participating in the agreement (http:// cites.org/eng/disc/parties/index.php).

Convention on Biological Diversity

The CBD, which was mentioned earlier in this chapter, was set up to conserve biodiversity and to promote the sustainable use of biological resources. The convention supports national efforts in the documentation and monitoring of biodiversity, the establishment of refuges and other protected areas, and the restoration of degraded ecosystems. It also supports goals that are related to the maintenance of traditional knowledge of sustainable resource use, the prevention of invasive species introductions, and the control of invasive species that are already

present. Finally, it funds education programs that promote public awareness of the value of natural resources.

Convention on the Conservation of Migratory Species of Wild Animals

The Convention on the Conservation of Migratory Species of Wild Animals (CMS) recognizes that certain migratory species cross national boundaries and require protection throughout their range. The convention (2014, http://www.cms.int/about/intro.htm) aims to "conserve terrestrial, aquatic and avian migratory species throughout their range." It was originally signed in Bonn, Germany, in 1979 and went into force in November 1983. According to the CMS (http://www.cms.int/about/partylist_e.pdf), as of February 2014, 119 nations were involved in the agreement. The United States and several other nations were not official parties to the agreement but nonetheless abide by its rules.

The CMS provides two levels of protection to migratory species. Appendix I species are endangered and strictly protected. Appendix II species are less severely threatened but would nonetheless benefit from international cooperative agreements.

World Commission on Protected Areas

The UN's World Conservation Protection Centre is the leading international body dedicated to the selection, establishment, and management of national parks and protected areas. It helps establish natural areas around the world for the protection of plant and animal species and maintains a database of protected areas. Protected areas often consist of a core zone, in which wildlife cannot legally be disturbed by human beings, and a buffer zone, a transitional space that acts as a shield for the core zone. On the periphery are areas for managed human living. According to the World Conservation Protection Centre, in "About Protected Areas" (2014, http:// www.unep-wcmc.org/about-protected-areas_163.html), a protected area is defined as "a clearly defined geographical space, recognised, dedicated and managed, through legal or other effective means, to achieve the long term conservation of nature with associated ecosystem services and cultural values."

Conservation biology theory suggests that protected areas should be as large as possible to increase biological diversity and to buffer refuges from outside pressures. The world's largest protected areas are the Ar-Rub'al-Khali Wildlife Management Area (Saudi Arabia), the Cape Churchill Wildlife Management Area (Canada), Great Barrier Reef Marine Park (Australia), Greenland National Park (Greenland), the Northern Wildlife Management Zone (Saudi Arabia), and the Qiangtang Nature Reserve (China).

FACTORS THAT CONTRIBUTE TO SPECIES ENDANGERMENT

Wildlife populations can be harmed by extreme weather events and other natural phenomena, such as floods, droughts, storms, disease, and wild fires. For example, Chapter 6 describes the adverse effects in 2005 of Hurricane Katrina on imperiled baby sea turtles. The strong tides and waves impeded the tiny creatures from crawling from their nesting beaches to the sea. Natural stressors have always existed, and animal and plant species have evolved to avoid or survive them. In addition, society takes certain actions to minimize the negative impacts of natural stressors on imperiled species. For example, people helped the baby sea turtles reach the sea safely. Government agencies at the federal, state, and local levels work in concert with private organizations and citizen volunteers to carry out activities such as these when natural disasters occur. The USFWS is a major player in this respect. In "Natural Disasters and Other Emergencies" (2014, http://refugeassociation.org/advocacy/funding/refuge-system/emergency-and-natural-disasters/), the National Wildlife Refuge Association notes that "baby sea turtles, nesting birds and many endangered animals are often in the path of natural disasters. The ability of the U.S. Fish and Wildlife Service ... to respond quickly to these disasters can determine the fate of these vulnerable creatures."

Natural phenomena can play a role in species loss, particularly when a species is isolated and/or low in number. However, experts suggest the primary cause of wildlife loss is the destructive effect of human activities. For example, Navjot S. Sodhi, Barry W. Brook, and Corey J. A. Bradshaw state in "Causes and Consequences of Species Extinctions" (S. A. Levin, ed., *The Princeton Guide to Ecology*, 2009) that "the major 'systematic drivers' of modern species loss are changes in land use (habitat loss degradation and fragmentation), overexploitation, invasive species, disease, climate change (global warming) connected to increasing concentration of atmospheric carbon dioxide, and increases in nitrogen deposition." Anthropomorphic (human-linked) activities can also cause or allow natural stressors to be more damaging to wildlife than they would be otherwise. For example, exposure to pollution can weaken a species and make it more susceptible to disease or drought.

The major anthropomorphic factors mentioned by Sodhi, Brook, and Corey that contribute to species loss are described in the following sections.

Changes in Land Use

For millennia humans have been changing the land to meet their needs and in the process destroying natural habitat. Raising crops, grazing livestock, logging, filling swamps, building dams, mining, and developing land for housing and commerce are major types of land use changes that greatly impact wildlife populations. Many of these activities produce negative secondary impacts as well. For example, agricultural activity can result in soil erosion, pollution from pesticides and fertilizers, and runoff into aquatic habitats. Finally, human recreational activity, particularly the use of off-road vehicles, results in the destruction of natural habitat and stresses wildlife populations.

HABITAT FRAGMENTATION. Human land-use patterns often result in the fragmentation of natural habitat areas that are available to species. For example, building a road through a forest or converting part of a meadow into a farm or subdivision fragments the large area that used to be available to species into smaller separated pieces. Habitat fragmentation can have significant effects on species. Small populations can become isolated, so that dispersal from one habitat patch to another is impossible. Smaller populations are also more likely to become extinct. Finally, because there are more "edges" when habitats are fragmented, there can be increased exposure to predators and vulnerability to disturbances that are associated with human activity.

Overexploitation

The National Wildlife Federation (2014, http://www.nwf.org/wildlife/threats-to-wildlife/overexploitation.aspx) defines overexploitation as "the over use of wildlife and plant species by people for food, clothing, pets, medicine, sport and many other purposes." As noted earlier, overhunting led to the extinction of several U.S. species including passenger pigeons and heath hens. Numerous cases will be presented in this book of endangered species in decline due to overuse by humans. As with other stressors, overexploitation can indirectly harm ecosystems and human interests. For example, Sodhi, Brook, and Bradshaw describe the unexpected consequences of overfishing of large pelagic sharks, such as great white sharks. Lowering the population of this superpredator "resulted in an increase in rays and skates that eventually suppressed commercially important scallop populations."

Invasive Species

Invasive species are also known as exotic, nuisance, or nonnative species. Basically, they are species that have been introduced directly or indirectly by humans into a new environment. Invasive species that thrive disrupt their new ecosystems in multiple ways. They compete with the established species for food, shelter, and other resources. They may also carry "new" diseases or other pathogens to which the existing species do not have natural resistance. Predatory invasive species are particularly harmful. As will be described in Chapter 6, some endangered island bird populations have been decimated by nonnative predators. Nearly all of Guam's native birds have been wiped out by the brown tree snake, an invasive species that likely arrived on the island decades ago via cargo ships. Introduced species that are genetically similar to established species can wreak havoc if interbreeding produces sterile offspring or offspring with a predominantly exotic genetic makeup. Over time, the native species can disappear completely as its unique genetic blueprint fades out of existence.

Disease

Disease has always posed a threat to wildlife, but its scope and hazard have greatly increased due to human interference in ecosystems. Animals and plants have evolved defense and immunity mechanisms that naturally help protect them from diseases to which they have been regularly exposed. Nevertheless, "new" diseases (e.g., from introduced species) can be devastating because the victims have no natural resistance. Likewise, wildlife already stressed by habitat changes, pollution, or other human-induced problems are more susceptible to disease.

Climate Change

The earth's temperature is regulated by many factors, including energy inputs and outputs, chemical processes, and physical phenomena. Radiation from the sun passes through the earth's atmosphere and warms the planet. (See Figure 1.4.) In turn, the earth emits infrared radiation. Some of this outgoing infrared radiation does not escape into outer space but is trapped beneath the atmosphere to provide a warm "blanket" for the planet. The amount of trapped energy depends on several variables, including the composition of the atmosphere. Certain gases, such as carbon dioxide and methane, naturally trap heat beneath the atmosphere in the same way that glass panels keep heat from escaping from a greenhouse. This natural greenhouse effect keeps the earth warm and habitable for life. Scientists believe massive combustion (burning) of fossil fuels, such as oil and natural gas, introduced large amounts of carbon dioxide, methane, and other heat-trapping gases into the atmosphere over the last century. This buildup has been increasing the earth's temperature above that expected from the natural greenhouse effect, an effect known as global warming. Global warming is bringing about climate change, which has numerous consequences to the planet's environment, ecosystems, and inhabitants.

Continued warming of the earth would alter habitats drastically, with serious consequences for many species. The Intergovernmental Panel on Climate Change (IPCC) is an international body of scientists and policy makers that publishes reports on climate change. In *Climate Change 2007: Impacts, Adaptation, and Vulnerability* (2007, http://www.ipcc.ch/), the IPCC reports that "observational evidence from all continents and most

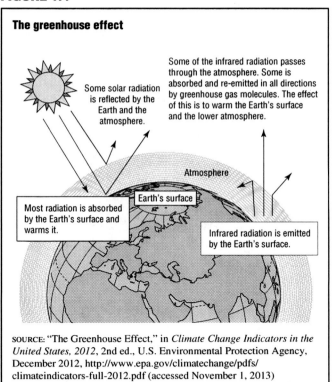

FIGURE 1.4

The greenhouse effect

Some solar radiation is reflected by the Earth and the atmosphere.

Some of the infrared radiation passes through the atmosphere. Some is absorbed and re-emitted in all directions by greenhouse gas molecules. The effect of this is to warm the Earth's surface and the lower atmosphere.

Atmosphere

Earth's surface

Most radiation is absorbed by the Earth's surface and warms it.

Infrared radiation is emitted by the Earth's surface.

SOURCE: "The Greenhouse Effect," in *Climate Change Indicators in the United States, 2012*, 2nd ed., U.S. Environmental Protection Agency, December 2012, http://www.epa.gov/climatechange/pdfs/climateindicators-full-2012.pdf (accessed November 1, 2013)

oceans shows that many natural systems are being affected by regional climate changes, particularly temperature increases." The consequences include an earlier occurrence of springtime events and a poleward movement in the ranges of plant and animal species. Warming temperatures in natural water bodies are causing range changes for algae, plankton, and fish species. IPCC scientists estimate that approximately 20% to 30% of animal and plant species have an increased risk of extinction if the global average temperature increases by more than 2.7 to 4.5 degrees Fahrenheit (1.5 to 2.5 degrees Celsius).

Increases in Nitrogen Deposition

Nitrogen is a key nutrient for plant growth. Human activities, however, such as use of nitrogen-rich fertilizers and the combustion of fossil fuels have introduced massive amounts of nitrogen into the environment. Excessive nitrogen concentrations in soils and water bodies upset the natural chemical balance needed to maintain healthy ecosystems. For example, rivers, lakes, and streams can become too acidic, putting wildlife at risk. This is especially problematic for species such as fish and amphibians (e.g., frogs) that are highly sensitive to acid content. Over-enrichment of soils with nitrogen can greatly change the mix of plants growing in a particular ecosystem as some species respond with vigorous growth and others falter. Such alterations disrupt the existing food webs further and stress the ecosystem inhabitants.

CHAPTER 2
THE ENDANGERED SPECIES ACT

The Endangered Species Act (ESA) of 1973 is considered to be one of the most far-reaching laws ever enacted by any nation for the preservation of wildlife. The passage of the ESA resulted from alarm at the decline of many species worldwide, as well as from recognition of the importance of preserving species diversity. The purpose of the ESA is to identify species that are either endangered (at risk of extinction throughout all or a significant portion of their range) or threatened (likely to become endangered in the future). Except for recognized insect pests, all animals and plants are eligible for listing under the ESA. Listed species are protected without regard to either commercial or sport value.

The ESA is also one of the most controversial and contentious laws ever passed. It affects the rights of private landowners and how they manage their property if endangered species are found there. It also allows private individuals and groups to sue federal agencies for alleged failures in carrying out the law. The result has been a flood of litigation since the 1990s by conservation organizations. They believe that full and effective implementation of the ESA will help ensure the survival of imperiled species. However, critics charge that the ESA has saved virtually no species, puts too many restrictions on land and water development projects, and is too expensive for the results that it achieves.

THE ESA: A LANDMARK LAW

The roots of the ESA lay in the Endangered Species Preservation Act, which was passed in 1966. This act established a process for listing species as endangered and provided some measure of protection. The first species to be listed are shown in Table 2.1. The Endangered Species Conservation Act of 1969 provided protection to species facing worldwide extinction, prohibiting their import and sale within the United States.

Passed by Congress in 1973, the ESA was substantially amended in 1978, 1982, and 1987. Table 2.2 describes the key sections of the amended law. The ESA is administered by the U.S. Department of the Interior (DOI) through the U.S. Fish and Wildlife Service (USFWS). The U.S. Department of Commerce, through the National Marine Fisheries Service (NMFS), is responsible for most marine (ocean-based) species and those that are anadromous (migrate between freshwaters and marine waters). The two agencies are often referred to collectively as the "ESA agencies." It should be noted, however, that other federal agencies have input into the ESA process. For example, the Biological Resources Division of the U.S. Geological Survey conducts research on species for which the USFWS has management authority.

Citizen Involvement

One of the hallmarks of the ESA is the broad latitude that it provides U.S. citizens to participate in the implementation and enforcement of the law. Individuals and groups can petition the ESA agencies to list specific species under the law. So long as the petitions meet defined screening criteria, the agencies must take further action on them. During the 1990s private groups devoted to conservation and animal protection began flooding the agencies with listing petitions for hundreds of imperiled species. The law includes specific time deadlines for completion of certain tasks by the ESA agencies. For example, they must make a decision on each new listing petition within 90 days. Nevertheless, as will be explained throughout this chapter, the agencies have struggled (and often failed) to meet the legally required deadlines as their workload has greatly outpaced their resources.

Section 11 (http://www.fws.gov/endangered/laws-policies/section-11.html) of the ESA allows private citizens or groups to file lawsuits against the ESA agencies for any alleged failures to carry out the law, including

TABLE 2.1

First list of endangered species, 1967

In accordance with section 1(c) of the Endangered Species Preservation Act of October 15, 1966 (80 Stat. 926; 16 U.S.C. 668aa(c) I [the Secretary of the Interior] find after consulting the states, interested organizations, and individual scientists, that the following listed native fish and wildlife are threatened with extinction.

Mammals

- Indiana bat—*Myotis sodalis*
- Delmarva Peninsula fox squirrel—*Sciurus niger cinereus*
- Timber wolf—*Canis lupus lycaon*
- Red wolf—*Canis niger*
- San Joaquin kit fox—*Vulpes macrotis mutica*
- Grizzly bear—*Ursus horribilis*
- Black-footed ferret—*Mustela nigripes*
- Florida panther—*Felis concolor coryi*
- Caribbean monk seal—*Monachus tropicalis*
- Guadalupe fur seal—*Arctocephalus philippi townsendi*
- Florida manatee or Florida sea cow—*Trichechus manatus latirostris*
- Key deer—*Odocoileus virginianus clavium*
- Sonoran pronghorn—*Antilocapra americana sonoriensis*

Birds

- Hawaiian dark-rumped petrel—*Pterodroma phaeopygia sandwichensis*
- Hawaiian goose (nene)—*Branta sandvicensis*
- Aleutian Canada goose—*Branta canadensis leucopareia*
- Tule white-fronted goose—*Anser albifrons gambelli*
- Laysan duck—*Anas laysanensis*
- Hawaiian duck (or koloa)—*Anas wyvilliana*
- Mexican duck—*Anas diazi*
- California condor—*Gymnogyps californianus*
- Florida Everglade kite (Florida Snail Kite)—*Rostrhamus sociabilis plumbeus*
- Hawaiian hawk (or ii)—*Buteo solitarius*
- Southern bald eagle—*Haliaeetus t. leucocephalus*
- Attwater's greater prairie chicken—*Tympanuchus cupido attwateri*
- Masked bobwhite—*Colinus virginianus ridgwayi*
- Whooping crane—*Grus americana*
- Yuma clapper rail—*Rallus longirostris yumanensis*
- Hawaiian common gallinule—*Gallinula chloropus sandvicensis*
- Eskimo curlew—*Numenius borealis*
- Puerto Rican parrot—*Amazona vittata*
- American ivory-billed woodpecker—*Campephilus p. principalis*
- Hawaiian crow (or alala)—*Corvus hawaiiensis*
- Small Kauai thrush (puaiohi)—*Phaeornia pulmeri*
- Nihoa millerbird—*Acrocephalus kingi*
- Kauai oo (or oo aa)—*Moho braccatus*
- Crested honeycreeper (or akohekohe)—*Palmeria dolei*
- Akiapolaau—*Hemignathus wilsoni*
- Kauai akialoa—*Hemignathus procerus*
- Kauai nukupuu—*Hemignathus lucidus hanapepe*

- Laysan finchbill (Laysan finch)—*Psittirostra c. cantans*
- Nihoa finchbill (Nihoa finch)—*Psittirostra cantans ultima*
- Ou—*Psittirostra psittacea*
- Palila—*Psittirostra bailleui*
- Maui parrotbill—*Pseudonestor xanthophyrys*
- Bachman's warbler—*Vermivora bachmanii*
- Kirtland's warbler—*Dendroica kirtlandii*
- Dusky seaside sparrow—*Ammospiza nigrescens*
- Cape Sable sparrow—*Ammospiza mirabilis*

Reptiles and Amphibians

- American alligator—*Alligator mississippiensis*
- Blunt-nosed leopard lizard—*Crotaphytus wislizenii silus*
- San Francisco garter snake—*Thamnophis sirtalis tetrataenia*
- Santa Cruz long-toed salamander—*Ambystoma macrodactylum croceum*
- Texas blind salamander—*Typhlomolge rathbuni*
- Black toad, Inyo County toad—*Bufo exsul*

Fishes

- Shortnose sturgeon—*Acipenser brevirostrum*
- Longjaw Cisco—*Coregonus alpenae*
- Paiute cutthroat trout—*Salmo clarki seleniris*
- Greenback cutthroat trout—*Salmo clarki stomias*
- Montana Westslope cutthroat trout—*Salmo clarki*
- Gila trout—*Salmo gilae*
- Arizona (*Apache*) trout—*Salmo sp.*
- Desert dace—*Eremichthys acros*
- Humpback chub—*Gila cypha*
- Little Colorado spinedace—*Lepidomeda vittata*
- Moapa dace—*Moapa coriacea*
- Colorado River squawfish—*Ptychocheilus lucius*
- Cui-ui—*Chasmistes cujus*
- Devils Hole pupfish—*Cyprinodon diabolis*
- Commanche Springs pupfish—*Cyprinodon elegans*
- Owens River pupfish—*Cyprinodon radiosus*
- Pahrump killifish—*Empetrichthys latos*
- Big Bend gambusia—*Gambusia gaigei*
- Clear Creek gambusia—*Gambusia heterochir*
- Gila topminnow—*Poeciliopsis occidentalis*
- Maryland darter—*Etheostoma sellare*
- Blue pike—*Stizostedion vitreum glaucum*

SOURCE: Stewart L. Udall, "Native Fish and Wildlife Endangered Species," in *Federal Register*, vol. 32, no. 48, March 11, 1967

TABLE 2.2

Key sections of the Endangered Species Act

Section	Description
4	Addresses the listing and recovery of species and designation of critical habitat.
6	Focuses on cooperation with the states and authorizes FWS and NOAA fisheries to provide financial assistance to states that have entered into cooperative agreements supporting the conservation of endangered and threatened species.
7	Requires all federal agencies, in consultation with FWS or NOAA fisheries, to use their authorities to further the purpose of the ESA and to ensure that their actions are not likely to jeopardize the continued existence of listed species or result in destruction or adverse modification of critical habitat.
8	Outlines the procedures for international cooperation.
9	Defines prohibited actions, including the import and export, take, illegally taken possession of illegally taken species, transport, or sale of endangered or threatened species.
10	Lays out the guidelines under which a permit may be issued to authorize prohibited activities, such as take of endangered or threatened species.
10(a)(1)(A)	Allows for permits for the taking of threatened or endangered species for scientific purposes or for purposes of enhancement of propagation or survival.
10(a)(1)(B)	Allows for permits for incidental taking of threatened or endangered species.

FWS = Fish and Wildlife Services.
NOAA = National Oceanic and Atmospheric Administration.
ESA = Endangered Species Act.

SOURCE: Adapted from "Endangered Species Act of 1973, as Amended," in *Endangered Species Glossary*, U.S. Department of the Interior, U.S. Fish and Wildlife Service, April 2005, http://www.fws.gov/endangered/esa-library/pdf/glossary.pdf (accessed November 1, 2013) failing to meet the mandated deadlines. Conservation groups have seized on the so-called citizen suit provision and filed numerous lawsuits against the agencies. The USFWS, in particular, has found itself mired in litigation since the 1990s. As a consequence, the agency's ESA scope of work and future planning are driven in large part by legal agreements that it has reached with plaintiffs that have sued it in court. Some critics complain that the ESA process has been hijacked by private groups with their own agendas. The groups respond that they are simply exercising the rights of citizen involvement that were built into the law. Many critics blame Congress for not changing the law to be more flexible or for not funding the agencies sufficiently so that they can better meet the ever-mounting demands placed on them under the ESA.

Cost Considerations

Another remarkable feature of the ESA is the relative lack of consideration it requires for the economic consequences of protecting endangered and threatened species. For example, it does not require the agencies to consider costs when they determine whether a species should be listed under the law. As noted in Chapter 1, this "saving nature for nature's sake" stance is highly controversial and deeply criticized by people who believe the financial costs of protecting imperiled plants and animals should be considered. As this chapter will explain, there are provisions in the law for assessment of the economic impacts of some ESA-related actions, such as the designation of critical habitat. Overall, however, the law requires that science rather than economics underlie many of the decisions regarding imperiled species.

LISTING SPECIES UNDER THE ESA
Definition of Species

The original ESA defined the word *species* to include species, subspecies, or "smaller taxa." Taxa is the plural of taxon, which is a grouping on the taxonomic table. In 1978 the ESA was amended to define a smaller taxon for vertebrates (animals with a backbone) as a distinct population segment (DPS). A DPS is a distinct population of vertebrates capable of interbreeding with each other that live in a specific geographical area. A DPS is usually described using geographical terms, such as northern or southern, or by a given latitude or longitude. In 1991 the NMFS developed a policy defining the DPS for Pacific salmon populations. Salmon are anadromous, and most salmon migrate in groups at particular times of the year. Each of these groups is called a stock. The NMFS developed the term *evolutionarily significant unit* (ESU) to refer to a distinct stock of Pacific salmon.

In summary, the word *species* as used in the ESA can mean a species, a subspecies, a DPS (vertebrates only), or an ESU (Pacific salmon only).

Listing Considerations

According to the USFWS, in "Listing a Species as Threatened or Endangered: Section 4 of the Endangered Species Act" (June 2011, http://www.fws.gov/endangered/esa-library/pdf/listing.pdf), the ESA stipulates five considerations for listing a species:

- The present or threatened destruction, modification, or curtailment of its habitat or range

- Overutilization for commercial, recreational, scientific, or educational purposes

- Disease or predation

- The inadequacy of existing regulatory mechanisms

- Other natural or manmade factors affecting its survival

Section 4 (http://www.fws.gov/endangered/laws-policies/section-4.html) of the law requires the agencies to base their listing determinations "solely on the basis of the best scientific and commercial data available." Thus, the ESA does not require economic factors to be considered during the listing process.

The primary status codes assigned to listed species are E for endangered and T for threatened. However, there are many other status codes for specific types of listings. (See Table 2.3.)

TABLE 2.3

Endangered Species Act status codes

Code	Description
E	Endangered
T	Threatened
EmE	Emergency listing, endangered
EmT	Emergency listing, threatened
EXPE, XE	Experimental population, essential
EXPN, XN	Experimental population, non-essential
SAE, E(S/A)	Similarity of appearance to an endangered taxon
SAT, T(S/A)	Similarity of appearance to a threatened taxon
PE	Proposed endangered
PT	Proposed threatened
PEXPE, PXE	Proposed experimental population, essential
PEXPN, PXN	Proposed experimental population, non-essential
PSAE, PE(S/A)	Proposed similarity of appearance to an endangered taxon
PSAT, PT(S/A)	Proposed similarity of appearance to a threatened taxon
C	Candidate taxon, ready for proposal
D3A	Delisted taxon, evidently extinct
D3B	Delisted taxon, invalid name in current scientific opinion
D3C	Delisted taxon, recovered
DA	Delisted taxon, amendment of the act
DM	Delisted taxon, recovered, being monitored first five years
DO	Delisted taxon, original commercial data erroneous
DP	Delisted taxon, discovered previously unknown additional populations and/or habitat
DR	Delisted taxon, taxonomic revision (improved understanding)
AD	Proposed delisting
AE	Proposed reclassification to endangered
AT	Proposed reclassification to threatened

SOURCE: "Endangered Species Act Status Codes," in *USFWS Threatened and Endangered Species System (TESS)*, U.S. Department of the Interior, U.S. Fish and Wildlife Service, undated, http://ecos.fws.gov/tess_public/html/db-status.html (accessed November 1, 2013)

As of November 2013, there were 1,516 U.S. species (644 animals and 872 plants) listed under the ESA. (See Table 1.2 in Chapter 1.) Most (468) of the animals were endangered, while 176 were threatened. Likewise, 720 of the plants were endangered, while 152 were threatened. In addition, there were 625 foreign species on the list, including 564 animals and one plant listed as endangered and 58 animals and two plants listed as threatened.

The Listing Process

The process by which a species becomes listed under the ESA is a legal process with specifically defined steps. Successful listing results in regulations that are legally enforceable within all U.S. jurisdictions. At various stages of the listing process, the USFWS or the NMFS publishes its actions in the *Federal Register* (https://www.federal register.gov/), an official document that is compiled daily by the National Archives and Records Administration in Washington, D.C., and printed/published digitally by the U.S. Government Printing Office. The *Federal Register* details specific legal actions of the federal government, such as rules, proposed rules, notices from federal agencies, executive orders, and miscellaneous presidential documents.

There are three ways for the ESA listing process to be initiated:

- Submittal of a petition to the USFWS or the NMFS
- Initiative of the USFWS or the NMFS
- Emergency designation by the USFWS or the NMFS

Figure 2.1 diagrams the most common listing process under the ESA, one that begins with a petition submittal. The listing process is described in detail by Joy Nicholopoulos in "Endangered Species Listing Program" (*Endangered Species Bulletin*, vol. 24, no. 6, November–December 1999) and by the USFWS in "Listing a Species as Threatened or Endangered: Section 4 of the Endangered Species Act" (February 2001, http://library.fws.gov/Pubs9/listing .pdf).

PETITION SUBMITTAL. The process for listing a new species under the ESA begins with a formal petition from a person, organization, or government agency. This petition is submitted to the USFWS for terrestrial and freshwater species or to the NMFS for marine and anadromous species. All listing petitions must be backed by published scientific data supporting the need for listing the species under the ESA. Within 90 days of petition receipt, the USFWS or the NMFS is supposed to determine whether there is "substantial information" to suggest that a species might require listing. If so, the species then undergoes a status review.

STATUS REVIEW. A status review is a detailed biological assessment of a particular species. During the petition

FIGURE 2.1

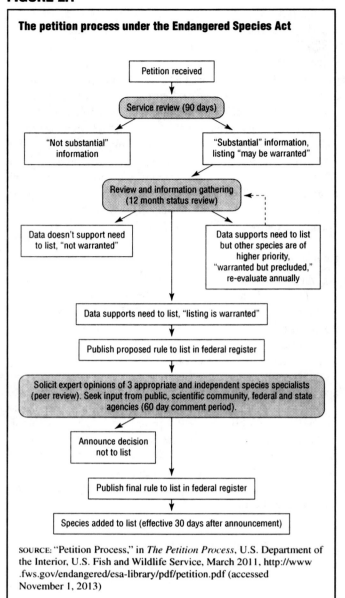

The petition process under the Endangered Species Act

SOURCE: "Petition Process," in *The Petition Process*, U.S. Department of the Interior, U.S. Fish and Wildlife Service, March 2011, http://www .fws.gov/endangered/esa-library/pdf/petition.pdf (accessed November 1, 2013)

process a status review helps the agencies determine whether a species should be listed and, if so, what its listing should be (endangered or threatened).

In *Endangered Species Petition Management Guidance* (July 1996, http://www.nmfs.noaa.gov/pr/pdfs/laws/ petition_management.pdf), the USFWS and the NMFS define a status review as "the act of reviewing all the available information on a species to determine if it should be provided protection under the ESA. A status review should also use the knowledge of experts; the greater the extent to which Service biologists can build an external consensus using the expertise of various parties (e.g., Federal, State, Tribal, University, Heritage programs), the better." Comments and information are also requested from the general public through publication of a notice in the *Federal Register*.

In general, a status review covers the following elements:

- Biology, life history, and reproductive factors of the species
- Genetic information
- Habitat characteristics
- Abundance and population trends
- Threats to species survival and well-being
- Conservation measures
- Existing regulatory mechanisms protecting the species

The ESA does not require the agencies to consider economic factors during status reviews. Each status review is supposed to be completed within 12 months. There are three possible determinations from a status review:

- Listing is not warranted
- Listing is warranted but precluded
- Listing is warranted

LISTING IS NOT WARRANTED. A finding that listing is not warranted must be accompanied by information explaining why the data presented do not support the petitioned action or why there are not enough data to make an appropriate determination.

LISTING IS WARRANTED BUT PRECLUDED—CANDIDATE SPECIES. The ESA agencies may decide that a species should be proposed for listing, but must wait while they deal with higher priorities. In other words, they acknowledge that a species deserves protection under the ESA, but they choose to devote their resources to what they consider to be more pressing needs. The on-hold species are officially called "candidate species."

The USFWS indicates in "Candidate Species: Section 4 of the Endangered Species Act" (March 2011, http://www.fws.gov/endangered/esa-library/pdf/candidate_species.pdf) that candidate species are assigned a listing priority number (LPN) ranging from 1 to 12, with lower numbers (1 to 3) indicating greater priority compared with other candidates. (See Table 2.4.) Priority is determined based on three considerations:

- The magnitude of the threats facing the species
- The immediacy of the threats facing the species
- The taxonomic uniqueness of the species

Candidate species are reevaluated annually to confirm that their listing status and LPN remain appropriate. The USFWS describes the reevaluation of each of the candidate species under its jurisdiction in a publication called a Candidate Notice of Review (CNOR). CNORs are published (typically annually) in the *Federal Register*. CNORs

TABLE 2.4

Listing priority numbers for candidate species

Threat			
Magnitude	Immediacy	Taxonomy	Priority
High	Imminent	Monotypic genus	1
		Species	2
		Subspecies/population	3
	Non-imminent	Monotypic genus	4
		Species	5
		Subspecies/population	6
Moderate to low	Imminent	Monotypic genus	7
		Species	8
		Subspecies/population	9
	Non-imminent	Monotypic genus	10
		Species	11
		Subspecies/population	12

SOURCE: John J. Fay and W. L. Thomas, "Table 1. Priorities for Listing or Reclassification from Threatened to Endangered," in "Fish and Wildlife Service: Endangered and Threatened Species Listing and Recovery Priority Guidelines," *Federal Register*, vol. 48, no. 184, September 21, 1983, http://www.fws.gov/endangered/esa-library/pdf/1983_LPN_Policy_FR_pub.pdf (accessed November 1, 2013)

dating back to 1994 are available at http://www.fws.gov/endangered/what-we-do/cnor.html.

The candidate reevaluations continue until the species is proposed for listing or until its status improves sufficiently to remove it from consideration for listing. Because they are not officially listed, candidate species do not enjoy the protection mechanisms of the ESA. Nonetheless, the ESA agencies work with state wildlife agencies and other groups to help preserve and improve the status of candidate species, hoping that populations will recover sufficiently such that the species will not require listing in the future.

As of February 2014, the most recent CNOR was published in November 2013 (http://www.fws.gov/endangered/esa-library/pdf/2013_11_22_CNOR.pdf) and included a total of 146 candidate species. Most of the USFWS candidates were flowering plants (47), followed by insects (29) and freshwater fish species (11). (See Table 2.5.) In addition, the NMFS (http://www.nmfs.noaa.gov/pr/species/esa/candidate.htm) had 24 candidate species as of November 2013. (See Table 2.5.) Most of the NMFS candidates were marine and anadromous fish species (17).

LISTING IS WARRANTED: THE PROPOSAL PROCESS. If a status review indicates that listing is warranted, the agency with jurisdiction officially proposes the species for listing under the ESA. This declaration is made in the *Federal Register*. The agency first asks at least three independent biological experts to verify that the petitioned species requires listing. After that, input from the public, other federal and state agencies, and the scientific community is welcomed. The period of public comment typically lasts 60 days, but may be extended in some cases. Within 45 days of proposal issuance interested parties can

TABLE 2.5

Candidate species by group type as of November 2013

Species type	Number
Under U.S. Fish and Wildlife Service jurisdiction	
Amphibians	6
Arachnids	1
Birds	10
Clams	6
Conifers and cycads	1
Crustaceans	4
Ferns and allies	4
Freshwater fish	11
Flowering plants	47
Insects	29
Marine mammals	1
Reptiles	7
Snails	10
Terrestrial mammals	9
Total	**146**
Under National Marine Fisheries Service jurisdiction	
Marine invertebrates	5
Marine mammals	1
Marine reptiles	1
Marine and anadromous fish	17
Total	**24**

SOURCE: Adapted from "Table 1—Candidate Notice of Review (Animals and Plants)," in *Endangered and Threatened Wildlife and Plants; Review of Native Species That Are Candidates for Listing as Endangered or Threatened*, U.S. Department of the Interior, U.S. Fish and Wildlife Service, November 22, 2013, http://www.fws.gov/endangered/esa-library/pdf/2013_11_22_ CNOR.pdf (accessed December 14, 2013) and "Candidates for Listing (24 Candidate 'Species')," in *Candidate and Proposed Species under the Endangered Species Act (ESA)*, U.S. Department of Commerce, National Oceanic and Atmospheric Administration, National Marine Fisheries Service, November 26, 2013, http://www.nmfs.noaa.gov/pr/species/esa/candidate.htm (accessed December 16, 2013)

TABLE 2.6

Species proposed for listing under the Endangered Species Act, November 2013

Species type	Number
Under U.S. Fish and Wildlife Service jurisdiction	
Amphibians	6
Birds	5
Fishes	5
Flowering plants	15
Insects	4
Reptiles	2
Terrestrial mammals	8
Total	**45**
Under National Marine Fisheries Service jurisdiction	
Marine invertebrates	66*
Marine and anadromous fish	14
Total	**80**

*Includes two already listed coral species under consideration for proposed reclassification from threatened to endangered

SOURCE: Adapted from "Table 1—Candidate Notice of Review (Animals and Plants)," in *Endangered and Threatened Wildlife and Plants; Review of Native Species That Are Candidates for Listing as Endangered or Threatened*, U.S. Department of the Interior, U.S. Fish and Wildlife Service, November 22, 2013, http://www.fws.gov/endangered/esa-library/pdf/2013_11_22_CNOR.pdf (accessed December 14, 2013) "Proposed for Listing (80 Proposed 'Species')," in *Candidate and Proposed Species under the Endangered Species Act (ESA)*, U.S. Department of Commerce, National Oceanic and Atmospheric Administration, National Marine Fisheries Service, November 26, 2013, http://www.nmfs.noaa.gov/pr/species/esa/candidate.htm (accessed December 16, 2013)

request that public hearings be held on the issues involved with listing. Such hearings are also held in cases where public interest is high in the listing outcome.

As shown in Table 2.6, there were 45 species under USFWS jurisdiction and 80 species under NMFS jurisdiction that were proposed for listing under the ESA as of November 2013. The largest numbers were marine invertebrates (66), flowering plants (15), and marine and anadromous fish species (14).

FINAL DECISION ON LISTING. Once a species begins the proposal process, the USFWS or the NMFS must ultimately take one of three possible actions:

- Withdraw the proposal—the biological information is found not to support listing the species

- Extend the proposal period—there is substantial disagreement within the scientific community regarding the listing; only one six-month extension is allowed, and then a final decision must be made

- Publish a final listing rule in the *Federal Register*— the listing becomes effective 30 days after publication, unless otherwise indicated

EMERGENCY LISTING. The ESA authorizes the USFWS or the NMFS to issue temporary emergency listings for species when evidence indicates an immediate and significant risk to the well-being of a species (e.g., following a natural disaster). Two designations are possible: endangered emergency listing and threatened emergency listing. The listing must be published in the *Federal Register* and is effective for only 240 days. During this time the normal status review procedure continues.

Petitioners also have the right under the ESA to ask the USFWS or the NMFS for an emergency listing for a species.

The USFWS (http://ecos.fws.gov/tess_public/pub/ad HocSpeciesCountForm.jsp) indicates that as of February 2014 there were no emergency listings in effect for endangered or threatened species.

PROTECTIONS AND ACTIONS TRIGGERED BY LISTING

In "Threatened and Endangered Species" (April 4, 2013, http://www.fws.gov/carlsbad/TEspecies/Recovery/5YearReview.htm) and "Listing and Critical Habitat: Overview" (July 15, 2013, http://www.fws.gov/endangered/what-we-do/listing-overview.html), the USFWS describes the protections and actions that are triggered when a species is listed under the ESA.

Five-Year Status Reviews

Section 4(c)(2)(A) of the ESA requires a status review of the condition and situation of a listed species at least every five years to determine whether it still requires government protection. As the number of listed species has increased over the years so has the number of required five-year reviews, further stressing agency resources.

USFWS records indicate that the so-called five-year reviews are seldom performed on time. In fact, they are frequently late by several years or even decades. This chronic tardiness has spurred substantial litigation against the agency. As will be explained later in this chapter, development and industry groups are keen to have five-year reviews performed for listed species that they believe have recovered sufficiently to be delisted or downlisted (reclassified from endangered to threatened). In contrast, conservation groups want five-year status reviews to be conducted in a timely manner for threatened species that they believe should be uplisted from threatened to endangered status.

Taking, Possessing, or Trading Listed Species

The ESA makes illegal the taking of listed species. For animal species, taking is defined as killing, harming, harassing, pursuing, or removing the species from the wild. For plants, taking means collecting or "maliciously" damaging endangered plants on federal lands. The ESA also outlaws removing or damaging listed plants on state and private lands "in knowing violation of State law or in the course of violating a State criminal trespass law." The USFWS notes that some state laws specifically prohibit the taking of federally listed plants and animals.

The USFWS explains in "Permits for Native Species under the Endangered Species Act" (March 2013, http://www.fws.gov/endangered/esa-library/pdf/permits.pdf) that it is also illegal under the ESA to possess, ship, deliver, carry, transport, sell, or receive any listed species that was taken in violation of the law. Likewise, the import, export, and interstate or foreign sales of listed species are prohibited except for permitted conservation purposes.

Civil and criminal penalties can be levied for violations of these provisions; exemptions, however, are allowed under certain sections of the ESA.

SECTION 4(D) EXEMPTIONS. Section 4(d) of the ESA (http://www.fws.gov/endangered/laws-policies/section-4.html) allows the USFWS to issue regulations governing the conservation of threatened species and those listed as experimental populations. As a result, "special" rules have been issued that grant exemptions from the taking, possession, and import/export/sales provisions for some

threatened species and experimental populations. For example, grizzly bears can be harmed "in self-defense or in defense of others." However, such taking has to be reported to authorities within a specified period. An updated listing of species with section 4(d) exemptions is available at http://ecos.fws.gov/tess_public/pub/special Rule.jsp?listings=0&type=4D.

INCIDENTAL TAKE PERMITS AND HABITAT CONSER-VATION PLANS. When the original ESA was passed, it included exceptions that allowed the taking of listed species only for scientific research or other conservation activities authorized by the act. In 1982 Congress added a provision in section 10 of the ESA that allows "incidental take" of listed species of wildlife by nonfederal entities. Incidental take is defined as take that is incidental to, but not the purpose of, an otherwise lawful activity. Incidental taking cannot appreciably reduce the likelihood of the survival and recovery of listed species in the wild. The incidental take provision was added to allow private landowners some freedom to develop their land even if it provides habitat to listed species.

To obtain an incidental take permit, an applicant has to prepare a Habitat Conservation Plan (HCP). The HCP process is described by the USFWS in "Habitat Conservation Plans under the Endangered Species Act" (April 2011, http://www.fws.gov/endangered/esa-library/pdf/hcp.pdf). An HCP describes the impacts that are likely to result from the taking of the species and the measures the applicant will take to minimize and mitigate the impacts. HCPs are generally partnerships drawn up by people at the local level who are working with officials from the USFWS or the NMFS. The plans frequently represent compromises between developers and environmentalists.

Included in the agreement is a "no surprise" provision that assures landowners that the overall cost of species protection measures will be limited to what has been agreed to under the HCP. In return, landowners make a long-term commitment to conservation as negotiated in the HCP. Many HCPs include the preservation of significant areas of habitat for endangered species.

ENHANCEMENT OF SURVIVAL PERMITS. Another type of permit issued under the ESA is the enhancement of survival permit. This permit applies to species that are candidate species or are likely to become candidate species. It authorizes future incidental take (should the species become listed) by nonfederal landowners in exchange for proactive management of the species on their property. Permit applicants must agree to participate in a Candidate Conservation Agreement with Assurances (CCAA) or a Safe Harbor Agreement (SHA). These agreements provide assurances to landowners that no additional future regulatory restrictions will be imposed.

SUBSISTENCE TAKING. Besides the previously mentioned taking exemptions offered by the ESA, the native peoples of Alaska who rely on certain endangered or threatened animals for food or other products needed for subsistence are exempted from the taking rule under the Marine Mammal Protection Act. This act is described in detail in Chapter 3.

Critical Habitat

Under the ESA, the USFWS or the NMFS must decide whether critical habitat should be designated for a listed species. Critical habitat is specific geographical areas of land, water, and/or air space that contain features essential for the conservation of a listed species and that may require special management and protection. For example, these could be areas that are used for breeding, resting, and feeding. If the agency decides that critical habitat should be designated, a proposal notice is published in the *Federal Register* for public comment. If it is decided that critical habitat is needed, then the final boundaries are published in the *Federal Register*.

The role of critical habitat is often misunderstood by the public. Critical habitat designation does not set up a refuge or sanctuary for a species in which no development can take place. It can provide additional protection for a specific geographical area that might not occur without the designation. For example, if the USFWS determines that an area not currently occupied by a species is needed for species recovery and designates that area as critical habitat, any federal actions involving that area have to avoid adverse modifications. Critical habitat designation has no regulatory impact on private landowners unless they wish to take actions on their land that involve federal funding or permits.

The original ESA did not provide a time limit for the setting of critical habitat. In 1978 the law was amended to require that critical habitat be designated at the same time a species is listed. However, the designation is only required "when prudent." For example, the USFWS or the NMFS can refuse to designate critical habitat for a species if doing so would publicize the specific locations of organisms known to be targets for illegal hunting or collection. Historically, both agencies have broadly used the "when prudent" clause to justify not setting critical habitat for many listed species. This has been a contentious issue between the government and conservation groups.

Notices regarding proposed new or revised critical habitat designations must be placed in the *Federal Register* so that public comment can be obtained and considered before a designation is finalized.

Section 4(b)(2) of the ESA requires the ESA agencies to consider economic and other impacts when designating critical habitat. In August 2013 the USFWS (http://www.gpo.gov/fdsys/pkg/FR-2013-08-28/html/2013-20994.htm)

TABLE 2.7

Number of U.S. endangered and threatened species with critical habitat specified, November 2013

Mammals	32
Birds	28
Reptiles	14
Amphibians	15
Fish	76
Clams	37
Snails	14
Insects	36
Arachnids	8
Crustaceans	12
Corals	2
Flowering plants	388
Ferns and allies	16
Total	**678**

SOURCE: Adapted from "Listed Species with Critical Habitat," in *Species Reports*, U.S. Department of the Interior, U.S. Fish and Wildlife Service, November 1, 2013, http://ecos.fws.gov/tess_public/pub/criticalHabitat.jsp?nmfs=1 (accessed November 1, 2013)

indicated that beginning in October 2013 the economic analyses reports will be completed and published for public comment at the same time that critical habitat is proposed.

As of November 2013, critical habitat had been designated for 678 U.S. species. (See Table 2.7.) This represented 45% of the 1,516 U.S. species listed under the ESA at that time. (See Table 1.2 in Chapter 1.) Plants made up more than half of the listed species for which critical habitat had been designated.

Experimental Populations

For some species, primarily mammals, birds, fish, and aquatic invertebrates, recovery efforts include the introduction of individuals into new areas. Typically, this is accomplished by moving a small group of imperiled animals from an established area to one or more other locations within the species' historical range of distribution.

Experimental populations of a species are not subject to the same rigorous protections under the ESA as other members of the species. Experimental populations can be considered threatened, even if the rest of the species is listed as endangered. In addition, the USFWS can designate an experimental population as essential or nonessential. A nonessential designation indicates that the survival of this population is not believed essential to the survival of the species as a whole. A nonessential experimental population is treated under the law as if it is proposed for listing, not already listed. This results in less protection under the ESA.

As of November 2013, there were 62 experimental populations listed under the ESA, all nonessential. (See Table 2.8.) It should be noted that some species have multiple experimental populations.

TABLE 2.8

Experimental populations, November 2013

Species type	Number
Birds	6
Clams	31
Fishes	16
Insects	1
Snails	2
Terrestrial mammals	6
Total	**62**

SOURCE: Adapted from "Listing Status: Experimental Population (Essential), Experimental Population (Non-Essential)," in *Species Reports*, U.S. Department of the Interior, U.S. Fish and Wildlife Service, November 5, 2013, http://ecos.fws.gov/tess_public/pub/adHocSpeciesForm.jsp (accessed November 5, 2013)

Actions by Federal Agencies

Section 7 of the ESA includes restrictions on federal agencies (and their nonfederal agency permit applicants) regarding endangered and threatened species. These restrictions are described by the USFWS in "Consultations with Federal Agencies: Section 7 of the Endangered Species Act" (April 2011, http://www.fws.gov/endangered/esa-library/pdf/consultations.pdf). Specifically, the federal agencies must "aid in the conservation of listed species" and "ensure that their activities are not likely to jeopardize the continued existence of listed species or adversely modify designated critical habitats." This applies to any activities that are funded, authorized, or permitted by these federal agencies or carried out on lands or waters managed by them.

According to the USFWS, there are two processes through which federal agencies (known as action agencies) comply with section 7 of the ESA as they plan projects or activities that might impact listed species: informal consultation or formal consultation. In either case, the first step is for the action agency to coordinate with the USFWS or the NMFS early in the process to determine which, if any, listed species are within the project area and to determine whether the project might affect the listed species or its critical habitat. If the action agency and the USFWS or the NMFS (whichever has jurisdiction) agree that the project will not jeopardize the listed species, then the project may proceed. The same is true if the project can be easily modified to prevent adverse effects. In either case, an informal consultation is said to have taken place.

If the action agency makes a preliminary determination that the project is likely to adversely affect listed species, then it may initiate a formal consultation. The action agency provides detailed information about the project and the listed species to the USFWS or the NMFS. The governing agency then issues a report called a "biological opinion" that determines whether the proposed action is likely to have an adverse effect, and if so, recommends "reasonable and prudent alternatives that could allow the project to move forward."

Recovery Plans

The ESA requires that a recovery plan be developed and implemented for every listed species unless "such a plan will not promote the conservation of the species." The USFWS and the NMFS are directed to give priority to those species that are most likely to benefit from having a plan in place. The recovery potential of species is ranked from 1 to 18 by the USFWS. (See Table 2.9.) Low rankings indicate a greater likelihood that the species can be recovered. Priority is based on the degree of threat, the potential for recovery, and taxonomy (genetic distinctiveness). In addition, rankings can be appended with the letter C when species recovery is in conflict with

TABLE 2.9

U.S. Fish and Wildlife Service recovery potential priority ranking system

Degree of threat	Recovery potential	Taxonomy	Priority	Conflict
High	High	Monotypic genus	1	1C 1
	High	Species	2	2C 2
	High	Subspecies	3	3C 3
	Low	Monotypic genus	4	4C 4
	Low	Species	5	5C 5
	Low	Subspecies	6	6C 6
Moderate	High	Monotypic genus	7	7C 7
	High	Species	8	8C 8
	High	Subspecies	9	9C 9
	Low	Monotypic genus	10	10C 10
	Low	Species	11	11C 11
	Low	Subspecies	12	12C 12
Low	High	Monotypic genus	13	13C 13
	High	Species	14	14C 14
	High	Subspecies	15	15C 15
	Low	Monotypic genus	16	16C 16
	Low	Species	17	17C 17
	Low	Subspecies	18	18C 18

SOURCE: John J. Fay and W. L. Thomas, "Table 3. Recovery Priority," in "Fish and Wildlife Service: Endangered and Threatened Species Listing and Recovery Priority Guidelines," *Federal Register*, vol. 48, no. 184, September 21, 1983, and *Federal Register*, vol. 48, no. 221, November 15, 1983 (correction), http://www.fws.gov/endangered/esa-library/pdf/48fr43098-43105.pdf (accessed November 12, 2013)

TABLE 2.10

National Marine Fisheries Service recovery potential priority ranking system

Magnitude of threat	Recovery potential	Conflict	Priority
High	High	Conflict	1
		No conflict	2
	Low to moderate	Conflict	3
		No conflict	4
Moderate	High	Conflict	5
		No conflict	6
	Low to moderate	Conflict	7
		No conflict	8
Low	High	Conflict	9
		No conflict	10
	Low to moderate	Conflict	11
		No Conflict	12

SOURCE: William J. Fox, Jr., "Table 3. Species Recovery Priority," in "National Oceanic and Atmospheric Administration: Endangered and Threatened Species Listing and Recovery Priority Guidelines," *Federal Register*, vol. 55, no. 116, June 15, 1990, http://www.nmfs.noaa.gov/pr/pdfs/fr/fr55-24296.pdf (accessed November 12, 2013)

economic activities. Species with a C designation have higher priority than other species within the same numerical ranking. The NMFS uses a different rating system that ranges from 1 (highest recovery potential) to 12 (lowest recovery potential). (See Table 2.10.)

Each recovery plan must include the following three elements:

- Site-specific management actions to achieve the plan's goals

- Objective and measurable criteria for determining when a species is recovered

- Estimates of the amount of time and money that will be required to achieve recovery

The USFWS describes in "Endangered Species Recovery Program" (June 2011, http://www.fws.gov/end angered/esa-library/pdf/recovery.pdf) a recovery plan as "a road map with detailed site-specific management actions for private, Federal, and State cooperation in conserving listed species and their ecosystems." Recovery plans include precisely defined milestones for recovery achievement. For example, recovery may be considered accomplished when a certain number of individuals is reached and specifically named threats are eliminated. The USFWS notes, however, that a recovery plan is not a regulatory document.

As of November 2013, most (1,145 or 76%) of the 1,516 listed species in the United States at that time had recovery plans in place. (See Table 1.2 in Chapter 1.)

TRACKING RECOVERY PLANS. Notices regarding proposed new or revised recovery plans must be placed in the *Federal Register* so that public comment can be obtained and considered before a plan is finalized. A searchable database of recovery plans is available at the USFWS website (http://ecos.fws.gov/tess_public/TESSWebpage Recovery?sort=1). The database also includes some information about the implementation and scheduling of recovery plan activities. Information on the progress (or lack thereof) toward recovery is provided in the five-year status review reports on a species-by-species basis; however, as noted earlier, many of the five-year reviews are not conducted in a timely manner. During 2009 the agencies prepared brief action plans for selected "spot-light species" that provide information about recovery plan goals and the progress made toward achieving them. According to the USFWS, in "Species Information" (September 27, 2013, http://www.fws.gov/north east/ecologicalservices/species.html), the spotlight species were "a representative group" of species that had detailed conservation plans in place. The action plans can be accessed at the USFWS website (http://ecos.fws .gov/tess_public/) for individual species.

DELISTING UNDER THE ESA

Delisting occurs when a species is removed from the candidate list, the proposed list, or the final list of endangered and threatened species. Delisting takes place for a variety of reasons, as indicated by the D codes in Table 2.3. In general, delisting occurs when the USFWS or the NMFS finds that a species has recovered or become extinct, or on various procedural grounds, including discovery of additional habitats or populations. The USFWS notes in "Delisting a Species: Section 4 of the Endangered Species Act" (April 2011, http://www.fws.gov/endan gered/esa-library/pdf/delisting.pdf) that the delisting process for a species believed recovered is similar to the listing process. The agency assesses population data, recovery achievements, and threats to the species. A proposal for delisting is published in the *Federal Register* for review and comment by scientists and the public. Expert opinions are obtained from three independent species specialists. All the collected information is analyzed and a final decision on delisting is published in the *Federal Register*. Under the ESA, the USFWS or the NMFS (in cooperation with state agencies) is required to monitor for at least five years any species that has been delisted due to recovery. This is accomplished through a post-delisting monitoring strategy that goes through peer review (review by qualified scientists) and public comment before being finalized.

Entities (species or distinct populations) that have been delisted as of November 2013 are shown in Table 2.11. Of the 59 delisted entities, 31 had recovered, 10 became extinct, and the remaining 18 had procedural issues.

PRIVATE-PARTY PETITIONS

As noted earlier, the ESA allows private parties (e.g., individuals and nongovernmental organizations [NGOs])

TABLE 2.11

Delisted U.S. and foreign species, November 1, 2013

Date species first listed	Date delisted	Species name	Reason delisted
05/18/1984	06/19/2006	Agave, Arizona (Agave arizonica)	Original data in error—not a listable entity
07/27/1979	06/04/1987	Alligator, American Entire (Alligator mississippiensis)	Recovered
12/06/1979	10/01/2003	Barberry, Truckee (Berberis (=Mahonia) sonnei)	Original data in error—taxonomic revision
02/17/1984	02/06/1996	Bidens, cuneate (Bidens cuneata)	Original data in error—taxonomic revision
08/27/1984	02/23/2004	Broadbill, Guam (Myiagra freycineti)	Extinct
04/28/1976	08/31/1984	Butterfly, Bahama swallowtail (Heraclides andraemon bonhotei)	Original data in error—act amendment
11/28/1979	06/24/1999	Cactus, Lloyd's hedgehog (Echinocereus lloydii)	Original data in error—taxonomic revision
12/07/1979	09/22/1993	Cactus, spineless hedgehog (Echinocereus triglochidiatus var. inermis)	Original data in error—not a listable entity
09/17/1980	08/27/2002	Cinquefoil, Robbins' (Potentilla robbinsiana)	Recovered
03/11/1967	09/02/1983	Cisco, longjaw (Coregonus alpenae)	Extinct
07/05/1979	09/02/2011	Coneflower, Tennessee purple (Echinacea tennesseensis)	Recovered
06/02/1970	05/23/2012	Crocodile, Morelet's (Crocodylus moreletii)	Recovered
09/05/1985	02/18/2011	Daisy, Maguire (Erigeron maguirei)	Recovered
07/24/2003	07/24/2003	Deer, Columbian white-tailed Douglas County DPS (Odocoileus virginianus leucurus)	Recovered
06/02/1970	09/12/1985	Dove, Palau ground (Gallicolumba canifrons)	Recovered
03/11/1967	07/25/1978	Duck, Mexican U.S.A. only (Anas diazi)	Original data in error—taxonomic revision
03/11/1967	08/08/2007	Eagle, bald lower 48 States (Haliaeetus leucocephalus)	Recovered
06/02/1970	08/25/1999	Falcon, American peregrine (Falco peregrinus anatum)	Recovered
06/02/1970	10/05/1994	Falcon, Arctic peregrine (Falco peregrinus tundrius)	Recovered
06/02/1970	09/12/1985	Flycatcher, Palau fantail (Rhipidura lepida)	Recovered
04/30/1980	12/04/1987	Gambusia, Amistad (Gambusia amistadensis)	Extinct
04/29/1986	06/18/1993	Globeberry, Tumamoc (Tumamoca macdougalii)	Original data in error—new information discovered
03/11/1967	03/20/2001	Goose, Aleutian Canada (Branta canadensis leucopareia)	Recovered
10/11/1979	11/27/1989	Hedgehog cactus, purple-spined (Echinocereus engelmannii var. purpureus)	Original data in error—taxonomic revision
12/30/1974	03/09/1995	Kangaroo, eastern gray (Macropus giganteus)	Recovered
12/30/1974	03/09/1995	Kangaroo, red (Macropus rufus)	Recovered
12/30/1974	03/09/1995	Kangaroo, western gray (Macropus fuliginosus)	Recovered
12/08/1977	02/23/2004	Mallard, Mariana (Anas oustalet)	Extinct
05/27/1978	09/14/1989	Milk-vetch, Rydberg (Astragalus perianus)	Original data in error—new information discovered
06/02/1970	09/21/2004	Monarch, Tinian (old world flycatcher) (Monarcha takatsukasae)	Recovered
06/02/1970	09/12/1985	Owl, Palau (Pyrroglaux podargina)	Recovered
06/14/1976	01/09/1984	Pearlymussel, Sampson's (Epioblasma sampsoni)	Extinct
06/02/1970	12/17/2009	Pelican, brown except U.S. Atlantic coast, FL, AL (Pelecanus occidentalis)	Recovered
06/02/1970	02/04/1985	Pelican, brown U.S. Atlantic coast, FL, AL (Pelecanus occidentalis)	Recovered
07/13/1982	09/22/1993	Pennyroyal, Mckittrick (Hedeoma apiculatum)	Original data in error—new information discovered
03/11/1967	09/02/1983	Pike, blue (Stizostedion vitreum glaucum)	Extinct
10/13/1970	01/15/1982	Pupfish, Tecopa (Cyprinodon nevadensis calidae)	Extinct
03/10/1997	04/14/2006	Pygmy-owl, cactus ferruginous AZ pop. (Glaucidium brasilianum cactorum)	Original data in error—not a listable entity
04/05/1990	11/04/2013	Sea-lion, Steller Eastern population (Eumetopias jubatus)	Recovered
04/10/1979	10/28/2008	Seal, Caribbean monk (Monachustropicalis)	Extinct
04/17/1989	06/14/2013	Shagreen, Magazine Mountain entire (Mesodon magazinensis)	Recovered
09/26/1986	02/28/2000	Shrew, Dismal Swamp southeastern (Sorex longirostris fisheri)	Original data in error—new information discovered
12/14/1992	09/24/2010	Snail, Utah valvata (Valvata utahensis)	Original data in error—new information discovered
09/03/1986	11/28/2011	Snake, Concho water (Nerodia paucimaculata)	Recovered
08/30/1999	09/15/2011	Snake, Lake Erie water subspecies range clarified (Nerodia sipedon insularum)	Recovered
03/11/1967	12/12/1990	Sparrow, dusky seaside (Ammodramus maritimus nigrescens)	Extinct
06/04/1973	10/12/1983	Sparrow, Santa Barbara song (Melospiza melodia graminea)	Extinct
12/14/1992	09/05/2007	Springsnail, Idaho (Pyrgulopsis idahoensis)	Original data in error—taxonomic revision
07/31/1985	03/04/2013	Squirrel, Virginia northern flying entire (Glaucomys sabrinus fuscus)	Recovered
05/22/1997	08/18/2005	Sunflower, Eggert's (Helianthus eggertii)	Recovered
12/18/1977	11/22/1983	Treefrog, pine barrens FL pop. (Hyla andersonii)	Original data in error—new information discovered
09/13/1996	04/26/2000	Trout, coastal cutthroat Umpqua R. (Oncorhynchus clarkii clarkii)	Original data in error—taxonomic revision
06/14/1976	02/29/1984	Turtle, Indian flap-shelled (Lissemys punctata punctata)	Original data in error—erroneous data
06/16/1994	06/16/1994	Whale, gray except where listed (Eschrichtius robustus)	Recovered
04/10/1978	01/27/2012	Wolf, gray MN (Canis lupus)	Recovered
01/27/2012	04/02/2009	Wolf, gray Western Great Lakes DPS (Canis lupus)	Recovered
05/05/2011	05/05/2011	Wolf, gray Northern Rocky Mountain DPS (delisted, except WY) (Canis lupus)	Recovered
05/05/2011	09/30/2012	Wolf, gray WY, EXPN population (Canis lupus)	Recovered
07/19/1990	10/07/2003	Woolly-star, Hoover's (Eriastrum hooveri)	Recovered

DPS = Distinct population segment; pop. = Population; R. = River.

SOURCE: "Delisting Report," in *Species Reports*, U.S. Department of the Interior, U.S. Fish and Wildlife Service, November 1, 2013, http://ecos.fws.gov/tess_public/pub/delistingReport.jsp (accessed November 1, 2013) to submit listing petitions to the federal government. The NGOs are typically environmental or conservation groups that have the funding and expertise to develop petitions containing the required scientific data supporting the need for listing. Since the passage of the law in 1973, some NGOs have flooded the USFWS and the NMFS with listing petitions. According to D. Noah Greenwald, Kieran Suckling, and Martin Taylor, in "The Listing Record" (Dale D. Goble, J. Michael Scott, and Frank W. Davis, eds., *The Endangered Species Act at Thirty: Renewing the Conservation Promise*, 2006), the vast majority of the listings that occurred between 1996 and 2004 were driven by private-party petitions. Since 2004 private parties have submitted petitions covering hundreds of additional species.

The USFWS or the NMFS must determine within 90 days whether a petition contains "substantial information" suggesting that a species may require listing under the ESA. If listing is found to be warranted, the responsible agency is supposed to complete a status review for the species within 12 months. These time constraints have proven infeasible given the large number of petitions coming into the agencies and the large number of species involved. As a result, NGOs have filed numerous lawsuits against the agencies for failing to comply with ESA-mandated deadlines.

Since the 1990s the USFWS has repeatedly complained that many of its decisions and activities are driven by court orders, rather than by scientific priorities. The agency has also suggested that NGOs have taken advantage of ESA provisions that allow citizen lawsuits. Critics claim the groups flood the USFWS with petitions so that lawsuits can be brought when the agency is unable to respond in a timely manner. Deborah Zabarenko notes in "Deal Aims to Cut Endangered Species Red Tape" (Reuters.com, May 10, 2011) that between 1994 and 2006 the USFWS received an average of approximately 17 petitions annually; however, between 2007 and May 2011 the agency received 1,230 petitions.

Environmentalists argue that the lawsuits are necessary because the USFWS fails to do the job assigned to it under the ESA.

CANDIDATE SPECIES BACKLOG

The USFWS has also been repeatedly sued for designating species as candidate species. As noted earlier, this designation means the USFWS acknowledges that the species deserves protection under the ESA, but believes that more pressing priorities must come first. The agency's September 1997 CNOR (http://www.gpo.gov/fdsys/pkg/FR-1997-09-19/html/97-24805.htm) included 207 candidate species. Subsequent annual CNORs (http://www.fws.gov/endangered/what-we-do/earlier-notices.html) continued to include 200 or more candidate species, much to the displeasure of conservation and wildlife NGOs.

The USFWS notes in "Improving ESA Implementation" (August 29, 2013, http://www.fws.gov/endangered/improving_ESA/listing_workplan.html) that multiple lawsuits dealing with candidate species were bundled together and resolved in late 2011 through legal settlements that were reached separately with the suing NGOs. Overall, the agency agreed to make listing decisions by 2017 for over 250 species included in the November 2010 CNOR (http://www.fws.gov/endangered/what-we-do/cnor-2010.html) and to make critical habitat determinations for any of these species that become listed. In addition, the agency set a timetable for reviewing previously submitted petitions for hundreds of species. In exchange, the NGOs involved in the settlements agreed to restrictions on their ESA petitioning and litigation activities through 2017.

The work called for under the legal settlements represents an increase in workload for the USFWS. It is uncertain whether Congress will fund the agency sufficiently to allow the work to be completed as planned. The timetable can also be derailed if other NGOs submit numerous petitions or file several ESA-related lawsuits over the coming years. However, the USFWS CNOR published in November 2013 included only 146 candidates. (See Table 2.5.) Thus, the agency had made some progress in reducing the number of candidate species.

In *USFWS Endangered Species Act Listing Workplan: FY13–FY18 MDL Packages and Other Court Settlement Agreements* (March 3, 2013, http://www.fws.gov/Endangered/improving_ESA/FY13-18_ESA_Listing_workplan.pdf), the USFWS lays out its internal deadlines (including court-ordered deadlines) for reducing the candidate species backlog in accordance with the legal settlements. The work plan, which covers more than 400 species, also includes species from the backlog of petitions that have been submitted to the agency.

Equal Access to Judgment Act

Critics assert that NGOs benefit financially from ESA-related lawsuits at the taxpayers' expense because of the Equal Access to Judgment Act (EAJA). The EAJA, passed by Congress in 1980 and signed into law by President Ronald Reagan (1911–2004), requires the federal government to pay the attorneys' fees of eligible individuals, nonprofit organizations, and other entities when these parties sue the federal government and prevail in court. NGOs have filed and won so many ESA-related lawsuits that they are believed to have collected many millions of dollars in legal fees from the government. The exact figures are unknown because the government does not compile or disclose the information.

Critics claim that litigious NGOs abuse the EAJA by submitting numerous ESA listing petitions and then suing when the government is unable to meet the mandated deadlines. The groups then collect attorneys' fees that fund additional listing petitions and lawsuits.

Overprotection Lawsuits

Overprotection lawsuits are typically filed by private parties whose economic interests are threatened by ESA measures. Examples include farmers, ranchers, landowners and developers, industry groups and associations, and the operators or users of natural resources, such as water and irrigation districts. The parties may be opposed to listings or designation of critical habitat for particular species or they may attempt to compel the federal government to delist or downlist species.

One of the most famous overprotection cases in ESA history concerns the polar bear, which was proposed in 2007 for listing as threatened. As will be explained in Chapter 3, the listing is unique because the most significant threat to the species' survival is believed to be climate change, specifically the loss of habitat due to continuing global warming. The Pacific Legal Foundation (PLF) notes in "PLF Challenges Unwarranted Polar Bear Listing" (2013, http://www.pacificlegal.org/cases/PLF-challenges-unwarranted-polar-bear-listing) that it sued the government in 2008 on behalf of the California Cattlemen's Association on various legal grounds. In June 2011 a federal court ruled against the PLF. The organization appealed, but lost. In October 2013 the U.S. Supreme Court refused to consider the case, which essentially settled the matter.

As noted earlier, the USFWS has historically been late in completing five-year reviews that are required by the ESA. Groups that allege the ESA is overprotective use legal action to force the agency to conduct the reviews for species they believe have recovered or improved in population. The PLF explains in "If Feds Concede a Species Isn't 'Endangered,' It Shouldn't Stay on the 'Endangered' List" (2014, http://www.pacificlegal.org/) that in 2005 it entered into a settlement agreement with the agency over the latter's failure to conduct status reviews for nearly 200 listed species in California. By 2008 the reviews for more than half of the species had been completed and resulted in recommendations for six of the species: the delisting of the Inyo California towhee (a bird) and the downlisting of the arroyo toad, the Indian Knob mountain balm (a plant), the Lane Mountain milkvetch (a plant), the Modoc sucker (a fish), and the Santa Cruz cypress (a plant). However, the agency did not finalize the decisions over the following year, spurring a petition from the PLF. In January 2011 the USFWS agreed to perform status reviews on the six species. As noted earlier, the ESA requires a status review to be completed within a year.

In April 2013 the PLF sued the USFWS for failing to meet the status review deadline. In September 2013 the agency (http://www.gpo.gov/fdsys/pkg/FR-2013-09-03/pdf/2013-21313.pdf) officially proposed that the Santa Cruz cypress be reclassified as threatened. Two months later the USFWS (http://www.gpo.gov/fdsys/pkg/FR-2013-11-04/pdf/2013-26122.pdf) officially proposed the Inyo California towhee for delisting. In February 2014 the agency (http://www.gpo.gov/fdsys/pkg/FR-2014-02-13/pdf/2014-01526.pdf) officially proposed delisting the Modoc sucker. As of February 2014, final decisions on the three proposals had not been published. In December 2013 the USFWS (http://www.gpo.gov/fdsys/pkg/FR-2013-12-11/pdf/2013-29410.pdf) announced its status review finding that the Indian Knob mountain balm did not warrant downlisting from endangered to threatened. As of February 2014, the status reviews for the other two contested species had not been completed.

Environment and Natural Resources Division

The U.S. Department of Justice's Environment and Natural Resources Division (ENRD) handles litigation cases that are associated with the nation's environmental and conservation laws, including the ESA. The ENRD provides in *Overview of the Endangered Species Act and Highlights of Recent Litigation* (January 2004, http://www.abanet.org/environ/committees/endangered/OverviewoftheESA.pdf) a brief summary of the several hundred ESA-related lawsuits that had reached the courts as of early 2004. The ENRD notes that some ESA litigation involved broad issues, such as the function of the law and the scope of the duties of the USFWS and the NMFS under the law. However, the vast majority of lawsuits focused on particular species. ENRD-litigation summaries for individual years since 2004 are available at http://www.justice.gov/enrd/Current_topics.html.

U.S. Supreme Court Cases

One of the foremost legal cases in ESA history involved a tiny fish called the snail darter in the Little Tennessee River. The ENRD reports in "*Tennessee Valley Authority v. Hill*: The Snail Darter Case" (November 2010, http://www.justice.gov/enrd/Tennessee_Valley_Authority_vs_Hill.html) that a biologist discovered the fish in the river in 1973, the same year that the ESA became law. At that time the Tennessee Valley Authority (TVA; a federally owned corporation) was building the Tellico Dam near Knoxville, Tennessee. The dam was to provide hydroelectric power and flood control by backing up the river into a 30-mile (48.3-kilometer) reservoir. In 1975 the USFWS declared the snail darter an endangered species and designated the Little Tennessee River as its critical habitat. Completion of the nearly finished dam—on which $78 million of tax money had already been spent—was put on hold while a massive legal battle was fought.

In 1978 the U.S. Supreme Court ruled in *Tennessee Valley Authority v. Hill* (437 U.S. 153) that protection of the snail darter outweighed the economic loss of abandoning the dam. The ENRD notes that the Supreme Court acknowledged "the perceived absurdity in forfeiting tens of millions of dollars of public funds for a small fish," but points out that the ESA did not include any provisions for cost-benefit analysis. In other words, the apparent intent of the ESA was to protect imperiled species regardless of the cost.

The decision was hailed as a great victory by environmental and conservation groups, but was extremely unpopular otherwise. Congress added new language to section 7 of the ESA allowing costs to be considered when federally funded or managed projects conflict with the needs of imperiled species. In addition, a separate bill was passed exempting the Tellico Dam from the ESA requirements for the snail darter. In 1979 the dam was completed, and the tiny fish was presumed exterminated. However, during the early 1980s more populations of the snail darter were discovered in Tennessee rivers and streams. In 1984 the USFWS downlisted the species from endangered to threatened and rescinded its critical habitat designation. As of February 2014, the snail darter remained on the list of threatened species.

In "ESA in the Supreme Court" (November 2010, http://www.justice.gov/enrd/4714.htm), the ENRD notes that four other notable ESA-related cases have reached the U.S. Supreme Court:

- *Babbitt v. Sweet Home Chapter of Communities for a Better Oregon* (515 U.S. 687 [1985])—the court affirmed the DOI's interpretation of taking under the ESA to include "significant modification or degradation where it actually kills or injures wildlife."

- *Bennett v. Spear* (520 U.S. 154 [1997])—the court broadened the right of individuals (and groups) to sue the federal government over ESA issues.

- *National Association of Home Builders v. Defenders of Wildlife* (551 U.S. 644 [2007])—the court affirmed that only specific types of federal actions fall under section 7 of the ESA.

- *Winter v. Natural Resources Defense Council* (555 U.S. 7 [2008])—the court overruled lower court decisions that had placed restrictions on the U.S. Navy's use of sonar during submarine training exercises off the coast of California. The lower courts had found in favor of plaintiffs, which argued that the sonar harmed marine mammals protected by federal laws, including the ESA.

THE GOD SQUAD

The snail darter controversy prompted Congress to amend the ESA in 1978 by creating a committee, informally dubbed "the God Squad," with the power to grant exemptions from section 7 of the law based on economic considerations. As noted earlier, section 7 includes restrictions on federal agencies (and their nonfederal agency permit applicants) regarding endangered and threatened species. The restrictions apply only to activities that are funded, authorized, or permitted by federal agencies or carried out on lands or waters managed by them. In "*Tennessee Valley Authority v. Hill*: The Snail Darter Case," the ENRD indicates that the God Squad considered but rejected exempting the TVA dam project from ESA requirements.

Over the decades the God Squad provision has been used very infrequently considering that thousands of projects subject to section 7 requirements are undertaken each year. As of December 2013, only three projects were known to have undergone God Squad consideration. They are described in detail by Erick Yuknis of Boston College in "Would a 'God Squad' Exemption under the Endangered Species Act Solve the California Water Crisis?" (*Boston College Environmental Affairs Law Review*, vol. 38, no. 2, May 1, 2011). According to Yuknis, the God Squad convened during the late 1970s to hear two cases: the TVA snail darter case and a case involving construction of the Grayrocks dam in Wyoming. Conservation groups feared that changing river flows would harm whooping crane populations; the species was listed as endangered under the ESA. The God Squad ultimately voted to exempt the project from the section 7 requirements; however, by the time the decision was made the contesting parties had reached a compromise agreement to complete the dam but accommodate the water needs of the whooping crane.

During the early 1990s controversy erupted in the Pacific Northwest over logging of old-growth trees on federal lands, an activity overseen by the Bureau of Land Management (BLM). The forests are home to populations of the northern spotted owl, which in 1990 was designated a threatened species under the ESA. Chapter 8 of this book describes in detail the bitter battle that raged between logging interests (with the support of the federal government) and conservationists over BLM's attempts to allow logging on dozens of tracts of federal land. Yuknis notes that a God Squad was convened and ultimately decided to exempt some of the logging activities from section 7 requirements. However, its decision was moot because the parties had in the meantime developed a compromise plan to proceed.

ESA SPENDING

Various federal agencies spend money to uphold the ESA. The primary agencies are the USFWS and the NMFS. For accounting purposes, the federal government operates on a fiscal year (FY) that runs from October through September. Thus, FY 2014 covers October 1,

2013, through September 30, 2014. Each year by the first Monday in February the U.S. president must present a proposed budget to the U.S. House of Representatives. This is the amount of money that the president estimates will be required to operate the federal government during the next fiscal year. It should be noted that Congress can take many months, even more than a year, to finalize and enact a federal budget. This has been particularly true during the 21st century due to fierce disagreements within Congress about government spending. For example, lawmakers were unable to agree on a budget for FY 2013 and instead passed a continuing resolution that generally kept funding at the previous year's level.

Table 2.12 shows funding enacted for FY 2012, allocated under a continuing resolution for FY 2013, and requested for FY 2014 for the USFWS endangered species program. For FY 2014, $185.4 million was requested. Nearly half of the money was allocated to recovery programs ($86.5 million), followed by consultations with other agencies and HCPs ($64.8 million), listing and critical habitat activities ($22.6 million), and candidate species conservation ($11.5 million).

The NMFS does not provide a breakdown of its ESA activities for the budget process.

Species Expenditures

Section 18 of the ESA requires the USFWS to file an annual report detailing certain expenditures that were made for the conservation of threatened and endangered species under the act. In *Federal and State Endangered and Threatened Species Expenditures: Fiscal Year 2012* (September 2013, http://www.fws.gov/endangered/esa-library/pdf/2012.EXP.FINAL.pdf), the USFWS indicates that nearly $1.4 billion was spent by federal agencies in FY 2012 to protect more than 1,400 specific entities (species, subspecies, DPS, or ESU) under the ESA.

ESA EXPENDITURES BY SPECIES. Table 2.13 shows the 20 species with the highest reported expenditures under the ESA in FY 2012. Together, these species accounted for nearly $924 million in spending. The list is dominated by fish species. Approximately $263.1 million was spent on the steelhead, followed by $240.7 million for the chinook salmon. Both species are anadromous, as are coho salmon, sockeye salmon, and chum salmon, and are found in the waters of the Pacific Northwest. The other fish on the list (excluding the Atlantic salmon) are freshwater species. There are two marine (ocean-based) mammals on the list: the Steller sea lion and the West Indian manatee. The list also contains several terrestrial mammal, bird, and reptile species.

How best to use the funds that are allocated to endangered species has been a contentious issue for years. The majority of the money spent in FY 2012 was devoted to only a few species.

The number of species being added to the federal threatened and endangered species list is expected to grow. Although vertebrate species dominated the list during the early years of the act, by the 21st century plants and invertebrate animals made up a much greater proportion

TABLE 2.12

U.S. Fish and Wildlife Service budget details for 2012, 2013, and proposed for 2014

[Dollars in thousands]

Appropriation: Resource management	2013 full yr. CR (PL. 112–175)	2012 enacted	Fixed costs	Internal transfers	Program changes	2014 president's budget
Ecological services						
Endangered species						
Candidate conservation	11,439	11,337	226	−33	0	11,530
Listing	20,997	20,869	294	−55	1,514	22,622
Critical habitat					−2,945	
Listing					4,459	
Consultation/HCP	61,673	60,943	918	−190	3,080	64,751
Renewable energy					1,500	
Science for pesticide consultations					1,000	
Tribal consultation					510	
General program activities					70	
Recovery	81,483	82,806	952	−230	3,015	86,543
Wolf Livestock Demonstration Program					−998	
State of the Birds Activities					−995	
Cooperative Recovery					1,900	
General program activities					3,108	
Endangered species subactivity total	**175,592**	**175,955**	**2,390**	**−508**	**7,609**	**185,446**

Notes: CR = Continuing resolution. PL = Public Law. HCP = Health Care Provider.

SOURCE: Adapted from "2014 Budget at a Glance," in *The United States Department of the Interior, Fish and Wildlife Service: Budget Justifications and Performance Information, Fiscal Year 2014*, U.S. Department of the Interior, U.S. Fish and Wildlife Service, 2013, http://www.fws.gov/budget/2014/FWS%202014%20Budget%20Justifications.pdf (accessed November 1, 2013)

TABLE 2.13

The 20 listed species with the highest expenditures under the Endangered Species Act, fiscal year 2012

Rank	Species	Species total
1	Steelhead (Oncorhynchus (=Salmo) mykiss)	$263,138,542
2	Salmon, chinook (Oncorhynchus (=Salmo) tshawytscha)	$240,689,663
3	Sturgeon, pallid (Scaphirhynchus albus)	$53,827,474
4	Salmon, coho (Oncorhynchus (=Salmo) kisutch)	$44,477,995
5	Sea-lion, steller (Eumetopias jubatus)	$40,214,833
6	Woodpecker, red-cockaded (Picoides borealis)	$37,900,480
7	Trout, bull (Salvelinus confluentus)	$37,697,010
8	Salmon, sockeye (Oncorhynchus (=Salmo) nerka)	$29,816,576
9	Salmon, chum (Oncorhynchus (=Salmo) keta)	$20,920,045
10	Owl, northern spotted (Strix occidentalis caurina)	$20,465,308
11	Smelt, delta (Hypomesus transpacificus)	$17,263,815
12	Flycatcher, southwestern willow (Empidonax traillii extimus)	$16,841,162
13	Bat, Indiana (Myotis sodalis)	$15,028,862
14	Sturgeon, white (Acipenser transmontanus)	$13,632,338
15	Plover, piping (Charadrius melodus)	$12,648,485
16	Sucker, razorback (Xyrauchen texanus)	$12,415,575
17	Tortoise, desert (Gopherus agassizii)	$12,334,481
18	Manatee, West Indian (Trichechus manatus)	$11,955,724
19	Wolf, gray (Canis lupus)	$11,770,973
20	Salmon, Atlantic (Salmo salar)	$10,913,156

SOURCE: Adapted from "Table 2. Species Ranked in Descending Order of Total FY2012 Reported Expenditures, Not Including Land Acquisition Costs," in *Federal and State Endangered and Threatened Species Expenditures: Fiscal Year 2012*, U.S. Department of the Interior, U.S. Fish and Wildlife Service, 2012, http://www.fws.gov/endangered/esa-library/pdf/2012.EXP.FINAL.pdf (accessed November 4, 2013)

of the listed species. (See Table 1.2 in Chapter 1.) These species are politically more difficult to defend than either mammals or birds, which are more inherently appealing to most Americans because of the "warm and fuzzy" factor. The ESA agencies struggle under intense legal and political pressures to decide which species to protect first.

Grants to State, Territory, and Local Governments

The ESA is a federal law and is implemented and enforced by federal agencies. However, the federal government cooperates with state, territorial, and local governments to carry out ESA measures. As of November 2013, listed species were found in every state and most U.S. territories. (See Table 1.3 in Chapter 1.) Some species are found in more than one state. However, each species (or DPS) is regulated under the ESA by range (the geographical area a species is known or believed to occupy). Thus, a range can cover two or more states.

Primarily the federal ESA agencies coordinate with state agencies (such as fish and wildlife agencies) in carrying out conservation programs. Section 6 of the ESA authorizes the federal government to operate the Cooperative Endangered Species Conservation Fund to provide grants to states to support their conservation efforts. The USFWS indicates in the press release "U.S. Fish and Wildlife Service Boosts State Endangered Species Conservation Efforts with $32 Million in Grants" (July 9, 2013, http://www.fws.gov/southeast/news/2013/039.html) that $32 million in grants were awarded to

20 states in July 2013. Example uses of the grant money include:

- Statewide HCPs that cover certain activities of all the landowners in each jurisdiction and may address multiple species

- Land acquisitions by the states to complement the conservation objectives in approved HCPs or to secure habitat for endangered and threatened species with approved recovery plans

- State baseline surveys and inventories, document preparation, outreach, and planning activities associated with HCP development

THE POLITICAL HISTORY OF THE ESA

The ESA has become one of the most controversial, litigious, and politically polarizing laws in U.S. history. Oddly enough, it did not start out that way. According to J. Michael Scott, Frank W. Davis, and Dale D. Goble, in "Introduction" (Dale D. Goble, J. Michael Scott, and Frank W. Davis, eds., *The Endangered Species Act at Thirty: Renewing the Conservation Promise*, 2006), the original act enjoyed broad bipartisan support from members of both major political parties. The bills establishing the ESA were passed unanimously by the U.S. Senate and almost unanimously in the U.S. House of Representatives. Although Congress had a Democratic majority at the time, the Republican president Richard M. Nixon (1913–1994) supported the ESA and signed the final bill into law in 1973. Environmental issues were a high priority during the early 1970s, and numerous sweeping environmental laws were passed during this time. Scott, Davis, and Goble describe passage of the ESA as "an idealistic and perhaps naive attempt to preserve humanity by preserving other species in the ecological support system that makes life possible." Certainly, its original supporters did not foresee the bitter contention that this law would later arouse.

The original law was very restrictive, in that it prohibited taking under almost all circumstances. The controversial snail darter court case and other litigation prompted Congress to make the ESA more permissive and flexible via amendments in 1978 and 1982. The 1982 amendment was particularly striking because it allowed for incidental take under certain circumstances, a concession that bothered environmentalists. The amendment was also notable for ending the possibility of using economic considerations in listing species. In 1981 President Reagan signed Executive Order 12291 (http://www.archives.gov/federal-register/codification/executive-order/12291.html) to "reduce the burdens of existing and future regulations." One requirement of this broad executive order was that federal agencies had to weigh the economic costs against the benefits of regulations. Reagan was a conservative Republican who opposed what he viewed as the overregulation of business and private interests. Congress responded by adding language in the 1982 ESA amendment that listing determinations would be made "solely on the basis of the best scientific and commercial data available." Thus, economic costs are not a consideration during the ESA listing process. This decision remains highly controversial and is bitterly opposed by many industrial and commercial interests.

By the early 1990s conservative Republicans enjoyed much greater political power in the United States. In general, Republicans believe the ESA violates private property rights and stifles economic growth by curbing development. They charge that environmental protection often results in the loss of jobs and business profits. During the spring of 1995 the Republican-controlled Congress imposed a moratorium on new ESA listings, and the law itself was in jeopardy. The authorization for funding the ESA had expired at the end of FY 1992. In 1993 and 1994 the Democratic-controlled Congress appropriated annual funds to keep the ESA going; however, the Republican-controlled Congress that took power in 1995 refused to do so. According to Scott, Davis, and Goble, this open congressional "hostility" toward the ESA spurred Bruce Babbitt (1938–), the U.S. secretary of the interior, to make changes. He added so-called incentive-based strategies "to try and reconcile endangered species conservation with economic development." These reforms included the HCPs, CCAAs, and SHAs described earlier in this chapter for private landowners. During the spring of 1996 funding was restored for the ESA, and the listing moratorium ended.

In 2000 the Republican George W. Bush (1946–) was elected president. Bush favored less government regulation of business and industry. He espoused a so-called new environmentalism that promoted conservation and cooperation at the local level over federal government prohibitions. During his eight years in office only 61 new listings were made under the ESA. (See Figure 1.2 in Chapter 1.) This historically low number was criticized and hailed as proof that the administration tried to undermine the intent of the law. There were also many accusations of political bullying of DOI scientists by administration officials.

The Bush administration supported legislative efforts to amend the ESA to change its scientific process and be less restrictive on private property owners, businesses, and industry. However, these legislative efforts failed to pass. The administration also attempted to reform the ESA through procedural policy changes and rule interpretations. For example, in December 2008, the last full month of the Bush administration, the DOI issued a rule relaxing the mandatory requirement that federal agencies consult with the ESA agencies as required by section 7 of the law. These consultations became optional under certain circumstances. The rule was greeted positively by business interests and negatively by environmentalists, who considered it a last-ditch effort by the Bush administration to weaken the ESA.

Bush was succeeded by the Democrat Barack Obama (1961–) in January 2009. Months later, Obama reversed the Bush administration's rule regarding section 7 consultations under the ESA. Conservation and animal protection groups were further pleased in 2011, when the USFWS forged a legal agreement to move forward with listing decisions for hundreds of candidate species that had languished on hold for years.

However, some decisions made by the ESA agencies under the Obama administration have angered advocates for endangered species. For example, in December 2010 the USFWS (http://www.gpo.gov/fdsys/pkg/FR-2010-12-14/pdf/2010-31140.pdf#page=1) officially proposed listing the dune sagebrush lizard (formerly a candidate species) under the ESA with a status of endangered. The lizard is found in southeastern New Mexico and western Texas, areas that have extensive oil and gas exploration activities. In 2012 the USFWS announced that it would not finalize the proposed listing under the ESA. In "Obama Administration Cancels Endangered Species Listing for Lizard" (June 13, 2012, http://www.humanevents.com/2012/06/13/obama-administration-cancels-endangered-species-listing-for-lizard/), Audrey Hudson explains that the listing was abandoned after the USFWS negotiated an agreement with "oil and gas developers and other stakeholders to protect 650,000 acres of land as habitat for the creature in Texas and New Mexico." Administration officials praised the agreement as a means for balancing economic and conservation interests. According to Hudson, "The unprecedented agreement commits the states and other stakeholders to decades of conservation efforts estimated to cost millions of dollars, thereby avoiding a certain shutdown of all oil and gas development near the lizard's habitat and save thousands of jobs." However, conservation groups were unhappy with the decision. Hudson notes that "environmentalists accused the Obama administration of selling out to energy companies and criticized the decision."

ASSESSING THE ESA
Private Property Rights

The issue of private property rights is a prime concern among ESA critics, particularly industry and development groups. One measure they strongly support is compensation for the loss of use of land. For example, the National Stone, Sand, and Gravel Association states in *Endangered Species Act Reform* (2014, http://www.nssga.org/endangered-species-act-reform/), "ESA mandates have severely restricted the use and value of privately owned property. When severe restrictions occur without compensation by the federal government, the Act shifts to individual citizens costs and burdens that should be shared by all citizens. The ESA must be modified to justly compensate landowners in a timely fashion when private property is preserved in a habitat conservation plan."

Evading the ESA

ESA critics also complain that the law provides no incentive for private landowners to participate in the conservation process. In fact, there is evidence that some people actively evade the law to prevent government restrictions on their land use. This claim is supported by Dean Lueck and Jeffrey A. Michael in "Preemptive Habitat Destruction under the Endangered Species Act" (*Journal of Law and Economics*, vol. 46, no. 1, 2003). The researchers examined land-use data between 1984 and 1990 for approximately 1,000 forest plots in North Carolina. As will be described in Chapter 8, the red-cockaded woodpecker is an endangered bird found in scattered forested habitats in the Southeast. It has been listed under the ESA since 1970. Lueck and Michael find that landowners with forest plots near areas known to contain the imperiled birds were much more likely to harvest and sell their timber than landowners with plots located farther from the birds. In addition, the plots closest to the birds were harvested when the trees were younger (and subsequently smaller and worth less). The researchers surmise that landowners with plots close to the birds rushed to harvest their trees before the trees became home to the imperiled species. Lueck and Michael call this "preemptive habitat destruction." The landowners evaded potential future ESA restrictions on their land use by destroying the very habitat that might attract and harbor the birds.

A more dire evasion technique allegedly used by some landowners is described by the colorful phrase "shoot, shovel, and shut up." The phrase was supposedly coined by Ralph R. Reiland, an economics professor known for his conservative views, in a column for the *Pittsburgh Tribune-Review*. In "Shoot, Shovel & Shut Up" (April 5, 2005, http://www.pittsburghlive.com/x/pittsburghtrib/opinion/columnists/reiland/s_187542.html), Reiland discusses the Lueck and Michael study and provides anecdotal stories about private landowners he claims have been economically harmed by ESA land-use restrictions. Reiland, like many ESA opponents, asserts that preemptive habitat destruction and "shoot, shovel and shut up" strategies are practiced by private landowners to avoid government interference with how they manage their land. As a result, these strategies thwart the preservation of the very species that the ESA is supposed to protect. This is presented as evidence that the ESA is a failed law.

Recovery Rate Controversy

One of the most frequent criticisms leveled against the ESA is that it has achieved recovery for few species since its passage in 1973. As shown in Table 2.11 and discussed earlier, only 31 U.S. entities (species or DPS) had been delisted due to recovery under the ESA as of November 2013. (Some of the recovered mammal entities are not entire species, but subpopulations of the wider population.) Considering that 1,516 species were listed under the ESA as of November 2013, the recovery rate was around 2%. (See Table 1.2 in Chapter 1.) This low recovery rate is often touted by ESA opponents as proof that the act has failed.

ESA proponents take a different stance on this issue. For example, Verlyn Klinkenborg asks in "Last One" (*National Geographic*, January 2009): "How many species might have vanished without it?" Conservation groups maintain that rates of full recovery and delisting are not adequate measures of ESA success because it can take many decades for a species to recover after being listed under the ESA.

CHAPTER 3
MARINE MAMMALS

Marine mammals live in and around the ocean. They are warm-blooded, breathe air, have hair at some point during their life, give birth to live young (as opposed to laying eggs), and nourish their young by secreting milk. Whales, dolphins, porpoises, seals, sea lions, sea otters, manatees, dugongs (manatee relatives), polar bears, and walruses fall into this category.

In "Research Themes—Role of Marine Mammals in Marine Ecosystems" (April 22, 2013, http://www.dfo-mpo .gc.ca/science/coe-cde/cemam/themes/ecosystem-eng.html), Fisheries and Oceans Canada (FOC) notes that marine mammals play a crucial role in the oceanic food web, particularly in the predator-prey balance. Some species, such as killer whales and polar bears, are called apex predators, meaning they are at the top of their respective food chains and as healthy adults are not preyed on by any other animals (except humans). Killer whales and polar bears do prey on lesser marine mammals, including seals. These two apex predators and many other marine mammals consume massive amounts of fish, which often puts them into conflict with humans over the valuable food source. Some marine mammal species prey on aquatic invertebrates (animals lacking a backbone) such as shrimp, crabs, and krill. Whatever their position in the food web, marine mammals are important to their ecosystems. The FOC explains, "In some cases marine mammals play a very clear role in structuring marine ecosystems. For example sea otter predation on sea urchins reduces grazing pressure, which allows the proliferation of kelp bed forests. This leads to the development of new ecosystems and an increase in marine fauna density and diversity."

For centuries, marine mammals of interest to humans for food, fur, or other commodities were hunted without restraint. As will be explained in this chapter, some species were driven to the brink of extinction by overhunting. Although modern restrictions and protections have largely eliminated that particular threat to marine mammals, much damage has already been done. In addition, new threats have arisen, including climate change due to global warming, entanglement of the animals in fishing gear and marine debris, and strikes from ships and boats in the world's busy waterways.

Marine mammals enjoy a relatively high level of public support and legal protection. During the 1960s the television show *Flipper* entertained U.S. audiences with stories about a highly intelligent and loveable dolphin that befriended and helped a family. Tourist attractions such as Marineland in Florida and SeaWorld in California began featuring acrobatic dolphins and whales in popular shows. The growing environmental movement seized on the public interest in marine mammals and lobbied for measures to protect animals that many people believed to be extremely smart and sociable.

At the time, purse-seine fishing was widely practiced by commercial tuna fishers in the eastern tropical Pacific Ocean. This fishing method involved the use of enormous nets, often hundreds of miles long, that were circled around schools of tuna. Many dolphins were inadvertently captured because they tend to mingle with fleets of tuna in that part of the ocean. Nontargeted animals that are captured during commercial fishing activities are called bycatch. Dolphin bycatch became a major public issue. Hauling in the enormous tuna-filled nets was a long process. As a result, the air-breathing dolphins were trapped for long periods underwater and often drowned. Public outcry over these killings and general concern for the welfare of marine mammals led Congress to pass the Marine Mammal Protection Act of 1972.

THE MARINE MAMMAL PROTECTION ACT
The Marine Mammal Protection Act (MMPA) was passed in 1972 and was substantially amended in 1994. The original act noted that "certain species and population

stocks of marine mammals are, or may be, in danger of extinction or depletion as a result of man's activities." However, it was acknowledged that "inadequate" information was available concerning the population dynamics of the animals being protected.

The MMPA prohibits the taking (hunting, killing, capturing, and harassing) of marine mammals. The act also bars the importation of most marine mammals or their products. Exceptions are occasionally granted for scientific research, public display in aquariums, traditional subsistence hunting by Alaskan Natives, and some incidental capture during commercial fishing operations. The goal of the MMPA is to maintain marine populations at or above "optimum sustainable" levels.

Whales, dolphins, seals, and sea lions were put under the jurisdiction of the National Marine Fisheries Service (NMFS), an agency of the National Oceanic and Atmospheric Administration (NOAA) in the U.S. Department of Commerce. Polar bears, sea and marine otters, manatees, dugongs, and walruses were placed under the jurisdiction of the U.S. Fish and Wildlife Service (USFWS), an agency of the U.S. Department of the Interior.

The MMPA requires the NMFS and the USFWS to conduct periodic surveys to estimate populations and to predict population trends for marine mammals in three regions of U.S. waters: the Pacific Ocean coast (excluding Alaska), the Atlantic Ocean coast (including the Gulf of Mexico), and the Alaskan coast. The survey results are published in an annual *Stock Assessment Report* (*SAR*) by

the NMFS (http://www.nmfs.noaa.gov/pr/sars/) and the USFWS (http://www.fws.gov/alaska/fisheries/mmm/reports.htm).

The MMPA was passed a year before the Endangered Species Act (ESA). The MMPA was driven largely by public affection for marine mammals, rather than by specific knowledge about impending species extinction. Eugene H. Buck and Harold F. Upton of the Congressional Research Service explain in *Fishery, Aquaculture, and Marine Mammal Issues in the 112th Congress* (November 4, 2011, http://www.fas.org/sgp/crs/misc/R41613.pdf) that "while some critics assert that the MMPA is scientifically irrational because it identifies one group of organisms for special protection unrelated to their abundance or ecological role, supporters note that the MMPA has accomplished much by way of promoting research and increased understanding of marine life as well as encouraging attention to incidental bycatch mortalities of marine life by commercial fishing and other maritime industries."

THE ENDANGERED SPECIES ACT

As shown in Table 2.1 in Chapter 2, the first list of native endangered species issued in 1967 included only three marine mammal species: the Caribbean monk seal, the Guadalupe fur seal, and the Florida manatee (or Florida sea cow). Over the following decades additional marine mammals were added as information became available on their population status. As of November 2013, there were 20 species of marine mammals listed as endangered or threatened in the United States. (See Table 3.1.) In addition,

TABLE 3.1

Endangered and threatened aquatic mammals, November 2013

Common name	Scientific name	Note	Listing status[a]	Year listed	U.S. or U.S./foreign listed
Bearded seal (1 DPS[b])	Erignathus barbatus	Beringia DPS (Alaska stock)	T	2012	US/foreign
Beluga whale (1 DPS)	Delphinapterus leucas	Toothed; Cook Inlet stock	E	2008	US/foreign
Blue whale	Balaenoptera musculus	Baleen plate	E	1970	US/foreign
Bowhead whale	Balaena mysticetus	Baleen plate	E	1970	US/foreign
False killer whale (1 DPS)	Pseudorca crassidens	Hawaiian stock	E	2012	US
Finback (or Fin) whale	Balaenoptera physalus	Baleen plate	E	1970	US/foreign
Guadalupe fur seal	Arctocephalus townsendi	Eared	T	1985	US/foreign
Hawaiian monk seal	Monachus schauinslandi	Earless	E	1976	US
Humpback whale	Megaptera novaeangliae	Baleen plate	E	1970	US/foreign
Killer whale (1 DPS)	Orcinus orca	Toothed; Southern resident stock	E	2005	US/foreign
North Atlantic right whale	Eubalaena glacialis	Baleen plate	E	1970	US/foreign
Northern Sea otter	Enhydra lutris kenyoni	North Pacific Ocean stock	T	2005	US
North Pacific right whale	Eubalaena japonica	Baleen plate	E	1970	US/foreign
Polar bear	Ursus maritimus	Sea ice is primary habitat	T	2008	US/foreign
Ringed seal (1 subspecies)	Phoca hispida hispida	Arctic subspecies (Alaska stock)	T	2012	US/foreign
Sei whale	Balaenoptera borealis	Baleen plate	E	1970	US/foreign
Southern sea otter	Enhydra lutris nereis	California stock	T	1977	US/foreign
Sperm whale	Physeter catodon (=macrocephalus)	Toothed	E	1970	US/foreign
Steller sea-lion (1 DPS)	Eumetopias jubatus	Western stock	T; E	1990; 1997	US/foreign
West Indian manatee	Trichechus manatus	Florida stock	E	1967	US/foreign

[a]T = Threatened; E = Endangered.
[b]DPS = Distinct population segment.

SOURCE: Adapted from "Marine Mammals," in *Endangered and Threatened Marine Mammals*, U.S. Department of Commerce, National Oceanic and Atmospheric Administration, National Marine Fisheries Services, November 1, 2013, http://www.nmfs.noaa.gov/pr/species/esa/mammals.htm (accessed November 4, 2013)

TABLE 3.2

Foreign endangered and threatened aquatic mammals, November 2013

Common name	Scientific name	Listing status[a]	Historic range
Amazonian manatee	Trichechus inunguis	E	South America (Amazon River basin)
Bearded seal	Erignathus barbatus	T	Russia (Sea of Okhotsk)
Cameroon clawless otter	Aonyx congicus (=congica) microdon	E	Cameroon, Nigeria
Chinese River dolphin	Lipotes vexillifer	E	China
Cochito (Vaquita porpoise)	Phocoena sinus	E	Mexico (Gulf of California)
Dugong	Dugong dugon	E	East Africa to southern Japan, including U.S.A. (Trust Territories)
Giant otter	Pteronura brasiliensis	E	South America
Gray whale (1 DPS[b])	Eschrichtius robustus	E	North Pacific Ocean—coastal and Bering Sea, formerly North Atlantic Ocean
Indus River dolphin	Platanista minor	E	Pakistan (Indus River and tributaries)
Long-tailed otter	Lontra (=Lutra) longicaudis (incl. platensis)	E	South America
Marine otter	Lontra (=Lutra) felina	E	Peru south to Straits of Magellan
Mediterranean monk seal	Monachus monachus	E	Mediterranean, Northwest African Coast and Black Sea
Ringed seal	Phoca hispida	T; E	Arctic Ocean, Sea of Okhotsk, Baltic Sea
Saimaa seal	Phoca hispida saimensis	E	Finland (Lake Saimaa)
Southern right whale	Eubalaena australis	E	Southern hemisphere
Southern river otter	Lontra (=Lutra) provocax	E	Chile, Argentina
Spotted seal	Phoca largha	T	Bering Sea, Sea of Japan, and Sea of Okhotsk
West African manatee	Trichechus senegalensis	T	West Coast of Africa from Senegal River to Cuanza River

[a]E = Endangered; T = Threatened.
[b]DPS = Distinct population segment.

SOURCE: Adapted from "Marine Mammals," in *Endangered and Threatened Marine Mammals*, U.S. Department of Commerce, National Oceanic and Atmospheric Administration, National Marine Fisheries Services, November 1, 2013, http://www.nmfs.noaa.gov/pr/species/esa/mammals.htm (accessed November 4, 2013)

there were 18 foreign species listed as endangered or threatened. (See Table 3.2.) As of November 2013, no marine mammals had been delisted under the ESA due to extinction. (See Table 2.11 in Chapter 2.) Two species—the gray whale (1994) and the eastern population of the Steller sea lion (2013)—have been delisted due to recovery, which will be explained later in this chapter.

During fiscal year 2012, $86.2 million was spent by federal and state agencies on the 10 marine mammal species with the highest spending that year. (See Table 3.3.)

As of November 2013, ESA-listed endangered and threatened marine mammals fell into six main categories: whales, dolphins and porpoises, seals and sea lions, sea otters, manatees and dugongs, and polar bears.

WHALES

Whales are in the order Cetacea (along with dolphins and porpoises). Cetaceans are marine mammals that live in the water all the time and have torpedo-shaped nearly hairless bodies. (See Figure 3.1.) There are approximately 70 known whale species. The so-called great whales are the largest animals on the earth. In general, the great whale species range in size from 30 to 100 feet (9.1 to 30.5 meters [m]) in length. There are 13 whale species normally considered to be great whales. The blue whale is the largest of these species.

Whales are found throughout the world's oceans; however, many species are concentrated in cold northern waters. Although they are warm-blooded and do not

TABLE 3.3

The 10 listed marine mammal entities with the highest expenditures under the Endangered Species Act, fiscal year 2012

Ranking	Species	Expenditure
1	Sea-lion, Steller (Eumetopias jubatus)—western pop.	$22,254,726
2	Sea-lion, Steller (Eumetopias jubatus)—eastern pop.	$17,960,107
3	Manatee, West Indian (Trichechus manatus)	$11,955,724
4	Whale, North Atlantic Right (Eubalaena glacialis)	$9,905,912
5	Whale, bowhead (Balaena mysticetus)	$5,614,736
6	Whale, humpback (Megaptera novaeangliae)	$4,626,033
7	Seal, Hawaiian monk (Monachus schauinslandi)	$4,594,393
8	Bear, polar (Ursus maritimus)	$4,438,621
9	Whale, Beluga (Delphinapterus leucas)—Cook Inlet DPS	$2,655,502
10	Whale, sperm (Physeter catodon (=macrocephalus))	$2,162,842

DPS = Distinct population segment.

SOURCE: Adapted from "Table 2. Species Ranked in Descending Order of Total FY2012 Reported Expenditures, Not Including Land Acquisition Costs," in *Federal and State Endangered and Threatened Species Expenditures: Fiscal Year 2012*, U.S. Department of the Interior, U.S. Fish and Wildlife Service, 2012, http://www.fws.gov/endangered/esa-library/pdf/2012.EXP.FINAL.pdf (accessed November 4, 2013)

have fur, whales can survive in cold waters because they have a thick layer of dense fat and tissue known as blubber lying just beneath the skin. This blubber layer can be up to 1 foot (30.5 centimeters) thick in larger species.

Most whales have teeth and are in the suborder Odontoceti. By contrast, the handful of whales in the suborder Mysticeti filter their food through strong flexible plates called baleen. (See Figure 3.2.) Baleen is informally known as "whalebone." It is composed of a

FIGURE 3.1

Humpback whales. ©*Jan Kratochvila/Shutterstock.*

FIGURE 3.2

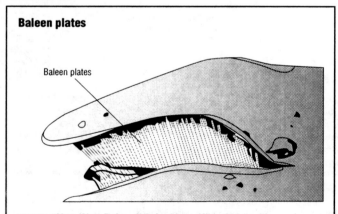

Baleen plates

Baleen plates

SOURCE: "How Were Baleen Whales Named?" in *Marine Mammal Education Web: Baleen Whales*, National Oceanic and Atmospheric Administration, Alaska Fisheries Science Center, National Marine Mammal Laboratory, undated, http://www.afsc.noaa.gov/nmml/ education/cetaceans/baleen1.php (accessed November 4, 2013)

substance similar to human fingernails. Baleen whales strain large amounts of water to obtain their food, mostly zooplankton, tiny fish, and crustaceans. Nearly all the great whales are baleen whales.

Imperiled Whale Populations

As of November 2013, 11 whale species had been listed for protection under the ESA in U.S. waters: beluga whales, blue whales, bowhead whales, false killer whales, finback whales, humpback whales, killer whales, North Atlantic right whales, North Pacific right whales, sei whales, and sperm whales. (See Table 3.1.) Most of these species have baleen plates. In 1994 the NMFS delisted a stock of the gray whale due to recovery. (See Table 2.11 in Chapter 2.) According to the agency, in "Gray Whale (*Eschrichtius robustus*)" (May 13, 2013, http://www.nmfs .noaa.gov/pr/species/mammals/cetaceans/graywhale.htm), the species as a whole was first listed in 1970 under a precursor law to the ESA. In 1994 the eastern North Pacific (California) population was delisted because the whales "had recovered to near their estimated original population size."

The right whale is the most endangered of the great whales. It was once the "right" whale to hunt because it swims slowly, prefers shallow coastal waters, and floats when it dies. According to the NMFS, in "North Atlantic Right Whales (*Eubalaena glacialis*)" (December 6, 2013, http://www.nmfs.noaa.gov/pr/species/mammals/ cetaceans/rightwhale_northatlantic.htm), right whales first received international protection from whaling during the 1930s. In 1973 the right whale was listed as endangered under the ESA. Since then, three distinct species have been determined: the North Atlantic right whale (*E. glacialis*) and the North Pacific right whale (*E. japonica*) in the Northern Hemisphere and the southern right whale (*E. australis*) in the Southern Hemisphere. The NMFS reports that the North Atlantic right whale can be further subdivided into two geographical populations: western and eastern. The latter is believed to be "nearly extinct." The NMFS estimates its population in the "low tens of animals." The western North Atlantic right whale population includes an estimated 400 individuals and is considered "critically" endangered.

Threats to Whales

Whale populations are imperiled due to a long history of hunting by humans. As early as the eighth century humans hunted whales for meat and baleen. Whales were relatively easy for fishermen to catch because the animals spend a great deal of time at the surface of the ocean and provide a large target for harpoons. Advances in shipbuilding and the invention of the steam engine allowed fishermen greater access to whale populations, even those in Arctic areas that had previously been out of reach. By the 19th century large numbers of whales were being killed for blubber and baleen. Blubber was rendered to extract whale oil, which was used to light lamps. Baleen was valued for making fans, corsets, and other consumer goods.

On December 2, 1946, the representatives of 14 nations signed the International Convention for the Regulation of Whaling (http://iwc.int/convention), which formed the International Whaling Commission (IWC). The signatory nations were Argentina, Australia, Brazil, Canada, Chile, Denmark, France, the Netherlands, New Zealand, Peru, South Africa, the Soviet Union, the United Kingdom, and the United States. The IWC was formed as a means to regulate the industry and limit the number and type of whales that could be killed. The MMPA banned commercial whaling in U.S. waters.

Centuries of whaling severely depleted whale populations. Low birth rates and high mortality rates due to a variety of factors have prevented many species from recovering. Like other marine animals, whales are endangered by water pollution and loss or degradation of habitat. However, the NMFS notes that the biggest threats to the right whale and other imperiled whale species are entanglement in fishing gear and ship strikes. For example, Allison G. Henry et al. report in *Mortality Determinations for Baleen Whale Stocks along the Gulf of Mexico, United States East Coast, and Atlantic Canadian Provinces, 2007–2011* (March 2013, http://nefsc.noaa .gov/publications/crd/crd1318/crd1318.pdf) on their

investigation of the causes of death for 306 baleen whales known to have died in U.S. and Canadian waters between 2007 and 2011. The researchers indicate that for 236 of the animals the cause of death could not be determined with certainty. Another 14 whales were found to have died from natural causes and 56 from human interactions: 28 from entanglement and 28 from ship strikes.

ENTANGLEMENT IN FISHING GEAR. In "What Kinds of Fishing Gear Most Often Entangle Right Whales?" (*Right Whale News*, November 2005), the NMFS describes a study by researchers at Duke University that found that lobster pot gear, mostly buoy lines, were particularly problematic. It was concluded "that any line rising vertically in the water column poses a significant entanglement risk" to North Atlantic right whales.

The Woods Hole Oceanographic Institution (WHOI) indicates in the press release "Study Reveals How Fishing Gear Can Cause Slow Death of Whales" (May 21, 2013, http://www.whoi.edu/main/news-releases?tid=362 2&cid=169130) that approximately 75% of known North Atlantic right whales "bear scars of fishing lines that cut into their flesh." Whales that drag gear, particularly buoyant equipment, have trouble getting food and migrating. In addition, they expend large amounts of energy due to the extra weight they are pulling. Together, these problems can contribute to what the WHOI calls "slow death."

WHOI scientists participate in the Marine Mammal Health and Stranding Response Program, which includes the Atlantic Large Whale Entanglement Response Program. Under the latter program rescue teams approach whales entangled in gear, sedate the animals if necessary, and cut away the gear. For example, in 2010 the WHOI reports that aerial survey teams spotted an emaciated whale with gear tangled around its mouth and fins and trailing behind it. A rescue team sedated the animal and cut away almost all the gear. Data provided by a monitoring chip placed on the whale indicated it dived to much greater depths and for longer durations after the removal. In 2011, however, the whale was found dead. A necropsy (animal autopsy) revealed "that effects of the chronic entanglement were the cause of death."

SHIP STRIKES. NOAA (http://nefsc.noaa.gov/publica tions/crd/) publishes numerous reports annually, some of which provide data on ship strikes on large whales in U.S. and Canadian waters. As of February 2014, the most recent report was "Mortality and Serious Injury Determinations for Baleen Whale Stocks along the Gulf of Mexico, United States East Coast and Atlantic Canadian Provinces, 2006–2010" (June 29, 2012, http://nefsc.noaa .gov/publications/crd/crd1211/). According to NOAA, the researchers documented 58 ship strikes during the study period of 2006 through 2010. However, the researchers cautioned that the actual number could be much higher because of the difficulties involved in detecting, confirming, and documenting the events.

The NMFS states in "Ship Strike Reduction" (July 10, 2013, http://www.nero.noaa.gov/shipstrike/) that "collision with vessels is the leading human-caused source of mortality for the endangered North Atlantic right whale." The animals are particularly vulnerable because they move rather slowly and spend a lot of time in coastal waters at or near the surface.

The Right Whale Sighting Advisory System (RWSAS) is a notification system operated by NOAA to reduce collisions between ships and right whales. Whale sightings and other detects are reported to the RWSAS and alerts are passed on to mariners in the area. Table 3.4 shows that 570 right whale sightings and detects were reported to the RWSAS in 2012. The largest number of sightings (288) was associated with aerial whale search surveys. During calving season (from November through April) the NMFS performs aerial surveys and alerts ships about whales in their vicinity. In addition, federal law requires that ships remain 500 yards (457 meters) from right whales. There are also routing requirements and speed limits for large vessels traveling in U.S. coastal waters that are frequented by right whales. Any sightings of dead, injured, or entangled whales must be reported to authorities.

Whale Recovery Plans

Table 3.5 provides information about whale species listed as endangered under the ESA in U.S. waters in 2013 (note that the false killer whale is not included because it was only listed in 2012). Critical habitat had been designated for four of the species or distinct population segments (DPS). Recovery plans had been developed or were under development for almost all the listed whales. The populations of bowhead, humpback, and North Atlantic right whales were believed to be increasing, whereas the populations of beluga whale (Cook Inlet DPS) and killer whale (southern resident DPS) were believed to be decreasing. Information was inadequate to determine population trends for the other whale species.

Table 3.5 also shows the recovery priority numbers assigned by the NMFS to each endangered whale species. Priority numbers can range from a value of 1 (highest priority) to 12 (lowest priority). The North Atlantic right whale has a priority level of 1, indicating strong concern about its abundance and chances for survival as a species.

TABLE 3.4

Right whale sightings reported to the Right Whale Sighting Advisory System, by source, 2012

	Jan	Feb	Mar	Apr	May	Jun	Jul	Aug	Sep	Oct	Nov	Dec	Total #	%
(a) Northeast														
Aerial survey	33	69	72	50	5	5	12				2	13	261	59%
Shipboard survey	6		19	5	26						2	7	65	14%
Whale watch			1	12		1	1	3	3				21	5%
Coast guard		2	8	10	1								21	5%
Commercial/fishing			2	2		1	2			1		1	9	2%
Opportunistic	3	17	14	16	1	2	2	6	1	1		4	67	15%
Total #	42	88	116	95	33	9	17	9	4	2	4	25	444	100%
(b) Mid-Atlantic														
Aerial survey														
Shipboard survey														
Whale watch								2					2	10%
Coast guard		2	2						1				5	25%
Commercial/fishing			1		2								3	15%
Opportunistic	5		1	2				1			1		10	50%
Total #	5	2	4	2	2			3	1		1		20	100%
(c) Canada														
Aerial survey					4	14	8				1		27	25%
Shipboard survey					15	8		30	23	1			77	73%
Whale watch														
Coast guard														
Commercial/fishing														
Opportunistic											1	1	2	2%
Total #					19	22	8	30	23	1	2	1	106	100%

SOURCE: Jennifer Gatzke et al., "Table 3. The Total Number of Right Whale Sighting Reports to the Right Whale Sighting Advisory System (RWSAS) in 2012 by Reporting Source and Month within the (A) Northeast Region (Maine through New York), (B) Mid-Atlantic Region (New Jersey through Virginia), and (C) Canadian Waters," in *North Atlantic Right Whale Sighting Survey (NARWSS) and Right Whale Sighting Advisory System (RWSAS) 2012 Results Summary*, U.S. Department of Commerce, National Oceanic and Atmospheric Administration, National Marine Fisheries Service, Northeast Fisheries Science Center, March 2013, http://nefsc.noaa.gov/publications/crd/crd1308/ (accessed November 4, 2013)

TABLE 3.5

Endangered U.S. whale species, 2013

Species (DPS)[a]	Date listed or reclassified	Endangered Species Act status	Population trend	Recovery priority number[b]	Status of recovery plan	Date 5-year status review completed	Critical habitat
Beluga whale (Cook Inlet DPS)	10/22/2008	Endangered	Declining	2	Under development	N/A	Final
Blue whale	06/02/1970	Endangered	Unknown	5	Completed 07/1998	N/A	None
Bowhead whale	06/02/1970	Endangered	Increasing	7	None	N/A	None
Fin whale	06/02/1970	Endangered	Unknown	9	Completed 07/2010	12/2011	None
Humpback whale	06/02/1970	Endangered	Increasing	5	Completed 11/1991	In progress	None
Killer whale (Southern resident DPS)	11/18/2005	Endangered	Declining	3	Completed 01/2008	03/2011	Final
North Atlantic right whale	06/02/1970; 03/06/2008	Endangered	Increasing	1	Completed 05/2005	09/2012	Final
North Pacific right whale	06/02/1970; 03/06/2008	Endangered	Unknown	4	Draft completed 01/2013	07/2012	Final
Sei whale	06/02/1970	Endangered	Unknown	11	Completed 12/2011	06/2012	None
Sperm whale	06/02/1970	Endangered	Unknown	5	Completed 12/2010	01/2009	None

[a]DPS: Distinct population segment.
[b]Recovery priority numbers are designated according to guidelines published by the National Marine Fisheries Service on June 15, 1990 (55 FR 24296). Priorities are designated from 1 (high) to 12 (low) based on the following factors: degree of threat, recovery potential, and conflict with development projects or other economic activity.

SOURCE: Adapted from "Species Status," in *Celebrating 40 Years: Recovering Threatened and Endangered Species FY 2011–2012 Report to Congress*, U.S. Department of Commerce, National Oceanic and Atmospheric Administration, National Marine Fisheries Services, July 2013, http://www.nmfs.noaa.gov/pr/laws/esa/noaa_esa_report_072213.pdf (accessed November 4, 2013)

In *Recovery Plan for the North Atlantic Right Whale* (August 2004, http://ecos.fws.gov/docs/recovery_plan/whale_right_northatlantic.pdf), the NMFS lists five goals for recovering the species. In order of importance, the goals are:

- Significantly reduce sources of human-caused death, injury and disturbance

- Develop demographically-based recovery criteria

- Identify, characterize, protect and monitor important habitats

- Monitor the status and trends of abundance and distribution of the western North Atlantic right whale population

- Coordinate federal, state, local, international and private efforts to implement the recovery plan

Imperiled Whales around the World

The International Union for Conservation of Nature (IUCN) indicates in *Red List of Threatened Species Version 2013.2* (http://www.iucnredlist.org/about/summary-statistics) that in November 2013 the following whale species were threatened:

- North Atlantic right whale

- North Pacific right whale

- Sperm whale

- Blue whale

- Fin whale

- Sei whale

The IUCN notes that it lacked sufficient data to determine the status of more than two dozen other whale species.

All of the species were deemed threatened by the IUCN. In addition, the southern right whale and one DPS of the gray whale were listed under the ESA as of November 2013. (See Table 3.1 and Table 3.2.)

INTERNATIONAL WHALING CONTROVERSIES. As noted earlier, the IWC was formed in 1946 to regulate the commercial whaling industry and limit the number and type of whales that can be killed. In 1986 the IWC banned commercial whaling after most whale populations were placed under Appendix I of the Convention on International Trade in Endangered Species of Wild Fauna and Flora (CITES) agreement. In 1991 Iceland dropped out of the IWC over the commercial whaling ban. It rejoined in 2002, but as of February 2014 it refused to abide by the ban. Norway also does not adhere to the ban. Commercial whalers and some scientists argue that some whale species are not imperiled and thus can be hunted, assuming that reasonable catch limits are employed.

The IWC (http://iwc.int/members.htm) indicates that as of 2014 it had 89 member nations. The commission allows whaling for "subsistence" purposes by native peoples, for example, Alaskan Eskimos. It also allows whaling for "scientific purposes." Conservation and wildlife groups have complained for decades that some IWC member countries, particularly Japan, kill many whales under this loophole and sell the meat commercially. In addition, Iceland and Norway openly hunt whales for commercial purposes and sell the meat primarily in Japanese markets.

DOLPHINS AND PORPOISES

Dolphins and porpoises are toothed cetaceans. They are similar in shape; however, dolphins are generally larger than porpoises and prefer shallower, warmer waters. Dolphins tend to have long bottlenoses and cone-shaped teeth, whereas porpoises have flatter noses and teeth. As of November 2013, there were no U.S. species of dolphins or porpoises listed under the ESA.

Imperiled Foreign Dolphins and Porpoises

Most dolphin and porpoise populations around the world are hardy and not in danger of extinction. However, there are several species that are in trouble due to limited geographical distribution. According to the IUCN, in *Red List of Threatened Species Version 2013.2*, nine dolphin and porpoise species were considered threatened in 2013. The most imperiled (those with a critically endangered rating) were the baiji (also known as the Chinese River dolphin) and the cochito (or vaquita, which is found in Mexico). Both species, along with the Indus River dolphin of Pakistan were on the ESA list of foreign species as of November 2013. (See Table 3.2.)

Protection of Prevalent Dolphins

Although they are not considered endangered or threatened, dolphins receive special consideration under U.S. law because of public concern about them. Dolphins are believed to be highly intelligent. In addition, many people have been exposed to dolphins through marine entertainment parks, movies, television shows, and even personal encounters and sightings at tourist beaches. As a result, there is widespread public fondness for the animals.

Dolphins are protected by the MMPA and by laws that are designed to limit their capture during tuna fishing. In 1990 large U.S. tuna canning companies announced they would no longer purchase tuna caught in a manner that endangered dolphins. The companies began labeling their products "Dolphin Safe" if their practices met specific standards established by the U.S. government.

The Dolphin Protection Consumer Information Act of 1990 specifies that tuna exported from or sold in the United States cannot include the "Dolphin Safe" label or similar claims if the tuna are harvested on the high seas via driftnet fishing or in specified waters using purse-seine fishing. There are, however, exceptions for tuna caught using the latter method, such as when an independent observer from an acceptable program verifies that the methods used were not harmful to dolphins. According to Lorraine Mitchell of the Economic Research Service, in "Dolphin-Safe Tuna Labeling" (January 24, 2001, http://www.ers.usda.gov/ersDownload Handler.ashx?file=/media/532244/aer793f.pdf), dolphin-safe fishing methods are enforced under the MMPA, in that "passage of the Act required observers on each U.S. boat to verify that dolphins and other marine mammals were not dying in large numbers."

The International Dolphin Conservation Program Act of 1992 reduced the number of legally permitted dolphin deaths. This act also made the United States a dolphin-safe zone in 1994, when it became illegal to sell, buy, or ship tuna products obtained using methods that kill dolphins.

SEALS AND SEA LIONS

Seals and sea lions are considered pinnipeds. This designation comes from the Latin word *pinnipedia*, which means "feather or fin foot." Pinnipeds have finlike flippers. Although they spend most of their time in the ocean, pinnipeds come on shore to rest, breed, give birth, and nurse their young. Areas preferred for breeding, birthing, and nursing are called rookeries. Pinnipeds not yet of reproductive age congregate at shore areas known as haul-outs.

Seals and sea lions were hunted extensively through the early 1900s for their blubber, fur, and meat. They continue to be imperiled by human encroachment of haul-out beaches, entanglement in marine debris and fishing nets, incidental catches, disease, and lack of food due to competition from humans for prey species.

Imperiled Seal and Sea Lion Populations

As of 2013, there were five U.S. species of seals and sea lions listed under the ESA. (See Table 3.6.) Another U.S. species, the Caribbean monk seal, was formerly listed, but is now believed to be extinct. It was officially delisted in 2008. (See Table 2.11 in Chapter 2.) The ESA-listed species were as follows:

- Bearded seal—the Beringia DPS is found in U.S. waters around Alaska. (See Figure 3.3.) The NMFS indicates in "Bearded Seal (*Erignathus barbatus*)" (May 17, 2013, http://www.nmfs.noaa.gov/pr/species/mammals/pinnipeds/beardedseal.htm) that the species depends on Arctic waters and sea ice for its habitat. The Alaska stock numbers around 250,000 to 300,000 individuals; however, population trends have not been determined. Possible threats to the DPS include bycatch in fishing gear and loss of sea ice due to global warming and climate change.

- Guadalupe fur seal—found in U.S. and Mexican waters west of Baja, California. According to the NMFS, in "Guadalupe Fur Seal (*Arctocephalus townsendi*)" (August 20, 2013, http://www.nmfs.noaa.gov/pr/species/mammals/pinnipeds/guadalupefurseal.htm), the species was heavily hunted during the 1700s and 1800s and is imperiled by fishing gear entanglement. The agency notes that the species "is slowly recovering from the brink of extinction." Scientists believe the population numbers about 10,000 individuals and is increasing each year.

TABLE 3.6

Endangered and threatened U.S. seal and sea lion species, 2013

Species (DPS)[a]	Date listed or reclassified	Endangered Species Act status	Population trend	Recovery priority number[b]	Status of recovery plan	Date 5-year status review completed	Critical habitat
Bearded seal							
Berengia DPS	12/28/2012	Threatened	Unknown	None	None	N/A	None
Guadalupe fur seal	12/16/1985	Threatened	Increasing	10	None	N/A	None
Hawaiian monk seal	11/23/1976	Endangered	Declining	1	Completed 03/1983; Revision completed 08/2007	08/2007	Final
Ringed seal							
Arctic subspecies	12/28/2012	Threatened	Unknown	None	None	N/A	None
Steller sea lion							
Western population	4/5/1990; 11/26/1990; 5/5/1997[c]	Endangered	Mixed	7	Completed 12/1992; Revision completed 03/2008	In progress	Final

N/A = Not applicable.
[a]DPS: Distinct population segment.
[b]Recovery priority numbers are designated according to guidelines published by the National Marine Fisheries Service on June 15, 1990 (55 FR 24296).
Priorities are designated from 1 (high) to 12 (low) based on the following factors: degree of threat, recovery potential, and conflict with development projects or other economic activity.
[c]This species was first listed as threatened via a 240-day emergency rule on 4/5/1990, then officially listed as threatened in a final rule on 11/26/1990. NMFS separated the species into western and eastern DPSs via final rule on 5/5/1997, which maintained the eastern DPS as threatened and reclassified the western DPS as endangered.

SOURCE: Adapted from "Species Status," in *Celebrating 40 Years: Recovering Threatened and Endangered Species FY 2011–2012 Report to Congress*, U.S. Department of Commerce, National Oceanic and Atmospheric Administration, National Marine Fisheries Services, July 2013, http://www.nmfs.noaa.gov/pr/laws/esa/noaa_esa_report_072213.pdf (accessed November 4, 2013)

FIGURE 3.3

Approximate distribution of bearded seals

Alaska

SOURCE: B. M. Allen and R. P. Angliss, "Figure 11. Approximate Distribution of Bearded Seals (Shaded Area)," in *Alaska Marine Mammal Stock Assessments, 2012*, U.S. Department of Commerce, National Oceanic and Atmospheric Administration, National Marine Fisheries Service, Alaska Fisheries Science Center, March 2013, http://www.nmfs.noaa.gov/pr/sars/pdf/ak2012.pdf (accessed November 5, 2013)

- Hawaiian monk seal—native to the waters around Hawaii and found only there. In "Hawaiian Monk Seal (*Monachus schauinslandi*)" (February 27, 2013, http://www.nmfs.noaa.gov/pr/species/mammals/pinni

peds/hawaiianmonkseal.htm), the NMFS notes that the species is "one of the rarest marine mammals in the world." It was hunted almost to extinction during the 1800s. Its population in the 21st century has been declining at about 4% annually due to low genetic diversity, food limitations, and a host of human-related causes, including entanglement in marine debris and bycatch in fishing gear. Only about 1,200 individuals are believed to exist.

- Ringed seal—the Arctic subspecies (*Phoca hispida hispida*) is found in U.S. waters around Alaska. (See Figure 3.4.) According to the NMFS, in "Ringed Seal (*Phoca hispida*)" (May 17, 2013, http://www.nmfs.noaa.gov/pr/species/mammals/pinnipeds/ringedseal.htm), the subspecies numbers around 249,000 individuals, but its population trend is unknown. Like other Arctic pinnipeds, the ringed seal is dependent on sea ice for habitat. Global warming is considered the primary threat to its existence, but bycatch in fishing gear is also a problem.

- Steller sea lion—there are two DPS within U.S. waters along the West Coast and around Alaska and the Aleutian Islands. (See Figure 3.5.) In "Steller Sea Lion (*Eumetopias jubatus*)" (December 11, 2013, http://www.nmfs.noaa.gov/pr/species/mammals/pinnipeds/stellersealion.htm), the NMFS indicates that the entire species was classified as threatened when it was first listed in 1990. By then, historic stocks had been depleted by hunting and intentional killing by fisherman due to competition for food fish. In 1997 the western DPS was uplisted to endangered, a listing it

FIGURE 3.4

Approximate distribution of ringed seals

SOURCE: B. M. Allen and R. P. Angliss, "Figure 12. Approximate Distribution of Ringed Seals (Shaded Area)," in *Alaska Marine Mammal Stock Assessments, 2012*, U.S. Department of Commerce, National Oceanic and Atmospheric Administration, National Marine Fisheries Service, Alaska Fisheries Science Center, March 2013, http://www.nmfs.noaa.gov/pr/sars/pdf/ak2012.pdf (accessed November 5, 2013)

maintained in 2013. In contrast, the eastern DPS was delisted in 2013 due to recovery. Figure 3.6 shows its increasing population abundance numbers since the late 1970s. Continuing threats to the Steller sea lion include fishing impacts (such as entanglement), boat and ship strikes, pollution and habitat degradation, offshore oil and gas exploration, and poaching (illegal hunting). In fiscal year 2012 species-specific expenditures under the ESA for the western and eastern populations of Steller sea lions totaled more than $40 million. (See Table 3.3.) The Steller sea lion ranked fifth in spending that year among all species covered by the ESA. (See Table 2.13 in Chapter 2.)

Table 3.6 lists information about population trends, recovery priority numbers, critical habitat designations, and the recovery plan status for the pinnipeds listed under the ESA. As of 2013, critical habitat and recovery plans had been developed for the Hawaiian monk seal and Steller sea lion (western DPS). Recovery priority numbers assigned by the NMFS can range from a value of 1 (highest priority) to 12 (lowest priority). The Hawaiian monk seal had a priority level of 1, indicating strong concern about its abundance and chances for survival as a species.

Imperiled Foreign Seals and Sea Lions

According to the IUCN, in *Red List of Threatened Species Version 2013.2*, 10 seal and sea lion species were considered threatened in 2013. The most imperiled were the Mediterranean monk seal and the Hawaiian monk seal. As of November 2013, five foreign seal species were listed under the ESA. (See Table 3.2.)

SEA OTTERS

Sea otters are the smallest marine mammals in North America. They are furry creatures that grow to be about 4 feet (1.2 m) in length and weigh up to 65 pounds (30 kilograms [kg]). Otters are related to weasels and mink and are members of the Mustelidae family. Sea otters are almost entirely aquatic and inhabit relatively shallow waters along the rocky coasts of the North Pacific Ocean. They eat a wide variety of marine invertebrate. They use rocks and other objects to smash open the hard shells of clams and crabs to get the meat inside.

Although they inhabit cold waters, sea otters do not have a blubber layer to keep them warm. Instead, they have extremely dense fur coats and high metabolism rates. Their fur coats are waterproof, but only if kept clean. This makes sea otters susceptible to water contaminants, such as oil.

Imperiled Otter Populations

At one time sea otters were populous along the entire U.S. West Coast from Southern California to Alaska. Their thick and lustrous fur, however, made them a target of intensive hunting for many centuries. By the dawn of the 20th century sea otters were on the brink of extinction. In 1911 they became protected under the International Fur Seal Treaty, and their numbers began to increase.

Biologists recognize two distinct populations: the northern sea otter and the southern sea otter. The northern sea otter extends from Russia across the Aleutian Islands and the coast of Alaska south to the state of Washington. As shown in Figure 3.7, there are three stocks: Southwest Alaska, Southcentral Alaska, and Southeast Alaska. Only the Southwest Alaska stock is listed under the ESA. It had a listing of threatened as of November 2013. The southern sea otter is found only off the California coast. It was also listed as threatened under the ESA. (See Table 3.1.)

NORTHERN SEA OTTERS. As of February 2014, the most recently published *SAR* for northern sea otters was a draft report dated April 2013. The USFWS indicates in *Draft Revised Northern Sea Otter (Enhydra lutris kenyoni): Southwest Alaska Stock* (http://www.fws.gov/alaska/fisheries/mmm/seaotters/pdf/Draft%20Southwest%20Alaska%20Sea%20Otter%20April%202013.For%20Surname.pdf) that the southwestern stock includes nearly 55,000 individuals. Although this number has increased slightly in recent years, the long-term trend is negative, as this stock has declined by more than 50% since the 1980s. The USFWS notes that "there is no evidence of

FIGURE 3.5

Range and rookeries of Steller sea lions

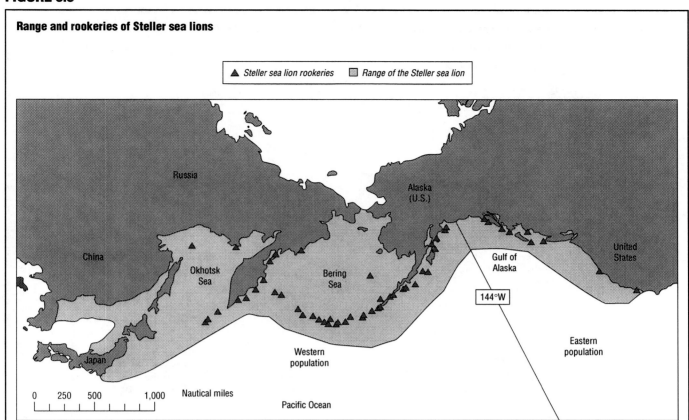

▲ Steller sea lion rookeries   ▨ Range of the Steller sea lion

SOURCE: "Figure 13. Steller Sea Lion Range and Rookeries," in *Biennial Report to Congress on the Recovery Program for Threatened and Endangered Species October 1, 2008–September 30, 2010*, U.S. Department of Commerce, National Oceanic and Atmospheric Administration, National Marine Fisheries Service, 2011, http://www.nmfs.noaa.gov/pr/pdfs/laws/esabiennial2010.pdf (accessed November 3, 2013)

recovery"; however, the overall population trend appears to have stabilized.

The causes of the huge population decline since the 1980s are hotly debated by scientists. In *Southwest Alaska Distinct Population Segment of the Northern Sea Otter (*Enhydra lutris kenyoni*) Recovery Plan* (July 2013, http://ecos.fws.gov/docs/recovery_plan/Recovery%20Plan%20SW%20AK%20DPS%20Sea%20Otter%20Aug13.pdf), the USFWS fingers predation by killer whales as the main cause. The agency rates this threat of moderate to high importance to the future recovery of the southwestern stock. Numerous other threats of low to moderate importance are also named, including oil spills, subsistence harvest (harvest by Alaska's native peoples), infectious disease, and poaching. Table 3.7 shows the estimated carrying capacity in number of animals for the five management units the USFWS has established for the stock. In total, the area is believed capable of supporting more than 211,000 individuals. As of 2007, the population accounted for only a quarter of the carrying capacity. Table 3.7 also shows the population numbers that would likely spur the agency to delist the stock due to recovery or to uplist it to endangered status.

SOUTHERN SEA OTTERS. Southern (or California) sea otters were designated as a threatened species in 1977. (See Figure 3.8.) At that time, the animals inhabited a small stretch of coastline in central California. Scientists feared that this isolated population was in grave danger of being wiped out by a single catastrophe, such as an oil spill. In 1987 the USFWS decided to establish an "experimental population" of sea otters at another location. Over the next few years more than 100 sea otters were moved, a few at a time, to San Nicolas Island. (See Figure 3.9.) It was hoped that these translocated animals would thrive and develop an independent growing colony. The venture, however, achieved only limited success. Many of the otters swam back to their original habitat; others died, apparently from the stress of moving. During the early 1990s the transport effort was abandoned. In December 2012 the USFWS (http://www.fws.gov/Ventura/docs/frno tices/77%20FR%2075266.pdf) officially ended the program. The agency indicates that the program resulted in a small colony of approximately 50 otters at the island, but "its ability to become established and persist is uncertain."

Figure 3.10 shows annual survey results for southern sea otters between 1983 and 2012. These surveys were

FIGURE 3.6

Abundance of the eastern distinct population segment (DPS) of the Steller sea lion, 1980–2010

[Estimated abundance of Steller sea lions by region in the eastern DPS]

Growth rate 4.18% (3.71%–4.62%)

Note: SEAK = Southeast Alaska. BC = British Columbia. CA = California. OR = Oregon.
Points are observed pup counts mulitplied by 4.5, which is an estimate of total population abundance.

SOURCE: "Figure 2. Estimated Abundance for the Eastern DPS of Steller Sea Lion," in *Celebrating 40 Years: Recovering Threatened and Endangered Species FY 2011–2012 Report to Congress*, U.S. Department of Commerce, National Oceanic and Atmospheric Administration, National Marine Fisheries Services, July 2013, http://www.nmfs.noaa.gov/pr/laws/esa/noaa_esa_report_072213.pdf (accessed November 4, 2013)

FIGURE 3.7

Approximate distribution of northern sea otters in Alaska waters

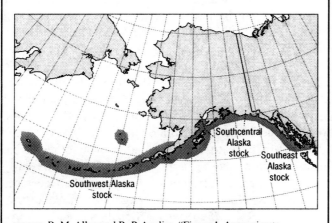

SOURCE: B. M. Allen and R. P. Angliss, "Figure 1. Approximate Distribution of Northern Sea Otters in Alaska Waters (Shaded Area)," in *Alaska Marine Mammal Stock Assessments, 2012*, U.S. Department of Commerce, National Oceanic and Atmospheric Administration, National Marine Fisheries Service, Alaska Fisheries Science Center, March 2013, http://www.nmfs.noaa.gov/pr/sars/pdf/ak2012.pdf (accessed November 5, 2013)

conducted during the springtime and count both independent otters and pups. In general, the population increased over this period. In the press release "California's Sea Otter Numbers Continue Slow Climb" (September 12, 2013, http://www.usgs.gov/newsroom/article.asp?ID=3687), the U.S. Geological Survey notes that the spring 2013 survey indicated a total population of 2,941 individuals.

The USFWS states in *Final Revised Recovery Plan for the Southern Sea Otter (*Enhydra lutis nereis*)* (February 24, 2003, http://ecos.fws.gov/docs/recovery_plans/2003/030403.pdf) that the primary recovery objective is to manage human activities that can damage or destroy habitat. Specifically, the agency sets a goal to "protect the population and reduce or eliminate the identified potential limiting factors related to human activities, including: managing petroleum exploration, extraction, and tankering to reduce the likelihood of a spill along the California coast to insignificant levels; minimizing contaminant loading and infectious disease; and managing fishery interactions to reduce sea otter mortality incidental to commercial fishing to insignificant levels."

TABLE 3.7

Recovery plan details for the southwest stock of northern sea otters

Management unit	Carrying capacity (K)	Delisting abundance	Uplisting abundance	2007 abundance estimate	Status (%K)
Western Aleutian	63,897	31,309	2,556	6,451	0.10
Eastern Aleutian	30,697	15,042	1,228	2,291	0.07
Bristol Bay	36,898	18,080	1,476	11,253	0.30
South Alaska Peninsula	33,476	16,403	1,339	4,724	0.14
Kodiak, Kamishak, Alaska Peninsula	46,086	22,582	1,843	28,955	0.63
Total	**211,054**	**103,417**	**8,442**	**53,674**	**0.25**

SOURCE: "Table 18. Examples of Estimates That Are Developed by PVA Models Using Available Data through 2007," in *Southwest Alaska Distinct Population Segment of the Northern Sea Otter (Enhydra lutris kenyoni) Recovery Plan*, U.S. Department of the Interior, U.S. Fish and Wildlife Service, July 2013, http://ecos.fws.gov/docs/recovery_plan/Recovery%20Plan%20SW%20AK%20DPS%20Sea%20Otter%20Aug13.pdf (accessed November 5, 2013)

FIGURE 3.8

Southern sea otter. ©*U.S. Fish and Wildlife.*

The USFWS indicates that southern sea otters can be considered for delisting under the ESA when the average population level over a three-year period exceeds 3,090 animals. Population trends through 2013 have been encouraging. Absent any catastrophic events, the southern sea otter could achieve delisting within the next decade.

Foreign Species of Otters

According to the IUCN, in *Red List of Threatened Species Version 2013.2*, two sea otter species—the marine otter (*Lontra felina*) and the sea otter (*Enhydra lutris*)—were considered threatened in 2013. Two other otter species that are not truly sea-dwelling, but typically inhabit coastal areas, are also considered threatened.

As of November 2013, five foreign otter species were listed as endangered under the ESA. (See Table 3.2.) They populate areas of Africa and South America.

MANATEES AND DUGONGS

Manatees are large stout mammals that inhabit freshwaters and coastal waterways. (See Figure 3.11.) They are from the Sirenian order, along with dugongs. There are only five Sirenian species, and all are endangered or extinct. Scientists believe Steller's sea cow, the only species of cold-water manatee, was hunted to extinction during the 1700s.

The West Indian manatee, also known as the Florida manatee, primarily swims in the rivers, bays, and estuaries of Florida and surrounding states. As of November 2013, this species was listed as endangered under the ESA. (See Table 3.1.)

Manatees are often called "sea cows" and can weigh up to 2,000 pounds (900 kg). They swim just below the surface of the water and feed on vegetation. West Indian manatees migrate north during the summer, though generally no farther than the North Carolina coast. During the winter many manatees huddle around warm-water discharges from power plants and other industrial facilities. Although this can keep them warm, scientists worry that overcrowding in small areas makes the animals more susceptible to sickness.

Imperiled Manatee Populations

In most years biologists conduct surveys during cold weather to determine the number of Florida manatees remaining in the wild. The Florida Fish and Wildlife Research Institute explains in "Population Monitoring and Aerial Surveys" (2014, http://myfwc.com/research/manatee/projects/population-monitoring/) that surveys were not conducted in 2008, 2012, and 2013 due to "warmer than average weather." The survey results are estimates based on surveys conducted at known wintering habitats. According to the Florida Fish and Wildlife Research Institute, in "Manatee Synoptic Surveys" (2014, http://myfwc.com/research/manatee/projects/population-monitoring/synoptic-surveys/), the January 2011 survey found 4,834 manatees living along the Florida coast. This number compares with 1,267 reported in 1991 (the first year of the survey) and 5,077 reported in 2010. Many manatees have scars on their backs from motorboat propellers—these allow individual manatees to be recognized. In fact,

FIGURE 3.9

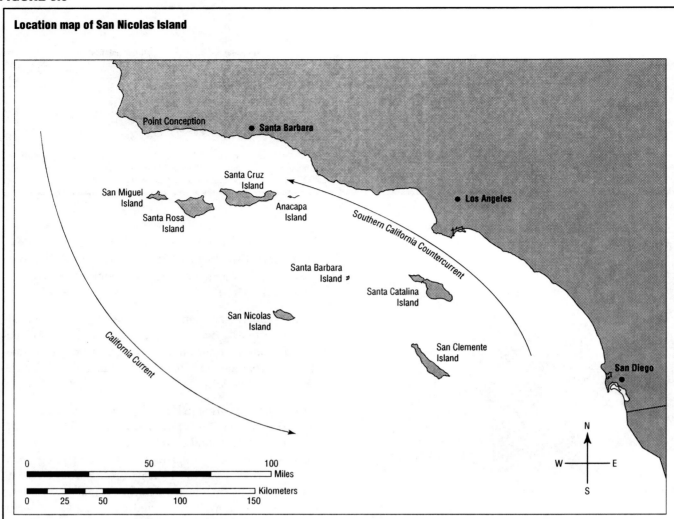

Location map of San Nicolas Island

SOURCE: "Figure 4-1. Main Surface Currents of the Southern California Bight," in *Final Supplemental Environmental Impact Statement: Translocation of Southern Sea Otters*, U.S. Department of the Interior, U.S. Fish and Wildlife Service, November 2012, http://www.fws.gov/ventura/species_information/ so_sea_otter/fseis/Final%20Supplemental%20EIS%20on%20the%20Translocation%20of%20Southern%20Sea%20Otters%20-%20Volume%201.pdf (accessed November 5, 2013)

motorboat strikes are the major documented cause of manatee mortalities. Manatees are large and swim slowly at the surface of the water. They often cannot move away from boats quickly enough to avoid being hit. As a result, several Florida waterways have been declared boat-free zones to protect manatees from boat collisions. There are also areas where boaters are required to lower their speed.

Other threats to manatee survival include disease, natural pathogens, and cold-water temperatures. Although the animals can live up to 50 to 60 years, they have naturally low birth rates, which makes it difficult for their population to rebound.

Regulating Water Activities

The Florida manatee was on the first list of endangered species published in 1967. (See Table 2.1 in Chapter 2.)

According to the USFWS (August 26, 2011, http://www .fws.gov/northflorida/Manatee/Documents/MPARules/ June11_KB_Proposed_Rule/20110621_frn_Federal_Regis ter_Notice_for_Proposed_Kings_Bay_Manatee_Rule.html), in 1979 the agency "adopted a regulatory process to provide a means for establishing manatee protection areas in waters under the jurisdiction of the United States where manatees were taken by waterborne activities." The regulatory process is codified at 50 Code of Federal Regulations (http://ecfr .gpoaccess.gov/), part 17, subpart J.

As noted earlier, the MMPA and the ESA prohibit taking of marine mammals and listed species, respectively. Between 1980 and 1998 the USFWS designated seven manatee protection areas in and around Crystal River/Kings Bay on the western coast of Florida. The bay is fed by warm spring waters and is a major manatee

FIGURE 3.10

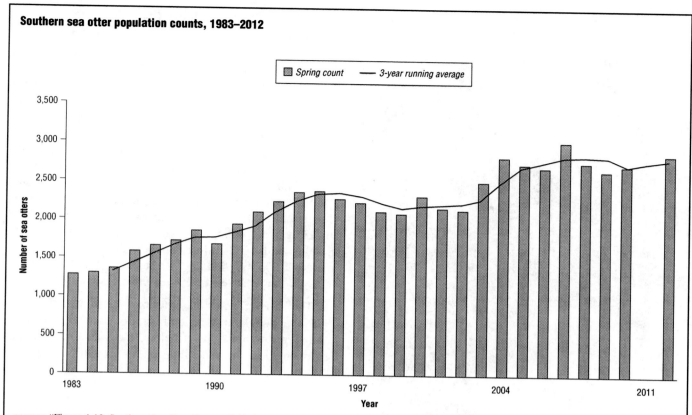

Southern sea otter population counts, 1983–2012

SOURCE: "Figure 4-19. Southern Sea Otter Counts 1983–2012 (Mainland Population)," in *Final Supplemental Environmental Impact Statement: Translocation of Southern Sea Otters*, U.S. Department of the Interior, U.S. Fish and Wildlife Service, November 2012, http://www.fws.gov/ventura/species_information/so_sea_otter/fseis/Final%20Supplemental%20EIS%20on%20the%20Translocation%20of%20Southern%20Sea%20Otters%20-%20Volume%201.pdf (accessed November 5, 2013)

habitat, both during cold and warm weather. However, the bay is also used for commercial boating and is a popular recreation area that features an active "manatee viewing industry." As a result, the USFWS reports that the bay has suffered increasing problems with manatee harassment and fatal boat strikes.

In 2000 a coalition of 18 environmental and wildlife groups and three individuals sued the USFWS and the state of Florida over manatee protection measures. In 2001 a settlement with the federal government was reached in *Save the Manatee Club v. Ballard.* According to the USFWS, in the press release "Settlement Reached in Manatee Lawsuit" (January 4, 2001, http://www.fws.gov/southeast/news/2001/r01-001.html), the agency agreed to a time table for completing the following actions:

- Designate additional manatee protection areas
- Revise the manatee recovery plan
- Develop regulations allowing manatee taking under the MMPA
- Coordinate with the U.S. Army Corps of Engineers to improve procedures for reviewing permit applications for the construction of boating facilities in manatee

habitat and improve the related consultation process required under the ESA

As of May 2013, the USFWS (http://www.fws.gov/northflorida/Manatee/Documents/MPARules/index-federal-mpa-maps.htm) had established 19 manatee protection areas (five sanctuaries and 14 refuges) in 12 counties along the central western coast of Florida. In addition, the Florida Fish and Wildlife Conservation Commission (http://myfwc.com/wildlifehabitats/managed/manatee/protection-zones/) had designated dozens of "manatee protection zones" with specific watercraft speed limit restrictions.

Foreign Manatee and Dugong Species

According to the IUCN, in *Red List of Threatened Species Version 2013.2*, three manatee species—the South American manatee, the West Indian manatee, and the West African manatee—and the only remaining dugong species were considered threatened in 2013.

As of November 2013, the species found in western Africa and in and around the Amazon River in South America were listed under the ESA and were in grave danger of extinction due to illegal hunting, deforestation, habitat destruction, and water pollution. (See Table 3.2.)

FIGURE 3.11

West Indian manatee (Florida manatee). ©*Kipling Brock/Shutterstock.*

The only remaining dugongs live in the coastal waters of the Indian Ocean and the Pacific Ocean. Their populations are also considered imperiled. Dugongs around the tiny island of Palau in the western Pacific Ocean are listed as endangered under the ESA.

POLAR BEARS

Polar bears are the largest of the bear species. They are believed to have evolved from grizzly bears hundreds of thousands of years ago. Polar bears have stocky bodies and can weigh up to 1,400 pounds (635 kg) when fully grown. They are relatively long lived and have small litters, typically only a cub or two per litter. Their fur includes water-repellent guard hairs and a dense undercoat that is white to pale yellow in color. They have large paddle-like paws that help make them excellent swimmers.

Polar bears are considered a marine mammal because sea ice is their primary habitat. They are found throughout the Arctic and near-Arctic regions of the Northern Hemisphere. The bears prefer coastal sea ice and other areas in which water conditions are conducive to providing prey. Seals are their primary food source, particularly ringed seals. As described earlier, the Arctic subspecies

of the ringed seal was listed under the ESA with a status of threatened as of November 2013. (See Table 3.1.)

The USFWS notes in the fact sheet "Polar Bear *Ursus maritimus*" (May 2012, http://www.fws.gov/alaska/fisheries/endangered/pdf/polarbear_factsheet_v2.pdf) that there are 20,000 to 25,000 bears worldwide. There are two stocks of polar bears in the United States; both are in and around Alaska: the southern Beaufort Sea stock and the Chukchi/Bering Sea stock. (See Figure 3.12.) There is extensive overlap between the two stocks. As of February 2014, the most recent *SARs* for the polar bear stocks were dated January 2010. According to the USFWS, in *Polar Bear (*Ursus maritimus*): Southern Beaufort Sea Stock* (January 1, 2010, http://alaska.fws.gov/fisheries/mmm/stock/final_sbs_polar_bear_sar.pdf), scientists estimate that the southern Beaufort population consists of approximately 1,500 individuals. The bears are found mostly in areas that have at least 50% ice cover.

The USFWS notes that after passage of the MMPA in 1972 the populations of both stocks increased, due to hunting restrictions. Nevertheless, the southern Beaufort Sea population showed "little or no growth" during the 1990s and declined by approximately 3% per year between 2001 and 2005. Reduced sea ice, particularly during the summer and fall, is believed to be a factor in the decline.

In *Polar Bear (*Ursus maritimus*): Chukchi/Bering Seas Stock* (January 1, 2010, http://alaska.fws.gov/fisheries/mmm/stock/final_cbs_polar_bear_sar.pdf), the USFWS indicates that the Chukchi/Bering Sea stock population is roughly estimated at 2,000 bears. However, the number is uncertain due to logistical challenges (e.g., the vast and difficult terrain) and the passage of the animals into Russian territory. The USFWS notes that this stock faces "different stressors" than those affecting the southern Beaufort Sea stock. In particular, the Chukchi/Bering Sea stock endures "increased harvest in Russia" and a greater loss of sea ice during the summer. The population of the stock is believed to be declining.

Listing Controversy

In 2005 the USFWS was petitioned by the Center for Biological Diversity (later joined by the Natural Resources Defense Council and Greenpeace) to list the polar bear as threatened throughout its range. Due to a heavy workload, the agency failed to issue a 90-day finding to the petition. The organizations sued, and in February 2006 the agency issued its 90-day finding, noting that there was sufficient scientific information to warrant the listing. In January 2007 the polar bear was officially proposed for listing as a threatened species.

Following a legal challenge, the USFWS was forced to make a decision by May 15, 2008. On that date the agency officially listed the polar bear as threatened. The USFWS also issued a "special rule" under section 4(d)

FIGURE 3.12

Map of polar bear stocks near Alaska

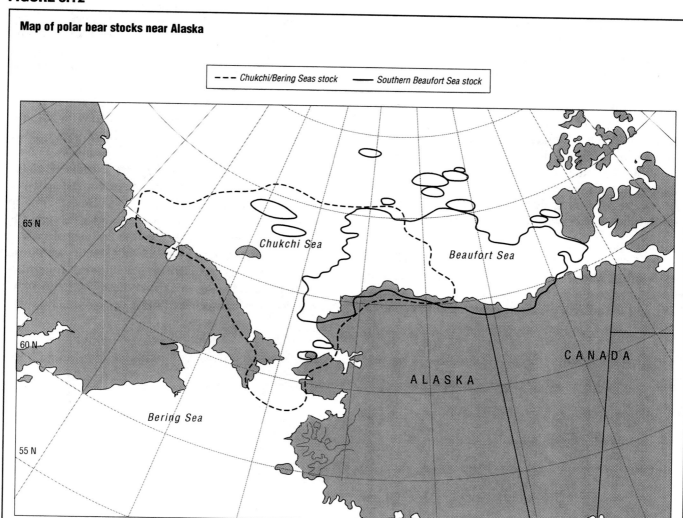

--- --- Chukchi/Bering Seas stock   ——— Southern Beaufort Sea stock

SOURCE: B. M. Allen and R. P. Angliss, "Figure 1. Map of the Southern Beaufort Sea and the Chukchi/Bering Seas Polar Bear Stocks," in *Alaska Marine Mammal Stock Assessments, 2012*, U.S. Department of Commerce, National Oceanic and Atmospheric Administration, National Marine Fisheries Service, Alaska Fisheries Science Center, March 2013, http://www.nmfs.noaa.gov/pr/sars/pdf/ak2012.pdf (accessed November 5, 2013)

of the ESA adopting the existing conservation regulatory requirements for polar bears under the MMPA and the CITES agreement. In other words, activities already authorized in these regulations would take precedence over the general prohibitions under U.S. law that apply to threatened species. Such activities include take, import and export, and shipment in interstate or foreign commerce for commercial purposes.

The USFWS notes in "Endangered and Threatened Wildlife and Plants; 12-Month Petition Finding and Proposed Rule to List the Polar Bear (*Ursus maritimus*) as Threatened throughout Its Range" (*Federal Register*, vol. 72, no. 5, January 9, 2007) that melting and thinning sea ice have already stressed polar bear populations. Computer models indicate these conditions are expected to worsen in the future as temperatures continue to warm. Polar bears have evolved to move on ice. They have special

suckers on their paws to help them walk on the ice. They are poorly suited to walking on ground and expend a great deal of energy when they are forced to do so because of a lack of sea ice. In addition, warmer temperatures are degrading the snowy birthing dens of ringed seals, the major prey of the polar bears, and endangering seal pup survival. Thus, both populations face problems due to the warming of their icy ecosystems.

Following the USFWS listing of the polar bear in 2008, the state of Alaska sued the USFWS arguing that the listing was not justified. The article "Alaska Sues to Overturn Polar Bear Protection" (WashingtonPost.com, November 16, 2009) explains that Alaska feared the listing would threaten oil development in the state, particularly of offshore reserves. In June 2011 a federal judge rejected the suit and ruled that the USFWS followed proper procedures in listing the polar bear.

Environmentalists hoped the listing status granted to polar bears under the ESA would facilitate legal restrictions on oil and gas exploration in Alaska and on U.S. emissions of carbon dioxide (a suspected cause of global warming). However, the 4(d) rule issued for the polar bear specifically noted that the incidental take of the species due to oil and gas exploration is already allowed under regulations of the MMPA. In addition, the administration of President Barack Obama (1961–) decided not to use the ESA listing as a mechanism for restricting carbon dioxide emissions. As of February 2014, the administration had attempted to achieve passage of environmental legislation to curb U.S. carbon dioxide emissions, but those efforts had been rebuffed by Congress.

The National Snow and Ice Data Center (NSIDC) in Boulder, Colorado, monitors ice coverage in the Arctic Sea. The NSIDC website (http://nsidc.org/arcticseaicenews/charctic-interactive-sea-ice-graph/) includes an interactive chart that shows Arctic Sea ice extent, which it defines as the area of the ocean with at least 15% sea ice. The ice extent varies seasonally throughout the year peaking around March and declining to its lowest level around September. According to the NSIDC, the average minimum ice extent over the period 1979 through 2000 was 2.6 million square miles (6.7 million square kilometers [km]). In 2012 the ice extent reached a new record low of 1 million square miles (3.4 million square km). In 2013 the minimum was slightly higher at 2 million square miles (5.1 million square km), but still below the historical average minimum. Scientists worry that continued global warming will further diminish the ice extent and seriously stress polar bear populations. In "Polar Bears: Time to Prepare for the Worst" (Discovery.com, February 8, 2013), Kieran Mulvaney describes the findings of various studies showing the negative effects of a smaller ice extent, such as polar bears are increasingly suffering from malnourishment and having to expend more energy to swim greater distances between ice floes.

CHAPTER 4
FISH

Fish are cold-blooded vertebrates with fins. They occur in nearly all permanent water environments, from deep oceans to remote alpine lakes and desert springs. Marine fish inhabit the salty waters of oceans and seas, whereas freshwater fish inhabit inland rivers, lakes, and ponds. Some fish species migrate between fresh- and marine waters. These include species called anadromous fish that are born in freshwater, migrate to the ocean to spend their adulthood, and then return to freshwater to spawn.

Fish are the most diverse vertebrate group on the planet and include thousands of different species. The largest known fish are the whale sharks, which can grow to be more than 50 feet (15.2 meters [m]) long and weigh several tons. At the other end of the spectrum is *Paedocypris progenetica*, a tiny fish discovered in Sumatra, Indonesia, that is less than 0.3 of an inch (0.8 of a centimeter [cm]) in length.

FishBase (http://www.fishbase.org/search.php) is a comprehensive online database of scientific information about fish. It was developed by the WorldFish Center of Malaysia in collaboration with the United Nations Food and Agriculture Organization and is supported by many government and research institutions. As of December 2013, FishBase contained information on 32,700 fish species around the world. Scientists report that only a small fraction of these species have been assessed for their conservation status.

Historically, imperiled fish species have drawn far less public attention than other species, such as marine mammals. The disappearance of large food fish species does garner concern because of their commercial importance to humans. Every fish species, however, plays some role in its respective ecosystem and food web. The U.S. Fish and Wildlife Service (USFWS) makes this point in "The Pallid Sturgeon, a Missouri River 'Dinosaur'" (October 16, 2009, http://www.fws.gov/mountain-prairie/feature/sturgeon.html), which discusses the pallid sturgeon,

an endangered species once common to midwestern rivers. The agency notes, "The imperiled status of this species is a result of alteration of the natural habitat of the Missouri and Mississippi rivers. And like a canary in a coal mine, the plight of the pallid sturgeon serves warning that the overall health of the ecosystem has suffered." The USFWS continues, "Species interact in complex ways, and survival of all native species in a given region is an indicator of a healthy ecosystem. If one species declines, others can become negatively affected. Recovery programs for any species, such as the pallid sturgeon, aim to restore the critical balance that exists between all members of a healthy ecosystem."

As of November 2013, there were 156 fish species listed under the Endangered Species Act (ESA) in the United States. (See Table 1.2 in Chapter 1.) Four fish species have been delisted because of extinction: Tecopa pupfish (1982), blue pike (1983), longjaw cisco (1983), and Amistad gambusia (1987). (See Table 2.11 in Chapter 2.) All were freshwater fish. The Tecopa pupfish and the Amistad gambusia were found in isolated habitats in springs in California and Texas, respectively. The longjaw cisco and the blue pike were once plentiful fish in the Great Lakes region and disappeared because of overfishing and other stresses. As of November 2013, no fish species had been delisted because of recovery.

In *Federal and State Endangered and Threatened Species Expenditures: Fiscal Year 2012* (September 2013, http://www.fws.gov/endangered/esa-library/pdf/2012 .EXP.FINAL.pdf), the USFWS indicates that more than $200 million was spent under the ESA during fiscal year (FY) 2012 on imperiled fish.

GENERAL THREATS TO FISH

Fish species have become endangered and threatened in the United States for a variety of reasons, both natural and anthropogenic (caused by humans). Most fish are not imperiled by a single threat to their survival, but by multiple threats that combine to produce daunting challenges to recovery. Some scientists believe natural threats, such as disease, have been aggravated by human actions that stress fish populations. Dams and other structures that are used for power generation, flood control, irrigation, and navigation have dramatically changed water flow patterns in many rivers. These impediments disrupt migration patterns and affect water temperature and quality. Likewise, the dredging of river and stream beds to produce channels and the filling of wetlands and swamps have changed water habitats.

Dams

Dams affect rivers, the lands abutting them, the water bodies they join, and aquatic wildlife throughout the United States. Water flow is reduced or stopped altogether downstream of dams, altering aquatic habitats and drying wetlands. Arthur C. Benke and Colbert E. Cushing, the editors of *Rivers of North America* (2005), note that it is difficult to find any river in the United States that has not been dammed or channeled. According to Benke and Cushing, "All human alterations of rivers, regardless of whether they provide services such as power or drinking water supply, result in degradation."

The U.S. Army Corps of Engineers maintains the National Inventory of Dams (NID; http://geo.usace.army.mil/pgis/f?p=397:5:0::NO). As of February 2014, the inventory included more than 87,000 dams throughout the country. To be included in this inventory, dams have to be at least 6 feet (1.8 m) tall or hold back a minimum of 15 acre-feet (4.9 million gallons [18.5 million liters]) of water. Dams are built for a variety of purposes. The most frequent purposes listed in the NID are recreation, fire protection, and flood control.

Although only a small percentage of the dams listed with the NID produce hydroelectric power, these dams tend to be the largest in size and affect large watersheds. These structures provide many challenges to aquatic species, besides impeding water flow and migration paths. Turbines operate like massive underwater fans. Passage through running turbine blades can result in the death of many small aquatic creatures that are unable to escape their path. Some modern hydroelectric dams include stairlike structures called fish ladders that provide migrating fish a watery path to climb up and over the dams.

SNAIL DARTERS. The snail darter, a small fish species related to perch, was at the center of a dam-building controversy during the 1970s. The USFWS listed the snail darter as endangered in 1975. At the time it was believed to exist only in the Little Tennessee River, and this area was designated as critical habitat for the species. That same year the Tellico Dam was near completion on the Little Tennessee River, and the filling of the Tellico Reservoir would have destroyed the entire habitat of the snail darter. A lawsuit was filed to prevent this from happening. The case went all the way to the U.S. Supreme Court, which ruled in *Tennessee Valley Authority v. Hill* (437 U.S. 153 [1978]) that under the ESA species protection must take priority over economic and developmental concerns. One month after this ruling Congress amended the ESA to allow for exemptions under certain circumstances.

In late 1979 the Tellico Dam received an exemption, and the Tellico Reservoir was filled. The snail darter is now extinct in that habitat. However, snail darter populations were later discovered in other river systems. In addition, the species has been introduced into several other habitats. Because of an increase in numbers, the snail darter was reclassified as threatened in 1984.

Entrainment and Impingement

Entrainment occurs when fish are pulled or diverted away from their natural habitat by mechanical equipment or other nonnatural structures in water bodies. A prime example is a freshwater intake structure in a river or lake. Small fish, in particular, are susceptible to being sucked into pipes through which water is being pumped out of a water body. Even if the pipe end is screened, the force of the suction can impinge (crush) fish against the screen, causing serious harm. In a more general sense entrainment refers to diversions that occur when fish accidentally feed through artificial water structures, such as gates, locks, or dams, and cannot return to their original location.

Excessive Sediment

Many river and stream banks and adjacent lands have been stripped of vegetation by timber harvesting, crop growing, and excessive grazing of livestock. This eliminates habitat for insects and other tiny creatures that serve as foodstuff for fish. It also aggravates erosion problems and allows large amounts of dirt to enter water bodies. Once in the water, this dirt is known as silt or sediment. Most of these particles settle to the bottom. However, sediment is easily stirred up by the movement of fish and other aquatic creatures, many of which spawn or lay eggs at the bed of their habitat. The dirt that remains in suspension in the water is said to make water turbid. The measure of the dirtiness (lack of clarity) of a water body is called its turbidity.

Freshwater aquatic creatures are sensitive to turbidity levels and choose their habitats based in part on their sediment preferences. Some fish prefer waters with large amounts of sediment. It provides cover that prevents predator fish from seeing them. Other species prefer clean waters with low turbidity levels. Excessive sediment may clog their gills or smother their eggs. (See Figure 4.1.)

FIGURE 4.1

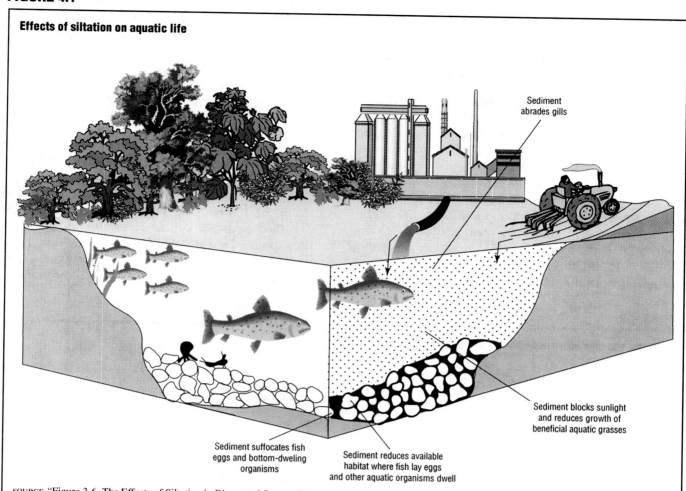

Effects of siltation on aquatic life

Sediment abrades gills

Sediment suffocates fish eggs and bottom-dweling organisms

Sediment reduces available habitat where fish lay eggs and other aquatic organisms dwell

Sediment blocks sunlight and reduces growth of beneficial aquatic grasses

SOURCE: "Figure 3-6. The Effects of Siltation in Rivers and Streams," in *National Water Quality Inventory: 1998 Report to Congress*, U.S. Environmental Protection Agency, June 2000, http://water.epa.gov/lawsregs/guidance/cwa/305b/upload/2000_06_28_305b_98report_chap3.pdf (accessed November 7, 2013)

Forestry and agricultural practices can drastically affect the sediment levels in a water system through the deforestation of banks and nearby lands. Excessive grazing of livestock along riverbanks can strip vegetation and permit large amounts of dirt to enter the water. Likewise, timber harvesting and crop production can expose loosened dirt to wind and rain that carry it into water bodies. Dams and diversion structures trap sediments behind them, interrupting the natural downstream flow of sediments that takes place in moving waters.

Chemical and Biological Pollutants

Water pollution poses a considerable threat to many aquatic species. Industrial pollution introduces metal and organic chemicals to water bodies. In agricultural areas there is runoff of manure, fertilizers, and pesticides. U.S. pesticide use during the 1960s centered around chlorine-containing organic compounds, such as dichlorodiphenyltrichloroethane (DDT) and chlordane. Scientists eventually learned that these chemicals are extremely persistent in the environment and have damaging effects on wildlife, particularly fish and bird species. DDT was banned in the United States in 1972 and chlordane in 1983; however, nearly four decades later both pesticides continue to show up in water, sediment, and fish samples.

In general, aquatic creatures are not killed outright by water contamination. A major exception is an oil spill, which can kill many creatures through direct contact. The more widespread and common threat is overall degradation of water quality and habitats because of pollutants. Exposure to contaminants can weaken the immune systems of aquatic animals and make them more susceptible to disease and to other health and reproductive problems.

Bioaccumulative contaminants are those that accumulate in the tissues of aquatic organisms at much higher concentrations than are found in the water body itself. This biomagnification effect occurs with mercury (a metal), the pesticides DDT and chlordane, and dioxins. Dioxins are a category of several hundred chlorinated organic compounds. Polychlorinated biphenyls (PCBs) are dioxins that were widely used to cool and lubricate electrical equipment before a 1977 ban on their manufacture. Bioaccumulative contaminants are a particular concern for fish at the higher end of the aquatic food chain, such as salmon and large freshwater species.

TOXIC POLLUTANT ADVISORIES. The states issue advisories to protect residents from the adverse health risk of eating fish that are contaminated with certain pollutants. The U.S. Environmental Protection Agency (EPA) provides a website (http://fishadvisoryonline.epa.gov/General.aspx) with an interactive map at which visitors can find the most recent fish advisory notices by state or water body. In addition, the EPA occasionally publishes national listings of the state advisories. As of February 2014, the most recent EPA summary was published in 2011. In *2010 Biennial National Listing of Fish Advisories* (September 2011, http://water.epa.gov/scitech/swguidance/fishshellfish/fishadvisories/upload/National-Listing-of-Fish-Advisories-Technical-Fact-sheet-2010.pdf), the EPA states that 4,600 advisories were in effect in 2010. The advisories covered approximately 1.5 million miles (2.4 million kilometers [km]) of river and 18.3 million acres (7.4 million hectares [ha]) of lakes. These values represented 41% of the total river miles and 44% of the total lake acres that were assessed for contamination in 2010.

As shown in Figure 4.2, the percentage of total river miles and lake acres under advisory has increased dramatically since 1993. The vast majority of the advisories issued in 2011 were due to mercury contamination (3,921). (See Table 4.1.) PCBs accounted for 1,102 of the advisories. Dioxins, DDT, and chlordane each accounted for much smaller numbers. All these chemicals are bioaccumulative. As shown in Table 4.1, the number

FIGURE 4.2

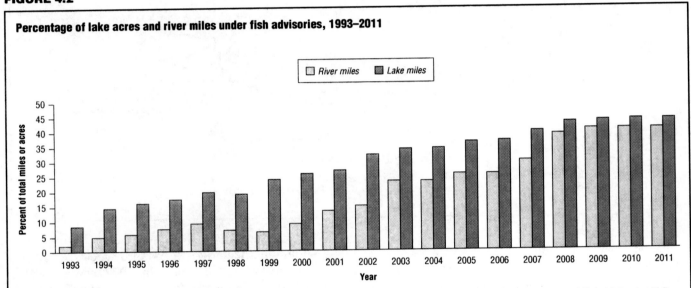

Percentage of lake acres and river miles under fish advisories, 1993–2011

SOURCE: "Figure 1. Percentage of Total Lake Acres and River Miles under Advisory from 1993 to 2011," in *2011 National Listing of Fish Advisories*, U.S. Environmental Protection Agency, December 2013, http://water.epa.gov/scitech/swguidance/fishshellfish/fishadvisories/loader.cfm?csModule=security/getfile&PageID=685927 (accessed January 24, 2014)

TABLE 4.1

Number of fish advisories and lake acres and river miles under fish advisories, by contaminant, 2010 and 2011

Contaminant	Number of waterbodies under advisory		Lake acres		River miles	
	2010	2011	2010	2011	2010	2011
Mercury	3,710	3,921	16,396,422	16,404,769	1,143,327	1,144,045
PCBs	1,084	1,102	6,071,877	6,080,041	131,224	131,657
Chlordane	60	60	824,290	824,290	53,893	53,893
Dioxins	128	129	35,400	35,400	2,333	2,333
DDT	58	67	876,470	876,571	68,884	68,927

SOURCE: "Table 1. Number of Waterbodies under Advisory and Size of Waters under Advisory, by Contaminant, for 2010 and 2011—as Documented in the NLFA Database," in *2011 National Listing of Fish Advisories*, U.S. Environmental Protection Agency, December 2013, http://water.epa.gov/scitech/swguidance/fishshellfish/fishadvisories/loader.cfm?csModule=security/getfile&PageID=685927 (accessed January 24, 2014) of advisories issued because of mercury and PCB contamination and the number of lake acres and river miles contaminated by mercury and PCBs increased between 2010 and 2011. The number of advisories issued because of dioxins and DDT increased only slightly between 2010 and 2011, whereas the number of advisories for chlordane remained the same during this one-year period.

Although the purpose of fish advisories is to protect human health, the underlying data illustrate that toxic pollutants pose a worrisome threat to the nation's fish species.

Unwelcome Guests: Injurious Invasive Fish

Historically, fish were generally geographically limited in their habitats, such as to streams, rivers, or lakes in a particular area. However, human intervention has allowed species to move into new habitats, sometimes thousands of miles from where they originated. Many fish species have been introduced purposely to new water bodies to improve sport and recreational fishing. Some species that are popular in aquariums have been intentionally dumped into the environment. Other species have been introduced unintentionally by migrating through human-built canals and locks, stowing away in the ballast water of ships, or escaping from research, breeding, and aquaculture (fish farming) facilities. Some introduced species are not problematic in their new habitats, but others cause ecological or economic harm by competing with native species for habitat and food, preying on them, or breeding with them. Injurious nonnative species are commonly called invasive species. Invasive species have played a role in the decline of some endangered and threatened species. For example, the threatened bull trout has become imperiled, in part, because of the introduction of nonnative brook trout to bull trout habitats. Because brook trout are an extremely popular sport and food fish, they are not considered by the public to be injurious.

Overcrowding

The overcrowding of stressed fish populations into smaller and smaller areas has contributed to hybridization (uncharacteristic mating between closely related species resulting in hybrid offspring). According to the USFWS, environmental degradation appears to inhibit natural reproductive instincts that historically prevented fish from mating outside their species. In addition, a shortage of suitable space for spawning has resulted in more mating between species. Cross-mating can be extremely detrimental to imperiled species because the offspring can be sterile.

IMPERILED FRESHWATER FISH

Freshwater fish listed under the ESA fall within the jurisdiction of the USFWS. They include a wide variety of species and are found all over the country. As of November 2013, there were 117 freshwater fish species

listed under the ESA. (See Table 4.2.) It should be noted that some species included experimental populations considered nonessential. As noted in Chapter 2, an experimental population is achieved by introducing a species to an area in which it is not currently found. The nonessential designation means that the survival of the experimental population is not believed essential to the survival of the species as a whole. Thus, the experimental population receives less protection under the ESA than does the species as a whole. Most of the imperiled fish species had recovery plans in place. In general, imperiled freshwater fish are small in size and are associated with flowing (lotic) waters, such as rivers and streams, rather than with still (lentic) waters, such as lakes and ponds.

Table 4.3 shows the 10 freshwater species with the highest expenditures under the ESA during FY 2012. Approximately $91.5 million was spent on only two of the fish: pallid sturgeon ($53.8 million) and bull trout ($37.7 million).

Pallid Sturgeon

The pallid sturgeon is a unique and rare freshwater fish that is sometimes called the "swimming dinosaur." It is descended from fish that were common more than 50 million years ago. The pallid sturgeon has a long flat snout and a slender body that ends with a pronounced tail fin. (See Figure 4.3.) Adults range in size from 3 to 5 feet (0.9 to 1.5 m) and typically weigh 25 to 50 pounds (11.3 to 22.7 kilogram [kg]). The fish is a bottom-feeder and prefers large rivers of relatively warm free-flowing water with high turbidity (high mud content).

Historically, the pallid sturgeon was found throughout the Mississippi and Missouri River systems from Montana and North Dakota south to the Gulf of Mexico. During the early 1900s specimens as large as 85 pounds (38.6 kg) and 6 feet (1.8 m) long were reported. Over the next century the fish virtually disappeared. In 1990 it was listed as endangered under the ESA. Three years later the USFWS published the first recovery plan for the species. In *Pallid Sturgeon Recovery Plan (Scaphirhynchus albus)* (November 1993, http://ecos.fws.gov/docs/recovery_plans/1993/931107.pdf), the agency blames human destruction and modification of habitat as the two primary causes for the pallid sturgeon's decline.

Pallid sturgeons are believed to be extremely sensitive to changes in the velocity and volume of river flows. They are nearly blind and forage along muddy river bottoms feeding on tiny fish and other creatures that prefer turbid waters. Dams and channelization have reduced the erosion of riverbank soil into the Missouri and Mississippi Rivers, their last remaining primary habitat. This has given other fish species with better eyesight an advantage over the pallid sturgeon at finding small prey. In addition, mating between the pallid

TABLE 4.2

Endangered and threatened freshwater fish species, November 2013

Common name	Scientific name	Listing status[a]	U.S.or U.S./foreign listed	Recovery plan date	Recovery plan stage[b]
Alabama cavefish	Speoplatyrhinus poulsoni	E	US	10/25/1990	RF(2)
Alabama sturgeon	Scaphirhynchus suttkusi	E	US	7/8/2013	F
Amber darter	Percina antesella	E	US	6/20/1986	F
Apache trout	Oncorhynchus apache	T	US	9/3/2009	RF(2)
Arkansas River shiner	Notropis girardi	T	US	None	—
Ash Meadows amargosa pupfish	Cyprinodon nevadensis mionectes	E	US	9/28/1990	F
Ash Meadows speckled dace	Rhinichthys osculus nevadensis	E	US	9/28/1990	F
Bayou darter	Etheostoma rubrum	T	US	7/10/1990	RF(1)
Beautiful shiner	Cyprinella formosa	T	US/foreign	3/29/1995	F
Big Bend gambusia	Gambusia gaigei	E	US	9/19/1984	F
Big Spring spinedace	Lepidomeda mollispinis pratensis	T	US	1/20/1994	F
Blackside dace	Phoxinus cumberlandensis	T	US	8/17/1988	F
Bluemask (=jewel) darter	Etheostoma sp.	E	US	7/25/1997	F
Blue shiner	Cyprinella caerulea	T	US	8/30/1995	F
Bonytail chub	Gila elegans	E	US	8/1/2002	RF(2)
Borax Lake chub	Gila boraxobius	E	US	2/4/1987	F
Boulder darter	Etheostoma wapiti	E; EXPN	US	7/27/1989	F
Bull trout	Salvelinus confluentus	T; EXPN	US	11/29/2002	D
Cahaba shiner	Notropis cahabae	E	US	4/23/1992	F
Cape Fear shiner	Notropis mekistocholas	E	US	10/7/1988	F
Cherokee darter	Etheostoma scotti	T	US	11/17/2000	F
Chihuahua chub	Gila nigrescens	T	US/foreign	4/14/1986	F
Chucky madtom	Noturus crypticus	E	US	None	—
Clear Creek gambusia	Gambusia heterochir	E	US	1/14/1982	F
Clover Valley speckled dace	Rhinichthys osculus oligoporus	E	US	5/12/1998	F
Colorado pikeminnow (=squawfish)	Ptychocheilus lucius	E; EXPN	US	8/28/2002	RF(2)
Comanche Springs pupfish	Cyprinodon elegans	E	US	9/2/1981	F
Conasauga logperch	Percina jenkinsi	E	US	6/20/1986	F
Cui-ui	Chasmistes cujus	E	US	5/15/1992	RF(2)
Cumberland darter	Etheostoma susanae	E	US	None	—
Delta smelt	Hypomesus transpacificus	T	US	11/26/1996	F
Desert dace	Eremichthys acros	T	US	5/27/1997	F
Desert pupfish	Cyprinodon macularius	E	US/foreign	12/8/1993	F
Devils Hole pupfish	Cyprinodon diabolis	E	US	9/28/1990	F
Devils River minnow	Dionda diaboli	T	US/foreign	9/13/2005	F
Diamond darter	Crystallaria cincotta	E	US	None	—
Duskytail darter	Etheostoma percnurum	E; EXPN	US	3/30/1994	F
Etowah darter	Etheostoma etowahae	E	US	11/17/2000	F
Foskett speckled dace	Rhinichthys osculus ssp.	T	US	4/27/1998	F
Fountain darter	Etheostoma fonticola	E	US	2/14/1996	RF(1)
Gila chub	Gila intermedia	E	US/foreign	None	—
Gila topminnow (incl. Yaqui)	Poeciliopsis occidentalis	E	US	3/5/1999	RD(1)
Gila trout	Oncorhynchus gilae	T	US	9/10/2003	RF(3)
Goldline darter	Percina aurolineata	T	US	11/17/2000	F
Greenback cutthroat trout	Oncorhynchus clarki stomias	T	US	3/1/1998	RF(2)
Grotto Sculpin	Cottus sp.	E	US	None	—
Hiko White River springfish	Crenichthys baileyi grandis	E	US	5/26/1998	F
Humpback chub	Gila cypha	E	US	9/19/1990	RF(2)
Hutton tui chub	Gila bicolor ssp.	T	US	4/27/1998	F
Independence Valley speckled dace	Rhinichthys osculus lethoporus	E	US	5/12/1998	F
June sucker	Chasmistes liorus	E	US	6/25/1999	F
Kendall Warm Springs dace	Rhinichthys osculus thermalis	E	US	12/26/2012	RD(1)
Lahontan cutthroat trout	Oncorhynchus clarkii henshawi	T	US	1/30/1995	F
Laurel dace	Chrosomus saylori	E	US	None	—
Leon Springs pupfish	Cyprinodon bovinus	E	US	8/14/1985	F
Leopard darter	Percina pantherina	T	US	5/3/1993	RD(1)
Little Colorado spinedace	Lepidomeda vittata	T	US	1/9/1998	F
Little Kern golden trout	Oncorhynchus aguabonita whitei	T	US	None	—
Loach minnow	Tiaroga cobitis	E	US/foreign	9/30/1991	F
Lost River sucker	Deltistes luxatus	E	US	4/16/2013	RF(1)
Maryland darter	Etheostoma sellare	E	US	10/17/1985	RF(1)
Moapa dace	Moapa coriacea	E	US	5/16/1996	RF(1)
Modoc Sucker	Catostomus microps	E	US	None	—
Mohave tui chub	Gila bicolor ssp. mohavensis	E	US	9/12/1984	F
Neosho madtom	Noturus placidus	T	US	9/30/1991	F
Niangua darter	Etheostoma nianguae	T	US	7/17/1989	F
Okaloosa darter	Etheostoma okaloosae	T	US	10/26/1998	RF(1)
Oregon chub	Oregonichthys crameri	T	US	9/3/1998	F
Owens pupfish	Cyprinodon radiosus	E	US	9/30/1998	F
Owens tui chub	Gila bicolor ssp. snyderi	E	US	9/30/1998	F

TABLE 4.2

Endangered and threatened freshwater fish species, November 2013 [CONTINUED]

Common name	Scientific name	Listing status[a]	U.S. or U.S./foreign listed	Recovery plan date	Recovery plan stage[b]
Ozark cavefish	Amblyopsis rosae	T	US	11/14/1989	F
Pacific eulachon	Thaleichthys pacificus	T	US	None	—
Pahranagat roundtail chub	Gila robusta jordani	E	US	5/26/1998	F
Pahrump poolfish	Empetrichthys latos	E	US	3/17/1980	F
Paiute cutthroat trout	Oncorhynchus clarkii seleniris	T	US	9/10/2004	RF(1)
Palezone shiner	Notropis albizonatus	E	US	7/7/1997	F
Pallid sturgeon	Scaphirhynchus albus	E	US	3/15/2013	RD(1)
Pecos bluntnose shiner	Notropis simus pecosensis	T	US	9/30/1992	F
Pecos gambusia	Gambusia nobilis	E	US	5/9/1983	F
Pygmy madtom	Noturus stanauli	E; EXPN	US	9/27/1994	F
Pygmy sculpin	Cottus paulus (=pygmaeus)	T	US	8/6/1991	F
Railroad Valley springfish	Crenichthys nevadae	T	US	3/15/1997	F
Razorback sucker	Xyrauchen texanus	E	US/foreign	8/28/2002	RF(1)
Relict darter	Etheostoma chienense	E	US	7/31/1994	D
Rio Grande silvery minnow	Hybognathus amarus	E; EXPN	US/foreign	2/22/2010	RF(1)
Roanoke logperch	Percina rex	E	US	3/20/1992	F
Rush darter	Etheostoma phytophilum	E	US	None	—
San Marcos gambusia	Gambusia georgei	E	US	2/14/1996	RF(1)
Santa Ana sucker	Catostomus santaanae	T	US	3/30/2012	O
Scioto madtom	Noturus trautmani	E	US	None	—
Shortnose sucker	Chasmistes brevirostris	E	US	4/16/2013	RF(1)
Shovelnose sturgeon	Scaphirhynchus platorynchus	SAT	US	None	—
Slackwater darter	Etheostoma boschungi	T	US	3/8/1984	F
Slender chub	Erimystax cahni	T; EXPN	US	7/29/1983	F
Smoky madtom	Noturus baileyi	E; EXPN	US	8/9/1985	F
Snail darter	Percina tanasi	T	US	5/5/1983	F
Sonora chub	Gila ditaenia	T	US/foreign	9/30/1992	F
Spikedace	Meda fulgida	E	US/foreign	9/30/1991	F
Spotfin chub	Erimonax monachus	T; EXPN	US	11/21/1983	F
Spring pygmy sunfish	Elassoma alabamae	T	US	None	—
Tidewater goby	Eucyclogobius newberryi	E	US	12/7/2005	F
Topeka shiner	Notropis topeka (=tristis)	E	US	None	—
Unarmored threespine stickleback	Gasterosteus aculeatus williamsoni	E	US	12/26/1985	RF(1)
Vermilion darter	Etheostoma chermocki	E	US	8/6/2007	F
Virgin River chub	Gila seminuda (=robusta)	E	US	4/19/1995	RF(2)
Waccamaw silverside	Menidia extensa	T	US	8/11/1993	F
Warm Springs pupfish	Cyprinodon nevadensis pectoralis	E	US	9/28/1990	F
Warner sucker	Catostomus warnerensis	T	US	4/27/1998	F
Watercress darter	Etheostoma nuchale	E	US	3/29/1993	RF(2)
White River spinedace	Lepidomeda albivallis	E	US	3/28/1994	F
White River springfish	Crenichthys baileyi baileyi	E	US	5/26/1998	F
White sturgeon	Acipenser transmontanus	E	US/foreign	9/30/1999	F
Woundfin	Plagopterus argentissimus	E; EXPN	US	4/19/1995	RF(2)
Yaqui catfish	Ictalurus pricei	T	US/foreign	3/29/1995	F
Yaqui chub	Gila purpurea	E	US/foreign	3/29/1995	F
Yellowcheek darter	Etheostoma moorei	E	US	None	—
Yellowfin madtom	Noturus flavipinnis	T; EXPN	US	6/23/1983	F

[a]E = Endangered; T = Threatened; SAT = Threatened due to similarity of appearance; EXPN = Experimental population, non-essential.
[b]F = Final; D = Draft; RD = Draft revision; RF = Final revision; O = Other.

SOURCE: Adapted from "Generate Species List," in *Species Reports*, U.S. Department of the Interior, U.S. Fish and Wildlife Service, November 2013, http://ecos.fws.gov/tess_public/pub/adHocSpeciesForm.jsp (accessed November 7, 2013), and "Listed FWS/Joint FWS and NMFS Species and Populations with Recovery Plans (Sorted by Listed Entity)," in *Recovery Plans Search*, U.S. Department of the Interior, U.S. Fish and Wildlife Service, November 2013, http://ecos.fws.gov/tess_public/pub/speciesRecovery.jsp?sort=1 (accessed November 7, 2013)

sturgeon and the shovelnose sturgeon in the lower Mississippi River has produced a population of hybrid sturgeon that is thriving compared with their imperiled parents. In 2007 the USFWS completed a five-year review on the pallid sturgeon and decided to maintain its listing as endangered. The species was given a recovery priority number of 2c. The USFWS ranks recovery priority on a scale from 1 to 18, with lower numbers indicating higher priority. The "c" designation means the recovery of this species is in conflict with economic activities in its region.

The USFWS published a draft revised recovery plan in January 2013. In *Draft Revised Recovery Plan for the Pallid Sturgeon* (Scaphirhynchus albus) (http://www.fws.gov/mountain-prairie/species/fish/pallidsturgeon/DrafRevisedRecoveryPlanMarch2013.pdf), the agency summarizes the information collected about the pallid sturgeon and notes "since listing, the status of the species has improved and is currently stable." The USFWS has a short-term goal to downlist the pallid sturgeon from endangered to threatened. This status change will be initiated when "a self-sustaining genetically diverse

TABLE 4.3

Freshwater fish species with the highest expenditures under the Endangered Species Act, fiscal year 2012

Ranking	Species	Expenditure
1	Sturgeon, pallid (Scaphirhynchus albus)	$53,827,474
2	Trout, bull (Salvelinus confluentus)	$37,697,010
3	Smelt, delta (Hypomesus transpacificus)	$17,263,815
4	Sturgeon, white (Acipenser transmontanus)	$13,632,338
5	Sucker, razorback (Xyrauchen texanus)	$12,415,575
6	Minnow, Rio Grande silvery (Hybognathus amarus)	$9,588,454
7	Chub, humpback (Gila cypha)	$9,005,463
8	Chub, bonytail (Gila elegans)	$5,998,367
9	Pikeminnow (=squawfish), Colorado (Ptychocheilus lucius)	$5,674,113
10	Sucker, Santa Ana (Catostomus santaanae)	$5,412,525

SOURCE: Adapted from "Table 2. Species Ranked in Descending Order of Total FY2012 Reported Expenditures, Not Including Land Acquisition Costs," in *Federal and State Endangered and Threatened Species Expenditures: Fiscal Year 2012*, U.S. Department of the Interior, U.S. Fish and Wildlife Service, 2012, http://www.fws.gov/endangered/esa-library/pdf/2012.EXP.FINAL.pdf (accessed November 4, 2013)

FIGURE 4.3

Pallid sturgeon

SOURCE: Mark P. Dryer and Alan J. Sandvol, "Pallid Sturgeon (Scaphirhynchus albus)," in *Recovery Plan for the Pallid Sturgeon (Scaphirhynchus albus)*, U.S. Department of the Interior, U.S. Fish and Wildlife Service, 1993, http://ecos.fws.gov/docs/recovery_plans/1993/931107.pdf (accessed November 12, 2013)

FIGURE 4.4

Bull trout

SOURCE: "Bull Trout," in *Bull Trout: Salvelinus confluentus*, U.S. Department of the Interior, U.S. Fish and Wildlife Service, January 2003, http://digitalmedia.fws.gov/cdm/ref/collection/document/id/190 (accessed November 12, 2013)

population" of 5,000 adults is obtained and maintained for at least two generations (20 to 30 years) in each of the four designated management units. The USFWS estimates that full recovery of the species could be achieved by around 2047 at a cost of $250 million if all the recovery tasks are completed and the recovery criteria are met. The recovery tasks cover a wide variety of activities, including data collection, habitat restoration, and a propagation and stocking program (raising pallid sturgeon in a hatchery and releasing them into the wild).

Bull Trout

Bull trout are relatively large fish that live in streams, lakes, and rivers. They can weigh more than 20 pounds (9.1 kg); however, those that inhabit small streams seldom exceed 4 pounds (1.8 kg) in weight. Bull trout are members of the char subgroup of the salmon family (Salmonidae). (See Figure 4.4.) Their backs are dark in color (green to brown) with small light-colored spots (crimson to yellow), and their undersides are pale. The fish prefer cold and clean inland waters in the Northwest.

Historically, bull trout were found throughout much of the northwestern United States and as far north as Alaska. Large populations have disappeared from major rivers, leaving mostly isolated pockets of smaller-sized fish in headwater streams. A variety of factors have contributed to the decline of the bull trout. The species is extremely sensitive to changes in water temperature and purity. Its survival is threatened by water pollution, degraded habitat, and dams and other diversion structures. In addition, the introduction of brook trout, a nonnative game fish, has been devastating. The two species are able to mate, but produce mostly sterile offspring, which is a genetic dead end for the imperiled bull trout.

The legal history of the bull trout is extensive. In 1992 three environmental groups petitioned the USFWS to list the fish as an endangered species under the ESA. In 1993 the agency concluded that listing the species was warranted, but low in priority. This set off a long series of court battles that culminated in 1999, when all bull trout in the coterminous United States (the lower 48 states) were listed as threatened under the ESA. In 2001 the Alliance for the Wild Rockies and Friends of the Wild Swan (two of the original petitioners) filed a lawsuit against the USFWS for failing to designate critical habitat for the bull trout. The following year the agency published a draft recovery plan for the species. In 2005 the USFWS designated critical habitat for the bull trout, but that designation was challenged by the Alliance for the Wild Rockies and Friends of the Wild Swan. In 2011 the USFWS designated revised critical habitat, this time consisting of 19,729 miles (31,751 km) of stream/coastal shoreline and 488,252 acres (197,589 ha) of lakes and reservoirs in five states: Idaho, Montana, Nevada, Oregon, and Washington. In the critical habitat rule the USFWS stated its intention to revise the 2002 recovery plan for the bull trout to include six recovery units: coastal, Columbia headwaters, mid-Columbia, Saint Mary, Upper Snake, and Klamath. (See Figure 4.5.) As of

FIGURE 4.5

Proposed recovery units for bull trout

SOURCE: "Figure 1. Bull Trout Recovery Units," in "Endangered and Threatened Wildlife and Plants; Revised Designation of Critical Habitat for Bull Trout in the Coterminous United States," *Federal Register*, vol. 75, no. 200, October 18, 2010, http://www.fws.gov/pacific/bulltrout/pdf/BTCHFR101810.pdf (accessed November 12, 2013)

February 2014, the proposed revised recovery plan for the bull trout had not been issued.

In "Status Review of Bull Trout Completed" (April 29, 2008, http://www.fws.gov/mountain-prairie/pressrel/ 08-37.htm), the USFWS lists four requirements for the bull trout's continued survival: "cold water, clean streambed gravel, complex stream habitat features and connected habitats for migration across the landscape." Bull trout are increasingly imperiled by too-warm and sediment-laden water, degradation of habitat and migration corridors (e.g., by dams), and past introductions of nonnative competing species of trout. In March 2012 the USFWS (http://www.gpo.gov/fdsys/pkg/FR-2012-03-06 /pdf/2012-5335.pdf) announced initiation of a five-year status review for dozens of species, including the bull trout. As of February 2014, the review results had not been published.

RECOVERY PLANS FOR FRESHWATER FISH. As of November 2013, there were recovery plans for more than 100 populations of listed freshwater fish populations. (See Table 4.2.) Most of the plans were finalized. The USFWS provides details of the plans in "Listed FWS/ Joint FWS and NMFS Species and Populations with Recovery Plans" (February 2014, http://ecos.fws.gov/tess _public/TESSWebpageRecovery?sort=1).

IMPERILED MARINE AND ANADROMOUS FISH

As noted earlier, marine fish inhabit the salty waters of seas and oceans. In reality, some species of fish thrive in both fresh- and marine waters. For example, anadromous fish migrate between freshwater and the sea for mating purposes. As of November 2013, there were 16 marine and anadromous fish species listed under the ESA. (See Table 4.4.) They are under the jurisdiction of the National Marine Fisheries Service (NMFS). The bocaccio, canary rockfish, and yelloweye rockfish are true marine species. They inhabit the Puget Sound in Washington.

The Atlantic sturgeon, gulf sturgeon, largetooth and smalltooth sawfish, Pacific eulachon, and shortnose sturgeon prefer coastal marine and estuarine waters (areas where saltwater and freshwater meet). The green sturgeon is anadromous and inhabits Pacific coast waters. Five other imperiled anadromous species are found in the Pacific Northwest:

- Chinook salmon
- Chum salmon
- Coho salmon
- Sockeye salmon
- Steelhead

In addition, there is an endangered species of Atlantic salmon that migrates between the Gulf of Maine and Maine's rivers.

Table 4.5 shows that $621.5 million was spent on the 10 listed marine and anadromous fish species with the highest expenses during FY 2012. As noted in Table 2.13 in Chapter 2, six of the species were among the 20 overall species with the highest spending during FY 2012: steelhead, chinook salmon, coho salmon, sockeye salmon, chum salmon, and Atlantic salmon. The steelhead topped the spending list with expenditures of $263.1 million.

TABLE 4.4

Endangered and threatened marine and anadromous fish species, November 2013

Common name	Scientific name	Listing status[a]	DPS[b] or entire species	U.S. coastal region
Atlantic salmon	Salmo salar	E	1 DPS	Atlantic Northeast
Atlantic sturgeon	Acipenser oxyrinchus oxyrinchus	E; T	5 DPS	Atlantic
Bocaccio	Sebastes paucispinis	E	1 DPS	Pacific Northwest
Canary rockfish	Sebastes pinniger	T	1 DPS	Pacific Northwest
Chinook salmon	Oncorhynchus (=Salmo) tshawytscha	E; T	9 DPS	Pacific
Chum salmon	Oncorhynchus (=Salmo) keta	T	2 DPS	Pacific Northwest
Coho salmon	Oncorhynchus (=Salmo) kisutch	E; T	4 DPS	Pacific
Green sturgeon	Acipenser medirostris	T	1 DPS	Pacific
Gulf sturgeon	Acipenser oxyrinchus desotoi	T	Entire species	Gulf of Mexico
Largetooth sawfish	Pristis perotteti	E	Entire species	Gulf of Mexico
Pacific eulachon	(Thaleichthys pacificus)	T	1 DPS	Pacific Northwest
Shortnose sturgeon	Acipenser brevirostrum	E	Entire species	Atlantic
Smalltooth sawfish	Pristis pectinata	E	Entire species	Atlantic & Gulf of Mexico
Sockeye salmon	Oncorhynchus (=Salmo) nerka	E; T	2 DPS	Pacific Northwest
Steelhead	Oncorhynchus (=Salmo) mykiss	E; T	11 DPS	Pacific
Yelloweye rockfish	Sebastes ruberrimus	T	1 DPS	Pacific Northwest

[a]E = Endangered; T = Threatened.
[b]DPS = Distinct population segment.

SOURCE: Adapted from "Status of Fish Species," in *Marine and Anadromous Fish*, U.S. Department of Commerce, National Oceanic and Atmospheric Administration, National Marine Fisheries Service, October 31, 2013, http://www.nmfs.noaa.gov/pr/species/fish/ (accessed November 7, 2013)

TABLE 4.5

Marine and anadromous fish species with the highest expenditures under the Endangered Species Act, fiscal year 2012

Ranking	Species	Expenditure
1	Steelhead (Oncorhynchus (=Salmo) mykiss)	$263,138,542
2	Salmon, chinook (Oncorhynchus (=Salmo) tshawytscha)	$240,689,663
3	Salmon, coho (Oncorhynchus (=Salmo) kisutch)	$44,477,995
4	Salmon, sockeye (Oncorhynchus (=Salmo) nerka)	$29,816,576
5	Salmon, chum (Oncorhynchus (=Salmo) keta)	$20,920,045
6	Salmon, Atlantic (Salmo salar)	$10,913,156
7	Sturgeon, North American green (Acipenser medirostris)	$3,605,068
8	Sturgeon, Atlantic (Acipenser oxyrinchus oxyrinchus)	$3,222,504
9	Sturgeon, shortnose (Acipenser brevirostrum)	$2,707,104
10	Sturgeon, gulf (Acipenser oxyrinchus desotoi)	$2,030,869

SOURCE: Adapted from "Table 2. Species Ranked in Descending Order of Total FY2012 Reported Expenditures, Not Including Land Acquisition Costs," in *Federal and State Endangered and Threatened Species Expenditures: Fiscal Year 2012*, U.S. Department of the Interior, U.S. Fish and Wildlife Service, 2012, http://www.fws.gov/endangered/esa-library/pdf/2012.EXP.FINAL.pdf (accessed November 4, 2013)

Pacific Salmonids

Pacific salmonids are found in waters of the northwestern United States and belong to the genus *Oncorhynchus*. There are five species of Pacific salmon: chinook, chum, coho, pink, and sockeye. As of November 2013, all but the pink salmon were listed under the ESA as endangered or threatened. (See Table 4.4.) A detailed discussion about Pacific salmonids is provided by the USFWS in "Pacific Salmon (*Oncorhynchus spp.*)" (2014, http://www.fws.gov/species/species_accounts/bio_salm.html).

Chinook salmon are the largest of the Pacific salmonids, averaging about 24 pounds (11 kg) in adulthood. (See Figure 4.6.) They spend two to seven years in the ocean and travel up to 2,500 miles (4,000 km) from their home streams. Chum, coho, and sockeye salmon adults average approximately 10 to 12 pounds (4.5 to 5.4 kg).

PERILS OF MIGRATION. Pacific salmon pose unique protection challenges because they are anadromous. Throughout their lifetime they spend time in both freshwater and the ocean. (See Figure 4.7.) Salmon eggs (or roe) are laid in the bottom gravel of cold freshwater streams, where they incubate for five to 10 weeks. Each egg ranges in size from 0.3 to 0.5 of an inch (0.8 to 1.3 cm) in size, depending on the species. The eggs hatch to release baby fish (or alevin) that are called fry as they mature. Once a fry reaches about 3 inches (7.6 cm) in length, it is called a fingerling. This typically takes less than a year.

At some point during their first two years the young salmon (now called smolts) migrate downstream to the ocean, where they spend several months or years of their adulthood. When they reach sexual maturity, males and females journey back to the streams where they were born to mate and deposit eggs. This is called spawning. Pacific salmon make the round-trip only once. They

FIGURE 4.6

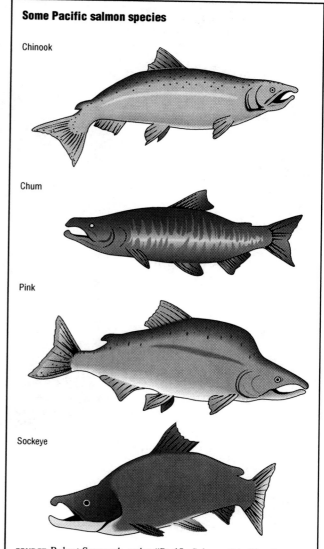

Some Pacific salmon species

Chinook

Chum

Pink

Sockeye

SOURCE: Robert Savannah, artist, "Pacific Salmons," in *Line Art (Drawings)*, U.S. Department of the Interior, U.S. Fish and Wildlife Service, undated, http://www.fws.gov/pictures/lineart/bobsavannah/pacificsalmons.html (accessed November 12, 2013)

expend all their energy swimming back upstream and die soon after the eggs are laid and fertilized. Their upstream habitats can be hundreds and even thousands of miles away from their ocean habitats. It is a long and dangerous journey both ways.

Predator fish and birds eat salmon fry, fingerlings, and smolts as they make their way to the ocean. Bears, birds, marine mammals, and humans prey on the adult fish as they migrate upstream. Waterfalls, rapids, dams, and other water diversions pose tremendous obstacles to Pacific salmon as they try to travel across long distances.

PROTECTED SALMON STOCKS. Salmon heading to the same general location travel upstream in groups called stocks (or runs). Stocks migrate at different times of the

FIGURE 4.7

Life cycle of Pacific salmon

SOURCE: "Salmon Lifecycle," in *Handouts*, U.S. Department of Commerce, National Oceanic and Atmospheric Administration, National Marine Fisheries Service, Northwest Fisheries Science Center, undated, http://www.nwfsc.noaa.gov/education/documents/salmon%20life%20cycle%20handout.pdf (accessed November 12, 2013)

year, depending on geographical and genetic factors. Endangered and threatened salmon are often identified by their water of origin (e.g., Snake River) and, in most cases, by their upstream migration season (e.g., spring). In 1990 the winter-run stock of chinook salmon from the Sacramento River was designated as threatened under the ESA, the first Pacific salmon to be listed. It was reclassified as endangered four years later. During the 1990s and the first decade of the 21st century the NMFS identified dozens of evolutionarily significant units (ESUs) of Pacific salmonids. As described in Chapter 2, the NMFS uses the term *ESU* to refer to a distinct stock of Pacific salmon.

According to the USFWS (http://ecos.fws.gov/species Profile/profile/speciesProfile.action?spcode=E06D), as of February 2014, nine chinook populations were listed under the ESA:

- Sacramento River winter-run ESU
- Upper Columbia River spring-run ESU
- California coastal ESU
- Snake River fall-run ESU
- Upper Willamette River ESU
- Puget Sound ESU
- Lower Columbia River ESU
- Central Valley spring-run ESU
- Snake River spring/summer-run ESU

The Sacramento River winter-run ESU and the upper Columbia River spring-run ESU were listed as endangered, while the remaining populations were listed as threatened.

The agency (February 24, 2014, http://ecos.fws.gov/ speciesProfile/profile/speciesProfile.action?spcode=E08A) also listed four coho salmon populations:

- Central California coast ESU
- Oregon coast ESU

- Lower Columbia River ESU
- Southern Oregon–Northern California coast ESU

Only the central California coast ESU was listed as endangered; the other three coho salmon ESUs were listed as threatened.

In addition, the USFWS (February 24, 2014, http://ecos.fws.gov/speciesProfile/profile/speciesProfile.action?spcode=E09Q) listed two chum salmon populations, the Columbia River and the Hood Canal summer-run, as threatened. Lastly, the agency (February 24, 2014, http://ecos.fws.gov/speciesProfile/profile/speciesProfile.action?spcode=E06Y) listed two sockeye salmon populations, the Snake River and the Ozette Lake, as endangered and threatened, respectively.

The protected stock descriptions for Pacific salmonids are complicated; some listings cover only "naturally spawned" fish while others include hatchery fish. Salmon raised in hatcheries that use specific government-approved genetic methods are covered under the ESA similarly to the wild populations. However, many other hatcheries propagate and release salmon species throughout the Pacific Northwest. According to the Washington Department of Fish and Wildlife (WDFW), in "Hatcheries: Salmon Recovery Relies on Support for Mass-Marking" (2014, http://wdfw.wa.gov/hatcheries/mass_marking.html), the vast majority of hatchery-grown salmon are marked so they can be distinguished from wild populations. A small knob called the adipose fin that protrudes from a salmon's back near the tail is removed before the fish are released from the hatcheries.

The mass-marking program, as it is called, was begun during the 1990s and is largely credited with allowing salmon fishing (a major commercial and recreational activity in the Pacific Northwest) to continue. The WDFW explains that "prior to mass-marking, restrictions imposed by new ESA listings threatened to close—or greatly curtail—historic salmon fisheries throughout the region. In addition to the recreational and cultural values involved, the potential loss of fishing opportunities presented a severe economic threat to fishing families and entire communities, especially in rural areas of the Northwest." Rather than closing all fishing along a particular waterway during a salmon run, fisheries managers can impose rules that allow anglers to keep only marked (hatchery-raised) salmon. Wild (unmarked) salmon must be returned to the water.

DECLINING POPULATIONS. Daniel L. Bottom et al. estimate in *Salmon at River's End: The Role of the Estuary in the Decline and Recovery of Columbia River Salmon* (August 2005, http://www.nwfsc.noaa.gov/assets/25/6294_09302005_153156_SARETM68Final.pdf) that between 11 million and 16 million salmon per year migrated upstream in waters of the northwestern United States before the arrival of European settlers. Extensive fishing and canning operations quickly decimated the salmon population. As early as 1893 federal officials warned that the future of salmon fisheries had a "disastrous outlook." During the 1890s hatcheries began operating and stocking rivers and streams with farm-raised salmon. Throughout the next century salmon populations were further stressed as natural river flows were dramatically altered with dams, navigational structures, and irrigation systems. By 2013 dozens of salmon hatcheries and hundreds of dams had been constructed in the Columbia River basin of the Pacific Northwest.

THREATS TO SURVIVAL. Biologists blame four main threats for the imperiled state of Pacific salmonids:

- Habitat degradation—channelization, dredging, water withdrawals for irrigation, wetland losses, and diking have changed river, stream, and estuary environments.
- Harvesting levels—overfishing for more than a century decimated salmon populations.
- Hatcheries—biologists fear that hatchery releases overburden estuaries with too many competing fish at the same time.
- Hydropower—impassable dams have rendered some historical habitats unreachable by salmon. Most modern dams have fish ladders. However, all dams affect water temperature, flow, and quality.

Besides these threats, scientists believe climate change and the presence of nonnative aquatic species have depleted salmon populations.

SEA LION PREDATION. In recent years wildlife officials have grown increasingly concerned about predation on imperiled Pacific salmon by sea lions in the lower Columbia River. The problem is particularly severe on the downstream side of the Bonneville Dam. The dam spans the lower Columbia River between Oregon and Washington and is located approximately 145 miles (233 km) upstream of the river's mouth at the Pacific Ocean. In "Columbia River Sea Lion Management" (2014, http://wdfw.wa.gov/conservation/sealions/questions.html), the WDFW notes that sea lions have consumed thousands of fish, some of which are listed under the ESA. The fish congregate below the dam during their migration upstream; the dam is equipped with fish ladders that provide the fish passage to upstream habitat. Each spring since 2002 trained observers at the dam have counted the numbers of sea lions preying on the fish and the number of fish eaten by the sea lions. The predators include California sea lions and Steller sea lions. The California sea lion is a thriving species that is not listed under the ESA, but is protected under the Marine Mammal Protection Act. The Steller sea lion (the eastern population) was a threatened species under the ESA, but was delisted in 2013 because of recovery.

According to the WDFW, hazing (the use of boats, underwater firecrackers, and rubber buckshot) is regularly conducted in an attempt to scare the sea lions away, but it only temporarily interrupts the feeding. In 2008 Idaho, Oregon, and Washington first received permission from the NMFS to remove or kill identifiable California sea lions that habitually prey on salmon at the dam. (The Steller sea lions have not been targeted because of their ESA status and because the WDFW indicates their primary prey at the dam is white sturgeon, which is not listed under the ESA.) The kill decision was challenged in court by the Humane Society of the United States (HSUS), which argued that the California sea lions were being used as scapegoats by authorities who do not want to reduce fishing limits. A long legal battle ensued; however, state authorities have repeatedly received approval from the NMFS to remove and kill the California sea lions. In "Judge Dismisses Humane Society Lawsuit That Opposed Killing Sea Lions at Bonneville Dam" (OregonLive.com, February 15, 2013), Scott Learn reports that in March 2012 the NMFS reauthorized the program through 2016 allowing the states to kill up to 92 of the animals during 2013. A subsequent lawsuit filed by the HSUS was dismissed by a judge.

In *2013 Adult Returns and 2014 Expectations: Columbia River, Preliminary Draft—December 12, 2013* (December 12, 2013, http://www.dfw.state.or.us/fish/OCRP/CRM/returns_and_expectations/docs/13_returns_14_expect.pdf), the WDFW indicates that 2013 was a good year for anadromous fish in the Columbia River. Counts of adults swimming upstream to spawn were higher than had been predicted for most species and runs. This was particularly true for Chinook salmon during the fall 2013 run (August to December 2013). According to Allen Thomas, in "'Incredible' Fall Chinook Run Forecast for Columbia" (Columbian.com, February 20, 2014) more than 1.2 million fall-run chinook salmon were counted at the Bonneville Dam, setting a new record. An even higher count was expected for the fall 2014 run. It was not clear if these high numbers would impact official efforts at the dam to reduce sea lion predation on imperiled Pacific salmon.

THE KLAMATH RIVER BASIN CONTROVERSY. The Klamath River originates in southern Oregon and flows southwest for more than 200 miles (320 km) across the southern part of Oregon and the northern part of California. (See Figure 4.8.) According to the NMFS, in *Klamath River Basin: 2009 Report to Congress* (June 30, 2009, http://www.nmfs.noaa.gov/pr/pdfs/klamath2009.pdf), the basin covers over 10 million acres (4 million ha) and was once the third-largest producer of salmon on the West Coast. Over the past 100 years the salmon populations have been reduced to a fraction of what they once were. Demand for water in the basin has grown dramatically and has sparked bitter battles among fishing, agricultural,

timber, mining, and environmental interests. These battles are complicated by the many stakeholders involved. The NMFS notes that approximately 6 million acres (2.4 million ha) in the basin are public lands. These include national wildlife refuges, national forests, national parks and monuments, and wild and scenic river designations—all managed by a variety of federal agencies and programs. In addition, approximately 96,000 acres (39,000 ha) are trust lands of six Native American tribes. The remaining 4 million acres (1.6 million ha) are in private hands. The basin is home to several anadromous species including stocks of chinook and coho salmon and steelhead. As mentioned earlier, the Southern Oregon–Northern California coast stock of coho salmon is listed as threatened under the ESA.

Since the 1990s federal, tribal, state, and local authorities and other stakeholders have been trying to craft a plan acceptable to all parties for managing water supplies and fisheries in the basin. Freshwater resource management in the West is largely handled by the Bureau of Reclamation (BOR) under the U.S. Department of the Interior (DOI). Until 2001 the BOR managed to balance competing water demands from users in the basin and maintain river and stream flows for fish. In 2001 the region was struck by a drought, and the BOR allowed large water diversions for irrigation purposes. The following year tens of thousands of dead salmon were found in the basin, apparently the victims of low water flow. The BOR responded with drastic water cuts to farmers. This led to a full-fledged water war among Native American tribes, commercial fishing interests, conservation groups, farmers, and local water districts. Ever since, BOR-developed operating plans for water flows in the Klamath River basin have been continually challenged in court.

In 2008 dozens of stakeholders (federal, state, and local government agencies; irrigation districts; property owners; Native American tribes; and private conservation organizations) crafted the Klamath Basin Restoration Agreement (KBRA; http://www.edsheets.com/Klamath docs.html). The KBRA seeks to restore thriving fish populations in the river and satisfy local needs for irrigation water and power generation.

Meanwhile, a separate legal battle raged over efforts by PacifiCorp, an Oregon-based utility company, to renew a federal license for four dams it owns on the Klamath River. According to the NMFS, the license expired in 2006, but PacifiCorp can continue to operate the dams under the terms and conditions of its old license until it obtains a new license. One of the dams is called Iron Gate, and it blocks upstream fish passage to the northern reaches of the basin. The old license did not require the company to provide fish ladders. However, the Federal Energy Regulatory Commission, which

FIGURE 4.8

Klamath River basin

SOURCE: "Figure ES-1. The Klamath Basin," in *Klamath Facilities Removal Public Draft Environmental Impact Statement/Environmental Impact Report*, U.S. Department of the Interior and California Department of Fish and Game, September 2011, http://klamathrestoration.gov/sites/klamathrestoration.gov/files/KlamathFacilitiesRemoval_EISEIR_09222011.pdf (accessed November 12, 2013)

oversees power companies, has included fish passage requirements as a condition of relicensing the dam. The NMFS notes that the fish passages could open up more than 350 miles (560 km) of historical habitat for salmon and other migrating fish species. In 2009 PacifiCorp reached an agreement—the Klamath Hydroelectric Settlement Agreement (KHSA)—with multiple stakeholders to remove the dams.

Implementation of the KBRA and the KHSA is the responsibility of the Klamath Basin Coordinating Council

(KBCC). In *Third Annual Report: Implementing the Klamath Basin Settlement Agreements* (October 2013, http://www.edsheets.com/Klamath/KBCC%20Third%20Annual%20Report%202013.pdf), the KBCC discusses the status of the agreements as of 2013. The organization notes that some implementation programs have been implemented, whereas others are on hold because of legislative and funding problems. In regards to the dam removal project, the KBCC indicates that federal agencies were still investigating the scientific and economic feasibility of the removal.

Steelhead

Steelhead are members of the *Oncorhynchus* genus and have the scientific name *Oncorhynchus mykiss*. (See Figure 4.9.) Freshwater steelhead are called rainbow trout. Anadromous steelhead are also trout, but they are associated with salmon because of similarities in habitat and behavior. Steelhead are found in the Pacific Northwest and are anadromous like salmon but have two major differences: steelhead migrate individually, rather than in groups, and can spawn many times, not just once.

According to the USFWS (http://ecos.fws.gov/spe ciesProfile/profile/speciesProfile.action?spcode=E08D), as of February 2014, 10 steelhead populations were listed under the ESA:

- Southern California coast
- Upper Willamette River
- Central Valley California
- Central California coast
- South central California coast
- Snake River Basin
- Middle Columbia River
- Upper Columbia River Basin
- Northern California
- Lower Columbia River

Only the Southern California coast population was listed as endangered; the other nine populations were listed as threatened. Steelhead face the same threats as Pacific salmon: habitat loss and alteration, overharvest-

FIGURE 4.9

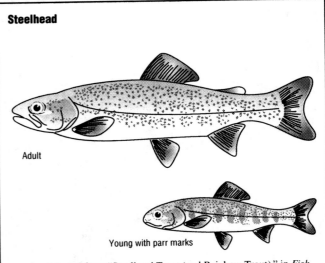

Steelhead

Adult

Young with parr marks

SOURCE: Adapted from "Steelhead Trout (and Rainbow Trout)," in *Fish of the Columbia River*, U.S. Department of Energy, Pacific Northwest National Laboratory, undated, http://ecology.pnnl.gov/rivers/colrvrfish/sh.htm (accessed November 7, 2013)

ing, dams and other water obstacles, and competition with hatchery fish.

The USFWS indicates that $263.1 million was spent on steelhead under the ESA during FY 2012. (See Table 4.5.)

Figure 4.10 shows the general locations of the ESA-listed salmon and steelhead populations as of October 2012. In addition, information is included on critical habitat designations and applicable rules.

Imperiled Fish around the World

The International Union for Conservation of Nature (IUCN) indicates in *Red List of Threatened Species Version 2013.2* (http://www.iucnredlist.org/about/summary-statistics) that 2,110 out of 11,172 species of evaluated fish were threatened in November 2013. The IUCN notes that there are 32,700 known fish species, so it is expected that many more fish species will be listed in the future as more evaluations are completed.

As of November 2013, the USFWS listed 12 foreign species of fish as endangered or threatened. (See Table 4.6.) All but one of the species were endangered. Most of the species are found in Asia.

FIGURE 4.10

Listing status and critical habitat designations for West Coast salmon and steelhead

(E) = Endangered   (T) = Threatened   (FCH) = Final critical habitat designated   ▨ Domain overlap

Puget Sound domain
- Puget Sound Chinook (T) [FCH 9/2/05]
- Hood Canal Summer Chum (T) [FCH 9/2/05]
- Ozette Lake Sockeye (T) [FCH 9/2/05]
- Puget Sound Steelhead (T) [CH under dev.; ANPR 1/10/11]

Interior Columbia domain
- Snake River Sockeye (E) [FCH 12/28/93]
- Snake River Fall Chinook (T) [FCH 12/28/93]
- Snake River Spring/Summer Chinook (T) [FCH 12/28/93; 10/25/99]
- Snake River Steelhead (T) [FCH 9/2/05]
- Upper Columbia River Spring Chinook (E) [FCH 9/2/05]
- Upper Columbia River Steelhead (T) [FCH 9/2/05]
- Middle Columbia River Steelhead (T) [FCH 9/2/05]

Oregon Coast domain
- Oregon Coast Coho (T) [FCH 2/11/08]

Southern Oregon/ Northern California Coast domain
- Southern Oregon/Northern California Coast Coho (T) [FCH 5/5/99]

Central Valley domain
- Sacramento River Winter Chinook (E) [FCH 6/16/93]
- Central Valley Spring Chinook (T) [FCH 9/2/05]
- Central Valley Steelhead (T) [FCH 9/2/05]

Willamette/Lower Columbia domain
- Columbia River Chum (T) [FCH 9/2/05]
- Lower Columbia River Coho (T) [CH Under dev.; ANPR 1/10/11]
- Lower Columbia River Chinook (T) [FCH 9/2/05]
- Lower Columbia River Steelhead (T) [FCH 9/2/05]
- Upper Willamette River Chinook (T) [FCH 9/2/05]
- Upper Willamette River Steelhead (T) [FCH 9/2/05]

North-Central California Coast domain
- Central California Coast Coho (E) [FCH 5/5/99]
- California Coastal Chinook (T) [FCH 9/2/05]
- Northern California Steelhead (T) [FCH 9/2/05]
- Central California Coast Steelhead (T) [FCH 9/2/05]

South-Central/Southern California Coast domain
- South-Central California Coast Steelhead (T) [FCH 9/2/05]
- Southern California Coast Steelhead (E) [FCH 9/2/05]

Critical habitat rules cites
- 6/16/93 (58 FR 33212) Final CHD for Sacramento River Winter-run Chinook
- 12/28/93 (58 FR 68543) Final CHD for Snake River Chinook and Sockeye
- 5/5/99 (64 FR 24049) Final CHD for Central CA Coast and SONCC Coho
- 10/25/99 (64FR57399) Revised CHD for Snake River Spring/Summer Chinook
- 9/2/05 (70 FR 52630) Final CHD for 12 ESUs of Salmon and Steelhead
- 2/11/08 (73 FR 7816) Final CHD for Oregon Coast Coho
- 1/10/11 (76 FR 1392) Advance Notice of Proposed Rulemaking; CHDs for Lower Columbia Coho and Puget Sound Steelhead

0   100   200 Miles

Note: ANPR = Advance Notice of Proposed Rulemaking. FCH = Final Critical Habitat. FR = Federal Register. T = Threatened. E = Endangered. ESU = Evolutionarily Significant Unit.

SOURCE: "Status of ESA Listings & Critical Habitat Designations for West Coast Salmon & Steelhead," in *West Coast Salmon & Steelhead Listings*, U.S. Department of Commerce, National Oceanic and Atmospheric Administration, National Marine Fisheries Service, October 31, 2012, http://www .westcoast.fisheries.noaa.gov/publications/protected_species/salmon_steelhead/status_of_esa_salmon_listings_and_ch_designations_map.pdf (accessed November 7, 2013)

TABLE 4.6

Foreign endangered and threatened fish species, November 2013

Common name	Scientific name	Listing status*	Historic range
Ala balik (trout)	Salmo platycephalus	E	Turkey
Asian bonytongue	Scleropages formosus	E	Thailand, Indonesia, Malaysia
Ayumodoki (loach)	Hymenophysa curta	E	Japan
Beluga sturgeon	Huso huso	T	Black Sea, Caspian Sea, Adriatic Sea and Sea of Azov.
Catfish	Pangasius sanitwongsei	E	Thailand
Cicek (minnow)	Acanthorutilus handlirschi	E	Turkey
Ikan temoleh (minnow)	Probarbus jullieni	E	Thailand, Cambodia, Vietnam, Malaysia, Laos
Mexican blindcat (catfish)	Prietella phreatophila	E	Mexico
Miyako tango (=Toyko bitterling)	Tanakia tanago	E	Japan
Nekogigi (catfish)	Coreobagrus ichikawai	E	Japan
Thailand giant catfish	Pangasianodon gigas	E	Thailand
Totoaba (seatrout or weakfish)	Cynoscion macdonaldi	E	Mexico (Gulf of California)

*E = Endangered; T = Threatened.

SOURCE: Adapted from "Generate Species List," in *Species Reports*, U.S. Department of the Interior, U.S. Fish and Wildlife Service, November 2013, http://ecos.fws.gov/tess_public/pub/adHocSpeciesForm.jsp (accessed November 8, 2013)

CHAPTER 5
CLAMS, SNAILS, CRUSTACEANS, AND CORALS

CLAMS, SNAILS, AND CRUSTACEANS

Clams, snails, and crustaceans are small aquatic creatures. They are invertebrates, meaning they lack an internal skeleton made of bone or cartilage. Clams and snails are in the phylum Mollusca. Mollusks have soft bodies that are usually enclosed in a thin hard shell made of calcium. The U.S. Fish and Wildlife Service (USFWS) uses the generic term *clam* to refer to clams and mussels, but there are physical and reproductive differences between the two creatures. In general, mussels are larger than clams and have an oblong lopsided shell, as opposed to the round symmetrical shell of the clam.

Crustaceans are a large class of creatures with a hard exoskeleton (external skeleton), appendages, and antennae. This class includes lobsters, shrimps, and crabs. Corals are marine creatures of the phylum Cnidaria, along with jellyfish and anemones.

As of November 2013, there were 160 U.S. and foreign species of clams (including mussels), snails, crustaceans, and corals listed under the Endangered Species Act (ESA) as endangered or threatened. (See Table 1.2 in Chapter 1.) As shown in Table 2.11 in Chapter 2, one species—Sampson's pearlymussel (1984)—has been delisted because of extinction. The mussel once inhabited southeastern rivers and was likely decimated decades ago by dam building and other habitat disturbances. In 2013 the USFWS delisted because of recovery the Magazine Mountain shagreen (a snail found in the Ozark Mountains in Arkansas). It was the first invertebrate to achieve that distinction under the ESA. According to the USFWS (http://www.gpo.gov/fdsys/pkg/FR-2013-05-15/html/2013-11541.htm), the snail was originally listed, in part, because of potential threats from planned military and state uses of Magazine Mountain. The U.S. Army (2013, http://www.asaie.army.mil/Public/ESOH/REEO/Central/docs/Central_Review_June_2013.pdf) notes that it abandoned its plans to use the area after the snail was

listed under the ESA in 1989. Other potential threats were minimized to protect the species and help realize its recovery.

Table 5.1 shows the 10 clam, snail, crustacean, and coral species with the highest expenditures under the ESA during fiscal year (FY) 2012. Just over $10.4 million was spent on activities to conserve these 10 species.

CLAMS AND MUSSELS

There were 88 U.S. species of clams and mussels listed under the ESA as of November 2013. (See Table 5.2.) Most had an endangered listing, and nearly all had recovery plans in place. The vast majority of imperiled clams and mussels in the United States are freshwater species that inhabit inland rivers, primarily in the Southeast. Conservation efforts for freshwater mussels include the captive breeding and reintroduction of some species, as well as measures to restore damaged habitats.

Mussels are bivalved (two-shelled) creatures encased in hard hinged shells made of calcium. The freshwater species can grow to be up to 6 inches (15.2 centimeters [cm]) in length. The United States, with nearly 300 species, has the greatest diversity of freshwater mussels in the world. According to the U.S. Geological Survey (USGS) in "Conservation of Southeastern Mussels" (December 14, 2012, http://fl.biology.usgs.gov/Southeastern_Aquatic_Fauna/Freshwater_Mussels/freshwater_mussels.html), approximately 90% of these creatures live in southeastern states. Most of them are found burrowed into the sand and gravel beds of rivers and streams making up the Mississippi River system. Mussels have a footlike appendage that acts like an anchor to hold them in place. They can use this appendage to move themselves slowly over small distances. Mussels tend to congregate in large groups called colonies.

TABLE 5.1

Clam, snail, crustacean, and coral species with the highest expenditures under the Endangered Species Act, fiscal year 2012

Ranking	Species	Group	Expenditure
1	Fairy shrimp, vernal pool (Branchinecta lynchi)	Crustacean	$2,190,217
2	Coral, elkhorn (Acropora palmata)	Coral	$1,173,382
3	Coral, staghorn (Acropora cervicornis)	Coral	$1,013,144
4	Abalone, white (Haliotis sorenseni)	Snail	$1,004,328
5	Snails, Oahu tree (Achatinella spp.)	Snail	$977,451
6	Abalone, black (Haliotis cracherodii)	Snail	$963,645
7	Tadpole shrimp, vernal pool (Lepidurus packardi)	Crustacean	$826,052
8	Higgins eye (pearlymussel) (Lampsilis higginsii)	Clam	$810,227
9	Fatmucket, Arkansas (Lampsilis powellii)	Clam	$791,720
10	Mucket, pink (pearlymussel) (Lampsilis abrupta)	Clam	$686,548

SOURCE: Adapted from "Table 2. Species Ranked in Descending Order of Total FY2012 Reported Expenditures, Not Including Land Acquisition Costs," in *Federal and State Endangered and Threatened Species Expenditures: Fiscal Year 2012*, U.S. Department of the Interior, U.S. Fish and Wildlife Service, 2012, http://www.fws.gov/endangered/esa-library/pdf/2012.EXP.FINAL.pdf (accessed November 4, 2013)

Mussels are filter-feeders. They have a siphoning system that sucks in food and oxygen from the water. Their gills can filter impurities out of the water. Thus, mussels are tiny natural water purifiers. They are also an indicator species in that their level of health and well-being is highly indicative of the overall condition of the freshwater systems in which they live.

Most mussel species have a unique way of spreading their offspring. A female mussel can produce several thousand eggs in a year. After the eggs are fertilized, they develop into larvae and are released. The larvae latch onto the fins or gills of passing fish and stay there until they have grown into baby clams. At that point they turn loose of the fish and drop to the river bottom. The larvae are called glochidia. It is believed that glochidia are harmless to the fish on which they hitchhike. This parasitic relationship allows mussels to spread and distribute beyond their usual range.

Mussel Declines

The decline of freshwater mussels began during the 1800s. Many of the creatures have an interior shell surface with a pearl-like sheen. These pearlymussels were in great demand as a source of buttons for clothing until the invention of plastic. Collectors also killed many mussels by prying them open looking for pearls. Until the 1990s mussel shells were ground up and used in the oyster pearl industry. Another cause for decline has been habitat disturbance, especially water pollution and the modification of aquatic habitats by dams. In addition, erosion due to strip mining and agriculture causes siltation that can actually bury and suffocate mussels. The invasive zebra mussel and quagga mussel have also harmed native freshwater mussel species, such as the Higgins eye pearlymussel, by competing with them for food and other resources.

Higgins Eye Pearlymussel

As shown in Table 5.1, more than $800,000 was spent under the ESA during FY 2012 on the Higgins eye pearlymussel. This freshwater species is native to the United States and is found in the waters of Illinois, Iowa, Minnesota, Missouri, Nebraska, and Wisconsin. According to the USFWS in "Higgins Eye Pearlymussel *Lampsilis higginsii*" (August 2012, http://www.fws.gov/midwest/endangered/clams/higginseye/higgins_fs.html), "Higgins eye are prey for wildlife like muskrats, otters, and raccoons; they filter water, which improves water quality; and mussel beds create microhabitats on river bottoms that provide food and cover for other aquatic life." The species was named after its discoverer, Frank Higgins, who found some of the mussels in the Mississippi River near Muscatine, Iowa, during the mid-1800s. Over the next few decades Muscatine developed a thriving pearl-button industry that lasted into the 1940s. Higgins eye was also harvested for the commercial pearl industry.

In 1976 the Higgins eye pearlymussel was listed as an endangered species under the ESA. More than a century of scavenging by humans had severely depleted the species. Dams, navigational structures, and water quality problems in the upper Mississippi River system were contributing factors to its decline. In 1983 the USFWS published its first recovery plan for the Higgins eye. The plan identified areas that were deemed essential habitat for the species and called for limits on construction and harvesting in those areas.

In May 2004 the USFWS published *Higgins Eye Pearlymussel (*Lampsilis higginsii*) Recovery Plan: First Revision* (http://ecos.fws.gov/docs/recovery_plans/2004/040714.pdf). The plan examines more recent threats to the pearlymussel's survival, primarily the pervasive spread of zebra mussels, an invasive species. It acknowledges that there is no feasible way to eliminate zebra mussels to the extent needed to benefit the Higgins eye. Instead, the plan focuses on developing methods to prevent new zebra mussel infestations and working to lessen the impacts of already infested populations.

TABLE 5.2

Endangered and threatened clam and mussel species, November 2013

Common name	Scientific name	Listing status[a]	U.S. or U.S./foreign listed	Recovery plan date	Recovery plan stage[b]
Alabama (=inflated) heelsplitter	Potamilus inflatus	T	US	4/13/1993	F
Alabama lampmussel	Lampsilis virescens	E; EXPN	US	7/2/1985	F
Alabama moccasinshell	Medionidus acutissimus	T	US	11/17/2000	F
Alabama pearlshell	Margaritifera marrianae	E	US	None	—
Altamaha Spinymussel	Elliptio spinosa	E	US	None	—
Appalachian elktoe	Alasmidonta raveneliana	E	US	8/26/1996	F
Appalachian monkeyface (pearlymussel)	Quadrula sparsa	E; EXPN	US	7/9/1984	F
Arkansas fatmucket	Lampsilis powellii	T	US	2/10/1992	F
Birdwing pearlymussel	Lemiox rimosus	E; EXPN	US	7/9/1984	F
Black clubshell	Pleurobema curtum	E	US	11/14/1989	F
Carolina heelsplitter	Lasmigona decorata	E	US	1/17/1997	F
Chipola slabshell	Elliptio chipolaensis	T	US	9/19/2003	F
Choctaw bean	Villosa choctawensis	E	US	None	—
Clubshell	Pleurobema clava	E; EXPN	US	9/21/1994	F
Coosa moccasinshell	Medionidus parvulus	E	US	11/17/2000	F
Cracking pearlymussel	Hemistena lata	E; EXPN	US	7/11/1991	F
Cumberland bean (pearlymussel)	Villosa trabalis	E; EXPN	US	8/22/1984	F
Cumberland elktoe	Alasmidonta atropurpurea	E	US	5/24/2004	F
Cumberlandian combshell	Epioblasma brevidens	E; EXPN	US	5/24/2004	F
Cumberland monkeyface (pearlymussel)	Quadrula intermedia	E; EXPN	US	7/9/1984	F
Cumberland pigtoe	Pleurobema gibberum	E	US	8/13/1992	F
Curtis pearlymussel	Epioblasma florentina curtisii	E	US	2/4/1986	F
Dark pigtoe	Pleurobema furvum	E	US	11/17/2000	F
Dromedary pearlymussel	Dromus dromas	E; EXPN	US	7/9/1984	F
Dwarf wedgemussel	Alasmidonta heterodon	E	US/foreign	2/8/1993	F
Fanshell	Cyprogenia stegaria	E; EXPN	US	7/9/1991	F
Fat pocketbook	Potamilus capax	E	US	11/14/1989	F
Fat three-ridge (mussel)	Amblema neislerii	E	US	9/19/2003	F
Finelined pocketbook	Lampsilis altilis	T	US	11/17/2000	F
Finerayed pigtoe	Fusconaia cuneolus	E; EXPN	US	9/19/1984	F
Flat pigtoe	Pleurobema marshalli	E	US	11/14/1989	F
Fluted kidneyshell	Ptychobranchus subtentum	E	US	None	—
Fuzzy pigtoe	Pleurobema strodeanum	T	US	None	—
Georgia pigtoe	Pleurobema hanleyianum	E	US	7/8/2013	D
Green blossom (pearlymussel)	Epioblasma torulosa gubernaculum	E	US	7/9/1984	F
Gulf moccasinshell	Medionidus penicillatus	E	US	9/19/2003	F
Heavy pigtoe	Pleurobema taitianum	E	US	11/14/1989	F
Higgins eye (pearlymussel)	Lampsilis higginsii	E	US	7/14/2004	RF(1)
James spinymussel	Pleurobema collina	E	US	9/24/1990	F
Littlewing pearlymussel	Pegias fabula	E	US	9/22/1989	F
Louisiana pearlshell	Margaritifera hembeli	T	US	12/3/1990	F
Narrow pigtoe	Fusconaia escambia	T	US	None	—
Neosho mucket	Lampsilis rafinesqueana	E	US	None	—
Northern riffleshell	Epioblasma torulosa rangiana	E	US	9/21/1994	F
Ochlockonee moccasinshell	Medionidus simpsonianus	E	US	9/19/2003	F
Orangefoot pimpleback (pearlymussel)	Plethobasus cooperianus	E; EXPN	US	9/30/1984	F
Orangenacre mucket	Lampsilis perovalis	T	US	11/17/2000	F
Ouachita rock pocketbook	Arkansia wheeleri	E	US	6/2/2004	F
Oval pigtoe	Pleurobema pyriforme	E	US	9/19/2003	F
Ovate clubshell	Pleurobema perovatum	E	US	11/17/2000	F
Oyster mussel	Epioblasma capsaeformis	E; EXPN	US	5/24/2004	F
Pale lilliput (pearlymussel)	Toxolasma cylindrellus	E	US	8/22/1984	F
Pink mucket (pearlymussel)	Lampsilis abrupta	E	US	1/24/1985	F
Purple bankclimber (mussel)	Elliptoideus sloatianus	T	US	9/19/2003	F
Purple bean	Villosa perpurpurea	E	US	5/24/2004	F
Purple cat's paw (=Purple cat's paw pearlymussel)	Epioblasma obliquata obliquata	E; EXPN	US	3/10/1992	F
Rabbitsfoot	Quadrula cylindrica cylindrica	T	US	None	—
Rayed bean	Villosa fabalis	E	US/foreign	None	—
Ring pink (mussel)	Obovaria retusa	E; EXPN	US	3/25/1991	F
Rough pigtoe	Pleurobema plenum	E; EXPN	US	8/6/1984	F
Rough rabbitsfoot	Quadrula cylindrica strigillata	E	US	5/24/2004	F
Round ebonyshell	Fusconaia rotulata	E	US	None	—
Scaleshell mussel	Leptodea leptodon	E	US	4/7/2010	F
Sheepnose mussel	Plethobasus cyphyus	E	US	None	—
Shiny pigtoe	Fusconaia cor	E; EXPN	US	7/9/1984	F
Shinyrayed pocketbook	Lampsilis subangulata	E	US	9/19/2003	F
Slabside pearlymussel	Lexingtonia dolabelloides	E	US	None	—
Snuffbox mussel	Epioblasma triquetra	E	US/foreign	None	—

TABLE 5.2

Endangered and threatened clam and mussel species, November 2013 [CONTINUED]

Common name	Scientific name	Listing status[a]	U.S. or U.S./foreign listed	Recovery plan date	Recovery plan stage[b]
Southern acornshell	Epioblasma othcaloogensis	E	US	11/17/2000	F
Southern clubshell	Pleurobema decisum	E	US	11/17/2000	F
Southern combshell	Epioblasma penita	E	US	11/14/1989	F
Southern kidneyshell	Ptychobranchus jonesi	E	US	None	—
Southern pigtoe	Pleurobema georgianum	E	US	11/17/2000	F
Southern sandshell	Hamiota australis	T	US	None	—
Speckled pocketbook	Lampsilis streckeri	E	US	1/2/1992	F
Spectaclecase (mussel)	Cumberlandia monodonta	E	US	None	—
Stirrupshell	Quadrula stapes	E	US	11/14/1989	F
Tan riffleshell	Epioblasma florentina walkeri (=E. walkeri)	E	US	10/22/1984	F
Tapered pigtoe	Fusconaia burkei	T	US	None	—
Tar River spinymussel	Elliptio steinstansana	E	US	5/5/1992	RF(1)
Triangular kidneyshell	Ptychobranchus greenii	E	US	11/17/2000	F
Tubercled blossom (pearlymussel)	Epioblasma torulosa torulosa	E; EXPN	US	1/25/1985	F
Turgid blossom (pearlymussel)	Epioblasma turgidula	E; EXPN	US	1/25/1985	F
Upland combshell	Epioblasma metastriata	E	US	11/17/2000	F
White catspaw (pearlymussel)	Epioblasma obliquata perobliqua	E	US	1/25/1990	F
White wartyback (pearlymussel)	Plethobasus cicatricosus	E; EXPN	US	9/19/1984	F
Winged mapleleaf	Quadrula fragosa	E; EXPN	US	6/25/1997	F
Yellow blossom (pearlymussel)	Epioblasma florentina florentina	E; EXPN	US	1/25/1985	F

[a]E = Endangered; T = Threatened; EXPN = Experimental population, non-essential.
[b]F = Final; RF = Final revision.

SOURCE: Adapted from "Generate Species List," in *Species Reports*, U.S. Department of the Interior, U.S. Fish and Wildlife Service, November 2013, http://ecos.fws.gov/tess_public/pub/adHocSpeciesForm.jsp (accessed November 7, 2013), and "Listed FWS/Joint FWS and NMFS Species and Populations with Recovery Plans (Sorted by Listed Entity)," in *Recovery Plans Search*, U.S. Department of the Interior, U.S. Fish and Wildlife Service, November 2013, http://ecos.fws.gov/tess_public/pub/speciesRecovery.jsp?sort=1 (accessed November 7, 2013)

The USFWS indicates in "Saving the Higgins Eye Pearlymussel" (January 3, 2013, http://www.fws.gov/midwest/Endangered/clams/higginseye/propagation_fs.html) that the Genoa National Fish Hatchery in Genoa, Wisconsin, specializes in capturing female Higgins eye pearlymussels that have not yet released their glochidia. The glochidia are removed via a syringe and placed in tanks or buckets that contain suitable host fish. The fish are either released into the environment or maintained at the hatchery until the glochidia are mature enough to live on their own. These juvenile mussels are then released into natural waters that are free from invasive mussel species.

In September 2010 the USFWS (http://www.gpo.gov/fdsys/search/citation.result.FR.action?federalRegister.volume=2010&federalRegister.page=55820&publication=FR) initiated a five-year review for several midwestern species, including the Higgins eye pearlymussel. As explained in Chapter 2, the ESA requires all listed species to be reviewed at least every five years to determine whether they still require ESA protection. As of February 2014, the results of the review had not been issued.

ZEBRA AND QUAGGA MUSSELS: AN INFESTATION. In 1988 an unwelcome visitor was discovered in the waters of Lake St. Clair, Michigan: a zebra mussel (*Dreissena polymorpha*). The zebra mussel is native to eastern Europe. It is smaller than the freshwater mussels found in the United States and has a different method for spreading its young. The larvae of zebra mussels do not require a fish host to develop into babies. They can attach to any hard surface under the water. This allows zebra mussels to spread much easier and quicker than their American counterparts.

It is believed that the first zebra mussels migrated to the United States in the ballast water of ships. This is water held in large tanks below deck to improve the stability and control of ships. Ballast water is pumped in and out as needed during a journey. Zebra mussels have also been found clinging to the hulls of small fishing boats and recreational craft. These boats are hauled overland on trailers, and this allows the creatures to travel great distances between inland water bodies.

Another foreign invader of concern is the quagga mussel (*Dreissena bugensis*), a native of the Ukraine in eastern Europe. In 1989 the mussel was first sighted in the United States in Lake Erie. By the mid-1990s it had spread to other lakes in the upper Midwest. In 2007 the mussel was discovered in lakes in Arizona, Nevada, and Southern California. This finding is particularly troubling to scientists because of the large concentration of imperiled aquatic species in southwestern water bodies.

Figure 5.1 shows a USGS map of zebra and quagga mussel distribution throughout the country as of 2012. These invasive species have spread from the Great Lakes south to the Gulf of Mexico and east to New England and

FIGURE 5.1

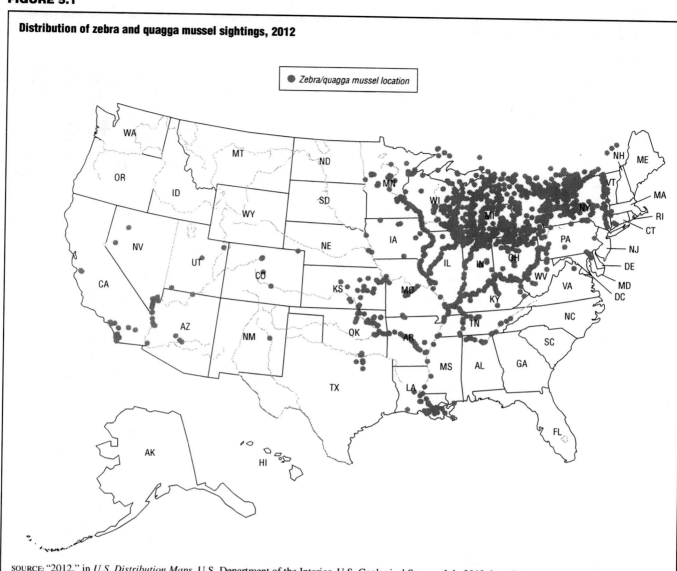

Distribution of zebra and quagga mussel sightings, 2012

● *Zebra/quagga mussel location*

SOURCE: "2012," in *U.S. Distribution Maps*, U.S. Department of the Interior, U.S. Geological Survey, July 2013, http://nas.er.usgs.gov/taxgroup/mollusks/zebramussel/maps/2012.gif (accessed November 8, 2013)

are beginning to show up in western waters. They have been found on boat hulls as far west as California. Throughout waterways in the Midwest, colonies of zebra mussels have clogged pipes and other structures that are used for municipal and industrial water supply. In addition, the pests have significantly degraded native mussel colonies by competing for available food, space, and resources.

Snails

Snails belong to the class Gastropoda of mollusks. They typically have an external spiral-shaped shell and a distinct head that includes sensory organs. Snails inhabit terrestrial (land), marine (ocean), and freshwater environments. Most land snails prefer moist, heavily vegetated locations and survive on a diet of vegetation and algae.

However, there are a few carnivorous (meat-eating) snail species. Snails are found throughout the United States. Most imperiled species are located in the West (including Hawaii) and the Southeast (primarily Alabama). Land snails are imperiled by a variety of factors including the destruction of habitat, being preyed on by rats and invasive carnivorous snails, and the spread of nonnative vegetation. Some marine snails have historically been prized by humans as a food source. Scientists say that snails play a valuable role in their ecosystems by recycling nutrients, such as nitrogen, that they ingest from food sources and then excrete back to the environment.

As of November 2013, there were 45 U.S. and U.S./foreign species of snails listed under the ESA. (See Table 5.3.) Most had an endangered listing and nearly all had recovery plans in place. As shown in Table 5.1,

TABLE 5.3

Endangered and threatened snail species, November 2013

Common name	Scientific name	Listing status[a]	U.S. or U.S./foreign listed	Recovery plan date	Recovery plan stage[b]
Alamosa springsnail	Tryonia alamosae	E	US	8/31/1994	F
Anthony's riversnail	Athearnia anthonyi	E; EXPN	US	8/13/1997	F
Armored snail	Pyrgulopsis (=Marstonia) pachyta	E	US	7/1/1994	D
Banbury Springs limpet	Lanx sp.	E	US	11/26/1995	F
Black abalone	Haliotis cracherodii	E	US	None	—
Bliss Rapids snail	Taylorconcha serpenticola	T	US	11/26/1995	F
Bruneau hot springsnail	Pyrgulopsis bruneauensis	E	US	9/30/2002	F
Chittenango ovate amber snail	Succinea chittenangoensis	T	US	8/21/2006	RF(1)
Chupadera springsnail	Pyrgulopsis chupaderae	E	US	None	—
Cylindrical lioplax (snail)	Lioplax cyclostomaformis	E	US	12/2/2005	F
Diamond Y springsnail	Pseudotryonia adamantina	E	US	None	—
Flat pebblesnail	Lepyrium showalteri	E	US	12/2/2005	F
Flat-spired three-toothed snail	Triodopsis platysayoides	T	US	5/9/1983	F
Gonzales tryonia	Tryonia circumstriata (=stocktonensis)	E	US	None	—
Interrupted (=Georgia) rocksnail	Leptoxis foremani	E	US	None	—
Iowa Pleistocene snail	Discus macclintocki	E	US	3/22/1984	F
Kanab ambersnail	Oxyloma haydeni kanabensis	E	US	10/12/1995	F
Koster's springsnail	Juturnia kosteri	E	US	None	—
Lacy elimia (snail)	Elimia crenatella	T	US	12/2/2005	F
Lanai tree snail	Partulina semicarinata	E	US	None	—
Lanai tree snail	Partulina variabilis	E	US	None	—
Morro shoulderband (=Banded dune) snail	Helminthoglypta walkeriana	E	US	9/28/1998	F
Newcomb's snail	Erinna newcombi	T	US	9/18/2006	F
Newcomb's tree snail	Newcombia cumingi	E	US	None	—
noonday globe	Patera clarki nantahala	T	US	9/7/1984	F
Oahu tree snails	Achatinella spp.	E	US	6/30/1992	F
Painted rocksnail	Leptoxis taeniata	T	US	12/2/2005	F
Painted snake coiled forest snail	Anguispira picta	T	US	10/14/1982	F
Pecos assiminea snail	Assiminea pecos	E	US/foreign	None	—
Phantom tryonia	Tryonia cheatumi	E	US	None	—
Plicate rocksnail	Leptoxis plicata	E	US	12/2/2005	F
Roswell springsnail	Pyrgulopsis roswellensis	E	US	None	—
Rough hornsnail	Pleurocera foremani	E	US	7/8/2013	D
Round rocksnail	Leptoxis ampla	T	US	12/2/2005	F
Royal marstonia (snail)	Pyrgulopsis ogmorhaphe	E	US	8/11/1995	F
San Bernardino springsnail	Pyrgulopsis bernardina	T	US	None	—
Slender campeloma	Campeloma decampi	E	US	None	—
Snake River physa snail	Physa natricina	E	US	11/26/1995	F
Socorro springsnail	Pyrgulopsis neomexicana	E	US	8/31/1994	F
Stock Island tree snail	Orthalicus reses (not incl. nesodryas)	T	US	5/18/1999	F
Three Forks springsnail	Pyrgulopsis trivialis	E	US	None	—
Tulotoma snail	Tulotoma magnifica	T	US	11/17/2000	F
Tumbling Creek cavesnail	Antrobia culveri	E	US	9/22/2003	F
Virginia fringed mountain snail	Polygyriscus virginianus	E	US	5/9/1983	F
White abalone	Haliotis sorenseni	E	US/foreign	1/12/2009	F

[a]E = Endangered; T = Threatened; EXPN = Experimental population, non-essential.
[b]F = Final; RF = Final revision; D = Draft.

SOURCE: Adapted from "Generate Species List," in *Species Reports*, U.S. Department of the Interior, U.S. Fish and Wildlife Service, November 2013, http://ecos.fws.gov/tess_public/pub/adHocSpeciesForm.jsp (accessed November 7, 2013), and "Listed FWS/Joint FWS and NMFS Species and Populations with Recovery Plans (Sorted by Listed Entity)," in *Recovery Plans Search*, U.S. Department of the Interior, U.S. Fish and Wildlife Service, November 2013, http://ecos.fws.gov/tess_public/pub/speciesRecovery.jsp?sort=1 (accessed November 7, 2013)

over $1 million was spent under the ESA in FY 2012 to conserve the white abalone.

White Abalone

The white abalone is a marine snail found along the West Coast from Southern California to northern Mexico. As a marine species, it is under the jurisdiction of the National Marine Fisheries Service (NMFS), an agency within the National Oceanic and Atmospheric Administration (NOAA). According to the NMFS in "White Abalone (*Haliotis sorenseni*)" (February 27, 2013, http://www .nmfs.noaa.gov/pr/species/invertebrates/whiteabalone.htm), the snail is a relative newcomer to the endangered species list, having been added in 2001. In addition, it is the first marine invertebrate ever to be listed under the ESA. In the listing rule, the NMFS (May 29, 2001, http://www.gpo .gov/fdsys/pkg/FR-2001-05-29/pdf/01-13430.pdf#page=1) indicated that it did not intend to designate critical habitat for the species because of fears about poaching (illegal hunting). The agency noted that the "abalone as a group continue to be highly prized and in demand as food by humans."

In October 2008 the NMFS published *Final White Abalone Recovery Plan (Haliotis sorenseni)* (http://ecos.fws.gov/docs/recovery_plan/whiteabalone.pdf), which describes the status of the species and the activities that are required to protect and recover it. According to the agency, recovery will be extremely difficult because white abalone populations have been reduced by 99% since the 1970s because of overharvesting by humans. In fact, the NMFS describes the current population size as "near zero." As such, no potential recovery date is given; however, the agency estimates that recovery will likely take "several decades and cost $20 million at a minimum."

"Breeding a Lifeline for Endangered White Abalone—The Conservation Value of Aquaculture" (August 27, 2012, http://www.nmfs.noaa.gov/aquaculture/homepage_stories/08_27_12abalone.html), the NMFS indicates that a population assessment conducted in 2010 found that the white abalone population had declined by 78 percent during the first decade of the 21st century. NOAA, in collaboration with other agencies and organizations, operates a captive breeding program for the species at the Bodega Marine Laboratory at the University of California at Davis. White abalone are difficult to propagate in captivity. However, NOAA indicates that the program has successfully reared thousands of the snails, and its goal is to achieve a sufficiently large number to create "a self-sustaining population in the wild."

Crustaceans

Crustaceans are a large class of mandibulate (jawed) creatures in the phylum Arthropoda. They are mostly aquatic and inhabit marine and freshwaters. In "Introduction to the Crustaceamorpha" (2013, http://www.ucmp.berkeley.edu/arthropoda/crustacea/crustaceamorpha.html), the University of California Museum of Paleontology notes that crustaceans are a highly varied species group and that "many serve as the main source of food for many fish and whales."

As of November 2013, there were 24 U.S. species listed as endangered or threatened under the ESA. (See Table 5.4.) Most had endangered listings and nearly all had recovery plans in place. Even though imperiled crustacean species are found throughout the United States, they are mostly located in California. Nearly $2.2 million was spent under the ESA during FY 2012 on one California crustacean: the vernal pool fairy shrimp. (See Table 5.1.)

VERNAL POOL FAIRY SHRIMP. The vernal pool fairy shrimp (*Branchinecta lynchi*) was listed under the ESA

TABLE 5.4

Endangered and threatened crustacean species, November 2013

Common name	Scientific name	Listing status[a]	U.S. or U.S./foreign listed	Recovery plan date	Recovery plan stage[b]
Alabama cave shrimp	Palaemonias alabamae	E	US	9/4/1997	F
Anchialine pool shrimp	Vetericaris chaceorum	E	US	None	—
California freshwater shrimp	Syncaris pacifica	E	US	7/31/1998	F
Cave crayfish	Cambarus zophonastes	E	US	9/26/1988	F
Cave crayfish	Cambarus aculabrum	E	US	10/30/1996	F
Conservancy fairy shrimp	Branchinecta conservatio	E	US	3/7/2006	F
Diminutive amphipod	Gammarus hyalleloides	E	US	None	—
Hay's Spring amphipod	Stygobromus hayi	E	US	None	—
Illinois cave amphipod	Gammarus acherondytes	E	US	9/20/2002	F
Kauai cave amphipod	Spelaeorchestia koloana	E	US	7/19/2006	F
Kentucky cave shrimp	Palaemonias ganteri	E	US	10/7/1988	F
Lee County cave isopod	Lirceus usdagalun	E	US	9/30/1997	F
Longhorn fairy shrimp	Branchinecta longiantenna	E	US	3/7/2006	F
Madison Cave isopod	Antrolana lira	T	US	9/30/1996	F
Nashville crayfish	Orconectes shoupi	E	US	2/8/1989	RF(1)
Noel's amphipod	Gammarus desperatus	E	US	None	—
Peck's cave amphipod	Stygobromus (=Stygonectes) pecki	E	US	2/14/1996	RF(1)
Riverside fairy shrimp	Streptocephalus woottoni	E	US	9/3/1998	F
San Diego fairy shrimp	Branchinecta sandiegonensis	E	US	9/3/1998	F
Shasta crayfish	Pacifastacus fortis	E	US	8/28/1998	F
Socorro isopod	Thermosphaeroma thermophilus	E	US	2/16/1982	F
Squirrel Chimney Cave shrimp	Palaemonetes cummingi	T	US	None	—
Vernal pool fairy shrimp	Branchinecta lynchi	T	US	3/7/2006	F
Vernal pool tadpole shrimp	Lepidurus packardi	E	US	3/7/2006	F

[a]E = Endangered; T = Threatened.
[b]F = Final; RF = Final revision.

SOURCE: Adapted from "Generate Species List," in *Species Reports*, U.S. Department of the Interior, U.S. Fish and Wildlife Service, November 2013, http://ecos.fws.gov/tess_public/pub/adHocSpeciesForm.jsp (accessed November 7, 2013), and "Listed FWS/Joint FWS and NMFS Species and Populations with Recovery Plans (Sorted by Listed Entity)," in *Recovery Plans Search*, U.S. Department of the Interior, U.S. Fish and Wildlife Service, November 2013, http://ecos.fws.gov/tess_public/pub/speciesRecovery.jsp?sort=1 (accessed November 7, 2013) as threatened in 1994. It is found in California and Oregon. The term *vernal* is from the Latin word for "spring." This species inhabits temporary small ponds and pools of water that appear during the rainy season (winter or springtime) and dry up during the dry season. Vernal pools are unique habitats, small temporary wetlands that harbor and nurture a rich variety of animals and plants. In "Vernal Pools Hold Waters of Life" (UTSanDiego.com, March 16, 2010), Mike Lee notes, "Researchers and wildlife advocates describe vernal ecosystems as biological gold mines. One of their most important functions is providing protein, in the form of tiny invertebrates, for amphibians and migrating birds."

The vernal pool fairy shrimp lay their eggs in vernal pools when they contain water. The eggs go dormant in the dirt when the pools become dry. Baby shrimp hatch only when exposed to water that is approximately 50 degrees Fahrenheit (10 degrees Celsius). Adults typically reach 0.4 to 1 inch (1 to 2.5 cm) in length. The shrimp have a life span of two to five months.

In 2003 critical habitat was designated for the vernal pool fairy shrimp along with several other species of vernal pool shrimp. In 2006 the USFWS published *Recovery Plan for Vernal Pool Ecosystems of California and Southern Oregon* (http://www.fws.gov/ecos/ajax/docs/recovery_plan/060614.pdf), a recovery plan that covers dozens of imperiled plant and animal species that inhabit vernal pool ecosystems in California and southern Oregon. The USFWS notes that vernal pool life forms are threatened by urban and agricultural development and by invasion of nonnative species. The recovery of vernal pool species will require an ecosystem-wide approach. The USFWS proposes establishing conservation areas and reserves to protect primary vernal pool habitat.

In May 2011 the USFWS (http://www.gpo.gov/fdsys/pkg/FR-2011-05-25/pdf/2011-12861.pdf) announced the initiation of a five-year review of the species. As of February 2014, the results of that review had not been published.

Imperiled Mollusks and Crustaceans around the World

According to the International Union for Conservation of Nature (IUCN), in *Red List of Threatened Species Version 2013.2* (November 2013, http://www.iucnredlist .org/about/summary-statistics), 1,898 species of mollusks and 723 species of crustaceans were threatened in 2013. For mollusks, this number accounted for 28% of the 6,809 species evaluated. The IUCN reports that approximately 85,000 mollusk species are known. Only 3,163 crustacean species were evaluated for the 2013 report. Threatened species accounted for 23% of this total. The IUCN notes that there are approximately 47,000 known species of crustaceans.

As shown in Table 5.5, only three foreign clam and snail species were listed under the ESA as of November 2013. All had endangered listings. They are found in Mexico and Papua New Guinea. No foreign crustacean species were listed under the ESA at that time.

CORALS

Corals are one of the most unusual members of the animal kingdom. Many people are familiar with coral reefs—vast and colorful undersea structures that are popular with scuba divers and snorkelers. (See Figure 5.2.) Most coral reefs are composed of many hundreds or thousands of individual coral organisms called polyps. Figure 5.3 shows a coral polyp with its common parts labeled. The polyp has an opening (or mouth) surrounded by tentacles that capture sea creatures for food. Following digestion in the polyp's stomach, waste materials are expelled out through the mouth.

Coral colonies provide key underwater habitats for numerous marine species, including fish and other aquatic creatures. Most reef-building coral polyps have a symbiotic (mutually beneficial) relationship with algae (tiny plant cells) called zooxanthellae. The algae perform photosynthesis, which creates oxygen and provides nutrients to the coral polyps, allowing them to grow and spread. Reef-building corals secrete calcium carbonate, a hard mineral compound that forms the reef skeleton. Zooxanthellae are also responsible for the bright and varied colors found in coral reefs. Without the algae, coral polyps are naturally translucent. Scientists believe zooxanthellae serve as sort of a "sunscreen" for warmwater corals, protecting them from the harsh ultraviolet rays of the sun.

TABLE 5.5

Foreign endangered and threatened clam, snail, crustacean, and coral species, November 2013

Common name	Scientific name	Group	Listing status*	Historic range
Tampico pearlymussel	Cyrtonaias tampicoensis tecomatensis	Clam	E	Mexico
Nicklin's pearlymussel	Megalonaias nicklineana	Clam	E	Mexico
Manus Island tree snail	Papustyla pulcherrima	Snail	E	Papua New Guinea

*E = Endangered.

SOURCE: Adapted from "Generate Species List," in *Species Reports*, U.S. Department of the Interior, U.S. Fish and Wildlife Service, November 2013, http://ecos .fws.gov/tess_public/pub/adHocSpeciesForm.jsp (accessed November 8, 2013)

FIGURE 5.2

Coral reefs are among the most diverse ecosystems in the world. They are also immediately threatened by global warming, which has caused unprecedented episodes of coral bleaching in recent years. ©Dennis Sabo/Shutterstock.

Coral reefs are the largest living structures on the earth. They are primarily found in coastal, tropical waters. These reefs are located in relatively shallow waters, making them more susceptible to human activities. The U.S. Commission on Ocean Policy states in *An Ocean Blueprint for the 21st Century: Final Report* (2004, http://govinfo.library.unt.edu/oceancommission/documents/full_color_rpt/000_ocean_full_report.pdf) that only 1% to 2% of warm-water corals are found in U.S. waters. Most warm-water corals are located in the waters of the South Pacific and around Indonesia. In addition, there are many cold-water reefs around the world that scientists are just beginning to study. These reefs are found in cold deep waters from depths of 100 feet (30.5 meters) to more than 3 miles (4.8 kilometers).

General Threats to Corals

In *An Ocean Blueprint for the 21st Century*, the Commission on Ocean Policy explains that coral reefs are imperiled by diseases and coastal development that spur the growth of unfriendly algae. Coastal development also increases the danger of the reefs being damaged by divers and boat anchors. Other serious threats to coral reef ecosystems include marine pollution, overfishing of species found around the corals, and destructive fishing methods used around the corals. The latter include explosives or chemicals, such as cyanide, that are used to stun coral inhabitants so they are easier to capture. Such methods are illegal and are known to be practiced in areas of Southeast Asia. The collection of tropical reef specimens for the aquarium trade has also damaged a number of species.

Perhaps the greatest immediate threat to coral reefs is rising water temperature due to global climate change. Overly warm water causes zooxanthellae to leave or be expelled from coral polyps. The resulting loss of color is known as coral bleaching. Bleached coral suffers from a lack of nutrients, becoming weak and lackluster and more susceptible to disease and other environmental stressors. Long-term zooxanthellae deficiencies can cause the coral to die. In "Susceptibility of Central Red Sea Corals during a Major Bleaching Event" (*Coral Reefs*, vol. 32, no. 2, June 2013), Kathryn A. Furby, Jessica Bouw-meester, and Michael L. Berumen state, "alarmingly, the frequency of bleaching events and mortalities has increased dramatically since 1979."

FIGURE 5.3

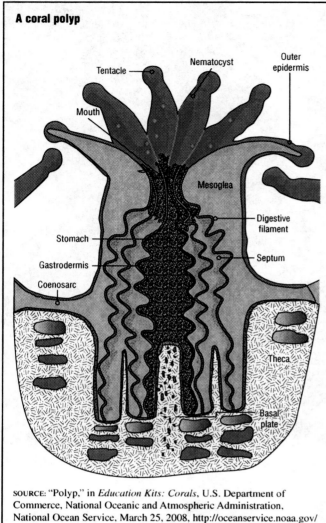

A coral polyp

Labels: Tentacle, Nematocyst, Outer epidermis, Mouth, Mesoglea, Digestive filament, Stomach, Septum, Gastrodermis, Coenosarc, Theca, Basal plate

SOURCE: "Polyp," in *Education Kits: Corals*, U.S. Department of Commerce, National Oceanic and Atmospheric Administration, National Ocean Service, March 25, 2008, http://oceanservice.noaa.gov/education/kits/corals/media/supp_coral01a.html (accessed November 12, 2013)

As described in Chapter 1, global climate change is believed to be triggered by excessive anthropogenic (human-caused) emissions of carbon dioxide into the atmosphere. NOAA explains in "What Is Ocean Acidification?" (2013, http://www.pmel.noaa.gov/co2/story/What+is+Ocean+Acidification%3F) that the increasing uptake of atmospheric carbon dioxide by the earth's oceans is lowering the pH (potential hydrogen; the level of acidity, a lower value indicates more acid) of the water and reducing the availability of carbonate ions to marine organisms that need them. The phenomenon is known as ocean acidification, and scientists fear that it poses a serious threat to the health of coral systems.

Imperiled U.S. Corals

NOAA periodically publishes a comprehensive report describing the condition of shallow-water coral reef ecosystems in the United States. As of February 2014, the most recent report was published in 2008. In *The State of Coral Reef Ecosystems of the United States and Pacific Freely Associated States: 2008* (July 2008, http://ccma.nos.noaa.gov/ecosystems/coralreef/coral2008/), NOAA's Coral Reef Conservation Program (CRCP) discusses the results of monitoring activities that were conducted by government, private, and academic entities engaged in assessing the condition of the nation's shallow-water coral reef ecosystems. According to the CRCP, approximately half the ecosystems were found to be in "poor" or "fair" condition.

As of November 2013, there were two U.S. species of coral listed as threatened under the ESA. (See Table 5.6.) The corals were Elkhorn coral (*Acropora palmata*) and Staghorn coral (*Acropora cervicornis*). Both species are branching corals found in the Caribbean, including the coastal waters of Florida, Puerto Rico, and the U.S. Virgin Islands. Their range extends to many tropical countries of Central and South America. Both species were listed under the ESA effective June 2006.

As marine creatures, corals are under the jurisdiction of the NMFS. In the original listing rule (December 14, 2007, http://www.nmfs.noaa.gov/pr/pdfs/fr/fr72-71102.pdf), the agency noted that the corals are primarily threatened by disease, hurricanes, and elevated sea surface temperatures. The NMFS called these threats "severe, unpredictable, [and] likely to increase in the foreseeable future." However, the corals are widely distributed. In addition, they reproduce asexually through a process called fragmentation in which branches break off and become reattached to the reef. This mechanism helps them recover from damaging events, such as hurricanes. As a result, the corals were not believed to be at risk of extinction throughout all or a significant part of their range. Thus, they were afforded a threatened, rather than an endangered ranking.

According to the NMFS (2012, https://www.federalregister.gov/articles/2012/12/07/2012-29350/endangered-and-threatened-wildlife-and-plants-proposed-listing-determinations-for-82-reef-building), in 2009 a private organization called the Center for Biological Diversity petitioned the agency to list 82 reef-building coral species under the ESA. During the biological study that ensued the agency also reviewed the status of the elkhorn and staghorn coral. In December 2012 the NMFS officially proposed uplisting the two species to endangered status noting that their populations had continued to decline and "the previous status review and listing determination underestimated the global climate change–associated impacts to *A. palmate* and *A. cervicornis*, based on our current knowledge of trends in emissions, likely warming scenarios, and ocean acidification." In addition, the agency proposed listing 66 of the petitioned coral species under the ESA—12 as endangered and 54 as threatened. The corals are found in the Caribbean and Indo-Pacific

TABLE 5.6

Endangered and threatened coral species, November 2013

Common name	Scientific name	Listing status*	U.S. or U.S./foreign listed	Recovery plan date	Recovery plan stage
Elkhorn coral	Acropora palmata	T	US/foreign	None	—
Staghorn coral	Acropora cervicornis	T	US/foreign	None	—

*T = Threatened.

SOURCE: Adapted from "Generate Species List," in *Species Reports*, U.S. Department of the Interior, U.S. Fish and Wildlife Service, November 2013, http://ecos .fws.gov/tess_public/pub/adHocSpeciesForm.jsp (accessed November 7, 2013), and "Listed FWS/Joint FWS and NMFS Species and Populations with Recovery Plans (Sorted by Listed Entity)," in *Recovery Plans Search*, U.S. Department of the Interior, U.S. Fish and Wildlife Service, November 2013, http://ecos.fws .gov/tess_public/pub/speciesRecovery.jsp?sort=1 (accessed November 7, 2013)

areas. As of February 2014, final decisions on the listing proposals had not been made.

Imperiled Corals around the World

In *Red List of Threatened Species Version 2013.2*, the IUCN indicates that 235 species of corals were threatened in 2013. This number accounted for 27% of the 856 species evaluated. According to the IUCN, approximately 2,175 coral species are known to scientists.

As of February 2014, no exclusively foreign coral species were listed as endangered or threatened under the ESA.

CHAPTER 6
AMPHIBIANS AND REPTILES

Amphibians and reptiles are collectively known by biologists as herpetofauna. In *Red List of Threatened Species Version 2013.2* (November 2013, http://www.iucnredlist.org/about/summary-statistics), the International Union for Conservation of Nature (IUCN) notes that there are 7,044 described amphibian species and 9,831 described reptile species. New species in both of these groups are being discovered every year, particularly in remote tropical regions that are only now being explored.

Most of the herpetofauna native to the United States are found in wetlands and riparian habitat (the banks and immediate areas around water bodies, such as rivers and streams). Biologists indicate that amphibians and reptiles play a crucial role in these ecosystems by controlling insects, processing dead organic matter into a form that is edible by smaller creatures, and providing an important link in the food chain.

Many herpetofauna species are under threat, primarily due to declines and degradation in their habitats in recent decades.

AMPHIBIANS

Amphibians are vertebrate animals in the taxonomic class Amphibia. They represent the most ancient group of terrestrial vertebrates. The earliest amphibians lived during the early Devonian era, some 400 million years ago. The three groups of amphibians that have survived to the present day are salamanders, frogs and toads, and caecilians.

Salamanders belong to the order Caudata (also called Urodela). They have moist smooth skin, slender bodies, four short legs, and long tails. This category includes the amphibians commonly known as newts (land-dwelling salamanders) and sirens (salamanders that have both lungs and gills).

Frogs and toads are in the order Anura. These amphibians do not have tails as adults. They have small bodies with two short front legs and two long back legs. (See Figure 6.1.) Their feet are webbed, and they are good jumpers and hoppers. True frogs belong to the family Ranidae, whereas true toads belong to the family Bufonidae. There are many other families in this order whose members are commonly described as frogs or toads. Many of the species go through a swimming tadpole stage before metamorphosing into an adult. However, in some species eggs hatch directly as juvenile froglets, which are miniature versions of the adults. Tadpoles are most often herbivorous (plant-eating), although there are some carnivorous (meat-eating) tadpoles, including cannibalistic species. Adults are carnivorous and catch prey with their sticky tongue.

Caecilians belong to the order Gymnophiona (also called Apoda) and share a common ancestor with the other amphibians, but look much different. They are often mistaken for worms or snakes. They have long slender bodies with no limbs and are found primarily in the tropics.

Amphi means "both," and amphibians get their name from the fact that many species occupy both aquatic and terrestrial habitats. In particular, many amphibian species undergo a dramatic change called metamorphosis, in which individuals move from an aquatic larval stage to a terrestrial adult stage. For example, in many frog species aquatic swimming tadpoles metamorphose into terrestrial jumping frogs. In the process, they lose their muscular swimming tails and acquire forelimbs and hind limbs. Many amphibian species occupy terrestrial habitats through most of the year, but migrate to ponds to breed. However, there are also species that are either entirely aquatic or entirely terrestrial. Whatever their habitat, amphibians generally require some moisture to survive. This is because amphibians pass some oxygen

FIGURE 6.1

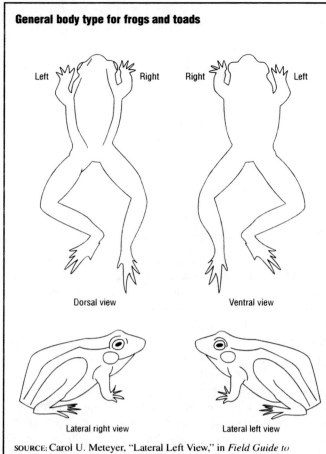

General body type for frogs and toads

Left   Right   Right   Left

Dorsal view   Ventral view

Lateral right view   Lateral left view

SOURCE: Carol U. Meteyer, "Lateral Left View," in *Field Guide to Malformations of Frogs and Toads with Radiographic Interpretations*, U.S. Department of the Interior, U.S. Geological Survey, 2000, http://www.nwhc.usgs.gov/publications/fact_sheets/pdfs/frog.pdf (accessed November 12, 2013)

and other chemicals in and out of their body directly through their skin, using processes that require water to function.

Many amphibian species are in serious decline because of factors such as habitat loss, pollution, and climate change. Amphibians are particularly vulnerable to pollution because their skin readily absorbs water and other substances from the environment. For this reason, amphibians are frequently considered biological indicator species, meaning that their presence, condition, and numbers are monitored as a gauge of the overall well-being of their habitat.

The U.S. Geological Survey (USGS) operates the Amphibian Research and Monitoring Initiative (http://armi.usgs.gov/) to study amphibian trends and causes of decline. In the press release "USGS Study Confirms U.S. Amphibian Populations Declining at Precipitous Rates" (May 22, 2013, http://www.usgs.gov/newsroom/article.asp?ID=3597), the agency summarizes the results of a study performed on nearly 50 amphibian species between

2002 and 2011 at dozens of sites around the United States. The USGS notes that "on average, populations of all amphibians examined vanished from habitats at a rate of 3.7 percent each year. If the rate observed is representative and remains unchanged, these species would disappear from half of the habitats they currently occupy in about 20 years." One troubling aspect of the study was that the declines were measured even on lands such as national parks and national wildlife refuges that are specifically managed for conservation purposes.

In April 2009 the Public Broadcasting Service (PBS) began televising the documentary *Frogs: The Thin Green Line* (http://www.pbs.org/wnet/nature/episodes/frogs-the-thin-green-line/video-full-episode/4882/), which focuses on the worldwide decline of frog species and the resulting effects on ecosystems and humans. Frogs are particularly important from an ecological standpoint, because they lie at the "middle" of the food chain. Tadpoles eat algae, a process that helps maintain clean water quality. Adult frogs eat insects, including insects such as mosquitoes and flies that can spread diseases to animals and humans. Frog eggs provide food for wasps and spiders. Fish and other aquatic creatures eat tadpoles, while birds and reptiles feed on adult frogs. Furthermore, PBS notes that scientists have discovered hundreds of chemicals in the skins of frogs, particularly tropical species. These chemicals hold promise in the development of anesthetics, painkillers, and other medicines that could greatly benefit humans.

THREATENED AND ENDANGERED SPECIES OF AMPHIBIANS

As of November 2013, there were 27 U.S. amphibian species listed as threatened or endangered under the Endangered Species Act (ESA). (See Table 6.1.) The list contains 16 species of salamander (including the Ozark hellbender) and 11 species of frogs and toads (including the coqui llanero, golden coqui, and the guajón, which are Puerto Rican frogs). Note that no caecilian species were listed. Most of the listed species were endangered and nearly all had recovery plans in place. Geographically, the list is dominated by western and southern states, primarily California and Texas. As shown in Table 2.11 in Chapter 2, no amphibian species have been delisted because of extinction or recovery under the ESA.

Table 6.2 shows the 10 amphibian species with the highest expenditures under the ESA during fiscal year (FY) 2012. Nearly $15.8 million was spent in an effort to conserve these species.

Imperiled Salamanders in the United States

Sixteen salamanders were listed under the ESA as of November 2013. (See Table 6.1.)

Some endangered salamanders, including many cave species, have highly restricted habitats. For example, the

TABLE 6.1

Endangered and threatened amphibian species, November 2013

Common name	Scientific name	Listing status[a]	U.S. or U.S./foreign listed	Recovery plan date	Recovery plan stage[b]
Arroyo (=arroyo southwestern) toad	Anaxyrus californicus	E	US/foreign	07/24/1999	F
Austin blind salamander	Eurycea waterlooensis	E	US	None	—
Barton Springs salamander	Eurycea sosorum	E	US	09/21/2005	F
California red-legged frog	Rana draytonii	T	US/foreign	09/12/2002	F
California tiger salamander	Ambystoma californiense	E; T	US	None	—
Cheat Mountain salamander	Plethodon nettingi	T	US	07/25/1991	F
Chiricahua leopard frog	Rana chiricahuensis	T	US/foreign	06/04/2007	F
Coqui llanero	Eleutherodactylus juanariveroi	E	US	None	—
Desert slender salamander	Batrachoseps aridus	E	US	08/12/1982	F
Dusky gopher frog	Rana sevosa	E	US	None	—
Frosted Flatwoods salamander	Ambystoma cingulatum	T	US	None	—
Golden coqui	Eleutherodactylus jasperi	T	US	04/19/1984	F
Guajon	Eleutherodactylus cooki	T	US	09/24/2004	F
Houston toad	Bufo houstonensis	E	US	09/17/1984	F
Jemez Mountains salamander	Plethodon neomexicanus	E	US	None	—
Jollyville Plateau salamander	Eurycea tonkawae	T	US	None	—
Mountain yellow-legged frog	Rana muscosa	E	US	None	—
Ozark hellbender	Cryptobranchus alleganiensis bishopi	E	US	None	—
Puerto Rican crested toad	Peltophryne lemur	T	US/foreign	08/07/1992	F
Red Hills salamander	Phaeognathus hubrichti	T	US	11/23/1983	F
Reticulated flatwoods salamander	Ambystoma bishopi	E	US	None	—
San Marcos salamander	Eurycea nana	T	US	02/14/1996	RF(1)
Santa Cruz long-toed salamander	Ambystoma macrodactylum croceum	E	US	07/02/1999	RD(2)
Shenandoah salamander	Plethodon shenandoah	E	US	09/29/1994	F
Sonora tiger salamander	Ambystoma tigrinum stebbinsi	E	US/foreign	09/24/2002	F
Texas blind salamander	Typhlomolge rathbuni	E	US	02/14/1996	RF(1)
Wyoming toad	Anaxyrus baxteri	E	US	09/11/1991	F

[a]E = Endangered; T = Threatened.
[b]F = Final; RF = Final revision.

SOURCE: Adapted from "Generate Species List," in *Species Reports*, U.S. Department of the Interior, U.S. Fish and Wildlife Service, November 2013, http://ecos.fws.gov/tess_public/pub/adHocSpeciesForm.jsp (accessed November 7, 2013), and "Listed FWS/Joint FWS and NMFS Species and Populations with Recovery Plans (Sorted by Listed Entity)," in *Recovery Plans Search*, U.S. Department of the Interior, U.S. Fish and Wildlife Service, November 2013, http://ecos.fws.gov/tess_public/pub/speciesRecovery.jsp?sort=1 (accessed November 7, 2013)

TABLE 6.2

Amphibian species with the highest expenditures under the Endangered Species Act, fiscal year 2012

Ranking	Species	Expenditure
1	Frog, California red-legged (Rana draytonii)	$6,388,743
2	Salamander, California tiger (Ambystoma californiense)	$4,526,609
3	Toad, arroyo southwestern) (Anaxyrus californicus)	$1,144,825
4	Frog, mountain yellow-legged (Rana muscosa)	$952,650
5	Frog, Chiricahua leopard (Rana chiricahuensis)	$898,484
6	Frog, dusky gopher (Rana sevosa)	$470,425
7	Toad, Wyoming (Bufo baxteri (=hemiophrys))	$380,428
8	Salamander, frosted flatwoods (Ambystoma cingulatum)	$365,606
9	Toad, Houston (Bufo houstonensis)	$324,540
10	Salamander, reticulated flatwoods (Ambystoma bishopi)	$313,250

SOURCE: Adapted from "Table 2. Species Ranked in Descending Order of Total FY2012 Reported Expenditures, Not Including Land Acquisition Costs," in *Federal and State Endangered and Threatened Species Expenditures: Fiscal Year 2012*, U.S. Department of the Interior, U.S. Fish and Wildlife Service, 2012, http://www.fws.gov/endangered/esa-library/pdf/2012.EXP.FINAL.pdf (accessed November 4, 2013)

Barton Springs salamander is found only in and around spring-fed pools in Zilker Park in Austin, Texas. The species was first listed as endangered in 1997. Urban development has contributed to degradation of the local groundwater that feeds the spring. In addition, flows from the spring have decreased because of increasing human use of groundwater from the aquifer. Finally, the Barton Springs salamander has been the subject of contentious debate between conservationists and those who wish to expand development around the area of the pools.

CALIFORNIA TIGER SALAMANDER. As shown in Table 6.2, $4.5 million was spent under the ESA during FY 2012 on the California tiger salamander. (See Figure 6.2.) According to the U.S. Fish and Wildlife Service (USFWS), in "California Tiger Salamander (*Ambystoma californiense*)" (February 24, 2014, http://ecos.fws.gov/species Profile/profile/speciesProfile.action?spcode=D01T), the salamander lives in terrestrial habitats and is relatively large, reaching a maximum length of about 8 inches (20.3 centimeters [cm]).

The ESA-listed populations are as follows:

- Sonoma County, California population—endangered

- Santa Barbara County, California population—endangered

FIGURE 6.2

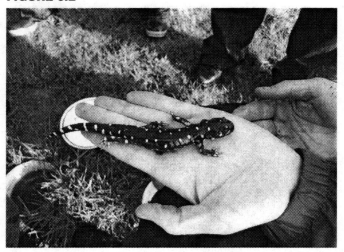

California tiger salamander. ©*U.S. Fish and Wildlife Service.*

• Central California distinct population segment (DPS), excluding the Sonoma and Santa Barbara County populations—threatened

Thus, the salamander is listed across a long swath of coastal California, an area that is characterized by residential and commercial development close to the coast and ranching and farming activities inland.

In *California Tiger Salamander* (Ambystoma californiense) *Santa Barbara County Distinct Population Segment: 5-Year Review—Summary and Evaluation* (November 2009, http://ecos.fws.gov/docs/five_year_review/doc3223.pdf), the USFWS indicates that the salamander lives mostly underground, but migrates to ponds and water pools to breed. Historically, the preferred breeding sites were vernal water bodies. (As explained in Chapter 5, the term *vernal* is from the Latin word for "spring." Vernal ponds and pools appear during the rainy season and dry up during the dry season.) The USFWS notes that the salamander is now found more often in human-made or human-modified water bodies, such as livestock ponds.

The USFWS states in "California Tiger Salamander: *Ambystoma californiense*" (July 29, 2009, http://www .fws.gov/sacramento/ES_Species/Accounts/Amphibians-Reptiles/Documents/california_tiger_salamander.pdf) that the salamander is imperiled by numerous threats, including habitat loss and fragmentation, intrusion of nonnative predators, and loss of mating partners.

In August 2011 the USFWS (http://www.gpo.gov/ fdsys/pkg/FR-2011-08-31/pdf/2011-21945.pdf) designated 47,383 acres (19,175 hectares [ha]) of critical habitat for the Sonoma County population of the California tiger salamander. The rule making followed years of court battles between the agency and the Center for Biological Diversity (a private conservation group) over the

appropriateness of and the proper extent for critical habitat. As of February 2014, critical habitat had not been designated for the Santa Barbara County or central California DPSs. Also, recovery plans had not been developed for any of the populations.

As noted earlier, a five-year review was published for the Santa Barbara County population in 2009. The purpose of a five-year review is to examine the status of listed species and determine whether to keep or change their ESA listings. The USFWS recommended that the endangered listing be maintained for the Santa Barbara population. In May 2010 and May 2011 the agency initiated five-year reviews for the central California and Sonoma County populations, respectively. As of February 2014, the results of the reviews had not been published.

In 2007 scientists reported that the genetic distinction of the California tiger salamander as a species is in serious doubt because of long-term interbreeding with the nonnative barred tiger salamander. Benjamin M. Fitzpatrick and H. Bradley Shaffer of the University of California, Davis, note in "Hybrid Vigor between Native and Introduced Salamanders Raises New Challenges for Conservation" (*PNAS*, vol. 104, no. 4, October 2, 2007) that the nonnative salamanders were introduced to California from Texas sometime during the late 1940s to the late 1950s as larval fish bait. Subsequent interbreeding with the native species has produced a vigorous and fertile hybrid offspring that has been dubbed a "super salamander." In "Tracking California's 'Super Salamanders'" (SCPR.org, September 12, 2013), Sanden Totten notes the hybrid salamanders are bigger and much more aggressive hunters than their forebears. One researcher told Totten, "What we found was, basically, in ponds that had hybrids they ate nearly everything in the pond. Hardly any frogs were able to survive. Hardly any larval newts." The rise of the "super salamander" presents a troubling problem for wildlife managers who fear for the survival of the California tiger salamander as a species. Scientists hope that the five-year status reviews underway for the central California and Sonoma County populations will provide some direction when they are published.

Imperiled Frogs and Toads in the United States

The 11 species of imperiled frogs and toads found in the United States are geographically diverse. Their habitats are located in the West, Southeast, and Puerto Rico.

CALIFORNIA RED-LEGGED FROGS. The California red-legged frog is the largest native frog in the western United States. The frog was made famous by Mark Twain's (1835–1910) short story "The Celebrated Jumping Frog of Calaveras County" (1865). The species experienced a significant decline during the mid-20th century because of loss and degradation of habitat. In 1996 the species was listed as threatened under the ESA. As noted in Table 6.2, $6.4 million was spent under the ESA during FY 2012 on conserving the California red-legged frog.

California red-legged frogs require riverside habitats that are covered by vegetation and are close to deepwater pools. They are extremely sensitive to habitat disturbance and water pollution—tadpoles are particularly sensitive to varying oxygen levels and siltation (mud and other natural impurities) during metamorphosis. The frogs require three to four years to reach maturity and have a normal life span of eight to 10 years.

Water reservoir construction and agricultural and residential development are the primary factors in the decline of this species. Biologists find that California red-legged frogs generally disappear from habitats within five years of a reservoir or water diversion project. The removal of vegetation associated with flood control and the use of herbicides and restructuring of landscapes further degrade remaining habitat. Finally, nonnative species have also attacked red-legged frog populations. These include alien fish predators as well as competing species such as bullfrogs.

In May 2002 the USFWS published *Recovery Plan for the California Red-Legged Frog (Rana aurora draytonii)* (http://ecos.fws.gov/docs/recovery_plans/2002/020528.pdf). The agency calls for eliminating threats in current habitats, restoring damaged habitats, and reintroducing populations into the historic range of the species. Critical habitat for the species was first set by the agency in 2001 and revised in 2006. In 2007 the Center for Biological Diversity filed a legal challenge arguing that the critical habitat designation was not sufficient. As a result, in March 2010 the USFWS (http://www.gpo.gov/fdsys/pkg/FR-2010-03-17/pdf/2010-4656.pdf#page=1) substantially increased the critical habitat from 450,000 acres (182,000 ha) to 1.6 million acres (660,000 ha).

In May 2011 the USFWS (http://www.gpo.gov/fdsys/pkg/FR-2011-05-25/pdf/2011-12861.pdf) initiated a five-year review for dozens of western species, including the California red-legged frog. As of February 2014, the results of the review had not been published.

Amphibian Deformities

Amphibian deformities first hit the spotlight during the mid-1990s, when reports about frogs with missing, extra, or misshapen limbs or other physical abnormalities began surfacing around the country. In *Field Guide to Malformations of Frogs and Toads* (April 2001, http://www.nwhc.usgs.gov/publications/fact_sheets/pdfs/frog.pdf), Carol U. Meteyer of the USGS indicates that as of 2000, frog malformations had been reported in more than 50 species of frogs and toads in 44 states.

The high incidence of amphibian deformities in some U.S. species in some areas appears to have multiple causes, as no single hypothesis accounts for all the different types of deformities seen. Probable causes include chemical contaminants, nutrient deficiencies, injuries (e.g., from predators), UV-B radiation, and parasites.

One of the difficulties associated with quantifying the scope of the problem is the lack of comprehensive data across populations. In 2013 the USFWS released the results of a study its scientists conducted on national wildlife refuges around the country. In press release "Landmark Study Reveals Low National Rate of Frog Abnormalities on Wildlife Refuges" (November 19, 2013, http://www.fws.gov/contaminants/Documents/News%20Release%20Abnormal%20Amphibians.pdf), the agency notes that the National Abnormal Amphibian Program sampled more than 68,000 frogs and toads on 152 national wildlife refuges compiling "one of the world's largest databases on amphibian abnormalities." The researchers found on average that 2% of the frogs and toads sampled had skeletal or eye abnormalities (the most commonly studied types of deformities in amphibians). This value was within the expected naturally occurring range of 0% to 2% for such abnormalities. Only 0.025% of the sampled frogs had extra limbs. Nevertheless, there were some geographical "hot spots" around the country in which the abnormality rate was much greater, as high as 40% in a few cases. The hot spots were found in the Mississippi River valley, the Central Valley of California, and parts of Alaska. The researchers did not investigate the possible causes of the deformities.

Foreign Amphibians in Danger

The IUCN reports in *Red List of Threatened Species Version 2013.2* that 1,950 amphibian species were threatened in 2013. This represented 31% of the 6,409 amphibian species evaluated, the highest percentage for any group of animals evaluated.

In "Amphibians" (February 21, 2014, http://www.iucn.org/about/work/programmes/species/our_work/amphibians/), the IUCN states that "extinctions and large scale declines of amphibian species have been variously attributed to habitat loss, pollution, fires, climate change, disease and over-exploitation. Action must be taken urgently to protect the remaining populations of amphibians across the world." James P. Collins and Martha L. Crump describe in *Extinction in Our Times: Global Amphibian Decline* (2009) the potential negative impacts of the loss of amphibian species, noting, "Amphibian declines and disappearances are important to all of us, because population fluctuations may reflect previously unknown problems in the environment. We know little concerning the consequences of species extinction on the capacity of ecosystems to deliver the goods and services on which all life

TABLE 6.3

Foreign endangered and threatened amphibian species, November 2013

Common name	Scientific name	Listing status*	Historic range
African viviparous toads	Nectophrynoides spp.	E	Tanzania, Guinea, Ivory Coast, Cameroon, Liberia, Ethiopia
Cameroon toad	Bufo superciliaris	E	Equatorial Africa
Chinese giant salamander	Andrias davidianus (=davidianus d.)	E	Western China
Goliath frog	Conraua goliath	T	Cameroon, Equatorial Guinea, Gabon
Israel painted frog	Discoglossus nigriventer	E	Israel
Japanese giant salamander	Andrias japonicus (=davidianus j.)	E	Japan
Monte Verde golden toad	Bufo periglenes	E	Costa Rica
Panamanian golden frog	Atelopus varius zeteki	E	Panama
Stephen Island frog	Leiopelma hamiltoni	E	New Zealand

*E = Endangered; T = Threatened.

SOURCE: Adapted from "Generate Species List," in *Species Reports*, U.S. Department of the Interior, U.S. Fish and Wildlife Service, November 2013, http://ecos .fws.gov/tess_public/pub/adHocSpeciesForm.jsp (accessed November 7, 2013)

depends, but we do know that amphibians play a key role in ecosystem health."

As of November 2013, there were nine foreign amphibian species listed as threatened or endangered under the ESA. (See Table 6.3.) This list included seven frog and toad species and two salamander species.

REPTILES

Reptiles belong to the class Reptilia. Although they may appear similar, reptiles differ from amphibians in that reptile skin is cornified (made of dead cells). All reptiles obtain oxygen from the air using lungs. Most reptiles lay shelled eggs, although some species, particularly lizards and snakes, give birth to live young. According to the IUCN, in *Red List of Threatened Species Version 2013.2*, 9,831 species of reptiles were described as of November 2013.

Reptiles include crocodilians, lizards, snakes, and turtles. Birds are also technically reptiles (birds and crocodiles are actually close relatives), but have historically been treated separately.

There are four taxonomic orders of reptiles:

- Squamata—thousands of species of lizards, anoles, iguanas, Gila monsters, monitors, skinks, geckos, chameleons, snakes (including asps, boas, pythons, and vipers), racerunners, whiptails, and amphisbaenians (worm lizards)

- Testudines—hundreds of species of turtles, terrapins, and tortoises

- Crocodilia—around two dozen species, including alligators, caimans, crocodiles, and gavials

- Rhynchocephalia—two species of tuataras found only in New Zealand

Lizards and snakes represent the largest group of reptiles. Many reptiles are in serious decline. Several

species are endangered because of habitat loss or degradation. In addition, humans hunt reptiles for their skins, shells, or meat. Global climate change has affected some reptile species, particularly turtles, in ominous ways— this is because in some reptiles ambient temperatures determine whether males or females are produced. Even a small increase in temperature can result in few or no males being born.

Natural disasters, such as hurricanes, can also negatively affect reptiles. For example, Christine Lagorio describes in "Katrina Displaces Sea Turtles" (CBSnews .com, August 29, 2005) the effects on nesting sea turtles by Hurricane Katrina, which struck the U.S. Gulf Coast in August 2005. Observers reported that newly hatched loggerhead sea turtles (an endangered species under the ESA) had difficulty making their way from their south Florida beach nests into the ocean because of the strong tides and waves produced by the storm. Lagorio notes that local residents, vacationers, and scientists from government agencies worked together to help temporarily rescue the struggling baby turtles until they could be released to the sea.

THREATENED AND ENDANGERED SPECIES OF REPTILES

As of November 2013, there were 35 U.S. reptile species listed as threatened or endangered under the ESA. (See Table 6.4.) Some species have dual status because they have separate populations in the United States. In addition, a few reptiles are listed as threatened because of similarity of appearance (SAT). This listing is applied to animals, such as the American alligator, that closely resemble imperiled species—in this case the American crocodile.

Except for sea turtles, most of the imperiled U.S. reptiles are geographically clustered in either the Southeast, California, or Puerto Rico and the Virgin Islands. Sea turtles spend most of their life at sea and come onto

TABLE 6.4

Endangered and threatened reptile species, November 2013

Common name	Scientific name	Listing status[a]	U.S. or U.S./foreign listed	Recovery plan date	Recovery plan stage[b]
Alabama red-belly turtle	Pseudemys alabamensis	E	US	1/8/1990	F
Alameda whipsnake (=striped racer)	Masticophis lateralis euryxanthus	T	US	4/7/2003	D
American alligator	Alligator mississippiensis	SAT	US	None	—
American crocodile	Crocodylus acutus	T	US/foreign	5/18/1999	F
Atlantic salt marsh snake	Nerodia clarkii taeniata	T	US	12/15/1993	F
Bluetail mole skink	Eumeces egregius lividus	T	US	5/18/1999	F
Blunt-nosed leopard lizard	Gambelia silus	E	US	9/30/1998	F
Bog (=Muhlenberg) turtle	Clemmys muhlenbergii	T; SAT	US	5/15/2001	F
Coachella Valley fringe-toed lizard	Uma inornata	T	US	9/11/1985	F
Copperbelly water snake	Nerodia erythrogaster neglecta	T	US	12/23/2008	F
Culebra Island giant anole	Anolis roosevelti	E	US	1/28/1983	F
Desert tortoise	Gopherus agassizii	T; SAT	US/foreign	5/6/2011	RF(1)
Eastern indigo snake	Drymarchon corais couperi	T	US	4/22/1982	F
Flattened musk turtle	Sternotherus depressus	T	US	2/26/1990	F
Giant garter snake	Thamnophis gigas	T	US	7/2/1999	D
Gopher tortoise	Gopherus polyphemus	T	US	12/26/1990	F
Green sea turtle	Chelonia mydas	E; T	US/foreign	10/29/1991	RF(1)
Hawksbill sea turtle	Eretmochelys imbricata	E	US/foreign	12/15/1993	RF(1)
Island night lizard	Xantusia riversiana	T	US	1/26/1984	F
Kemp's ridley sea turtle	Lepidochelys kempii	E	US/foreign	9/22/2011	RF(2)
Leatherback sea turtle	Dermochelys coriacea	E	US/foreign	1/12/1998	RF(1)
Loggerhead sea turtle	Caretta caretta	E; T	US/foreign	1/16/2009	RF(2)
Mona boa	Epicrates monensis monensis	T	US	4/19/1984	F
Mona ground iguana	Cyclura stejnegeri	T	US	4/19/1984	F
Monito gecko	Sphaerodactylus micropithecus	E	US	3/27/1986	F
New Mexican ridge-nosed rattlesnake	Crotalus willardi obscurus	T	US/foreign	3/22/1985	F
Olive ridley sea turtle	Lepidochelys olivacea	T	US/foreign	1/12/1998	RF(1)
Plymouth red-bellied turtle	Pseudemys rubriventris bangsi	E	US	5/6/1994	RF(2)
Puerto Rican boa	Epicrates inornatus	E	US	3/27/1986	F
Ringed map turtle	Graptemys oculifera	T	US	4/8/1988	F
Sand skink	Neoseps reynoldsi	T	US	5/18/1999	F
San Francisco garter snake	Thamnophis sirtalis tetrataenia	E	US	9/11/1985	F
St. Croix ground lizard	Ameiva polops	E	US	3/29/1984	F
Virgin Islands tree boa	Epicrates monensis granti	E	US/foreign	3/27/1986	F
Yellow-blotched map turtle	Graptemys flavimaculata	T	US	3/15/1993	F

[a]E = Endangered; T = Threatened; SAT = Threatened due to similarity of appearance.
[b]F = Final; D = Draft; RD = Draft revision; RF = Final revision.

SOURCE: Adapted from "Generate Species List," in *Species Reports*, U.S. Department of the Interior, U.S. Fish and Wildlife Service, November 2013, http://ecos.fws.gov/tess_public/pub/adHocSpeciesForm.jsp (accessed November 7, 2013), and "Listed FWS/Joint FWS and NMFS Species and Populations with Recovery Plans (Sorted by Listed Entity)," in *Recovery Plans Search*, U.S. Department of the Interior, U.S. Fish and Wildlife Service, November 2013, http://ecos.fws.gov/tess_public/pub/speciesRecovery.jsp?sort=1 (accessed November 7, 2013)

land only to nest and lay eggs. Because there are many potential nesting sites along the U.S. coasts, sea turtles are listed in many states.

The following is a breakdown of imperiled U.S. reptiles by taxonomic order:

- Squamata—19 species (10 snakes and nine lizards)

- Testudines—14 species

- Crocodilia—two species

As shown in Table 2.11 in Chapter 2, four reptile species—the American alligator (1987), Lake Erie water snake (2011), Concho water snake (2011), and Morelet's crocodile (2012)—have been delisted because of recovery. No reptile species have been delisted because of extinction.

The 10 listed reptile species with the highest expenditures under the ESA during FY 2012 are shown in

Table 6.5. The list is dominated by tortoise and sea turtle species.

Imperiled Tortoises in the United States

Terrestrial (land-dwelling) turtles inhabit inland areas and waterways; some species are generically called tortoises.

DESERT TORTOISES. The desert tortoise is a species native to the Sonoran and Mojave Deserts in the southwestern United States and into Mexico. The tortoise has evolved to survive for long periods on little water and to eat scrubby desert plants. Because of the extreme temperatures in its environment the tortoise spends much of its time in underground burrows that it makes. These burrows also provide habitat for numerous other desert animals. Rachelle Meyer of the U.S. Forest Service notes in "*Gopherus agassizii*" (2008, http://www.fs.fed.us/data

TABLE 6.5

Reptile species with the highest expenditures under the Endangered Species Act, fiscal year 2012

Ranking	Species	Expenditure
1	Tortoise, desert (Gopherus agassizii)	$12,334,481
2	Sea turtle, loggerhead (Caretta caretta)	$8,236,650
3	Sea turtle, green (Chelonia mydas)	$6,939,181
4	Snake, giant garter (Thamnophis gigas)	$5,947,661
5	Sea turtle, leatherback (Dermochelys coriacea)	$5,807,681
6	Sea turtle, hawksbill (Eretmochelys imbricata)	$5,436,912
7	Sea turtle, Kemp's ridley (Lepidochelys kempii)	$5,119,958
8	Tortoise, gopher (Gopherus polyphemus)	$2,388,354
9	Snake, eastern indigo (Drymarchon corais couperi)	$2,174,581
10	Turtle, bog (=Muhlenberg) (Clemmys muhlenbergii)—northern	$1,766,170

SOURCE: Adapted from "Table 2. Species Ranked in Descending Order of Total FY2012 Reported Expenditures, Not Including Land Acquisition Costs," in *Federal and State Endangered and Threatened Species Expenditures: Fiscal Year 2012*, U.S. Department of the Interior, U.S. Fish and Wildlife Service, 2012, http://www.fws.gov/endangered/esa-library/pdf/2012.EXP.FINAL.pdf (accessed November 4, 2013)

base/feis/animals/reptile/goag/all.html) that "desert tortoises share burrows with other desert tortoises and with several other animals including mammal, reptile, bird, and invertebrate species." The species include squirrels, woodrats, owls, snakes, Gila monsters, spiders, and scorpions. As such, the desert tortoise is considered a keystone species because it provides a major benefit to fellow species in its ecosystem who would greatly suffer from its demise.

The desert tortoise has dual listings under the ESA. (See Figure 6.3.) The population in Arizona, California, Nevada, and Utah was listed in 1980 as threatened except for those tortoises in Arizona south and east of the Colorado River. The latter were listed in 1990 as SAT. The population with a threatened listing is commonly known as the Mojave Desert population, whereas the population

FIGURE 6.3

The desert tortoise is threatened because of habitat destruction, livestock grazing, invasion of nonnative plant species, collection, and predation by ravens. ©*Ross Haley/U.S. Fish and Wildlife Service.*

with a SAT listing is commonly known as the Sonoran Desert population. In "Genetic Analysis Splits Desert Tortoise into Two Species" (June 28, 2011, http://www.usgs.gov/newsroom/article.asp?ID=2842), the USGS reports that in 2011 researchers determined that the two populations are actually two different species. The so-called Sonoran Desert population has been officially named the Morafka's desert tortoise (*Gopherus morafkai*).

The decline of the desert tortoise has resulted from collection by humans, predation of young turtles by ravens, off-road vehicles, invasive plant species, and habitat destruction due to development for agriculture, mining, and livestock grazing.

Desert tortoise populations are constrained by the fact that females do not reproduce until they are 15 to 20 years of age (individuals can live 80 to 100 years) and by small clutch sizes (i.e., small numbers of eggs per laying). Juvenile mortality is also extremely high, in large part because of predation by ravens, whose populations in the desert tortoise's habitat have risen with increasing urbanization of desert areas—human garbage provides food for ravens and power lines provide perches.

Approximately $12.3 million was spent under the ESA during FY 2012 on conservation measures for the Mojave Desert population of the desert tortoise. (See Table 6.5.) In September 2010 the USFWS published *Mojave Population of the Desert Tortoise (*Gopherus agassizii*): 5-Year Review—Summary and Evaluation* (http://ecos.fws.gov/docs/five_year_review/doc3572.DT%205Year%20Review_FINAL.pdf), in which the agency decided to maintain the population's threatened listing. In May 2011 the agency published *Revised Recovery Plan for the Mojave Population of the Desert Tortoise (*Gopherus agassizii*)* (http://ecos.fws.gov/docs/recovery_plan/RRP%20for%20the%20Mojave%20Desert%20Tortoise%20-%20May%202011_1.pdf). It estimates that the species can be recovered by 2025 at a cost of at least $159 million.

The Sonoran Desert tortoise DPS is considered a candidate species by the USFWS, meaning that the agency acknowledges that the species deserves protection under the ESA but is on hold while the USFWS deals with higher priorities. The species was listed in the *Candidate Notice of Review* (http://www.fws.gov/endangered/esa-library/pdf/2013_11_22_CNOR.pdf), which was published by the USFWS in November 2013. As explained in Chapter 2, in late 2011 the agency settled long-standing lawsuits involving candidate species by agreeing to make final listing decisions for all of them by 2017. The USFWS (2013, http://www.fws.gov/Endangered/improving_ESA/FY13-18_ESA_Listing_workplan.pdf) plans to make a decision on the Sonoran Desert tortoise DPS by the end of FY 2015.

FIGURE 6.4

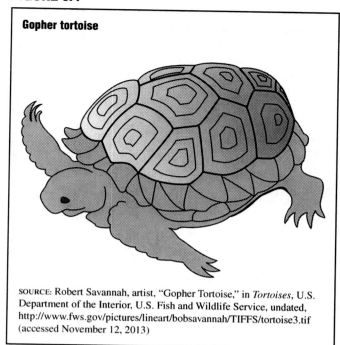

Gopher tortoise

SOURCE: Robert Savannah, artist, "Gopher Tortoise," in *Tortoises*, U.S. Department of the Interior, U.S. Fish and Wildlife Service, undated, http://www.fws.gov/pictures/lineart/bobsavannah/TIFFS/tortoise3.tif (accessed November 12, 2013)

FIGURE 6.5

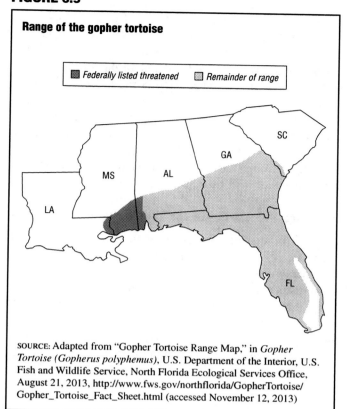

Range of the gopher tortoise

■ *Federally listed threatened*   ■ *Remainder of range*

SOURCE: Adapted from "Gopher Tortoise Range Map," in *Gopher Tortoise (Gopherus polyphemus)*, U.S. Department of the Interior, U.S. Fish and Wildlife Service, North Florida Ecological Services Office, August 21, 2013, http://www.fws.gov/northflorida/GopherTortoise/Gopher_Tortoise_Fact_Sheet.html (accessed November 12, 2013)

GOPHER TORTOISES. In 1987 the western population of the gopher tortoise was listed as threatened under the ESA. (See Figure 6.4.) This population is found west of the Tombigbee and Mobile Rivers in Alabama and across Mississippi and into Louisiana. (See Figure 6.5.) Gopher tortoises are land-dwelling turtles that prefer habitat in longleaf pine ecosystems with sandy soils. The tortoises spend much of their time in sandy burrows that often provide shelter for other animals, such as snakes and frogs. Thus, gopher tortoises are a keystone species in their ecosystems. A recovery plan for the gopher tortoise was completed in 1990. At that time the primary threats to the species were habitat degradation and illegal taking.

Coastal longleaf pine forests in the Southeast have been highly degraded by centuries of land development. As this habitat has become more fragmented, isolated pockets of the species have resulted in poor reproduction rates. Scientists fear that genetic drift and interbreeding are already occurring within the population. During the Great Depression (1929–1939) gopher tortoises were a highly prized meat source. Since that time their numbers have been further reduced by road strikes and collection for the pet trade. Natural predators include raccoons, foxes, snakes, and fire ants that prey on eggs or hatchlings.

In *Gopher Tortoise (Gopherus polvphemus) Recovery Plan* (December 26, 1990, http://ecos.fws.gov/docs/recovery_plan/901226.pdf), the USFWS notes that better management of government-owned forests in the region could help the survival status of the gopher tortoise. However, most lands with suitable habitat are privately owned and have already undergone, or are likely to undergo, development for agricultural, residential, or commercial purposes.

In 2001 the USFWS, in conjunction with the Mobile Area Water and Sewer System (MAWSS) and the conservation organizations Environmental Defense Fund and Southeastern Natural Resources, created a 222-acre (89.8-ha) gopher tortoise conservation bank near Big Creek Lake in Mobile, Alabama. Property owners can relocate gopher tortoises from their land to the conservation bank, which will remain undeveloped. As of 2013, the MAWSS (http://www.mawss.com/faq.html) charged $3,500 per gopher tortoise admitted to the bank. This money is used to manage the habitat. Each bank tortoise is also equipped with a radio collar so that the USFWS can monitor its movement.

As shown in Table 6.5, nearly $2.4 million was spent under the ESA during FY 2012 on the western population of the gopher tortoise. In April 2010 the USFWS (http://www.gpo.gov/fdsys/pkg/FR-2010-04-09/pdf/2010-8103.pdf#page=1) published notice of its intention to conduct a five-year review for 10 southeastern species, including the gopher tortoise. As of February 2014, the results of that review had not been published.

In 2006 the USFWS (September 9, 2009, http://www.gpo.gov/fdsys/pkg/FR-2009-09-09/pdf/E9-21481.pdf#page=1) received a petition submitted by two conservation groups—Save Our Big Scrub Inc. and Wild South—requesting that the eastern population of gopher tortoises be listed as threatened under the ESA. As shown in Figure 6.5, this population is found in Alabama (east of the Tombigbee and Mobile Rivers), Florida, Georgia, and into South Carolina. The species was listed in the *Candidate Notice of Review*, which was published by the USFWS in late 2013; however, it does not appear on the agency's scheduled work plan (http://www.fws.gov/Endangered/improving_ESA/FY13-18_ESA_Listing_workplan.pdf) for 2013 through 2018. Thus, it is not certain when a listing decision will be made.

Imperiled Sea Turtles in the United States

Sea (or marine) turtles are excellent swimmers and spend nearly their entire life in water. They feed on a wide array of food items, including mollusks, vegetation, and crustaceans. Some sea turtles are migratory, swimming thousands of miles between feeding and nesting areas. The latter are on beaches on which the turtles lay their eggs under the sand. Individuals are exposed to a variety of both natural and human threats. As a result, only an estimated one out of 10,000 sea turtles survives to adulthood.

There are seven species of sea turtles that exist worldwide. One species, the flatback turtle, occurs near Australia. The other six species—green sea turtle, hawksbill sea turtle, Kemp's ridley sea turtle, leatherback sea turtle, loggerhead sea turtle, and olive ridley sea turtle—spend part or all their life in U.S. territorial waters. As of November 2013, all six species were listed under the ESA. (See Table 6.4.) The green sea turtle, hawksbill sea turtle, Kemp's ridley sea turtle, leatherback sea turtle, and loggerhead sea turtle are shown in Figure 6.6.

ESA-listed sea turtles fall under the jurisdiction of the USFWS while they are on U.S. land and under the jurisdiction of the National Marine Fisheries Service (NMFS) while they are at sea. The populations and their ESA listings are as follows:

- Green sea turtle—endangered in Florida and threatened throughout the rest of its U.S. range, which includes Hawaii, the U.S. Virgin Islands, Puerto Rico, and the mainland coast from Texas to Massachusetts and from Southern California to Alaska. Key feeding grounds are in Florida coastal waters. Primary nesting sites are the Florida east coast, the U.S. Virgin Islands, Puerto Rico, and a remote atoll in Hawaii.

- Hawksbill sea turtle—endangered throughout its range, which is primarily around Hawaii, the U.S. Virgin Islands, Puerto Rico, and along the Gulf and southeast Florida coasts. Key nesting sites are in Puerto Rico, the U.S. Virgin Islands, Hawaii, and the southeast coast and keys of Florida.

FIGURE 6.6

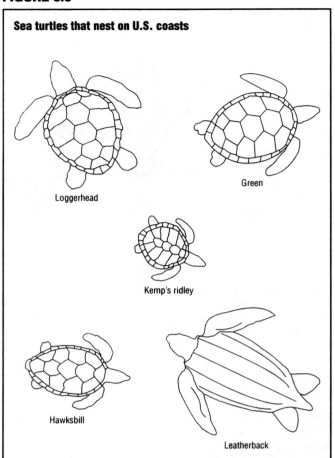

Sea turtles that nest on U.S. coasts

Loggerhead

Green

Kemp's ridley

Hawksbill

Leatherback

SOURCE: Adapted from "Untitled," in *You Can Help Protect Sea Turtles*, U.S. Department of the Interior, U.S. Fish and Wildlife Service, North Florida Ecological Services Office, July 2009, http://www.fws.gov/northflorida/SeaTurtles/20090700_You_Can_Help_ST.pdf (accessed November 12, 2013)

- Kemp's ridley sea turtle—endangered throughout its range, which includes waters along the Gulf and New England coasts. Primary nesting sites are in Mexico and Texas along the Gulf Coast.

- Leatherback sea turtle—endangered throughout its range, which includes waters around Hawaii, the U.S. Virgin Islands, Puerto Rico, and along the entire Atlantic coast. Major nesting locations are in the U.S. Virgin Islands and Georgia.

- Loggerhead sea turtle—two DPSs are found in U.S. waters: the endangered North Pacific Ocean DPS and the threatened Northwest Atlantic Ocean DPS. Primary nesting sites occur on the Gulf and east coast of Florida and in Georgia, South Carolina, and North Carolina.

- Olive ridley sea turtle—threatened throughout its range, which includes southwestern U.S. waters. Major nesting sites are in Mexico along the Pacific coast and in other tropical locations.

PROTECTING SEA TURTLES. Sea turtles are at risk of human interference in their aquatic habitats (i.e., ocean waters) and at their nesting locations on sandy beaches.

Shrimp trawling is recognized as one of the most deadly human activities for sea turtles in the Gulf of Mexico and the Caribbean. During the late 1970s the NMFS began developing turtle excluder devices (TEDs), which allow sea turtles to escape from shrimp nets. In "Turtle Excluder Device (TED) Chronology" (2013, http://www.dnr.sc.gov/seaturtle/teds.htm), the South Carolina Department of Natural Resources indicates that by the early 1980s the NMFS estimated that shrimp trawling killed more than 12,000 sea turtles annually. The NMFS developed a TED that was estimated to exclude 97% of sea turtles from shrimp nets, while allowing no shrimp to escape. (See Figure 6.7.)

Rusty Middleton notes in "Saving Sea Turtles" (TPWMagazine.com, June 2012) that a mandatory TED program was instituted by the NMFS in 1987, but it applies only to deepwater shrimp boats. Smaller skimmer trawlers are not required to use the devices. According to Middleton, the smaller boats are forbidden to shrimp in Texas waters, but make up about two-thirds of the shrimp fleet in Louisiana. Although the skimmer trawlers are supposed to limit their underwater trawling time, this requirement is difficult to enforce. In 2011 conservation groups filed a lawsuit against the NMFS after more than 900 dead turtles washed up on Gulf Coast beaches and necropsies (animal autopsies) revealed that most had died from drowning. In 2012 the agency reached an agreement with the groups and proposed issuance of new regulations on skimmer trawlers. However, the NMFS later changed its mind and did not issue the regulations.

In "National Fisheries Services Holds Off on New Turtle Excluder Device Rules" (NOLA.com, November 27, 2012), Benjamin Alexander-Bloch quotes an NMFS spokesperson defending the decision, who said, "Information we now have suggests the conservation benefit does not justify the burden this rule would place on the industry. We need more research looking at different options." Conservation groups accused the agency of bowing to political pressure from Louisiana officials wanting to protect the state's shrimpers. As of February 2014, the NMFS (http://sero.nmfs.noaa.gov/pr/Shrimp Fishery_SeaTurtle.htm) had not issued new TED regulations applicable to skimmer trawlers.

Under Public Law 101-162, Section 609, the United States bans the import of shrimp from countries that use harvesting methods deemed harmful to sea turtles. Each year the U.S. Department of State issues a list of nations that have been certified to import shrimp into the United States. Certification is based, in part, on the results of inspections conducted by the Department of State and the NMFS. On May 2, 2013, the Department of State (https://www.federalregister.gov/articles/2013/07/26/2013-18019/certifications-pursuant-to-section-609-of-public-law-101-162) listed 39 nations that were certified for shrimp imports under Section 609. Certification means that the shrimp were obtained using TEDs or in some other manner that does not endanger sea turtles. Shrimp imports are allowed from noncertified countries on a shipment-by-shipment basis if the respective governments can show that the shrimp were harvested in a manner not harmful to sea turtles.

Sea turtles bury their eggs in nests on sandy beaches and then return to the sea. The hatchlings emerge approximately 60 days later and must make a treacherous march to the water. During the short trip they are highly prone to predation by birds and other animals.

The building of beachfront resorts and homes has destroyed a large proportion of nesting habitat over the decades. New development projects must comply with the ESA and applicable state and local laws. For example, the Florida Fish and Wildlife Conservation Commission explains in "Marine Turtle Protection" (2014, http://myfwc.com/wildlifehabitats/managed/sea-turtles/protection/) that it works with the Florida Department of Environmental Protection to review permits for coastal construction to ensure that sea turtles and their habitats will not be harmed. Florida's Marine Turtle Protection Act (379.2431, Florida Statutes; http://www.leg.state.fl.us/) also governs projects that transfer sand from the sea bottom to the beach, a practice known as renourishment that is widely used to replace beach sand that erodes away. Renourishment can be detrimental to sea turtles

FIGURE 6.7

A bycatch reduction device designed to protect sea turtles

Water accelerator funnel
TED Grid
Fisheye BRD
TED escape opening

Notes: TED = Turtle excluder device. BRD = Bycatch reduction device.

SOURCE: Richard K. Wallace and Kristen M. Fletcher, "Figure 9," in *Understanding Fisheries Management: A Manual for Understanding the Federal Fisheries Management Process, Including Analysis of the 1996 Sustainable Fisheries Act*, 2nd ed., U.S. Department of Commerce, National Oceanic and Atmospheric Administration, National Sea Grant Office, Mississippi Alabama Sea Grant Consortium, 2001, http://nsgl.gso.uri.edu/masgc/masgch00001.pdf (accessed November 12, 2013) (and other species) if the newly sourced sand is too dense or compacted.

On beach areas where turtle nesting is known to take place, authorities typically erect barriers (such as fences) and post signs warning beachgoers not to interfere with the nests. Artificial lighting associated with coastal development also poses a problem—lights discourage females from nesting and cause hatchlings to become disoriented and wander inland instead of out to sea. As a result, some jurisdictions have regulations that govern beach lighting. For example, the Florida Fish and Wildlife Conservation Commission has developed a model local ordinance that serves as a guide for local governments that wish to regulate beach lighting. As of 2013, dozens of cities and counties within the state had adopted such ordinances.

Nesting sea turtles and hatchlings also benefit from the activities of numerous private conservation organizations and citizen volunteers that collaborate with government agencies. In "Current Sea Turtle Nesting Season" (February 23, 2014, http://www.nps.gov/pais/naturescience/current-season.htm), the National Park Service explains that it conducts "turtle patrols" on all of Texas's Gulf Coast beaches to detect and monitor nesting sea turtles and their nests. It is helped in these efforts by the USFWS and the NMFS and by private and academic groups such as Animal Rehabilitation Keep, Sea Turtle, Inc., the Sea Turtle Restoration Project, Texas A&M University, and the University of Texas.

Imperiled Snakes and Lizards

As of November 2013, there were 10 snakes (including whipsnakes and boas) and nine lizards (including skinks, anoles, iguanas, and geckos) listed as endangered or threatened under the ESA. (See Table 6.4.) The following sections discuss three of the species: giant garter snake, eastern indigo snake, and Monito gecko.

GIANT GARTER SNAKES. As shown in Table 6.5, approximately $5.9 million was spent under the ESA during FY 2012 on the giant garter snake. This species is found only in California. It prefers agricultural wetlands (such as rice fields), canals, ponds, streams, and other small water bodies. Extensive land development in the Central Valley of the state has severely depleted the snake's habitat. Other threats to its survival include invasive predatory fish, water pollution, and flood control activities. In 1993 the giant garter snake was listed as threatened under the ESA.

Aaron Cotter describes in "Building a Bank Takes More Than Just Snakes" (May 19, 2011, http://www.fws.gov/sacramento/outreach/featured-stories/Building BanksSnakes/outreach_featured-stories_BuildingBanks Snakes.htm) the Sutter Basin Conservation Bank in California. The 429-acre (174-ha) bank provides marshy habitat for giant garter snakes and offers banking credits for fees that are used to operate the bank. Cotter explains, "When a company or individual plans a project that will impact endangered species or other natural resources, they may buy credits at a conservation bank in order to offset any impacts. The bank owner then uses the money to protect and manage the resources within the bank."

In May 2011 the USFWS (http://www.gpo.gov/fdsys/pkg/FR-2011-05-25/pdf/2011-12861.pdf) published notice that it was initiating a five-year review of dozens of West Coast species, including the giant garter snake. As of February 2014, the results of the review had not been published.

EASTERN INDIGO SNAKES. As shown in Table 6.5, nearly $2.2 million was spent under the ESA during FY 2012 on the eastern indigo snake. This is a large thick-bodied black snake found only in Florida and Georgia. (See Figure 6.8.) In 1978 it was listed as threatened under the ESA. Its recovery plan was finalized in 1982. In May 2008 the USFWS published *Eastern Indigo Snake (Drymarchon couperi): 5-Year Review—Summary and Evaluation* (http://ecos.fws.gov/docs/five_year_review/doc1910 .pdf). The agency decided to maintain the snake's threatened listing because of continued threats to its habitat.

MONITO GECKOS. The endangered Monito gecko is a small lizard less than 2 inches (5 cm) long. (See Figure 6.9.) This species exists only on the 38-acre (15.4-ha) Monito Island off the Puerto Rican coast. Endangerment of the Monito gecko has resulted from human activity and habitat destruction. After World War II (1939–1945) the U.S. military used Monito Island as a site for bombing exercises, causing large-scale habitat destruction. In 1982 the USFWS observed only 24 Monito geckos on the island. In 1985 Monito Island was designated as critical habitat for the species. The

FIGURE 6.8

Eastern indigo snake. ©*fivespots/Shutterstock.*

FIGURE 6.9

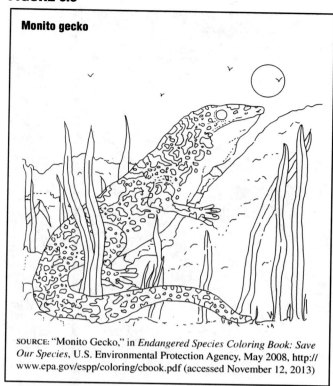

Monito gecko

SOURCE: "Monito Gecko," in *Endangered Species Coloring Book: Save Our Species*, U.S. Environmental Protection Agency, May 2008, http://www.epa.gov/espp/coloring/cbook.pdf (accessed November 12, 2013)

has a narrower, more pointed snout and an indentation in its upper jaw that allows a tooth to be seen when its mouth is closed.

The American alligator has a unique history under the ESA. It was on the first list of endangered species published in 1967. During the 1970s and 1980s populations of the species in many states rebounded in abundance and could have been delisted. Instead, it was reclassified as threatened. This measure was taken, in part, because federal officials acknowledged a certain amount of "public hostility" toward the creatures and were concerned that delisting would open the population to excessive hunting. Also, it was feared that the American alligator was so similar in appearance to the highly endangered American crocodile that delisting the alligator might lead to accidental taking of the crocodile species. By 1987 the alligator was considered fully recovered in the United States. As of November 2013, the alligator was listed as SAT. (See Table 6.4.)

The American crocodile is considered a success story of the ESA. When the species was originally listed as endangered in 1975, less than 300 individuals existed. Over the next three decades the species thrived and expanded its nesting range to new locations on the east and west coasts of Florida. In 2005 the USFWS initiated a five-year status review of the species. In 2007 the western DPS of the species in Florida was downlisted from endangered to threatened. At that time an estimated 2,000 American crocodiles lived in the state, not including hatchlings. Figure 6.11 shows a map of the critical habitat for the American crocodile and areas for which the USFWS provides consultation services regarding the species.

Commonwealth of Puerto Rico is now managing the island for the gecko and as a refuge for seabirds; unauthorized human visitation is prohibited. In 2007 the USFWS initiated a five-year review of 18 Caribbean wildlife and plant species, including the Monito gecko. As of February 2014, the results of that review had not been published.

Imperiled Crocodilians

Crocodilians play a crucial role in their habitat. They control fish populations and dig water holes, which are important to many species in times of drought. The disappearance of alligators and crocodiles has a profound effect on the biological communities these animals occupy. There are two imperiled crocodilian species in the United States: the American alligator and the American crocodile. (See Figure 6.10.) They are similar in appearance with only slight differences. The crocodile

Threatened and Endangered Foreign Reptile Species

The IUCN reports in *Red List of Threatened Species Version 2013.2* that 879 reptile species were threatened in 2013. A total of 4,204 reptile species were evaluated out of the 9,831 known species.

As of November 2013, there were 83 totally foreign reptile species listed under the ESA. (See Table 6.6.) Most are found in the tropical regions of Africa, Mexico, South America, and Southeast Asia.

FIGURE 6.10

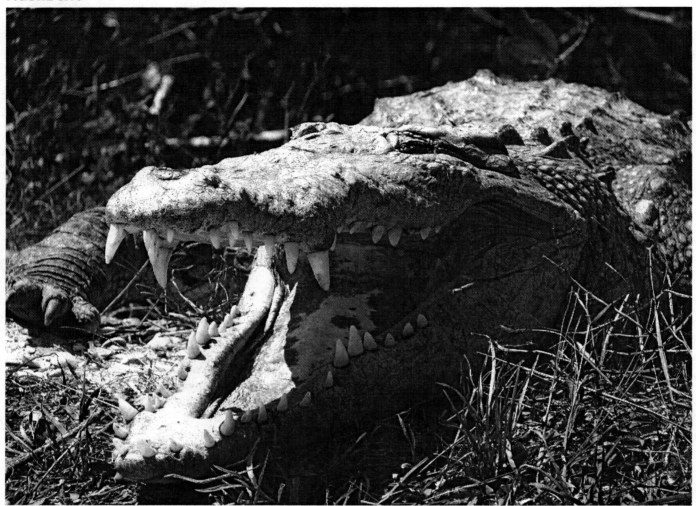

American crocodile. ©*U.S. Fish and Wildlife Service.*

FIGURE 6.11

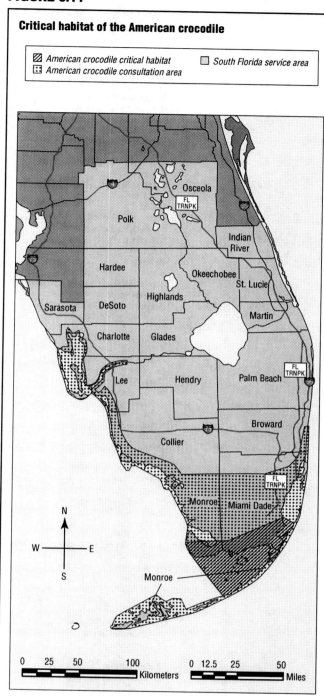

Critical habitat of the American crocodile

American crocodile critical habitat
American crocodile consultation area
South Florida service area

SOURCE: Adapted from "American Crocodile: Consultation Area Map," in *American Crocodile: Consultation Area*, U.S. Department of the Interior, U.S. Fish and Wildlife Service, South Florida Ecological Services Office, September 19, 2003, http://www.fws.gov/verobeach/ ReptilesPDFs/AmericanCrocodileConsultationArea.pdf (accessed November 12, 2013)

TABLE 6.6

Foreign endangered and threatened reptile species, November 2013

Common name	Scientific name	Listing status*	Historic range
Acklins ground iguana	Cyclura rileyi nuchalis	T	West Indies—Bahamas
African dwarf crocodile	Osteolaemus tetraspis tetraspis	E	West Africa
African slender-snouted crocodile	Crocodylus cataphractus	E	Western and central Africa
Allen's Cay iguana	Cyclura cychlura inornata	T	West Indies—Bahamas
American crocodile	Crocodylus acutus	E	Caribbean Sea, and Pacific Coast of Central and South America from Mexico to Ecuador
Andros Island ground iguana	Cyclura cychlura cychlura	T	West Indies—Bahamas
Anegada ground iguana	Cyclura pinguis	E	West Indies—British Virgin Islands (Anegada Island)
Angulated tortoise	Geochelone yniphora	E	Malagasy Republic (=Madagascar)
Apaporis River caiman	Caiman crocodilus apaporiensis	E	Colombia
Aquatic box turtle	Terrapene coahuila	E	Mexico
Aruba Island rattlesnake	Crotalus unicolor	T	Aruba Island (Netherland Antilles)
Barrington land iguana	Conolophus pallidus	E	Ecuador (Galapagos Islands)
Black caiman	Melanosuchus niger	E	Amazon basin
Black softshell turtle	Trionyx nigricans	E	Bangladesh
Bolson tortoise	Gopherus flavomarginatus	E	Mexico
Brazilian sideneck turtle	Phrynops hogei	E	Brazil
Broad-snouted caiman	Caiman latirostris	E; T	Brazil, Argentina, Paraguay, Uruguay
Brother's Island tuatara	Sphenodon guntheri	E	New Zealand (N. Brother's Island)
Brown Caiman	Caiman crocodilus fuscus (includes Caiman crocodilus chiapasius)	SAT	Mexico, Central America, Colombia, Ecuador, Venezuela, Peru
Burmese peacock turtle	Morenia ocellata	E	Burma
Cat Island turtle	Trachemys terrapen	E	West Indies—Jamaica, Bahamas
Cayman Brac ground iguana	Cyclura nubila caymanensis	T	West Indies—Cayman Islands
Central American river turtle	Dermatemys mawii	E	Mexico, Belize, Guatemala
Ceylon mugger crocodile	Crocodylus palustris kimbula	E	Sri Lanka
Chinese alligator	Alligator sinensis	E	China
Common caiman	Caiman crocodilus crocodilus	SAT	Brazil, Colombia, Ecuador, French Guiana, Guyana, Suriname, Venezuela, Bolivia, Peru
Congo dwarf crocodile	Osteolaemus tetraspis osborni	E	Congo River drainage
Cuatro Cienegas softshell turtle	Trionyx ater	E	Mexico
Cuban crocodile	Crocodylus rhombifer	E	Cuba
Cuban ground iguana	Cyclura nubila nubila	T	Cuba
Day gecko	Phelsuma edwardnewtoni	E	Indian Ocean—Mauritius
Desert monitor	Varanus griseus	E	North Africa to Aral Sea, through Central Asia to Pakistan, Northwest India
Exuma Island iguana	Cyclura cychlura figginsi	T	West Indies—Bahamas
Fiji banded iguana	Brachylophus fasciatus	E	Pacific—Fiji, Tonga
Fiji crested iguana	Brachylophus vitiensis	E	Pacific—Fiji
Galapagos tortoise	Geochelone nigra (=elephantopus)	E	Ecuador (Galapagos Islands)
Gavial	Gavialis gangeticus	E	Pakistan, Burma, Bangladesh, India, Nepal
Geometric turtle	Psammobates geometricus	E	South Africa
Grand Cayman ground iguana	Cyclura nubila lewisi	E	West Indies—Cayman Islands
Hierro giant lizard	Gallotia simonyi simonyi	E	Spain (Canary Islands)
Ibiza wall lizard	Podarcis pityusensis	T	Spain (Balearic Islands)
Inagua Island turtle	Trachemys stejnegeri malonei	E	West Indies—Bahamas (Great Inagua Island)
Indian (=Bengal) monitor	Varanus bengalensis	E	Iran, Iraq, India, Sri Lanka, Malaysia, Afghanistan, Burma, Vietnam, Thailand
Indian python	Python molurus molurus	E	Sri Lanka and India
Indian sawback turtle	Kachuga tecta tecta	E	India
Indian softshell turtle	Trionyx gangeticus	E	Pakistan, India
Jamaican boa	Epicrates subflavus	E	Jamaica
Jamaican iguana	Cyclura collei	E	West Indies—Jamaica
Komodo Island monitor	Varanus komodoensis	E	Indonesia (Komodo, Rintja, Padar, and western Flores Island)
Lar Valley viper	Vipera latifii	E	Iran
Loggerhead sea turtle	Caretta caretta	E; T	Mediterranean Sea, North Indian Ocean, Northeast Atlantic Ocean, South Pacific Ocean, South Atlantic Ocean, Southeast Indian Ocean, and Southwest Indian Ocean
Madagascar radiated tortoise	Geochelone radiata	E	Malagasy Republic (=Madagascar)
Maria Island ground lizard	Cnemidophorus vanzoi	E	West Indies—St. Lucia (Maria Islands)
Maria Island snake	Liophus ornatus	E	West Indies—St. Lucia (Maria Islands)
Mayaguana iguana	Cyclura carinata bartschi	T	West Indies—Bahamas
Mugger crocodile	Crocodylus palustris palustris	E	India, Pakistan, Iran, Bangladesh
Nile crocodile	Crocodylus niloticus	T	Africa, Middle East
Olive ridley sea turtle	Lepidochelys olivacea	E	Circumglobal in tropical and temperate seas

TABLE 6.6

Foreign endangered and threatened reptile species, November 2013 [CONTINUED]

Common name	Scientific name	Listing status*	Historic range
Orinoco crocodile	Crocodylus intermedius	E	South America—Orinoco River basin
Peacock softshell turtle	Trionyx hurum	E	India, Bangladesh
Philippine crocodile	Crocodylus novaeguineae mindorensis	E	Philippine Islands
River terrapin	Batagur baska	E	Malaysia, Bangladesh, Burma, India, Indonesia
Round Island bolyeria boa	Bolyeria multocarinata	E	Indian Ocean—Mauritius
Round Island casarea boa	Casarea dussumieri	E	Indian Ocean—Mauritius
Round Island day gecko	Phelsuma guentheri	E	Indian Ocean—Mauritius
Round Island skink	Leiolopisma telfairi	T	Indian Ocean—Mauritius
Saltwater crocodile	Crocodylus porosus	E; T	Southeast Asia, Australia, Papua New Guinea, Islands of the West Pacific Ocean
San Esteban Island chuckwalla	Sauromalus varius	E	Mexico
Serpent Island gecko	Cyrtodactylus serpensinsula	T	Indian Ocean—Mauritius
Short-necked or western swamp turtle	Pseudemydura umbrina	E	Australia
Siamese crocodile	Crocodylus siamensis	E	Southeast Asia, Malay Peninsula
South American red-lined turtle	Trachemys scripta callirostris	E	Colombia, Venezuela
Spotted pond turtle	Geoclemys hamiltonii	E	North India, Pakistan
Tartaruga	Podocnemis expansa	E	South America—Orinoco River and Amazon River basins
Three-keeled Asian turtle	Melanochelys tricarinata	E	Central India to Bangladesh and Burma
Tomistoma	Tomistoma schlegelii	E	Malaysia, Indonesia
Tracaja	Podocnemis unifilis	E	South America—Orinoco River and Amazon River basins
Tuatara	Sphenodon punctatus	E	New Zealand
Turks and Caicos iguana	Cyclura carinata carinata	T	West Indies—Turks and Caicos Islands
Watling Island ground iguana	Cyclura rileyi rileyi	E	West Indies—Bahamas
White Cay ground iguana	Cyclura rileyi cristata	T	West Indies—Bahamas
Yacare Caiman	Caiman yacare	T	Bolivia, Argentina, Peru, Brazil
Yellow monitor	Varanus flavescens	E	West Pakistan through India to Bangladesh

*E = Endangered; T = Threatened; SAT = Threatened due to similarity of appearance.

SOURCE: Adapted from "Generate Species List," in *Species Reports*, U.S. Department of the Interior, U.S. Fish and Wildlife Service, November 2013, http://ecos.fws.gov/tess_public/pub/adHocSpeciesForm.jsp (accessed November 7, 2013)

CHAPTER 7
TERRESTRIAL MAMMALS

Terrestrial animals are animals that inhabit the land. Mammals are warm-blooded, breathe air, have hair at some point during their life, give birth to live young (as opposed to laying eggs), and nourish their young by secreting milk.

The biggest cause of terrestrial mammalian decline and extinction is habitat loss and degradation. As humans convert forests, grasslands, rivers, and wetlands for various uses, they relegate many species to precarious existences in small, fragmented habitat patches. In addition, some terrestrial mammals have been purposely eliminated by humans. For example, bison (buffalo), elk, and beaver stocks were severely depleted in the United States following colonization by European settlers. All three species were nearly hunted to extinction by the end of the 1800s. The disappearance of native large game had consequences on other species. Wolves and other predators began preying on livestock and became the target of massive kill-offs by humans.

Some terrestrial mammal species have been imperiled, in part, because they are considered dangerous to human life. This has been the case for many bears, wolves, and mountain lions. Changing attitudes have led to interest in preserving all species, and conservation measures have allowed several terrestrial mammals to recover.

ENDANGERED AND THREATENED U.S. SPECIES

As of November 2013, there were 68 species of terrestrial mammals in the United States listed under the Endangered Species Act (ESA) as endangered or threatened. (See Table 7.1.) Nearly all had an endangered listing, meaning that they are at risk of extinction, and most had recovery plans in place.

The imperiled species fall into nine broad categories:

• Bats

• Bears

• Canines—foxes and wolves

• Deer, caribou, pronghorns, bighorn sheep, and bison

• Felines—jaguars, jaguarundis, lynx, ocelots, panthers, and pumas

• Ferrets

• Rabbits

• Rodents—beavers, mice, prairie dogs, rats, squirrels, and voles

• Shrews

Table 7.2 shows the 10 terrestrial mammal species with the highest expenditures under the ESA during fiscal year (FY) 2012. The Indiana bat was the most expensive ($15 million), followed by the gray wolf ($11.8 million) and the grizzly bear ($7.6 million).

Bats

Bats belong to the taxonomic order Chiroptera, which means "hand-wing." They are the only true flying mammals. They typically weigh less than 2 ounces (57 grams [g]) and have wingspans of less than 20 inches (51 centimeters [cm]). Most are insectivores, meaning that insects are their primary food source. As such, bats are valued by humans for keeping in check populations of insects that are agricultural pests or carry diseases (such as mosquitos). Bats prefer to sleep during the day and feed after dusk. Biologists believe that bats are vastly underappreciated for their role in controlling nighttime insect populations.

As of November 2013, 10 bat species were listed by the U.S. Fish and Wildlife Service (USFWS) as endangered or threatened under the ESA (see Table 7.1):

• Florida bonneted bat

• Gray bat

TABLE 7.1

Endangered and threatened terrestrial mammal species, November 2013

Common name	Scientific name	Listing status[a]	U.S. or U.S./foreign listed	Recovery plan date	Recovery plan stage[b]
Alabama beach mouse	Peromyscus polionotus ammobates	E	US	8/12/1987	F
Amargosa vole	Microtus californicus scirpensis	E	US	9/15/1997	F
American black bear	Ursus americanus	SAT	US	None	—
Anastasia Island beach mouse	Peromyscus polionotus phasma	E	US	9/23/1993	F
Black-footed ferret	Mustela nigripes	E; EXPN	US/foreign	4/23/2013	RD(2)
Buena Vista Lake ornate shrew	Sorex ornatus relictus	E	US	9/30/1998	F
Canada lynx	Lynx canadensis	T	US	9/14/2005	O
Carolina northern flying squirrel	Glaucomys sabrinus coloratus	E	US	9/24/1990	F
Choctawhatchee beach mouse	Peromyscus polionotus allophrys	E	US	8/12/1987	F
Columbian white-tailed deer	Odocoileus virginianus leucurus	E	US	6/14/1983	RF(1)
Delmarva Peninsula fox squirrel	Sciurus niger cinereus	E; EXPN	US	6/8/1993	RF(2)
Eastern puma (=cougar)	Puma (=Felis) concolor couguar	E	US/foreign	8/2/1982	F
Florida bonneted bat	Eumops floridanus	E	US	None	—
Florida panther	Puma (=Felis) concolor coryi	E	US	12/18/2008	RF(3)
Florida salt marsh vole	Microtus pennsylvanicus dukecampbelli	E	US	9/30/1997	F
Fresno kangaroo rat	Dipodomys nitratoides exilis	E	US	9/30/1998	F
Giant kangaroo rat	Dipodomys ingens	E	US	9/30/1998	F
Gray bat	Myotis grisescens	E	US	7/8/1982	F
Gray wolf	Canis lupus	E; EXPN	US/foreign	8/3/1987	RF(1)
Grizzly bear	Ursus arctos horribilis	E; EXPN	US	9/10/1993	RF(1)
Gulf Coast jaguarundi	Herpailurus (=Felis) yagouaroundi cacomitli	E	US/foreign	12/24/2012	RD(1)
Hawaiian hoary bat	Lasiurus cinereus semotus	E	US	5/11/1998	F
Hualapai Mexican vole	Microtus mexicanus hualpaiensis	E	US	8/19/1991	F
Indiana bat	Myotis sodalis	E	US	4/16/2007	RD(1)
Jaguar	Panthera onca	E	US/foreign	4/20/2012	O
Key deer	Odocoileus virginianus clavium	E	US	5/18/1999	F
Key Largo cotton mouse	Peromyscus gossypinus allapaticola	E	US	5/18/1999	F
Key Largo woodrat	Neotoma floridana smalli	E	US	5/18/1999	F
Lesser long-nosed bat	Leptonycteris curasoae yerbabuenae	E	US/foreign	3/4/1997	F
Little Mariana fruit bat	Pteropus tokudae	E	US	11/2/1990	F
Louisiana black bear	Ursus americanus luteolus	T	US	9/27/1995	F
Lower Keys marsh rabbit	Sylvilagus palustris hefneri	E	US	5/18/1999	F
Mariana fruit bat (=Mariana flying fox)	Pteropus mariannus mariannus	T	US	3/30/2010	RD(1)
Mexican long-nosed bat	Leptonycteris nivalis	E	US/foreign	9/8/1994	F
Morro Bay kangaroo rat	Dipodomys heermanni morroensis	E	US	1/25/2000	RD(1)
Mount Graham red squirrel	Tamiasciurus hudsonicus grahamensis	E	US	5/27/2011	RD(1)
Northern Idaho ground squirrel	Spermophilus brunneus brunneus	T	US	9/16/2003	F
Ocelot	Leopardus (=Felis) pardalis	E	US/foreign	8/26/2010	RD(1)
Ozark big-eared bat	Corynorhinus (=Plecotus) townsendii ingens	E	US	3/28/1995	RF(1)
Pacific pocket mouse	Perognathus longimembris pacificus	E	US	9/28/1998	F
Peninsular bighorn sheep	Ovis canadensis nelsoni	E	US/foreign	10/25/2000	F
Perdido Key beach mouse	Peromyscus polionotus trissyllepsis	E	US	8/12/1987	F
Point Arena mountain beaver	Aplodontia rufa nigra	E	US	6/2/1998	F
Preble's meadow jumping mouse	Zapus hudsonius preblei	T	US	None	—
Puma (=mountain lion)	Puma (=Felis) concolor (all subsp. except coryi)	SAT	US	None	—
Pygmy rabbit	Brachylagus idahoensis	E	US	1/23/2013	F
Red wolf	Canis rufus	E; EXPN	US	10/26/1990	RF(2)
Rice rat	Oryzomys palustris natator	E	US	5/18/1999	F
Riparian brush rabbit	Sylvilagus bachmani riparius	E	US	9/30/1998	F
Riparian woodrat (=San Joaquin Valley)	Neotoma fuscipes riparia	E	US	9/30/1998	F
Salt marsh harvest mouse	Reithrodontomys raviventris	E	US	2/10/2010	D
San Bernardino Merriam's kangaroo rat	Dipodomys merriami parvus	E	US	None	—
San Joaquin kit fox	Vulpes macrotis mutica	E	US	9/30/1998	F
San Miguel Island fox	Urocyon littoralis littoralis	E	US	9/14/2012	D
Santa Catalina Island fox	Urocyon littoralis catalinae	E	US	9/14/2012	D
Santa Cruz Island fox	Urocyon littoralis santacruzae	E	US	9/14/2012	D
Santa Rosa Island fox	Urocyon littoralis santarosae	E	US	9/14/2012	D
Sierra Nevada bighorn sheep	Ovis canadensis sierrae	E	US	2/13/2008	F
Sinaloan jaguarundi	Herpailurus (=Felis) yagouaroundi tolteca	E	US/foreign	None	—
Sonoran pronghorn	Antilocapra americana sonoriensis	E; EXPN	US/foreign	12/3/1998	RF(1)
Southeastern beach mouse	Peromyscus polionotus niveiventris	T	US	9/23/1993	F
St. Andrew beach mouse	Peromyscus polionotus peninsularis	E	US	12/28/2010	F
Stephens' kangaroo rat	Dipodomys stephensi (incl. D. cascus)	E	US	6/23/1997	D
Tipton kangaroo rat	Dipodomys nitratoides nitratoides	E	US	9/30/1998	F
Utah prairie dog	Cynomys parvidens	T	US	4/26/2012	RF(1)

TABLE 7.1

Endangered and threatened terrestrial mammal species, November 2013 [CONTINUED]

Common name	Scientific name	Listing status[a]	U.S. or U.S./foreign listed	Recovery plan date	Recovery plan stage[b]
Virginia big-eared bat	Corynorhinus (=Plecotus) townsendii virginianus	E	US	5/8/1984	F
Wood bison	Bison bison athabascae	T	US/foreign	None	—
Woodland caribou	Rangifer tarandus caribou	E	US/foreign	3/4/1994	RF(1)

[a]E = Endangered; T = Threatened; SAT = Threatened due to similarity of appearance; EXPN = Experimental population, non-essential.
[b]F = Final; D = Draft; RD = Draft revision; RF = Final revision; O = Other.

SOURCE: Adapted from "Generate Species List," in *Species Reports*, U.S. Department of the Interior, U.S. Fish and Wildlife Service, November 2013, http://ecos.fws.gov/tess_public/pub/adHocSpeciesForm.jsp (accessed November 7, 2013), and "Listed FWS/Joint FWS and NMFS Species and Populations with Recovery Plans (Sorted by Listed Entity)," in *Recovery Plans Search*, U.S. Department of the Interior, U.S. Fish and Wildlife Service, November 2013, http://ecos.fws.gov/tess_public/pub/speciesRecovery.jsp?sort=1 (accessed November 7, 2013)

TABLE 7.2

Terrestrial mammal species with the highest expenditures under the Endangered Species Act, fiscal year 2012

Rank	Species	Species total
1	Bat, Indiana (Myotis sodalis)	$15,028,862
2	Wolf, gray (Canis lupus)	$11,770,973
3	Bear, grizzly (Ursus arctos horribilis)	$7,632,156
4	Bear, Louisiana black (Ursus americanus luteolus)	$5,130,935
5	Lynx, Canada (Lynx canadensis)	$4,941,283
6	Wolf, red (Canis rufus)	$3,901,500
7	Fox, San Joaquin kit (Vulpes macrotis mutica)	$2,900,783
8	Bat, gray (Myotis grisescens)	$2,851,238
9	Ferret, black-footed (Mustela nigripes)	$2,663,541
10	Deer, Columbian white-tailed (Odocoileus virginianus leucurus)	$2,324,063

SOURCE: Adapted from "Table 2. Species Ranked in Descending Order of Total FY2012 Reported Expenditures, Not Including Land Acquisition Costs," in *Federal and State Endangered and Threatened Species Expenditures: Fiscal Year 2012*, U.S. Department of the Interior, U.S. Fish and Wildlife Service, 2012, http://www.fws.gov/endangered/esa-library/pdf/2012.EXP.FINAL.pdf (accessed November 4, 2013)

- Hawaiian hoary bat

- Indiana bat

- Lesser long-nosed bat

- Little Mariana fruit bat

- Mariana fruit bat

- Mexican long-nosed bat

- Ozark big-eared bat

- Virginia big-eared bat

Bats are imperiled for a variety of reasons, including habitat degradation, disturbance of hibernating and maternity colonies, direct extermination by humans, and the indirect effects of pesticide use on insects. During the first decade of the 21st century a new threat to bat survival emerged called white-nose syndrome (WNS). The U.S. Geological Survey (USGS) reports in "White-Nose Syndrome (WNS)" (January 27, 2014, http://www .nwhc.usgs.gov/disease_information/white-nose_syndrome/) that the disease was first documented during the winter of 2005–06. It is evidenced by the appearance of a white fungus on the muzzle, ears, and wings of afflicted bats. USGS researchers believe WNS is caused by a previously unknown fungus called *Geomyces destructans*. The agency notes that "millions of insect-eating bats in 22 states and five Canadian provinces have died from this devastating disease."

In May 2011 the USFWS published *A National Plan for Assisting States, Federal Agencies, and Tribes in Managing White-Nose Syndrome in Bats* (http://www.white nosesyndrome.org/sites/default/files/white-nose_syndrome _national_plan_may_2011.pdf), which provides information about WNS and lays out a national plan for collaboration between federal, state, tribal, and local agencies for managing bats that are imperiled by WNS. The USFWS indicates that cave bats (i.e., species that hibernate in caves or mines during the winter months) are most susceptible to WNS. Species that have been afflicted include the little brown bat, the big brown bat, the Indiana bat, the northern long-eared bat, the eastern small-footed bat, and the tricolored bat. In 2010 three additional species—the cave myotis, the gray bat, and the southeastern myotis—were found to be infected with the fungus, but not yet showing WNS symptoms. As shown in Table 7.1, the gray bat and the Indiana bat have endangered listings under the ESA.

In October 2013 the USFWS (http://www.gpo.gov/fdsys/pkg/FR-2013-10-02/pdf/2013-23753.pdf) published its decision regarding a petition submitted by the Center for Biological Diversity, a nonprofit conservation group, requesting that the eastern small-footed bat and the northern long-eared bat be listed as endangered under the ESA because of population declines caused by WNS. The agency decided against listing the eastern small-footed bat but officially proposed listing the northern long-eared bat as endangered. As of February 2014, the proposal had not been finalized.

INDIANA BATS. As shown in Table 7.2, more than $15 million was spent under the ESA during FY 2012 on the Indiana bat. It is a medium-sized, brown-colored bat found throughout a region encompassing the mid-Atlantic states and into the Midwest. The bats spend their winters in hibernation spots (or hibernacula) consisting primarily of large caves and abandoned mines. Figure 7.1 shows the breakdown by state of the hibernacula surveyed by the USFWS during the winter of 2012–13. Just over half a million bats were estimated to inhabit these hibernacula. Bats are extremely sensitive to any disturbances during hibernation. In "Indiana Bat" (2014, http://www.dec.ny.gov/animals/6972.html), the New York State Department of Environmental Conservation indicates that awakened bats become agitated and waste precious energy flying around frantically. This can leave them too weak and malnourished to survive the remainder of the winter. During the springtime adult females move to wooded areas and form maternity colonies. The loss of suitable habitat due to deforestation has disrupted this natural process. In addition, the bats have a low reproductive rate, producing only one baby per year. This makes it difficult for their populations to grow.

The Indiana bat was on the first list of endangered species, which was issued in 1967. (See Table 2.1 in Chapter 2.) In April 2007 the USFWS published *Indiana*

FIGURE 7.1

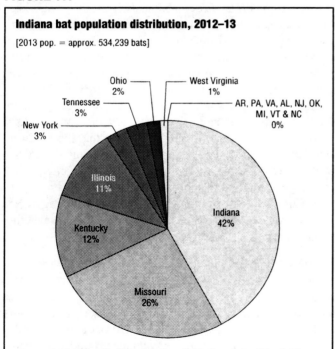

Indiana bat population distribution, 2012–13

[2013 pop. = approx. 534,239 bats]

- Ohio 2%
- West Virginia 1%
- Tennessee 3%
- AR, PA, VA, AL, NJ, OK, MI, VT & NC 0%
- New York 3%
- Illinois 11%
- Indiana 42%
- Kentucky 12%
- Missouri 26%

SOURCE: Andy King, "Indiana Bat Rangewide Population Distribution among Known Hibernacula in 17 States during the 2012–2013 Winter Survey," in *2013 Rangewide Population Estimate*, U.S. Department of the Interior, U.S. Fish and Wildlife Service, August 26, 2013, http://www.fws.gov/midwest/endangered/mammals/inba/pdf/2013inbaPop EstimateAug13.pdf (accessed November 10, 2013)

*Bat (*Myotis sodalis*) Draft Recovery Plan: First Revision* (http://ecos.fws.gov/docs/recovery_plan/070416.pdf). The USFWS estimated that there were 883,300 Indiana bats in the United States in 1965. The agency was optimistic that the species would be fully recovered by the 2020s. However, this was before WNS emerged. As noted earlier, WNS poses a new and serious threat to the survival of the Indiana bat and other cave-hibernating bat species.

In July 2011 the USFWS (http://www.gpo.gov/fdsys/pkg/FR-2011-07-26/pdf/2011-18893.pdf) initiated a five-year review for the Indiana bat. As of February 2014, the results of the review had not been published.

Bears

Bears belong to the Ursidae family. Their furry bodies are large and heavy, with powerful arms and legs and short tails. For the most part, they feed on fruits and insects, but they also eat meat.

As of November 2013, there were three bear species listed under the ESA as endangered or threatened in the United States: the American black bear, the Louisiana black bear, and the grizzly bear. (See Table 7.1; note that the polar bear is not included in this table because it is considered a marine mammal and is discussed in Chapter 3.) The American black bear is listed as threatened because of similarity of appearance (SAT). American black bears look similar to threatened Louisiana black bears. The listing is designed to prevent harmful actions by humans who might mistake Louisiana black bears for American black bears. Both species are found in Louisiana, Mississippi, and Texas. Grizzly bears inhabit Alaska and the northwestern states, primarily Idaho, Montana, Washington, and Wyoming.

In general, bears are endangered because of habitat loss. Some bears have been hunted because they are considered predatory or threatening, whereas others have been hunted for sport.

GRIZZLY BEARS. As shown in Table 7.2, $7.6 million was spent under the ESA during FY 2012 to conserve grizzly bears. They are large animals, standing 4 feet (1.2 meters [m]) high at the shoulder when on four paws and as tall as 7 feet (2.1 m) when upright. Males weigh 500 pounds (230 kilograms [kg]) on average but are sometimes as large as 900 pounds (410 kg). Females weigh 350 pounds (160 kg) on average. Grizzlies have a distinctive shoulder hump, which actually represents a massive digging muscle. Their claws are 2 to 4 inches (5.1 to 10.2 cm) long.

The grizzly bear was originally found throughout the continental United States, but was eventually eliminated from all but Alaska and a handful of western habitats. It was first listed as endangered in 1967. (See Table 2.1 in Chapter 2.) As of February 2014, the grizzly bear population in Alaska was thriving and not listed under the ESA. Two populations in the lower 48 states were listed:

- Portions of Idaho and Montana—experimental population, nonessential (as explained in Chapter 2, this listing means that the survival of this population is not believed essential to the survival of the species as a whole; thus, the population receives less protection under the ESA)

- Remainder of the lower 48 states—threatened

The USFWS indicates in "Grizzly Bear (*Ursus arctos horribilis*)" (February 25, 2014, http://ecos.fws.gov/species Profile/profile/speciesProfile.action?spcode=A001) that

over the decades it has published numerous recovery plans and supplements for specific populations of grizzly bears. Figure 7.2 shows the recovery zones that have been designated for the species. In "Grizzly Bear Conservation and Recovery" (http://www.fs.fed.us/biology/resources/pubs/issuepapers/Issueupdate_GrizRecovery_Sept2013.pdf), the U.S. Forest Service (USFS) provides an update as of September 2013 on the status of each recovery zone as follows:

- NCDE (North Continental Divide ecosystem in northwestern Montana)—population estimated at more than 900 individuals. The USFS anticipates that this population will be proposed for delisting during the second decade of the 21st century due to recovery.

FIGURE 7.2

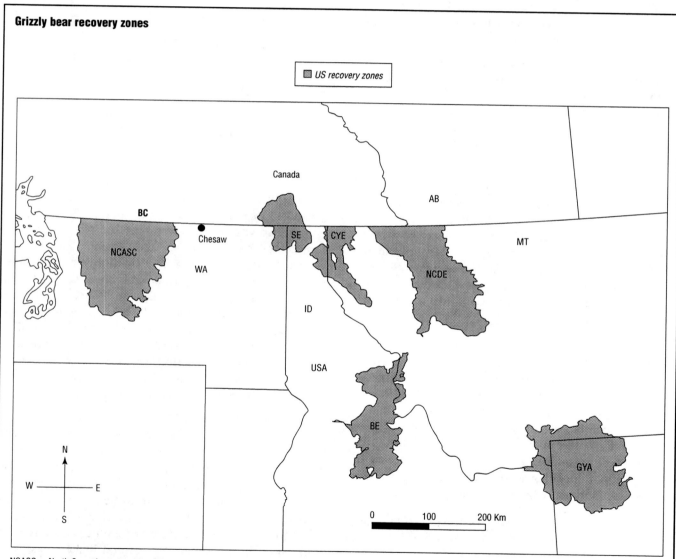

Grizzly bear recovery zones

NCASC = North Cascades ecosystem. SE = Selkirk ecosystem. CYE = Cabinet-Yaak ecosystem.
NCDE = North Continental Divide ecosystem. BE = Bitterroot ecosystem. GYA = Greater Yellowstone Area ecosystem.

SOURCE: Adapted from "Figure 1. Current Grizzly Bear Recovery Ecosystems," in *Grizzly Bear (Ursus arctos horribilis) 5-Year Review: Summary and Evaluation*, U.S. Department of the Interior, U.S. Fish and Wildlife Service, Grizzly Bear Recovery Office, August 2011, http://ecos.fws.gov/docs/five_year_review/doc3847.review_August%202011.pdf (accessed November 12, 2013)

- SE (Selkirk ecosystem in northeastern Washington and northern Idaho)—population estimated at a few dozen bears (i.e., a total of 100 individuals including those in the Cabinet-Yaak recovery zone). The USFWS has determined that the Selkirk population, along with those in the Cabinet-Yaak and North Cascades recovery zones, warrants uplisting from threatened to endangered status.

- CYE (Cabinet-Yaak ecosystem in northern Idaho and northwestern Montana)—population estimated at a few dozen bears (i.e., a total of 100 individuals counting those in the Selkirk recovery zone).

- NCASC (North Cascades ecosystem in north-central Washington)—according to the USFS this recovery zone holds "few bears."

- BE (Bitterroot ecosystem in eastern Idaho and western Montana)—grizzly bears have not been reintroduced into this recovery zone.

- GYA (Greater Yellowstone area ecosystem in eastern Idaho, southwestern Montana, and northwestern Wyoming)—the USFS notes that "the Yellowstone grizzly bear population is currently estimated at over 700 and continues to expand its range outside the recovery zone. Social tolerance for grizzly/human conflicts is decreasing."

Recovery efforts for the grizzly bear are coordinated by the Interagency Grizzly Bear Committee (IGBC), which was created in 1983. The IGBC (August 28, 2012, http://www.igbconline.org/index.php/who-we-are/about-the-igbc) is made up by representatives from the USFWS, the USGS, the USFS, the National Park Service, the Bureau of Land Management, the Canadian Wildlife Service, and the wildlife agencies of Idaho, Montana, Washington, and Wyoming.

In March 2007 the USFWS (http://frwebgate.access.gpo.gov/cgi-bin/getdoc.cgi?dbname=2007_register&docid=fr29mr07-14) established the GYA distinct population segment (DPS) of grizzly bears. As noted in Chapter 2, a DPS is a distinct population of a species that is capable of interbreeding and lives in a specific geographic area. In the rulemaking that created the DPS, the USFWS simultaneously delisted the DPS because of recovery (e.g., population gains). The delisting decision was challenged in court and overturned.

In August 2011 the USFWS published *Grizzly Bear (Ursus arctos horribilis): 5-Year Review—Summary and Evaluation* (http://ecos.fws.gov/docs/five_year_review/doc3847.review_August%202011.pdf), which summarized the lengthy and complicated legal history of the species under the ESA. The agency noted that between 1986 and 2007 it reviewed 10 petitions requesting listing status changes for individual grizzly bear populations.

The USFWS concluded that the CYE, NCDE, and SE populations warrant listing as endangered under the ESA. However, the uplisting actions were put on hold while the agency dealt with higher priorities. As of February 2014, the agency had not finalized the uplistings; thus, all three bear populations maintained their threatened listings.

Canines

Canine is the common term used to describe a member of the Canidae family of carnivorous (meat-eating) animals. This family includes coyotes, foxes, jackals, wolves, and domestic dogs.

As of November 2013, there were two wolf species and five fox species listed under the ESA in the United States (see Table 7.1):

- Gray wolf
- Red wolf
- San Joaquin kit fox
- San Miguel Island fox
- Santa Catalina Island fox
- Santa Cruz Island fox
- Santa Rosa Island fox

All the species were listed as endangered except for specific wolf DPSs.

WOLVES. Wolves were once among the most widely distributed mammals on the earth. Before European settlement, wolves ranged over most of North America, from central Mexico to the Arctic Ocean. Their decline was mostly due to hunting. In 1914 Congress authorized funding for the removal of all large predators, including wolves, from federal lands. By the 1940s wolves had been eliminated from most of the contiguous United States. In 1967 the gray wolf (which was then called the timber wolf) and the red wolf (which is shown in Figure 7.3) were on the first list of endangered species issued by the USFWS. (See Table 2.1 in Chapter 2.) By that time both species had all but disappeared.

In April 1994 the USFWS noted in *The Reintroduction of Gray Wolves to Yellowstone National Park and Central Idaho: Final Environmental Impact Statement* (http://www.fws.gov/mountain-prairie/species/mammals/wolf/eis_1994.pdf) the following: "Currently, as a result of natural dispersal of wolves from Canada over the past 15 years, about five wolf pack (65 wolves) live in northwest Montana. While lone wolves are occasionally seen or killed in the Yellowstone or central Idaho areas, wolf packs still do not exist in these areas." The agency outlined its decision to capture and release wolves in Yellowstone National Park and central Idaho. The USFWS acknowledged that reestablishing wolf packs in those areas would have some negative economic impacts due

FIGURE 7.3

The red wolf is found in the eastern United States. ©*U.S. Fish and Wildlife Service.*

to less spending by hunters (because of lower big game availability) and losses of livestock. However, the annual economic losses were estimated at less than $1 million annually. By contrast, the agency estimated that reintroduced wolves would result in an economic benefit of at least $23 million annually due to increased tourism and related spending.

The reintroductions began in 1995. Over a two-year period 66 gray wolves from southwestern Canada were introduced to Yellowstone National Park and central Idaho. Wolf reintroductions were not greeted with universal enthusiasm. Ranchers in particular were concerned that wolves would attack livestock. They were also worried that their land would be open to government restrictions as a result of the wolves' presence. Several measures were adopted to address the ranchers' concerns. The most significant was that ranchers would be reimbursed for livestock losses from a compensation fund. Until 2010 the fund was maintained by the Defenders of Wildlife, a private conservation group, and financed by private donors. In "Defenders of Wildlife Wolf Compensation Trust" (October 2009, http://www.defenders.org/sites /default/files/publications/statistics_on_payments_from _the_defenders_wildlife_foundation_wolf_compensation _trust.pdf), the Defenders of Wildlife states that between 1987 and October 2009 the fund paid out nearly $1.4 million to 893 ranchers, covering the losses of 3,832 livestock, mostly sheep and cattle. In 2010 the USFWS initiated its own compensation fund following passage of the Omnibus Public Lands Management Act of 2009, which established the Wolf Compensation and Prevention Program and provided $1 million in funding.

Wolf introductions were legally challenged in 1997, when the American Farm Bureau Federation initiated a lawsuit calling for the removal of wolves from Yellowstone. The farm coalition scored an initial victory, but in 2000 the 10th Circuit Court of Appeals in Denver, Colorado, overturned the decision on appeal by the U.S. Department of the Interior, the World Wildlife Fund, and other conservation groups.

As of November 2013, the listing status of the gray wolf was complicated because the USFWS recognized multiple populations of the species. In addition, efforts to delist gray wolf populations have been repeatedly challenged in court. The gray wolf was listed under the ESA as endangered throughout the lower 48 states, with the following exceptions or notes:

- Minnesota—this population was delisted in 2007 because of recovery and then relisted in September 2009 following a court order. As shown in Table 2.11 in Chapter 2, it was again delisted in 2012.

- Western Great Lakes DPS—the USFWS (http://www .gpo.gov/fdsys/pkg/FR-2011-12-28/pdf/2011-32825.pdf) designated this DPS in December 2011 and at the same time removed it from the ESA, noting that the DPS "does not meet the definitions of threatened or endangered under the Act."

- Portions of Arizona, New Mexico, and Texas— experimental population, nonessential of the Mexican gray wolf.

The northern Rocky Mountain DPS once consisted of wolves in eastern Washington and Oregon, a small part of north-central Utah, and all of Montana, Idaho, and Wyoming (excluding a nonessential experimental population). The DPS was the subject of intense litigation and political controversy. It was delisted in 2008, but that listing was vacated after 12 parties sued and prevailed in court. In April 2009 the USFWS again attempted to delist the DPS because of recovery, but the delisting was overturned in court. In April 2011 Congress passed a spending bill that included an amendment that essentially delisted the DPS. Actually, Congress (http://www.gpo .gov/fdsys/pkg/PLAW-112publ10/html/PLAW-112publ10 .htm) ordered the agency to reissue the April 2009 delisting rule and forbade any further "judicial review" of the decision. The latter condition triggered multiple lawsuits by conservation and wildlife groups alleging that the prohibition against judicial review of a congressional decision is unconstitutional. However, the congressional action was upheld in court.

In 2011 the USFWS officially delisted the northern Rocky Mountain DPS (excluding the Wyoming population). (See Table 2.11 in Chapter 2.) The following year the agency (http://www.gpo.gov/fdsys/pkg/FR-2012-09-10/pdf/2012-21988.pdf) delisted the Wyoming population.

In June 2013 the USFWS (http://www.fws.gov/south west/es/mexicanwolf/pdf/NR_wolf_press_release.pdf) proposed delisting the remaining gray wolves in the United States. At the same time, the agency (http://www.gpo.gov/fdsys/pkg/FR-2013-06-13/pdf/2013-13982.pdf) proposed listing the Mexican wolf (a subspecies of the gray wolf with the scientific name of *Canis lupus baileyi*) as endangered under the ESA. As of February 2014, these proposals had not been finalized. If they are finalized, the Mexican wolf will be the only gray wolf listed under the ESA.

Deer, Caribou, Pronghorns, Bighorn Sheep, and Bison

Deer and caribou are members of the Cervidae family, along with elk and moose. Pronghorn are the last surviving members of the Antilocapridae family and are often confused with antelopes. Bighorn sheep and bison belong to the large Bovidae family, which also contains antelopes, gazelles, and domesticated sheep, cattle, and goats. Although these species are diverse in taxonomy, the wild populations share a common threat: they are popular big game animals for hunters.

As of November 2013, there were seven species of big game listed under the ESA:

- Columbian white-tailed deer
- Key deer
- Peninsular bighorn sheep
- Sierra Nevada bighorn sheep
- Sonoran pronghorn
- Wood bison
- Woodland caribou

As shown in Table 7.1, most of these species had endangered listings and all but the wood bison had recovery plans in place.

COLUMBIAN WHITE-TAILED DEER. According to the USFWS, in "Columbian White-Tailed Deer: *Odocoileus virginianus leucurus*" (November 26, 2013, http://www.fws.gov/oregonfwo/species/data/columbianwhitetailed deer/), white-tailed deer occur throughout the United States. The Columbian white-tailed deer is the westernmost subspecies. Its historical range in Washington and Oregon is shown in Figure 7.4. Once quite populous, the subspecies was severely depleted by habitat disruption and loss. In 1968, when it was first listed as endangered under a precursor law to the ESA, only one "small" population was known to exist along the Columbia River, which forms most of the border between the two states. The USFWS notes that during the 1970s a second "small" population was found near Roseburg in Douglas County in southwestern Oregon. (See Figure 7.4.) As shown in Table 2.11 in Chapter 2, the latter population was delisted because of recovery in 2003. In November

FIGURE 7.4

Range of the Columbian white-tailed deer

- ▥ Columbia River population
- ▧ Roseburg population
- ▤ Historical range

SOURCE: "Figure 1. Historical and Current Range of the Columbian White-Tailed Deer," in *Columbian White-Tailed Deer Recovery Plan*, U.S. Department of the Interior, U.S. Fish and Wildlife Service, June 14, 1983, http://ecos.fws.gov/docs/recovery_plan/830614.pdf (accessed November 10, 2013)

2013 the USFWS published *Columbia River Distinct Population Segment of the Columbian White-Tailed Deer* (Odocoileus virginianus leucurus): *5-Year Review—Summary and Evaluation* (http://ecos.fws.gov/docs/five_year_review/doc4319.pdf), which recommended that the DPS be downlisted to threatened status because of continued population stability. As of February 2014, the agency had not officially proposed the downlisting action. As shown in Table 7.2, $2.3 million was spent under the ESA on the DPS during FY 2012.

Felines

Feline is the common term used for a member of the Felidae family. This diverse family includes bobcats, cheetahs, cougars, jaguars, jaguarundis, leopards, lions, lynx, panthers, pumas, tigers, and domesticated cats. All the wild species are under threat as development has left them with less natural habitat in which to live.

As of November 2013, there were eight wild feline species listed as endangered or threatened under the ESA in the United States:

- Canada lynx
- Eastern puma (= cougar)
- Florida panther
- Gulf coast jaguarundi
- Jaguar
- Ocelot
- Puma (= mountain lion)
- Sinaloan jaguarundi

Almost all these species had endangered listings. (See Table 7.1.) The exceptions were the Canada lynx, which was threatened, and the puma (= mountain lion), which in Florida was threatened because of similarity of appearance to the Florida panther. (See Figure 7.5.)

CANADA LYNXES. The Canada lynx is a medium-sized feline. Adults average 30 to 35 inches (76 to 89 cm) in length and weigh about 20 pounds (9 kg). The animal has tufted ears, a short tail, long legs, and large flat paws that allow it to walk on top of the snow. The Canada lynx inhabits cold, moist northern forests that are dominated by coniferous trees. Its primary food source is the snowshoe hare. Habitat modification, chiefly forest fragmentation due to timber harvesting, forest fire suppression, and human development, is blamed for imperiling both the snowshoe hare and the Canada lynx. In FY 2012 more than $4.9 million was spent under the ESA to conserve the Canada lynx. (See Table 7.2.)

In 1982 the USFWS designated the Canada lynx as a candidate species for listing. However, no action was taken on listing until 1994, when the agency proposed to list the species as threatened. The decision was challenged in court by a group of conservation organizations led by the Defenders of Wildlife. This began a protracted legal battle over the listing status and critical habitat designation for the species. As of February 2014, the USFWS (http://ecos.fws.gov/speciesProfile/profile/species Profile.action?spcode=A073) indicated that the threatened listing applied to the so-called contiguous United States DPS, including the populations in California, Colorado, Idaho, Maine, Michigan, Minnesota, Montana, Oregon, Utah, Washington, Wisconsin, and Wyoming.

In December 2009 the USFWS (http://frwebgate .access.gpo.gov/cgi-bin/getdoc.cgi?dbname=2009_register &docid=fr17de09-15) published a 12-month finding on a petition it had received in 2007 from seven conservation groups requesting that the DPS be expanded to include the mountains of north-central New Mexico. The agency concluded that the DPS change was warranted, but was "precluded by higher priority actions" (i.e., the DPS was deemed a candidate species). The decision was challenged in court and in September 2013 the USFWS (http://www.fws.gov/mountain-prairie/species/mammals/ lynx/09112013LynxTempFR.pdf) proposed to expand the contiguous United States DPS to include Canada lynx "everywhere they occur in the contiguous United States including New Mexico." In addition, the agency proposed to expand the existing critical habitat for the species. (See Figure 7.6.) As of February 2014, the proposals had not been finalized.

Ferrets

The ferret is a member of the Mustelidae family, along with badgers, mink, muskrats, otters, skunks, and weasels. Ferrets are small, furry creatures with long, skinny bodies typically less than 2 feet (0.6 m) long. They have short legs and elongated necks with small heads. Ferrets are carnivores; in the wild they feed on rodents, rabbits, reptiles, and insects.

As shown in Table 7.1, as of November 2013 there was one U.S. species of ferret listed under the ESA: the black-footed ferret, which is depicted in Figure 7.7.

FIGURE 7.5

Florida panther

SOURCE: Robert Savannah, artist, "Florida Panthers," in *Line Art (Drawings)*, U.S. Department of the Interior, U.S. Fish and Wildlife Service, undated, http://www.fws.gov/pictures/lineart/bobsavannah/ floridapanthers.html (accessed November 12, 2013)

FIGURE 7.6

Critical habitat for Canada lynx

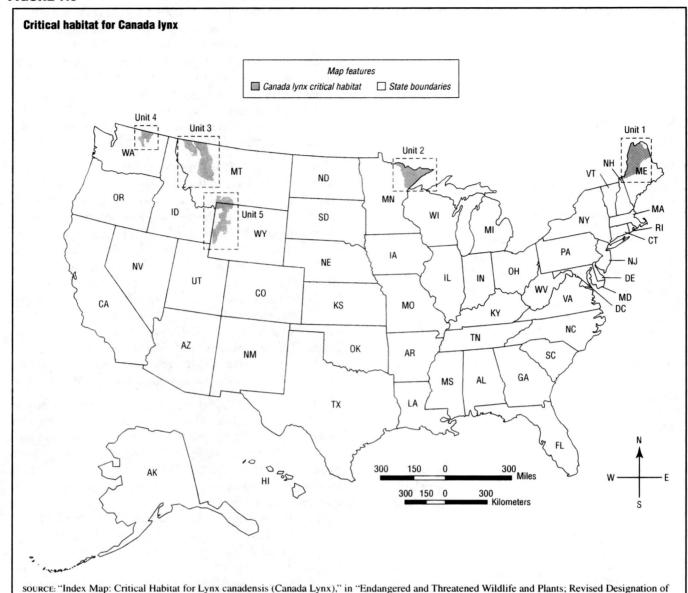

SOURCE: "Index Map: Critical Habitat for Lynx canadensis (Canada Lynx)," in "Endangered and Threatened Wildlife and Plants; Revised Designation of Critical Habitat for the Contiguous United States Distinct Population Segment of the Canada Lynx," *Federal Register*, vol. 74, no. 36, February 25, 2009, http://www.fws.gov/mountain-prairie/species/mammals/lynx/criticalhabitat_files/74FR8616.pdf (accessed November 12, 2013)

The species was listed as endangered, except in nonessential experimental populations in portions of Arizona, Colorado, Montana, South Dakota, Utah, and Wyoming.

BLACK-FOOTED FERRETS. The black-footed ferret is a small, furrow-digging mammal. It is a nocturnal creature and helps control populations of snakes and rodents, including its primary prey: black-tailed prairie dogs. The black-footed ferret once ranged over 11 Rocky Mountain states and parts of Canada. Its population has declined because of the large-scale conversion of prairie habitats to farmland and because its main prey, the prairie dog, has been nearly exterminated by humans. Prairie dogs are considered pests because they dig holes and tunnels just beneath the ground surface. These holes can cause

serious injury to horses or other large animals that step into them. Poisons that are used to kill prairie dogs may also kill some ferrets.

Black-footed ferret populations declined so drastically that the species was included on the first list of endangered species published in 1967. (See Table 2.1 in Chapter 2.) However, prairie dog poisonings continued, and by 1979 it was believed that the black-footed ferret was extinct. During the 1980s a small colony was discovered in Wyoming. These individuals were captured and entered into a captive breeding program. The Black-Footed Ferret Recovery Implementation Team was created in 1996 to integrate the efforts of dozens of agencies and nonprofit organizations working to save the species.

FIGURE 7.7

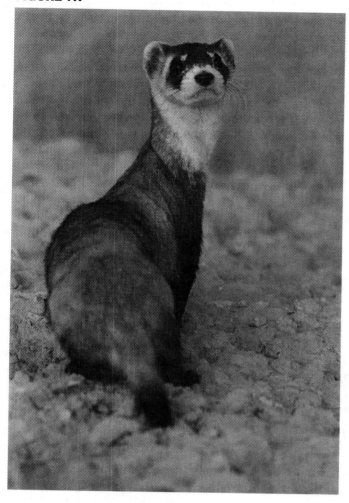

Black-footed ferret. ©*Laura Romin & Larry Dalton/Alamy.*

In November 2013 the USFWS published *Black-Footed Ferret Recovery Plan* (http://ecos.fws.gov/docs/recovery_plan/20131108%20BFF%202nd%20Rev.%20Final%20Recovery%20Plan.pdf). The agency cites the recovery criteria for the black-footed ferret as requiring 10 separate "successful" populations containing 1,500 breeding adults. As of 2013, only about 400 breeding adults were believed to exist in the wild. Another 300 animals were being managed in captive breeding facilities. The agency notes, "We believe that downlisting [from endangered to threatened status] of the black-footed ferret could be accomplished in approximately 10 years if conservation actions continue at existing reintroduction sites and if additional reintroduction sites are established."

Rabbits

Rabbits are members of the Leporidae family, along with hares. Rabbits are generally smaller than hares and have somewhat shorter ears. Both species have tall slender ears and short bodies with long limbs and thick soft fur. Domesticated rabbits are all descended from European species.

As of November 2013, there were three rabbit species listed as endangered under the ESA in the United States. (See Table 7.1.) The species and their primary locations are:

- Lower Keys marsh rabbit—Florida
- Pygmy rabbit—Columbia Basin DPS in Washington
- Riparian brush rabbit—California

All the species had recovery plans in place.

The USFWS published notices in April 2010 (http://www.gpo.gov/fdsys/pkg/FR-2010-04-08/pdf/2010-7915.pdf#page=1) and May 2010 (http://www.gpo.gov/fdsys/pkg/FR-2010-05-21/pdf/2010-12170.pdf#page=1) indicating that it was initiating five-year reviews for dozens of western species, including the pygmy rabbit Columbia Basin DPS and the riparian brush rabbit, respectively. As of February 2014, the results of the reviews had not been issued.

Rodents

Rodents are members of the order Rodentia, the single largest group of mammals. This order includes beavers, chipmunks, mice, prairie dogs, rats, squirrels, voles, and many other species. Rodents are characterized by their distinctive teeth, particularly a pair of chisel-shaped incisors in each jaw. Although most rodents are plant eaters, some species include insects in their diet.

As of November 2013, there were 28 rodent species listed under the ESA as endangered or threatened (see Table 7.1):

- Kangaroo rat—six species
- Mountain beaver—one species
- Mouse—10 species
- Prairie dog—one species
- Rat—three species
- Squirrel—four species
- Vole—three species

One imperiled rodent species of particular interest is the Utah prairie dog. The USFWS reports in *Federal and State Endangered and Threatened Species Expenditures: Fiscal Year 2012* (September 2013, http://www.fws.gov/endangered/esa-library/pdf/2012.EXP.FINAL.pdf) that in FY 2012 nearly $1.5 million was spent on this controversial species under the ESA.

UTAH PRAIRIE DOGS. Prairie dogs are members of the Sciuridae family, along with chipmunks and squirrels. (See Figure 7.8.) They are endemic (limited) to the United States and inhabit mostly arid grasslands. They are found from Montana and North Dakota south to Texas. The 19th-century explorers Meriwether Lewis

FIGURE 7.8

Prairie dog

SOURCE: Robert Savannah, artist, "Prairie Dogs," in *Line Art (Drawings)*, U.S. Department of the Interior, U.S. Fish and Wildlife Service, undated, http://www.fws.gov/pictures/lineart/bobsavannah/prairiedogs.html (accessed November 12, 2013)

(1774–1809) and William Clark (1770–1838) allegedly named the animals prairie dogs because of their barklike calls.

Before settlers moved into the West, it is believed that millions of prairie dogs inhabited the area. Prairie dogs are burrowing creatures and live in colonies. They produce holes, tunnels, and dirt mounds that can be damaging to land that is used for agriculture. The holes also pose a tripping hazard to horses and cattle. As a result, ranchers of the late 1800s and early 1900s tried to eradicate the prairie dog by using poison on a large scale. They were assisted in their efforts by the federal government.

According to the USFWS, in *Utah Prairie Dog* (Cynomys parvidens) *Draft Revised Recovery Plan* (August 2010, http://ecos.fws.gov/docs/recovery_plan/100917.pdf), by the mid-1970s the Utah population had been reduced to about 3,300 individuals. Massive poisoning by humans, disease (a form of plague), and loss of suitable habitat are blamed for the population decline. In 1973 the USFWS listed the species as endangered under the ESA.

Over the next decade conservation efforts led to an increase in its population, and angry farmers began reporting massive crop damage caused by the creatures. The state of Utah petitioned the USFWS to downlist the species from endangered to threatened, and in May 1984 the USFWS (http://ecos.fws.gov/docs/federal_register/fr838.pdf) did so. In addition, the agency established a section 4(d) rule under the ESA allowing the Utah Division of Wildlife Resources to issue permits to private landowners who wished to kill Utah prairie dogs on their property. Also, the USFWS began relocating Utah prairie dogs from private lands to federal-controlled lands. The USFWS (June 2, 2011, http://www.gpo.gov/fdsys/pkg/FR-2011-06-02/pdf/2011-13684.pdf) notes that its issuance of the 4(d) rule sparked years of litigation against the agency by conservation groups.

In May 2012 the agency published *Utah Prairie Dog (Cynomys parvidens): 5-Year Review—Summary and Evaluation* (http://www.fws.gov/mountain-prairie/species/mammals/utprairiedog/5-yearReview_UPD_May2012_FINAL_signed_(withRPappendix).pdf). The USFWS recommends that the species retain its threatened listing because of continuing problems with habitat loss and disease, noting, "Although recent Utah prairie dog population trends appear to be relatively stable, the species remains vulnerable to serious threats."

VIRGINIA NORTHERN FLYING SQUIRRELS. The Virginia (or West Virginia) northern flying squirrel is a small furry animal that grows to be about 12 inches (30.5 cm) long and weighs less than 5 ounces (142 g). (See Figure 7.9.) According to the USFWS, in *West Virginia Northern Flying Squirrel* (March 4, 2013, http://www.fws.gov/northeast/newsroom/wvnfsq.html), the species is a relic from the last Ice Age and has existed for at least 10,000 years. It is found only in the highest mountains along the West Virginia and Virginia border. Its historical habitat (old-growth spruce and other hardwood forests) was virtually eliminated by industrial logging between the 1880s and 1940s. In 1985, when the squirrel was listed as endangered under the ESA, biologists had captured only 10 individuals throughout its range and feared that it was in imminent danger of extinction. However, the species managed to survive over the following two decades as the hardwood forests rebounded. In 2008 the Virginia northern flying squirrel was delisted because of recovery. By 2009 its population was believed to be over 1,100 individuals. The USFWS notes that the squirrel's traditional forested habitat continues to spread because of protection efforts by federal and state government agencies and private conservation groups. However, in 2011 the delisting decision was overturned in court after being challenged by a coalition of nonprofit organizations. In June of that year the USFWS (http://www.gpo.gov/fdsys/pkg/FR-2011-06-17/pdf/2011-15111.pdf) reinstated

FIGURE 7.9

West Virginia northern flying squirrel

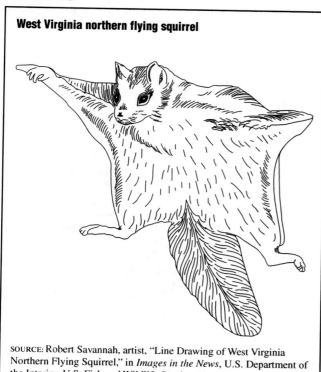

SOURCE: Robert Savannah, artist, "Line Drawing of West Virginia Northern Flying Squirrel," in *Images in the News*, U.S. Department of the Interior, U.S. Fish and Wildlife Service, Northeast Region, September 18, 2008, http://www.fws.gov/northeast/images.html (accessed November 13, 2013)

the endangered listing for the species. Another court battle followed, and in March 2013 the agency (https://www.federalregister.gov/articles/2013/03/04/2013-04932/endangered-and-threatened-wildlife-and-plants-reinstatement-of-removal-of-the-virginia-northern) again delisted the Virginia northern flying squirrel.

Shrews

Shrews belong to the order Soricomorpha, along with moles and their relatives. They are small furry animals about the size of mice. Shrews are primarily insectivores (insect eaters) with long snouts and small eyes.

As of November 2013, only one shrew, the Buena Vista Lake ornate shrew, was listed under the ESA. (See Table 7.1.) It was designated as endangered. According to the USFWS, in "Buena Vista Lake Ornate Shrew (*Sorex ornatus relictus*)" (February 26, 2014, http://ecos.fws.gov/speciesProfile/profile/speciesProfile.action?spcode=A0DV), the species is found in California and is about 4 inches (10 cm) long when fully grown, including a 1.5-inch (3.8-cm) tail. In *Buena Vista Lake Ornate Shrew (*Sorex ornatus relictus*): 5-Year Review—Summary and Evaluation* (September 2011, http://ecos.fws.gov/docs/five_year_review/doc3889.pdf), the agency noted that the species has lost more than 95% of its historic wetland habitat due to channelization and agricultural

and urban uses of water resources. The USFWS recommended maintaining an endangered listing for the shrew.

IMPERILED TERRESTRIAL MAMMALS AROUND THE WORLD

The International Union for Conservation of Nature (IUCN) indicates in *Red List of Threatened Species Version 2013.2* (http://www.iucnredlist.org/about/summary-statistics) that 1,143 mammal species were threatened as of November 2013. The IUCN does not break down the number by marine and terrestrial species. However, as noted in Chapter 3 the IUCN has designated as threatened approximately three dozen marine mammal species. Thus, around 1,100 terrestrial mammal species were considered threatened by the IUCN in 2013.

As of November 2013, the USFWS listed 259 totally foreign species of terrestrial mammals as endangered or threatened under the ESA. (See Table 7.3.) Many of the species are from groups that are also imperiled in the United States, such as bats, bears, big game, canines, felines, rabbits, and rodents. In addition, there are exotic animals not native to this country, particularly elephants, pandas, primates, and rhinoceros.

Big Cats

The IUCN (2013, http://www.iucnredlist.org/apps/redlist/details/15955/0) recognizes six subspecies of tigers that are believed to be extant (still in existence) in the wild:

- Amur tiger (or Siberian tiger, see Figure 7.10)—eastern Russia and northeastern China

- Bengal tiger—Indian subcontinent

- Northern Indochinese tiger—Indochina north of Malaya

- Malayan tiger—Malayan peninsula

- South China tiger—China

- Sumatran tiger—Sumatra

Wild tigers are found exclusively in Asia, from India to Siberia. Although the world tiger population surpassed 100,000 during the 19th century, experts fear that fewer than 10,000 remained by the turn of the 21st century. Besides habitat loss, countless tigers fall victim to the illegal wildlife trade every year. Many tiger body parts are used as ingredients in traditional Chinese medicine, and the big cats are also prized in the exotic pet industry. In addition, ecologists warn that tigers, which hunt deer, wild pigs, cattle, antelope, and other large mammals, are seriously threatened by the loss of prey, much of which consists of nonprotected species that are being eliminated by hunters. Many tiger populations have also been weakened by inbreeding, which increases the possibility of reproductive problems and birth defects.

TABLE 7.3

Foreign endangered and threatened terrestrial mammal species, November 2013

Common name	Scientific name	Listing status*	Historic range
Addax	Addax nasomaculatus	E	North Africa
African elephant	Loxodonta africana	T	Africa
African wild ass	Equus africanus	E	Somalia, Sudan, Ethiopia
African wild dog	Lycaon pictus	E	Sub-Saharan Africa
Andean cat	Felis jacobita	E	Chile, Peru, Bolivia, Argentina
Apennine chamois	Rupicapra rupicapra ornata	E	Italy
Arabian gazelle	Gazella gazella	E	Arabian Peninsula, Palestine, Sinai
Arabian oryx	Oryx leucoryx	E	Arabian Peninsula
Arabian tahr	Hemitragus jayakari	E	Oman
Argali	Ovis ammon	E; T	Afganistan, China, India, Kazakhstan, Kyrgyzstan, Mongolia, Nepal, Pakistan, Russia, Tajikistan, Uzbekistan
Asian elephant	Elephas maximus	E	South-central and southeastern Asia
Asian golden (=Temmnick's) cat	Catopuma (=Felis) temminckii	E	Nepal, China, Southeast Asia, Indonesia (Sumatra)
Asian tapir	Tapirus indicus	E	Burma, Laos, Cambodia, Vietnam, Malaysia, Indonesia, Thailand
Asian wild ass	Equus hemionus	E	Southwestern and Central Asia
Asiatic lion	Panthera leo persica	E	Turkey to India
Australian native mouse	Notomys aquilo	E	Australia
Australian native mouse	Zyzomys pedunculatus	E	Australia
Avahi	Avahi laniger (entire genus)	E	Malagasy Republic (=Madagascar)
Aye-aye	Daubentonia madagascariensis	E	Malagasy Republic (=Madagascar)
Babirusa	Babyrousa babyrussa	E	Indonesia
Bactrian camel	Camelus bactrianus	E	Mongolia, China
Bactrian deer	Cervus elaphus bactrianus	E	Tajikistan, Uzbekistan, Afghanistan
Baluchistan bear	Ursus thibetanus gedrosianus	E	Iran, Pakistan
Banded hare wallaby	Lagostrophus fasciatus	E	Australia
Banteng	Bos javanicus	E	Southeast Asia
Barbary deer	Cervus elaphus barbarus	E	Morocco, Tunisia, Algeria
Barbary hyena	Hyaena hyaena barbara	E	Morocco, Algeria, Tunisia
Barbary serval	Leptailurus (=Felis) serval constantina	E	Algeria
Barbary stag	Cervus elaphus barbarus	E	Tunisia, Algeria
Barred bandicoot	Perameles bougainville	E	Australia
Beaver (Mongolian)	Castor fiber birulai	E	Mongolia
Black colobus monkey	Colobus satanas	E	Equatorial Guinea, People's Republic of Congo, Cameroon, Gabon
Black-faced impala	Aepyceros melampus petersi	E	Namibia, Angola
Black-footed cat	Felis nigripes	E	Southern Africa
Black howler monkey	Alouatta pigra	T	Mexico, Guatemala, Belize
Black rhinoceros	Diceros bicornis	E	Sub-Saharan Africa
Bontebok	Damaliscus pygarus (=dorcas) dorcas	E	South Africa
Brazilian three-toed sloth	Bradypus torquatus	E	Brazil
Brindled nail-tailed wallaby	Onychogalea fraenata	E	Australia
Brown bear	Ursus arctos arctos	E	Palearctic
Brown bear	Ursus arctos pruinosus	E	China (Tibet)
Brown hyena	Parahyaena (=Hyaena) brunnea	E	Southern Africa
Brush-tailed rat-kangaroo	Bettongia penicillata	E	Australia
Buff-headed marmoset	Callithrix flaviceps	E	Brazil
Bulmer's fruit bat (=flying fox)	Aproteles bulmerae	E	Papua New Guinea
Bumblebee bat	Craseonycteris thonglongyai	E	Thailand
Cabrera's hutia	Capromys angelcabrerai	E	Cuba
Calamianes (=Philippine) deer	Axis porcinus calamianensis	E	Philippines (Calamian Islands)
Capped langur	Trachypithecus (=Presbytis) pileatus	E	India, Burma, Bangladesh
Cedros Island mule deer	Odocoileus hemionus cerrosensis	E	Mexico (Cedros Island)
Central American tapir	Tapirus bairdii	E	Southern Mexico to Colombia and Ecuador
Cheetah	Acinonyx jubatus	E	Africa to India
Chiltan (=wild goat) markhor	Capra falconeri (=aegragrus) chiltanensis	E	Chiltan Range of west-central Pakistan
Chimpanzee	Pan troglodytes	E; T	Africa
Chinchilla	Chinchilla brevicaudata boliviana	E	Bolivia
Clark's gazelle	Ammodorcas clarkei	E	Somalia, Ethiopia
Clouded leopard	Neofelis nebulosa	E	Southeastern and south-central Asia, Taiwan
Corsican red deer	Cervus elaphus corsicanus	E	Corsica, Sardinia
Costa Rican puma	Puma (=Felis) concolor costaricensis	E	Nicaragua, Panama, Costa Rica
Cotton-top marmoset	Saguinus oedipus	E	Costa Rica to Colombia
Crescent nail-tailed wallaby	Onychogalea lunata	E	Australia
Cuban solenodon	Solenodon cubanus	E	Cuba
Dama gazelle	Gazella dama	E	North Africa
Desert bandicoot	Perameles eremiana	E	Australia
Desert (=plain) rat-kangaroo	Caloprymnus campestris	E	Australia
Dhole	Cuon alpinus	E	C.I.S., Korea, China, India, Southeast Asia
Diana monkey	Cercopithecus diana	E	Coastal West Africa
Dibbler	Antechinus apicalis	E	Australia

TABLE 7.3

Foreign endangered and threatened terrestrial mammal species, November 2013 [CONTINUED]

Common name	Scientific name	Listing status*	Historic range
Douc langur	Pygathrix nemaeus	E	Cambodia, Laos, Vietnam
Drill	Mandrillus (=Papio) leucophaeus	E	Equatorial West Africa
Dwarf hutia	Capromys nana	E	Cuba
Eastern jerboa marsupial	Antechinomys laniger	E	Australia
Eastern native-cat	Dasyurus viverrinus	E	Australia
Eld's brow-antlered deer	Cervus eldi	E	India to Southeast Asia
False water rat	Xeromys myoides	E	Australia
Fea's muntjac	Muntiacus feae	E	Northern Thailand, Burma
Field's mouse	Pseudomys fieldi	E	Australia
Flat-headed cat	Prionailurus (=Felis) planiceps	E	Malaysia, Indonesia
Formosan rock macaque	Macaca cyclopis	T	Taiwan
Formosan sika deer	Cervus nippon taiouanus	E	Taiwan
Formosan yellow-throated marten	Martes flavigula chrysospila	E	Taiwan
Francois' langur	Trachypithecus (=Presbytis) francoisi	E	China (Kwangsi), Indochina
Gaimard's rat-kangaroo	Bettongia gaimardi	E	Australia
Gelada baboon	Theropithecus gelada	T	Ethiopia
Giant armadillo	Priodontes maximus	E	Venezuela and Guyana to Argentina
Giant panda	Ailuropoda melanoleuca	E	China
Giant sable antelope	Hippotragus niger varrani	E	Angola
Gibbons	Hylobates spp. (including Nomascus)	E	China, India, Southeast Asia
Goeldi's marmoset	Callimico goeldii	E	Brazil, Colombia, Ecuador, Peru, Bolivia
Golden langur	Trachypithecus (=Presbytis) geei	E	India (Assam), Bhutan
Golden-rumped tamarin	Leontopithecus spp.	E	Brazil
Goral	Naemorhedus goral	E	East Asia
Gorilla	Gorilla gorilla	E	Central and western Africa
Gould's mouse	Pseudomys gouldii	E	Australia
Gray (=entellus) langur	Semnopithecus (=Presbytis) entellus	E	China (Tibet), India, Pakistan, Kashmir, Sri Lanka, Sikkim, Bangladesh
Great Indian rhinoceros	Rhinoceros unicornis	E	India, Nepal
Grevy's zebra	Equus grevyi	T	Kenya, Ethiopia, Somalia
Guatemalan jaguarundi	Herpailurus (=Felis) yagouaroundi fossata	E	Mexico, Nicaragua
Guizhou snub-nosed monkey	Rhinopithecus brelichi	E	China
Haitian solenodon	Solenodon paradoxus	E	Dominican Republic, Haiti
Hartmann's mountain zebra	Equus zebra hartmannae	T	Namibia, Angola
Hispid hare	Caprolagus hispidus	E	India, Nepal, Bhutan
Indochina hog deer	Axis porcinus annamiticus	E	Thailand, Indochina
Indri lemur	Indri indri	E	Malagasy Republic (=Madagascar)
Iriomote cat	Prionailurus (=Felis) bengalensis iriomotensis	E	Japan (Iriomote Island, Ryukyu Islands)
Japanese macaque	Macaca fuscata	T	Japan (Shikoku, Kyushu and Honshu Islands)
Javan rhinoceros	Rhinoceros sondaicus	E	Indonesia, Indochina, Burma, Thailand, Sikkim, Bangladesh, Malaysia
Jentink's duiker	Cephalophus jentinki	E	Sierra Leone, Liberia, Ivory Coast
Kabul markhor	Capra falconeri megaceros	E	Afghanistan, Pakistan
Kashmir stag	Cervus elaphus hanglu	E	Kashmir
Koala	Phascolarctos cinereus	T	Australia
Kouprey	Bos sauveli	E	Vietnam, Laos, Cambodia, Thailand
Kuhl's (=Bawean) deer	Axis porcinus kuhli	E	Indonesia
Large desert marsupial-mouse	Sminthopsis psammophila	E	Australia
Large-eared hutia	Capromys auritus	E	Cuba
Leadbeater's possum	Gymnobelideus leadbeateri	E	Australia
Lemurs	Lemuridae (incl. genera Lemur, Phaner, Hapalemur, Lepilemur, Microcebus, Allocebus, Cheirogaleus, Varecia)	E	Malagasy Republic (=Madagascar)
Leopard	Panthera pardus	E; T	Africa, Asia
Leopard cat	Prionailurus (=Felis) bengalensis bengalensis	E	India, Southeast Asia
Lesser rabbit bandicoot	Macrotis leucura	E	Australia
Lesser slow loris	Nycticebus pygmaeus	T	Indochina
Lesueur's rat-kangaroo	Bettongia lesueur	E	Australia
L'hoest's monkey	Cercopithecus lhoesti	E	Upper eastern Congo R. Basin, Cameroon
Lion-tailed macaque	Macaca silenus	E	India
Little earth hutia	Capromys sanfelipensis	E	Cuba
Little planigale	Planigale ingrami subtilissima	E	Australia
Long-tailed langur	Presbytis potenziani	T	Indonesia
Long-tailed marsupial-mouse	Sminthopsis longicaudata	E	Australia
Lowland anoa	Bubalus depressicornis	E	Indonesia
Malabar large-spotted civet	Viverra civettina (=megaspila c.)	E	India
Mandrill	Mandrillus (=Papio) sphinx	E	Equatorial West Africa
Maned wolf	Chrysocyon brachyurus	E	Argentina, Bolivia, Brazil, Paraguay, Uruguay
Mantled howler monkey	Alouatta palliata	E	Mexico to South America
Marbled cat	Pardofelis (=Felis) marmorata	E	Nepal, Southeast Asia, Indonesia
Margay	Leopardus (=Felis) wiedii	E	U.S.A. (TX), Central and South America
Marsh deer	Blastocerus dichotomus	E	Argentina, Uruguay, Paraguay, Bolivia, Brazil

Common name	Scientific name	Listing status*	Historic range
McNeill's deer	Cervus elaphus macneilii	E	China (Sinkiang, Tibet)
Mexican bobcat	Lynx (=Felis) rufus escuinapae	E	Central Mexico
Mexican grizzly bear	Ursus arctos	E	Holarctic
Mexican prairie dog	Cynomys mexicanus	E	Mexico
Mhorr gazelle	Gazella dama mhorr	E	Morocco
Mongolian saiga (antelope)	Saiga tatarica mongolica	E	Mongolia
Moroccan gazelle	Gazella dorcas massaesyla	E	Morocco, Algeria, Tunisia
Mountain anoa	Bubalus quarlesi	E	Indonesia
Mountain (=Cuvier's) gazelle	Gazella cuvieri	E	Morocco, Algeria, Tunisia
Mountain pygmy possum	Burramys parvus	E	Australia
Mountain tapir	Tapirus pinchaque	E	Colombia, Ecuador and possibly Peru and Venezuela
Mountain zebra	Equus zebra zebra	E	South Africa
Musk deer	Moschus spp. (all species)	E	Central and eastern Asia
New Holland mouse	Pseudomys novaehollandiae	E	Australia
North Andean huemul	Hippocamelus antisensis	E	Ecuador, Peru, Chile, Bolivia, Argentina
North China sika deer	Cervus nippon mandarinus	E	China (Shantung and Chihli Provinces)
Northern swift fox	Vulpes velox hebes	E	U.S.A. (northern plains), Canada
Northern white rhinoceros	Ceratotherium simum cottoni	E	Zaire, Sudan, Uganda, Central African Republic
Numbat	Myrmecobius fasciatus	E	Australia
Orangutan	Pongo pygmaeus	E	Borneo, Sumatra
Pagi Island langur	Nasalis concolor	E	Indonesia
Pakistan sand cat	Felis margarita scheffeli	E	Pakistan
Pampas deer	Ozotoceros bezoarticus	E	Brazil, Argentina, Uruguay, Bolivia, Paraguay
Panamanian jaguarundi	Herpailurus (=Felis) yagouaroundi panamensis	E	Nicaragua, Costa Rica, Panama
Parma wallaby	Macropus parma	E	Australia
Pelzeln's gazelle	Gazella dorcas pelzelni	E	Somalia
Peninsular pronghorn	Antilocapra americana peninsularis	E	Mexico (Baja California)
Persian fallow deer	Dama mesopotamica (=dama m.)	E	Iraq, Iran
Philippine tarsier	Tarsius syrichta	T	Philippines
Pied tamarin	Saguinus bicolor	E	Brazil
Pig-footed bandicoot	Chaeropus ecaudatus	E	Australia
Pink fairy armadillo	Chlamyphorus truncatus	E	Argentina
Preuss' red colobus monkey	Procolobus (=Colobus) preussi (=badius p.)	E	Cameroon
Proboscis monkey	Nasalis larvatus	E	Borneo
Przewalski's horse	Equus przewalskii	E	Mongolia, China
Pudu	Pudu pudu	E	Southern South America
Purple-faced langur	Presbytis senex	T	Sri Lanka
Pygmy chimpanzee	Pan paniscus	E	Zaire
Pygmy hog	Sus salvanius	E	India, Nepal, Bhutan, Sikkim
Pyrenean ibex	Capra pyrenaica pyrenaica	E	Spain
Queensland hairy-nosed wombat (incl. Barnard's)	Lasiorhinus krefftii (formerly L. barnardi and L. gillespiei)	E	Australia
Queensland rat-kangaroo	Bettongia tropica	E	Australia
Quokka	Setonix brachyurus	E	Australia
Rabbit bandicoot	Macrotis lagotis	E	Australia
Red-backed squirrel monkey	Saimiri oerstedii	E	Costa Rica, Panama
Red-bellied monkey	Cercopithecus erythrogaster	E	Western Nigeria
Red-eared nose-spotted monkey	Cercopithecus erythrotis	E	Nigeria, Cameroon, Fernando Po
Red lechwe	Kobus leche	T	Southern Africa
Rio de Oro Dama gazelle	Gazella dama lozanoi	E	Western Sahara
Rodrigues fruit bat (=flying fox)	Pteropus rodricensis	E	Indian Ocean_Rodrigues Island
Ryukyu rabbit	Pentalagus furnessi	E	Japan (Ryukyu Islands)
Ryukyu sika deer	Cervus nippon keramae	E	Japan (Ryukyu Islands)
Sand gazelle	Gazella subgutturosa marica	E	Jordan, Arabian Peninsula
Saudi Arabian gazelle	Gazella dorcas saudiya	E	Israel, Iraq, Jordan, Syria, Arabian Peninsula
Scaly-tailed possum	Wyulda squamicaudata	E	Australia
Scimitar-horned oryx	Oryx dammah	E	North Africa
Seledang	Bos gaurus	E	Bangladesh, Southeast Asia, India
Serow	Naemorhedus (=Capricornis) sumatraensis	E	East Asia, Sumatra
Shansi sika deer	Cervus nippon grassianus	E	China (Shansi Province)
Shapo	Ovis vignei vignei	E	Kashmir
Shark Bay mouse	Pseudomys praeconis	E	Australia
Shortridge's mouse	Pseudomys shortridgei	E	Australia
Shou	Cervus elaphus wallichi	E	Tibet, Bhutan
Siamang	Symphalangus syndactylus	E	Malaysia, Indonesia
Sichuan snub-nosed monkey	Rhinopithecus roxellana	E	China
Sifakas	Propithecus spp.	E	Malagasy Republic (=Madagascar)
Simien fox	Canis simensis	E	Ethiopia
Singapore roundleaf horseshoe bat	Hipposideros ridleyi	E	Malaysia
Slender-horned gazelle	Gazella leptoceros	E	Sudan, Egypt, Algeria, Libya

TABLE 7.3

Foreign endangered and threatened terrestrial mammal species, November 2013 [CONTINUED]

Common name	Scientific name	Listing status*	Historic range
Smoky mouse	Pseudomys fumeus	E	Australia
Snow leopard	Uncia (=Panthera) uncia	E	Central Asia
South American (=Brazilian) tapir	Tapirus terrestris	E	Colombia and Venezuela south to Paraguay and Argentina
South Andean huemul	Hippocamelus bisulcus	E	Chile, Argentina
South China sika deer	Cervus nippon kopschi	E	Southern China
Southern bearded saki	Chiropotes satanas satanas	E	Brazil
Southern planigale	Planigale tenuirostris	E	Australia
Southern white rhinoceros	Ceratotherium simum ssp. simum	SAT	Angola, Botswana, Malawi, Mozambique, Namibia, South Africa, Sudan, Swaziland, and Zimbabwe
Spanish lynx	Felis pardina	E	Spain, Portugal
Spider monkey	Ateles geoffroyi frontatus	E	Costa Rica, Nicaragua
Spider monkey	Ateles geoffroyi panamensis	E	Costa Rica, Panama
Spotted linsang	Prionodon pardicolor	E	Nepal, Assam, Vietnam, Cambodia, Laos, Burma
Stick-nest rat	Leporillus conditor	E	Australia
Straight-horned markhor	Capra falconeri jerdoni	E	Afghanistan, Pakistan
Stump-tailed macaque	Macaca arctoides	T	India (Assam) to southern China
Sumatran rhinoceros	Dicerorhinus sumatrensis	E	Bangladesh to Vietnam to Indonesia (Borneo)
Swamp deer	Cervus duvauceli	E	India, Nepal
Swayne's hartebeest	Alcelaphus buselaphus swaynei	E	Ethiopia, Somalia
Tamaraw	Bubalus mindorensis	E	Philippines
Tana River mangabey	Cercocebus galeritus galeritus	E	Kenya
Tana River red colobus monkey	Procolobus (=Colobus) rufomitratus (=badius r.)	E	Kenya
Tasmanian forester kangaroo	Macropus giganteus tasmaniensis	E	Australia (Tasmania)
Tasmanian tiger	Thylacinus cynocephalus	E	Australia
Temnick's ground pangolin	Manis temminckii	E	Africa
Thin-spined porcupine	Chaetomys subspinosus	E	Brazil
Tibetan antelope	Pantholops hodgsonii	E	China, India, Nepal
Tiger	Panthera tigris	E	Temperate and tropical Asia
Tiger cat	Leopardus (=Felis) tigrinus	E	Costa Rica to northern Argentina
Tonkin snub-nosed monkey	Rhinopithecus avunculus	E	Vietnam
Toque macaque	Macaca sinica	T	Sri Lanka
Tora hartebeest	Alcelaphus buselaphus tora	E	Ethiopia, Sudan, Egypt
Uakari (all species)	Cacajao spp.	E	Peru, Brazil, Ecuador, Colombia, Venezuela
Urial	Ovis musimon ophion	E	Cyprus
Vancouver Island marmot	Marmota vancouverensis	E	Canada (Vancouver Island)
Vicuna	Vicugna vicugna	E	South America (Andes)
Visayan deer	Cervus alfredi	E	Philippines
Volcano rabbit	Romerolagus diazi	E	Mexico
Walia ibex	Capra walie	E	Ethiopia
Western giant eland	Taurotragus derbianus derbianus	E	Senegal to Ivory Coast
Western hare wallaby	Lagorchestes hirsutus	E	Australia
Western mouse	Pseudomys occidentalis	E	Australia
White-collared mangabey	Cercocebus torquatus	E	Senegal to Ghana; Nigeria to Gabon
White-eared (=buffy tufted-ear) marmoset	Callithrix aurita (=jacchus a.)	E	Brazil
White-footed tamarin	Saguinus leucopus	T	Colombia
White-nosed saki	Chiropotes albinasus	E	Brazil
Wild yak	Bos mutus (=grunniens m.)	E	China (Tibet), India
Woolly spider monkey	Brachyteles arachnoides	E	Brazil
Yarkand deer	Cervus elaphus yarkandensis	E	China (Sinkiang)
Yellow-footed rock wallaby	Petrogale xanthopus	E	Australia
Yellow-tailed woolly monkey	Lagothrix flavicauda	E	Andes of northern Peru
Yunnan snub-nosed monkey	Rhinopithecus bieti	E	China
Zanzibar red colobus monkey	Procolobus (=Colobus) pennantii (=kirki) kirki	E	Tanzania
Zanzibar suni	Neotragus moschatus moschatus	E	Zanzibar (and nearby islands)

*E = Endangered; T = Threatened; SAT = Threatened due to similarity of appearance.

SOURCE: Adapted from "Generate Species List," in *Species Reports*, U.S. Department of the Interior, U.S. Fish and Wildlife Service, November 2013, http://ecos.fws.gov/tess_public/pub/adHocSpeciesForm.jsp (accessed November 7, 2013)

Elephants

Elephants are the largest land animals on the earth. They are frequently described as the "architects" of the savanna habitats in which they live. Elephants dig water holes, keep forest growth in check, and open up grasslands that support other species, including the livestock of African herders. Elephants are highly intelligent, emotional animals and form socially complex herds. There are two species of elephants: African elephants and Asian elephants, both of which are highly endangered. The African elephant, which can weigh as much as 6 tons (5.4 tonnes [t]), is the larger species. (See Figure 7.11.)

Elephants have huge protruding teeth (tusks) made of ivory. Ivory is valued by humans for several reasons, particularly for use in making jewelry and figurines. Piano keys were also once made almost exclusively of ivory; however, this practice has ceased. The market for ivory has had tragic consequences for African elephants.

FIGURE 7.10

The Siberian tiger is one of the most endangered species in the world. It now occupies forest habitats in the Amur-Ussuri region of Siberia. ©Henner Damke/Shutterstock.

FIGURE 7.11

Elephants are highly intelligent and social animals. Once on the verge of extinction, elephants have recovered somewhat after a worldwide ban on the ivory trade. ©Four Oaks/Shutterstock.

In "Africa's Environment in Crisis" (November 2002, http://diglib1.amnh.org/articles/Africa/Africa_environment .pdf), Gordy Slack of the American Museum of Natural History states that their numbers dropped from between 5 million and 10 million individuals in 1930 to only 600,000 in 1989. As a result of this decline, the Convention on International Trade in Endangered Species of Wild Fauna and Flora (CITES) banned worldwide commerce in ivory and other elephant products in 1990. However, like rhinoceros horns, elephant tusks continue to be illegally traded. Thousands of African elephants are believed killed every year for their ivory.

Pandas

Few creatures have engendered more human affection than the giant panda, with its roly-poly character, small ears, and black eye patches on a snow-white face. Giant pandas are highly endangered. According to the IUCN (http://www.iucnredlist.org/apps/redlist/details/712/0), there were less than 2,500 adult giant pandas in the wild in 2013. Pandas are endemic to portions of southwestern China, where they inhabit a few fragmentary areas of high-altitude bamboo forest. Unlike other bear species, to which they are closely related, pandas have a vegetarian diet that consists entirely of bamboo.

Pandas have become star attractions at many zoos, where they draw scores of visitors. Zoos typically pay China millions of dollars for the loan of adult pandas. These funds are used to support panda conservation efforts in China, including the purchase of land for refuges as well as the development of habitat corridors to link protected areas.

Big Game

Most big game species are members of the Artiodactyla order. This order contains a variety of ungulates (hoofed animals), including antelopes, bison, buffalo, camels, deer, gazelles, goats, hartebeests, hippopotamuses, impalas, and sheep. Many of the wild species have been overhunted for their meat, bones, or horns. Horns are used in traditional Chinese medicine and are popular trophies for big game hunters. Big game species also face threats from domesticated livestock because of competition for habitat and food resources.

Primates

The endangerment of primate species is mostly due to loss of habitat and overhunting. Primates are dependent on large expanses of tropical forests, a habitat that is under siege worldwide. Countries with large numbers of primate species include Brazil, the Democratic Republic of Congo, Indonesia, and Madagascar. Many of the most endangered primate species are found in Madagascar, which has a diverse and unique primate fauna. Most of Madagascar's primate species are endemic.

Habitat loss, especially the fragmentation and conversion of tropical forests for road building and agriculture, contributes to the decline of nearly all imperiled primates. For example, in Indonesia and Borneo, which are home to most of the world's orangutans, deforestation has dramatically shrunk orangutan habitat. (See Figure 7.12.) Logging and extensive burning have caused many orangutans to flee the forests for villages, where they have been killed or captured by humans.

Some threatened primates face pressures from excessive hunting and poaching. They are also used in medical research because of their close biological relationship with humans. As of 2013, almost all countries had either

FIGURE 7.12

The orangutan is highly endangered, along with the majority of the world's primate species. ©*Eric Gevaert/Shutterstock.*

banned or strictly regulated the trade of primates, but these laws were often hard to enforce.

Rhinoceros

Rhinoceros are among the largest land mammals. They weigh up to 4 tons (3.6 t) and are herbivorous (plant-eating) grazers. The name *rhinoceros* consists of two Greek words meaning "nose" and "horn," and rhinos are in fact the only animals on the earth that have a horn on their nose. Rhinoceros are found in the wild only in Africa and Asia. Figure 7.13 shows an African white rhinoceros with two horns. The female may be identified by her longer, more slender primary horn.

Rhinoceros have roamed the earth for more than 40 million years, but in less than a century humans have reduced their populations to dangerously low levels. Hunting has been the primary cause of rhinoceros decline. Rhinoceros horn is highly prized as an aphrodisiac (although its potency has never been proven), as well as an ingredient in traditional Chinese medicine. Rhinoceros were first listed by CITES in 1976. This listing banned international trade in the species and its products. In 1992 CITES also started requiring the destruction of horn caches that were confiscated from poachers. Nonetheless, people continue to buy and consume rhinoceros horn, and many poachers are willing to risk death to acquire it.

FIGURE 7.13

The white rhinoceros is native to Africa and can weigh up to 8,000 pounds. ©*U.S. Fish and Wildlife Service.*

CHAPTER 8

BIRDS

Birds belong to the class Aves, which contains dozens of orders. Birds are warm-blooded vertebrates with wings, feathers, and light hollow bones. The vast majority of birds are capable of flight. In *Red List of Threatened Species Version 2013.2* (November 2013, http://www.iucnredlist.org/about/summary-statistics), the International Union for Conservation of Nature (IUCN) states that 10,065 species of birds have been identified around the world. An estimated 600 to 900 of these species spend all or part of their life in the United States.

Besides taxonomy, birds are broadly classified by their physical characteristics (such as feet or beak structure), eating habits, primary habitats, or migratory habits. For example, raptors (birds of prey) have curved beaks and talons that are well suited for catching prey. This category includes buzzards, eagles, hawks, owls, and vultures. Perching birds have a unique foot structure with three toes in front and one large flexible toe to the rear. Ducks and geese are known as open-water or swimming birds and have webbed feet. Habitat categories include seabirds, shore birds, and arboreal (tree-dwelling) birds. Some birds migrate over long distances, whereas others, such as turkeys and quail, do not migrate at all.

Birds include a particularly diverse group of species. As such they play a variety of different roles in their ecosystems. In "Ecosystem Services Provided by Birds" (*Annals of the New York Academy of Sciences*, vol. 1134, June 2008), Christopher J. Whelan, Daniel G. Wenny, and Robert J. Marquis note that birds benefit ecosystems by serving as "predators, pollinators, scavengers, seed dispersers, seed predators, and ecosystem engineers." These services also directly or indirectly benefit human society. Many bird species prey on insects that pose a threat to agricultural crops or carry disease. For example, the southwestern willow flycatcher (as its name implies) is a voracious consumer of insects, including mosquitoes.

ENDANGERED AND THREATENED U.S. SPECIES

As of November 2013, there were 94 bird species listed under the Endangered Species Act (ESA) as endangered or threatened in the United States. (See Table 8.1.) As shown in Table 2.11 in Chapter 2, four bird species—dusky seaside sparrow (1990), Guam broadbill (2004), Mariana mallard (2004), and Santa Barbara song sparrow (1983)—have been delisted under the ESA because of extinction. According to the National Park Service in "Island Views" (2007–08, http://www.nps.gov/chis/parknews/upload/2007-2008%20Park%20Newspaper%20for%20web3.pdf), the Santa Barbara song sparrow was decimated by habitat loss and feral cats on the island on which it lived. In "Countdown to Extinction" (NationalGeographic.com, January 2009), Verlyn Klinkenborg indicates the dusky seaside sparrow inhabited the salt marshes of Florida's Merritt Island until the last known individual died in 1987. Its body is preserved at the Florida Museum of Natural History. In "Listing Actions" (http://www.fws.gov/endangered/bulletin/2002/07-08/29-32.pdf), the USFWS notes that the Guam broadbill was lost primarily because of predation by the brown treesnake, an invasive species that was accidentally introduced to the island of Guam after World War II (1939–1945). Another Pacific Island species, the Mariana mallard, went extinct because of habitat loss and overhunting.

The vast majority of the listed species shown in Table 8.1 had an endangered listing as of November 2013, meaning that they are at risk of extinction. Nearly all had a recovery plan in place.

The imperiled birds come from many different genera (plural of genus) and represent a variety of habitats. Most are perching birds, seabirds, or shore birds. There are also a handful of other bird types, including woodpeckers and raptors, such as the northern spotted owl and the Puerto Rican broad-winged hawk.

TABLE 8.1

Endangered and threatened bird species, November 2013

Common name	Scientific name	Listing status[a]	U.S. or U.S./foreign listed	Recovery plan date	Recovery plan stage[b]
`O`u (honeycreeper)	Psittirostra psittacea	E	US	9/22/2006	RF(1)
Akekee	Loxops caeruleirostris	E	US	6/17/2010	O
Akiapola`au (honeycreeper)	Hemignathus munroi	E	US	9/22/2006	RF(1)
Akikiki	Oreomystis bairdi	E	US	6/17/2010	O
Ash-breasted tit-tyrant	Anairetes alpinus	E	US	None	—
Attwater's greater prairie-chicken	Tympanuchus cupido attwateri	E	US	4/26/2010	RF(2)
Audubon's crested caracara	Polyborus plancus audubonii	T	US	5/18/1999	F
Bachman's warbler (=wood)	Vermivora bachmanii	E	US/foreign	None	—
Black-capped vireo	Vireo atricapilla	E	US/foreign	9/30/1991	F
Blue-billed curassow	Crax alberti	E	US	None	—
Bridled white-eye	Zosterops conspicillatus conspicillatus	E	US	9/28/1990	F
Brown-banded antpitta	Grallaria milleri	E	US	None	—
California clapper rail	Rallus longirostris obsoletus	E	US	2/10/2010	D
California condor	Gymnogyps californianus	E; EXPN	US/foreign	4/25/1996	RF(3)
California least tern	Sterna antillarum browni	E	US/foreign	9/27/1985	RF(1)
Cape Sable seaside sparrow	Ammodramus maritimus mirabilis	E	US	5/18/1999	F
Coastal California gnatcatcher	Polioptila californica californica	T	US/foreign	None	—
Crested honeycreeper	Palmeria dolei	E	US	9/22/2006	RF(1)
Eskimo curlew	Numenius borealis	E	US/foreign	None	—
Everglade snail kite	Rostrhamus sociabilis plumbeus	E	US	5/18/1999	F
Florida grasshopper sparrow	Ammodramus savannarum floridanus	E	US	5/18/1999	F
Florida scrub-jay	Aphelocoma coerulescens	T	US	5/9/1990	F
Golden-cheeked warbler (=wood)	Dendroica chrysoparia	E	US/foreign	9/30/1992	F
Guam Micronesian kingfisher	Halcyon cinnamomina cinnamomina	E	US	11/14/2008	RF(1)
Guam rail	Rallus owstoni	E; EXPN	US	9/28/1990	F
Hawaii akepa (honeycreeper)	Loxops coccineus coccineus	E	US	9/22/2006	RF(1)
Hawaii creeper	Oreomystis mana	E	US	9/22/2006	RF(1)
Hawaiian (='alala) crow	Corvus hawaiiensis	E	US	4/17/2009	RF(1)
Hawaiian (=koloa) duck	Anas wyvilliana	E	US	1/19/2012	RF(2)
Hawaiian (='lo) hawk	Buteo solitarius	E	US	5/9/1984	F
Hawaiian common moorhen	Gallinula chloropus sandvicensis	E	US	1/19/2012	RF(2)
Hawaiian coot	Fulica americana alai	E	US	1/19/2012	RF(2)
Hawaiian dark-rumped petrel	Pterodroma phaeopygia sandwichensis	E	US	4/25/1983	F
Hawaiian goose	Branta (=Nesochen) sandvicensis	E	US	9/24/2004	RD(1)
Hawaiian stilt	Himantopus mexicanus knudseni	E	US	1/19/2012	RF(2)
Heinroth's shearwater	Puffinus heinrothi	T	US	None	—
Inyo California towhee	Pipilo crissalis eremophilus	T	US	4/10/1998	F
Ivory-billed woodpecker	Campephilus principalis	E	US/foreign	7/19/2010	F
Kauai `o`o (honeyeater)	Moho braccatus	E	US	9/22/2006	RF(1)
Kauai akialoa (honeycreeper)	Hemignathus procerus	E	US	9/22/2006	RF(1)
Kirtland's warbler	Dendroica kirtlandii	E	US/foreign	9/30/1985	RF(1)
Large Kauai (=kamao) thrush	Myadestes myadestinus	E	US	9/22/2006	RF(1)
Laysan duck	Anas laysanensis	E	US	9/22/2009	RF(1)
Laysan finch (honeycreeper)	Telespyza cantans	E	US	10/4/1984	F
Least Bell's vireo	Vireo bellii pusillus	E	US/foreign	5/6/1998	D
Least tern	Sterna antillarum	E	US	9/19/1990	F
Light-footed clapper rail	Rallus longirostris levipes	E	US	6/24/1985	RF(1)
Marbled murrelet	Brachyramphus marmoratus	T	US	9/24/1997	F
Mariana (=aga) crow	Corvus kubaryi	E	US	1/11/2006	RD(1)
Mariana common moorhen	Gallinula chloropus guami	E	US	9/30/1991	F
Mariana gray swiftlet	Aerodramus vanikorensis bartschi	E	US	9/30/1991	F
Masked bobwhite (quail)	Colinus virginianus ridgwayi	E	US/foreign	4/21/1995	RF(2)
Maui akepa (honeycreeper)	Loxops coccineus ochraceus	E	US	9/22/2006	RF(1)
Maui parrotbill (honeycreeper)	Pseudonestor xanthophrys	E	US	9/22/2006	RF(1)
Mexican spotted owl	Strix occidentalis lucida	T	US/foreign	12/18/2012	RF(1)
Micronesian megapode	Megapodius laperouse	E	US/foreign	4/10/1998	F
Mississippi sandhill crane	Grus canadensis pulla	E	US	9/6/1991	RF(3)
Molokai creeper	Paroreomyza flammea	E	US	9/22/2006	RF(1)
Molokai thrush	Myadestes lanaiensis rutha	E	US	9/22/2006	RF(1)
Newell's Townsend's shearwater	Puffinus auricularis newelli	T	US	4/25/1983	F
Nightingale reed warbler (old world warbler)	Acrocephalus luscinia	E	US	4/10/1998	F
Nihoa finch (honeycreeper)	Telespyza ultima	E	US	10/4/1984	F
Nihoa millerbird (old world warbler)	Acrocephalus familiaris kingi	E	US	10/4/1984	F
northern aplomado falcon	Falco femoralis septentrionalis	E; EXPN	US/foreign	6/8/1990	F
Northern spotted owl	Strix occidentalis caurina	T	US/foreign	7/1/2011	RF(1)
Nukupu`u (honeycreeper)	Hemignathus lucidus	E	US	9/22/2006	RF(1)

TABLE 8.1

Endangered and threatened bird species, November 2013 [CONTINUED]

Common name	Scientific name	Listing status[a]	U.S. or U.S./foreign listed	Recovery plan date	Recovery plan stage[b]
Oahu creeper	Paroreomyza maculata	E	US	9/22/2006	RF(1)
Oahu elepaio	Chasiempis sandwichensis ibidis	E	US	9/22/2006	RF(1)
Palila (honeycreeper)	Loxioides bailleui	E	US	9/22/2006	RF(1)
Piping plover	Charadrius melodus	E; T	US/foreign	5/12/1988	F
Po`ouli (honeycreeper)	Melamprosops phaeosoma	E	US	None	—
Puerto Rican broad-winged hawk	Buteo platypterus brunnescens	E	US	9/8/1997	F
Puerto Rican nightjar	Caprimulgus noctitherus	E	US	4/19/1984	F
Puerto Rican parrot	Amazona vittata	E	US	6/17/2009	RF(1)
Puerto Rican plain pigeon	Columba inornata wetmorei	E	US	10/14/1982	F
Puerto Rican sharp-shinned hawk	Accipiter striatus venator	E	US	9/8/1997	F
Red-cockaded woodpecker	Picoides borealis	E	US	3/20/2003	RF(2)
Roseate tern	Sterna dougallii dougallii	E; T	US/foreign	9/24/1993	F
Rota bridled white-eye	Zosterops rotensis	E	US	10/19/2007	F
San Clemente loggerhead shrike	Lanius ludovicianus mearnsi	E	US	1/26/1984	F
San Clemente sage sparrow	Amphispiza belli clementeae	T	US	1/26/1984	F
Short-tailed albatross	Phoebastria (=Diomedea) albatrus	E	US/foreign	5/20/2009	F
Small Kauai (=puaiohi) thrush	Myadestes palmeri	E	US	9/22/2006	RF(1)
Southwestern willow flycatcher	Empidonax traillii extimus	E	US/foreign	8/30/2002	F
Spectacled eider	Somateria fischeri	T	US/foreign	8/12/1996	F
Steller's eider	Polysticta stelleri	T	US	8/13/2008	F
Streaked horned lark	Eremophila alpestris strigata	T	US	None	—
Thick-billed parrot	Rhynchopsitta pachyrhyncha	E	US/foreign	7/2/2013	F
Western snowy plover	Charadrius alexandrinus nivosus	T	US/foreign	9/24/2007	F
White-necked crow	Corvus leucognaphalus	E	US	None	—
Whooping crane	Grus americana	E; EXPN	US/foreign	5/29/2007	RF(3)
Wood stork	Mycteria americana	E	US	1/27/1997	RF(1)
Yellow-shouldered blackbird	Agelaius xanthomus	E	US	11/12/1996	RF(1)
Yuma clapper rail	Rallus longirostris yumanensis	E	US	2/10/2010	RD(1)

[a]E = Endangered; T = Threatened; EXPN = Experimental population, non-essential.
[b]F = Final; D = Draft; RD = Draft revision; RF = Final revision; O = Other.

SOURCE: Adapted from "Generate Species List," in *Species Reports*, U.S. Department of the Interior, U.S. Fish and Wildlife Service, November 2013, http://ecos.fws.gov/tess_public/pub/adHocSpeciesForm.jsp (accessed November 7, 2013), and "Listed FWS/Joint FWS and NMFS Species and Populations with Recovery Plans (Sorted by Listed Entity)," in *Recovery Plans Search*, U.S. Department of the Interior, U.S. Fish and Wildlife Service, November 2013, http://ecos.fws.gov/tess_public/pub/speciesRecovery.jsp?sort=1 (accessed November 7, 2013)

Table 8.2 shows the 10 bird species with the highest expenditures under the ESA during fiscal year (FY) 2012. The three most expensive species were the red-cockaded woodpecker ($37.9 million), northern spotted owl ($20.5 million), and southwestern willow flycatcher ($16.8 million).

The following sections describe the categories of birds that are found on the list of endangered and threatened species.

Woodpeckers

Woodpeckers belong to the order Piciformes and the family Picidae. They are characterized by their physiology. They have hard chisel-like beaks and a unique foot structure with two toes pointing forward and two toes pointing backward. This allows them to take a firm grip on tree trunks and extend horizontally from vertical surfaces. Woodpeckers prefer arboreal habitats, primarily dead trees in old-growth forests. The birds hammer away at the bark on the trees to dig out insects living there. They often form deep cavities in the tree to use as roosting and nesting holes.

RED-COCKADED WOODPECKERS. The red-cockaded woodpecker is named for the red patches, or cockades,

TABLE 8.2

Bird species with the highest expenditures under the Endangered Species Act, fiscal year 2012

Ranking	Species	Expenditure
1	Woodpecker, red-cockaded (Picoides borealis)	$37,900,480
2	Owl, northern spotted (Strix occidentalis caurina)	$20,465,308
3	Flycatcher, southwestern willow (Empidonax traillii extimus)	$16,841,162
4	Plover, piping (Charadrius melodus)	$12,648,485
5	Tern, least (Sterna antillarum)	$9,969,552
6	Murrelet, marbled (Brachyramphus marmoratus)	$7,322,553
7	Stork, wood (Mycteria americana)	$6,872,943
8	Rail, Yuma clapper (Rallus longirostris yumanensis)	$4,386,407
9	Crane, whooping (Grus americana)	$4,319,966
10	Plover, western snowy (Charadrius alexandrinus nivosus)	$3,983,469

SOURCE: Adapted from "Table 2. Species Ranked in Descending Order of Total FY2012 Reported Expenditures, Not Including Land Acquisition Costs," in *Federal and State Endangered and Threatened Species Expenditures: Fiscal Year 2012*, U.S. Department of the Interior, U.S. Fish and Wildlife Service, 2012, http://www.fws.gov/endangered/esa-library/pdf/2012.EXP.FINAL.pdf (accessed November 4, 2013)

of feathers on the head of the male. (See Figure 8.1.) This species is found in old pine forests in the southeastern United States, where family groups (consisting of a

FIGURE 8.1

Red-cockaded woodpecker

SOURCE: Robert Savannah, artist, "Red Cockaded Woodpeckers," in *Line Art (Drawings)*, U.S. Department of the Interior, U.S. Fish and Wildlife Service, undated, http://www.fws.gov/pictures/lineart/bobsavannah/redcockadedwoodpeckers.html (accessed November 12, 2013)

breeding male and female as well as several helpers) nest within self-dug cavities in pine trees. Tree cavities serve as nesting sites and provide protection from predators. Because red-cockaded woodpeckers rarely nest in trees less than 80 years old, heavy logging has destroyed much of their former habitat.

The red-cockaded woodpecker is considered a keystone species, which as explained in chapter 1, means that other species are highly dependent on it, and its loss would have severe negative impacts on them. In "The Red-Cockaded Woodpecker's Role in the Southern Pine Ecosystem, Population Trends and Relationships with Southern Pine Beetles (August 1997, http://www.srs.fs.usda.gov/pubs/ja/ja_conners014.pdf), Richard N. Conner et al. of Texas A&M University, note that dozens of other species use the bird's cavities and conclude, "Because of the dependence of many other cavity nesters on Red-cockaded Woodpecker cavities, forest biodiversity would suffer substantially in the absence of this endangered woodpecker in southern pine ecosystems."

The red-cockaded woodpecker was first listed under the ESA in 1970. It is currently found in fragmented populations in the southeastern seaboard westward into Texas. As of February 2014, its most recent recovery plan was published in 2003. (See Table 8.1.)

In *Red-Cockaded Woodpecker (*Picoides borealis*): Five-Year Review—Summary and Evaluation* (October 2006, http://ecos.fws.gov/docs/five_year_review/doc787.pdf), the USFWS concludes that the endangered status listing is still appropriate for the species. The agency reports that over 6,000 active clusters (occupied territories) of the bird have been documented, up from about 4,700 active clusters reported during the early 1990s. However, the USFWS believes the bird still faces significant threats from the loss, degradation, and fragmentation of nesting and foraging habitat.

The USFWS indicates in "Red-Cockaded Woodpecker (*Picoides borealis*)" (2013, http://ecos.fws.gov/speciesProfile/profile/speciesProfile.action?spcode=B04F) that critical habitat has not been designated for the red-cockaded woodpecker. However, eight states (Alabama, Florida, Georgia, Louisiana, North Carolina, South Carolina, Texas, and Virginia) have established statewide Safe Harbor Agreements with the USFWS. These are voluntary agreements in which nonfederal landowners agree to conserve and manage listed species on their property. In exchange, the federal government provides assurances that it will not impose certain restrictions on the conservation activities. For example, if a landowner improves or expands red-cockaded woodpecker habitat and more of the birds move into the habitat, the landowner will not face increased regulatory requirements.

Passerines

Just over half of all bird species belong to the order Passeriformes and are called passerines. They are informally known as perching birds or songbirds, although not all passerines are truly songbirds. This order includes many well-known species, such as blackbirds, cardinals, crows, finches, larks, mockingbirds, sparrows, starlings, swallows, and wrens. Over one-third of the U.S. species of endangered and threatened birds listed in Table 8.1 are passerine (perching) birds. The following sections describe some species of note.

SOUTHWESTERN WILLOW FLYCATCHERS. As shown in Table 8.2, in FY 2012 over $16.8 million was spent under the ESA to conserve the southwestern willow flycatcher. (See Figure 8.2.) This small bird has a grayish-green back and wings with a pale yellow belly and a white-colored throat. The bird feeds on insects and prefers riparian areas (dense vegetation near rivers or streams) for its habitat. According to the Arizona Game and Fish Department in "Wild Kids" (June 2002, http://www.azgfd.gov/i_e/ee/resources/wild_kids/endangered46.pdf), the bird's scientific name (*Empidonax traillii extimus*) means "mosquito king."

The species was first listed as endangered in 1995. In August 2002 the USFWS published *Final Recovery Plan: Southwestern Willow Flycatcher (*Empidonax

FIGURE 8.2

Southwestern willow flycatcher

SOURCE: "Southwestern Willow Flycatcher," in *Songbirds: A Colorful Chorus*, U.S. Department of the Interior, U.S. Fish and Wildlife Service, January 2002, http://www.fws.gov/birds/songbird-fact-sheet.pdf (accessed November 11, 2013)

traillii extimus) (http://ecos.fws.gov/docs/recovery_plans/ 2002/020830c.pdf). At that time the agency reported that approximately 900 to 1,100 pairs of the bird were believed to exist. The species migrates from the southwestern United States to Mexico and Central and South America for the winter. It is endangered primarily because of the loss of riparian vegetation. In ranching areas this vegetation is often stripped by grazing livestock. Another factor in its decline is harm from brood parasites (bird species that lay their eggs in the nests of other species). Brown-headed cowbirds are brood parasites that threaten southwestern willow flycatchers. They lay their eggs in the flycatchers' nests, and the unsuspecting flycatchers raise the cowbirds' young as their own.

Since 1997 the USFWS has repeatedly designated and revised critical habitat for the southwestern willow flycatcher in response to litigation. In January 2013 the agency (http://www.gpo.gov/fdsys/pkg/FR-2013-01-03/pdf/ 2012-30634.pdf) designated 1,227 stream miles (1,975 stream kilometers [km]) in Arizona, California, Colorado, Nevada, New Mexico, and Utah.

In 2008 the USFWS launched a five-year status review of more than two dozen southwestern species, including the southwestern willow flycatcher. As of February 2014, the results of that review had not been published.

HAWAIIAN HONEYCREEPERS. Hawaiian honeycreepers are a group of songbirds endemic (limited) to Hawaii. The honeycreepers are named for the characteristic creeping behavior some species exhibit as they search for nectar.

Hawaiian honeycreepers are extremely diverse in their diet; different species are insect, nectar, or seed eaters. (The nectar-consuming honeycreepers are particularly valued for their role in pollinating flowering plants.) Species also differ in the shapes of their beaks and in plumage coloration. The birds are found in forest habitats at high elevations.

As of February 2014, 13 species of Hawaiian honeycreepers were listed under the ESA as endangered:

- Akekee
- Akiapola'au
- Crested honeycreeper
- Hawaii akepa
- Kauai akialoa
- Laysan finch
- Maui akepa
- Maui parrotbill
- Nihoa finch
- Nukupu'u
- 'O'u
- Palila
- Po'ouli

Some honeycreeper species are among the most endangered animals on the earth, with only a few individuals left. One of the primary factors involved in honeycreeper endangerment is loss of habitat. In addition, the introduction of predators that hunt birds or eat their eggs, such as cats, mongooses, and rats, have contributed to the decline of many species. The introduction of bird diseases, particularly those spread by introduced mosquitoes, has decimated honeycreeper populations. Finally, competition with introduced bird species for food and habitat has also been a significant cause of decline.

In *Revised Recovery Plan for Hawaiian Forest Birds* (September 22, 2006, http://ecos.fws.gov/docs/recovery _plan/060922a.pdf), the USFWS covers 19 endangered Hawaiian forest birds. The agency reports that 10 of these species have not been observed in at least a decade and may well be extinct. Most of these species are native to rain forests at elevations above 4,000 feet (1,200 meters [m]) on the islands of Hawaii (Big Island), Kauai, and Maui. Major threats to endangered forest species include habitat loss and modification, other human activity, disease, and predation. Of particular importance are nonnative plants, which have converted native plant communities to alien ecosystems that are unsuitable as habitat.

MIGRATORY SONGBIRDS. In the fact sheet "Neotropical Migratory Bird Basics" (2012, http://nationalzoo

.si.edu/scbi/migratorybirds/fact_sheets/default.cfm?id=9), Mary Deinlein of the Smithsonian Migratory Bird Center states that there are nearly 200 species of songbirds known as neotropical migrators. Every year these birds migrate between the United States and tropical areas in Mexico, the Caribbean, and Central and South America. Even though some songbirds are appreciated by humans for their beautiful songs and colorful plumage, migratory songbirds also play a vital role in many ecosystems. For example, during spring migration in the Ozarks, dozens of migratory bird species arrive and feed on the insects that inhabit oak trees, thereby helping control insect populations.

Migratory species are particularly vulnerable because they are dependent on suitable habitat in both their winter and spring ranges. In North America, land development has eliminated many forest habitats. Migratory songbird habitats are also jeopardized in Central and South America, where farmers and ranchers have been burning and clearing tropical forests to plant crops and graze livestock. Some countries, including Belize, Costa Rica, Guatemala, and Mexico, have set up preserves for songbirds, but improved forest management is needed to save them.

Raptors

The term *raptor* is derived from the Latin word *raptores*, which was once the order on the taxonomy table to which birds of prey were assigned. Eventually, scientists split the birds into three orders:

- Accipitriformes—buzzards, eagles, and hawks
- Falconiformes—falcons
- Strigiformes—owls

As of November 2013, there were less than a dozen raptors listed as endangered or threatened in the United States. (See Table 8.1.) Species of note include the northern spotted owl and the California condor.

NORTHERN SPOTTED OWLS. The northern spotted owl occupies old-growth forests in the Pacific Northwest, where it nests in the cavities of trees 200 years old or older. (See Figure 8.3.) The bird is called an indicator species, because its well-being is indicative of the overall well-being of the forests in which it lives. Its populations have declined primarily because of habitat loss. Most of the private lands in its range have been heavily logged, leaving only public lands, such as national forests and national parks, for habitat. In 1990 the northern spotted owl was listed under the ESA. Court battles began over continued logging in national forest habitats.

In 1992 the USFWS set aside 7 million acres (2.8 million hectares [ha]) as critical habitat for the species and published a recovery plan. Two years later the Northwest

FIGURE 8.3

The northern spotted owl, which inhabits old-growth forests in the Pacific Northwest, was the subject of a lengthy battle pitting environmentalists against logging interests. ©*U.S. Fish and Wildlife Service.*

Forest Plan (http://www.fs.fed.us/r5/nwfp/) was established. It reduced logging in 13 national forests by about 85% to protect northern spotted owl habitats. However, populations of the northern spotted owl continued to decline, this despite the unanticipated discovery of 50 pairs of nesting adults in California's Marin County, just north of the Golden Gate Bridge.

In November 2004 the USFWS published *Northern Spotted Owl: Five-Year Review—Summary and Evaluation* (http://ecos.fws.gov/docs/five_year_review/doc743 .pdf). The review was conducted as part of a settlement agreement for litigation that was filed by the American Forest Resource Council, the Rough & Ready Lumber Company, Swanson Group Inc., and the Western Council of Industrial Workers. The agency concluded that the bird should continue to have a threatened listing under the ESA. The USFWS found that habitat loss on federal lands had been minimized after the species was listed. This success was attributed to the Northwest Forest Plan.

However, the agency noted that the population of northern spotted owls in California, Oregon, and Washington continued to decline and that the species faced emerging threats from forest fires, West Nile virus, Sudden Oak Death (a plant disease that has killed hundreds of thousands of trees in California and Oregon), and competition for habitat from barred owls.

The settlement agreement also required the USFWS to review critical habitat based on economic impacts. In August 2008 the USFWS (http://frwebgate.access.gpo.gov/cgi-bin/getdoc.cgi?dbname=2008_register&docid=fr13au08-17) designated revised critical habitat that covered approximately 5.3 million acres (2.1 million ha) of federal lands in California, Oregon, and Washington. This represented nearly 1.6 million acres (647,000 ha) less than were originally designated in 1992. In November 2012 the agency (http://www.fws.gov/oregonfwo/species/data/NorthernSpottedOwl/Documents/11-21-12_NSO_PressRelease.pdf) revised critical habitat again to include 9.3 million acres (3.8 million ha) of federal lands and nearly 300,000 acres (121,406 acres) on state lands.

In October 2011 the USFWS (http://www.fws.gov/pacific/ecoservices/endangered/recovery/documents/NSO5-YrReview-R8SignedCopy10-26-2011.pdf) published the results of a five-year review for the northern spotted owl. The agency notes that data collected between 2006 and 2011 indicate the species population continued to decline at a rate of 2.7% per year. The decrease was blamed on habitat loss and the presence of barred owls which compete for habitat.

In June 2011 the USFWS issued *Revised Recovery Plan for the Northern Spotted Owl (*Strix occidentalis caurina*)* (http://ecos.fws.gov/docs/recovery_plan/RevisedNSORecPlan2011_1.pdf). Figure 8.4 shows the bird's current range divided into 12 physiographic provinces based on physical and environmental features. The agency indicates that competition from the barred owl is the most important threat facing the spotted owl. Other threats include ongoing habitat losses due to logging, wildfires, and other disturbances and lost habitat due to past actions. The USFWS estimates that at least $127.1 million will be required to fund recovery efforts over the next 30 years.

CALIFORNIA CONDORS. The California condor has a wingspan of more than 9 feet (2.7 m) and is among the continent's most impressive birds. Ten thousand years ago this species soared over most of North America. However, its range contracted at the end of the Ice Age, and eventually it was found only along the Pacific coast. Like other vulture species, the California condor is a carrion eater and feeds on the carcasses of deer, sheep, and smaller species such as rodents. Random shooting, egg collection, poisoning (particularly from lead in bullets used by hunters to kill game), and loss of habitat devastated the condor population. The species was listed as endangered in 1967. (See Table 2.1 in Chapter 2.) In the press release "California Condor Chick Takes Flight in Southern California" (AmericanCityandCounty.com, November 29, 2006), the USFWS states that by late 1984 only 15 condors remained in the wild. After seven of these birds died, the agency decided to capture the remaining population.

An intense captive breeding program for the California condor was initiated in 1987. (See Figure 8.5.) The breeding program was successful enough that California condors were released into the wild beginning in 1992. The introduced birds in parts of Arizona, Nevada, and Utah were designated a nonessential experimental population. (Nonessential experimental populations are not believed essential to the survival of a species as whole. Thus, they receive less rigorous protections under the ESA.) In March 2012 the USFWS announced in the press release "John McCamman, Former Director of California Department of Fish and Game, Named California Condor Recovery Coordinator" (March 21, 2012, http://www.fws.gov/cno/press/release.cfm?rid=372) that 217 of the birds were living in the wild.

Water Birds

Water birds live in and around bodies of water. Some prefer marine (ocean) habitats, and others are found only near freshwater. Many species inhabit swamps, marshes, and wetlands. These areas may be inland or intertidal (along the sea coast).

As of November 2013, there were more than two dozen water birds listed as endangered or threatened in the United States. (See Table 8.1.) They include a variety of species from many different taxonomic orders.

MIGRATORY SHORE BIRDS. Migratory shore birds are found most often in marshes, mudflats, estuaries, and other wetland areas where the sea meets freshwater. This category includes avocets, oystercatchers, plovers, sandpipers, shearwaters, snipes, and stilts. These birds vary greatly in size and color, but nearly all migrate over long distances. Most of them breed near the North Pole during the spring and spend their winters anywhere from the southern United States to South America. During their migrations the birds stop to rest and feed at specific locations, known as staging areas, in the United States. Major staging areas include Cheyenne Bottoms in Kansas, the Copper River delta in Alaska, Delaware Bay, the Great Salt Lake in Utah, and San Francisco Bay. The birds eat insect larvae (including mosquito larvae), leeches, worms, and aquatic invertebrates.

The piping plover is an imperiled migratory shorebird first listed under the ESA in 1985. The USFWS recognizes three distinct populations of the species. (See Figure 8.6.) As of February 2014, the Great Lakes

FIGURE 8.4

Range of the spotted owl

Physiographic Provinces

Olympic
Peninsula

Seattle

WA

Olympia

Western
Washington
Lowlands

Western
Washington
Cascades

Eastern
Washington
Cascades

Portland

Williamette
Valley

Salem

Newport

Oregon
Coast
Range

Bend

OR

Western
Oregon
Cascades

Eastern
Oregon
Cascades

Roseburg

Oregon
Klamath

N

W   E

S

Yreka

California
Klamath

California
Cascades

Arcata

NV

CA

Kilometers

0   50   100   150   200

0   50   100   150

Miles

California
Coast

Sacramento

San Francisco

SOURCE: "Figure A-1. Physiographic Provinces within the Range of the Spotted Owl in the United States," in *Revised Recovery Plan for the Northern Spotted Owl (Strix occidentalis caurina)*, U.S. Department of the Interior, U.S. Fish and Wildlife Service, June 28, 2011, http://www.fws.gov/arcata/es/birds/NSO/documents/USFWS2011RevisedRecoveryPlanNorthernSpottedOwl.pdf (accessed November 12, 2013)

FIGURE 8.5

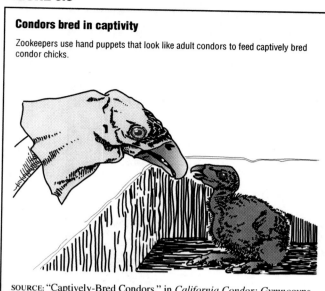

Condors bred in captivity

Zookeepers use hand puppets that look like adult condors to feed captively bred condor chicks.

SOURCE: "Captively-Bred Condors," in *California Condor: Gymnogyps californianus*, U.S. Fish and Wildlife Service, August 1998, http://digitalmedia.fws.gov/cdm/ref/collection/document/id/197 (accessed November 12, 2013)

population was listed as endangered. Piping plovers in the rest of the United States, including the northern Great Plains population and the Atlantic coast population, were listed as threatened. The birds breed and raise their young in northern areas during the spring and summer and migrate to the south Atlantic coast, the Gulf coast, and the Caribbean and Mexican coasts for the winter. As shown in Table 8.2, approximately $12.6 million was spent under the ESA during FY 2012 on the species. Recovery plans have been published for all three populations.

In September 2009 the USFWS published *Piping Plover (*Charadrius melodus*): 5-Year Review—Summary and Evaluation* (http://ecos.fws.gov/docs/five_year_review/doc3009.pdf) and concluded that no changes were warranted to its listings under the ESA. The agency noted that the endangered Great Lakes population contained only 63 breeding pairs, which was well below the recovery goal of 150 breeding pairs. The USFWS also indicated that all three populations face continuing threats to their survival from development of coastal lands in their breeding and wintering habitats.

Another imperiled migratory shorebird is the least tern. (See Figure 8.7.) The least tern is the smallest member of the gull and tern family. According to the Texas Parks and Wildlife Department in "Interior Least Tern (*Sterna antillarum athalassos*)" (2013, http://www.tpwd.state.tx.us/huntwild/wild/species/leasttern/), there are three North American populations of the least tern. An Atlantic coast population is not listed under the ESA. As of February 2014, the California least tern and what is

known as the interior population were listed as endangered. The latter is distributed throughout the nation's midsection from Montana to Texas and as far east as Tennessee. As shown in Table 8.2, in FY 2012 nearly $10 million was spent under the ESA on the least tern. In 2013 the USFWS (http://www.fws.gov/southeast/5year Reviews/5yearreviews/interiorLeastTern5yrReivew102413 .pdf) published a five-year status review for the interior least tern. The agency notes that the population is "biologically recovered." However, before officially recommending the bird for delisting the USFWS plans to confirm its assessment using computer modeling, obtain conservation agreements with other stakeholders (such as the states), and prepare a range-wide monitoring strategy and plan. As of February 2014, the interior least tern had not been proposed for delisting.

SEABIRDS. Seabirds spend most of their time out at sea, but they nest on land. They are also known as pelagic birds because pelagic means oceanic (associated with the open seas). Seabird species include albatrosses, auks and auklets, cormorants, gulls, kittiwakes, murres and murrelets, petrels, penguins, and puffins.

The marbled murrelet is one of a handful of seabirds listed under the ESA. The bird was first listed under the ESA in 1992; as of February 2014, it was designated as threatened in California, Oregon, and Washington. The marbled murrelet is about 9 inches (23 centimeters) long and has a distinctive two-tone pattern of light and dark markings. (See Figure 8.8.) The species prefers to nest in the trees of old-growth forests along the northwest Pacific coastline. Logging and other types of habitat degradation have resulted in population declines.

In June 2009 the USFWS published *Marbled Murrelet (*Brachyramphus marmoratus*): 5-Year Review* (http://ecos.fws.gov/docs/five_year_review/doc2417.pdf). The agency concluded that the marbled murrelet should retain its listing as threatened. However, the USFWS noted deep concern about "the apparent substantial downward trend of the population and the species' continued vulnerability from a broad range of threats" and indicated that "a change in listing status to endangered may be warranted in the future."

The USFWS received a petition from the American Forest Resource Council, the Carpenters Industrial Council of Douglas County, Oregon, and Ron Stuntzner (the founder of Stuntzner Engineering and Forestry) requesting that the California/Oregon/Washington distinct population segment (a distinct population of a species that is capable of interbreeding and lives in a specific geographic area) be delisted. After finding the request to be warranted, the agency initiated a status review. In January 2010 the USFWS (http://www.gpo.gov/fdsys/pkg/FR-2010-01-21/pdf/2010-951.pdf#page=1) declined to delist the bird because it "continues to be subject to a

FIGURE 8.6

Range of the piping plover

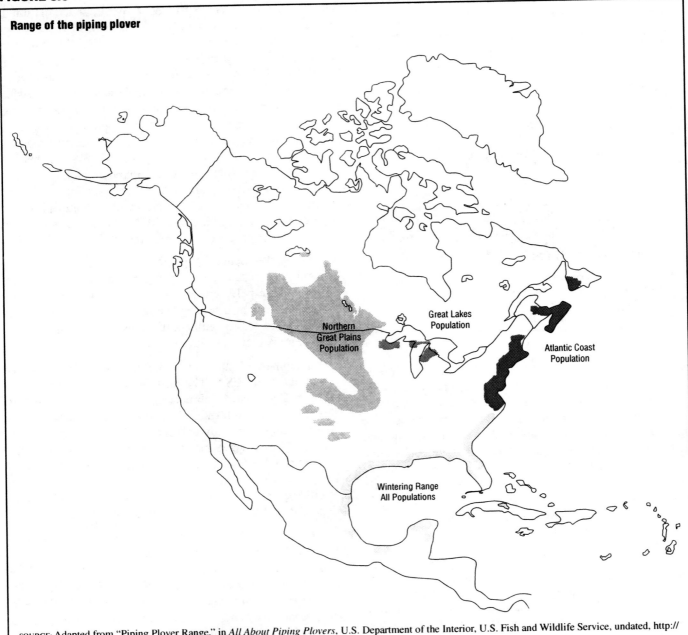

Northern
Great Plains
Population

Great Lakes
Population

Atlantic Coast
Population

Wintering Range
All Populations

SOURCE: Adapted from "Piping Plover Range," in *All About Piping Plovers*, U.S. Department of the Interior, U.S. Fish and Wildlife Service, undated, http://www.fws.gov/plover/piplchmaps/NA_range.gif (accessed November 12, 2013)

broad range of threats, such as nesting habitat loss, habitat fragmentation, and predation." The agency noted that even though some threats have been reduced since the species was first listed, new threats have arisen, such as becoming entangled in abandoned fishing gear and being harmed by algal blooms and declining quality of marine prey. As of February 2014, the agency maintained a threatened listing for the bird.

WADING BIRDS. Wading birds are unusual birds characterized by long skinny legs and extended necks and beaks. They wade in shallow waters of swamps, wetlands, and bays, where they feed on aquatic life forms.

Wading birds include species of crane, egret, ibis, and stork. As of February 2014, three wading birds of note were listed under the ESA: the wood stork, the whooping crane, and the Mississippi sandhill crane.

The wood stork weighs about 5 pounds (2.3 kilograms) and stands up to 3 feet (0.9 m) tall with a 5-foot (1.5-m) wingspan. At one time tens of thousands of the birds inhabited the southeastern coastline. In 1984 the species was listed under the ESA as endangered in Alabama, Florida, Georgia, and South Carolina. A recovery plan for the bird was published in 1999. At that time about 5,000 breeding pairs lived in the wild. Throughout

FIGURE 8.7

Least tern

SOURCE: Laurel Ovitt, artist, "Untitled," in *Threatened and Endangered Species: Least Tern Sterna antillarum Fact Sheet*, U.S. Department of Agriculture Natural Resources Conservation Service, November 2005, http://efotg.nrcs.usda.gov/references/public/MT/LeastTern.pdf (accessed November 12, 2013)

FIGURE 8.8

Marbled murrelet. ©*Encyclopaedia Britannica/Universal Images Group Limited/Alamy.*

the first decade of the 21st century populations declined in the Everglades in southern Florida, but increased in coastal areas farther north. In September 2010 the USFWS (http://www.gpo.gov/fdsys/pkg/FR-2010-09-21/pdf/2010-23138.pdf#page=1) published a 90-day finding on a petition to reclassify the wood stork from endangered to threatened. The petition was submitted by the Pacific Legal Foundation on behalf of the Florida Homebuilders Association. In December 2012 the USFWS (http://www.fws.gov/northflorida/woodstorks/2009_Petition/12-Month_Finding/20121226_frn_woodstork_p_reclassification_rule.pdf) officially proposed downlisting the wood stork to threatened status. As of February 2014, however, the change had not been finalized.

Standing 5 feet (1.5 m) tall, the whooping crane is North America's tallest bird and among the best-known endangered species in the United States. (See Figure 8.9.)

FIGURE 8.9

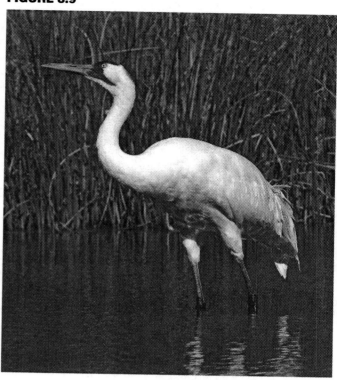

The whooping crane is highly endangered. Each year whooping cranes migrate from breeding grounds in Canada to wintering grounds in south Texas. ©*Al Mueller/Shutterstock.*

Its name comes from its loud and distinctive call, which can be heard for miles. Historically, whooping cranes lived in the Great Plains and along the southeastern coast of the United States. The birds were once heavily hunted for their meat as well as for their beautiful, long white feathers. In addition, the heavy loss of wetland areas in the United States deprived whooping cranes of much of their original habitat. In 1937 it was discovered that fewer than 20 whooping cranes were left in the wild in two small populations: a migratory population that nested in Canada and wintered on the Texas coast and a nonmigratory population that lived in Louisiana.

Every fall the migratory whooping cranes fly 2,500 miles (4,000 km) from nesting grounds in Wood Buffalo National Park in Canada, to Aransas, Texas, for the winter before returning north during the spring to breed. Whooping cranes return to the same nesting site each year with the same mate. In 1937 the Aransas National Wildlife Refuge was established in southern Texas to protect the species' wintering habitat. Conservation efforts for the whooping crane are coordinated with the Canadian government, which manages the birds' breeding areas.

As of February 2014, the whooping crane was listed under the ESA as endangered in Colorado, Kansas, Montana, Nebraska, North Dakota, Oklahoma, South Dakota, and Texas. Since 1993 three nonessential experimental populations have been designated in dozens of states from Wyoming to Florida. In 2001 the first introduced cranes in Wisconsin were led to their Florida wintering grounds along the migration route by ultralight aircraft. Ever since, the birds have been successfully migrating between their nesting and wintering grounds.

The Mississippi sandhill crane is a gray-colored bird that is about 4 feet (1.2 m) tall when standing upright. (See Figure 8.10.) It was first listed as endangered under the ESA in 1973. In September 1991 the USFWS (http://ecos.fws.gov/docs/recovery_plan/910906.pdf) published a recovery plan for the bird. At that time the species was in critical danger of becoming extinct with only one population existing in a small area of Jackson County, Mississippi. The bird was imperiled because of loss and degradation of its pine savanna habitat and reproductive isolation from other sandhill crane subspecies. The USFWS operates a captive breeding program at its Mississippi Sandhill Crane National Wildlife Refuge in Gautier, Mississippi. According to the agency (http://www.fws.gov/refuges/profiles/index.cfm?id=43615), as of 2014 the refuge was home to 110 to 130 of the birds, up from only 30 to 35 individuals reported during the 1970s.

OTHER BIRDS. Other types of birds listed under the ESA include nonmigratory shore birds, such as the California clapper rail and the Guam rail (a flightless bird); swimming birds, including coots, ducks, eiders, and geese; and ground-dwelling birds, such as the prairie chicken.

FIGURE 8.10

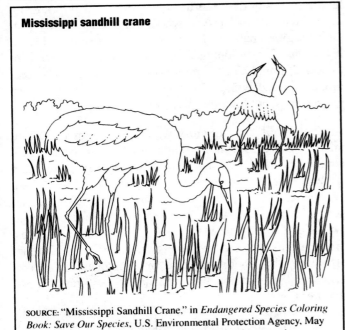

Mississippi sandhill crane

SOURCE: "Mississippi Sandhill Crane," in *Endangered Species Coloring Book: Save Our Species*, U.S. Environmental Protection Agency, May 2008, http://www.epa.gov/espp/coloring/cbook.pdf (accessed November 12, 2013)

GENERAL THREATS TO IMPERILED U.S. BIRD SPECIES

The driving force behind current declines in most imperiled bird species in the United States is the destruction, degradation, and fragmentation of habitat due to increasing human population size and consumption of resources. For example, natural habitats are lost because of agriculture, urban sprawl and other development, logging, mining, and road building. Other general threats include chemical contaminants, such as pesticides and oil, that are released to the environment and invasive species that prey on imperiled birds or compete with them for food and resources.

Pesticides

During the latter half of the 20th century pesticides and other toxic chemicals were recognized as a major cause of avian mortality and a primary factor in the endangerment of several species, including the bald eagle and the peregrine falcon. Many harmful pesticides, such as dichlorodiphenyltrichloroethane (DDT) and toxaphene, have been banned. The U.S. Environmental Protection Agency (EPA) evaluates the potential risks of pesticides to listed species and any designated critical habitat through a process called an "effects determination." The EPA (http://www.epa.gov/oppfead1/endanger/litstatus/effects/) has published the results of dozens of effects determinations on hundreds of imperiled species.

Oil

Another threat to imperiled birds is oil. During the 1970s and 1980s oil spills from seagoing tanker ships were a major environmental problem for coastal birds and seabirds. Birds coming into contact with spilled oil often died immediately, either from losing the insulation of their feathers or by ingesting lethal amounts of oil when they tried to clean themselves. (See Figure 8.11.) According to the Exxon Valdez Oil Spill Trustee Council (2013, http://www.evostc.state.ak.us/facts/qanda.cfm), the worst oil tanker spill in U.S. waters occurred on March 24, 1989, when the *Exxon Valdez* tanker released approximately 257,000 barrels of crude oil into Alaska's Prince William Sound. Hundreds of thousands of seabirds are estimated to have died as a result of the accident. Ever since, large-volume oil tanker spills have become much less common because of strict international regulation of oil tankers.

In April 2010 the largest oil spill in U.S. history occurred when an explosion on the Deepwater Horizon, an offshore drilling platform in the Gulf of Mexico, released nearly 5 million barrels of oil. The drilling platform was leased by the BP (formerly British Petroleum) oil company and located approximately 41 miles (66 km) off the coast of Louisiana. The oil spill affected

FIGURE 8.11

An oil-contaminated guillemot is cleaned after a spill. ©*Corepics VOF/Shutterstock.*

aquatic wildlife and water quality across a huge area of the Gulf of Mexico.

The U.S. Department of the Interior compiled a bird database as part of its Natural Resource Damage Assessment (NRDA) process, in which live and dead birds were collected following the spill. As of February 2014, the most recent NRDA database available was dated May 12, 2011. It should be noted that the data were provisional (i.e., not finalized) and that not all collected birds were necessarily killed or affected by the oil spill. The database (http://www.fws.gov/home/dhoilspill/pdfs/Bird%20Data%20Species%20Spreadsheet%2005122011.pdf) listed a total of 7,258 birds, including 6,381 dead birds. Of the latter, 2,121 were described as "visibly oiled." Nearly half of the visibly oiled dead birds were identified as laughing gulls. Other species in this category included the northern gannet (225), the brown pelican (152), and the royal tern (116). Comparison of the database against the ESA-listed bird species in Table 8.1 indicates that only two listed species were collected alive or dead: 106 least terns (of which 46 were visibly oiled dead birds) and one dead, but not visibly oiled, piping plover. It should be noted that dozens of birds included in the database are not identified by species.

A much greater threat to bird species than oil spills is oil field waste pits. These pits hold oil-containing water that is pumped out of the ground during oil extraction. In "Contaminant Issues—Oil Field Waste Pits" (2013, http://www.fws.gov/mountain-prairie/contaminants/contaminants1a.html), the USFWS notes that an estimated 500,000 to 1 million birds per year die in these pits and similar oil field wastewater facilities, such as lagoons. Birds mistake the pits and lagoons for freshwater and become oiled when they light on the water or dive into it after prey. The main avian victims are waterfowl. However, songbirds and raptors, such as hawks and owls, are also killed. It is unknown how many endangered and threatened species might be among the victims.

Invasive Species

Invasive species have damaged bird populations in some parts of the world, particularly those that occupy islands. Guam's unique bird fauna has been all but wiped out by the brown tree snake, an invasive species that probably arrived in ship cargo decades ago. According to the National Zoo in the fact sheet "Where Have the Birds of Guam Gone?" (2013, http://nationalzoo.si.edu/Animals/Birds/Facts/fact-guambirds.cfm), as many as

14,000 snakes may live in a single square mile (2.6 square km) in some Guam forest habitats. Nine out of 18 bird species have already gone extinct on Guam, including the Guam flycatcher, the Rufus fantail, the white-throated ground dove, and the cardinal honeyeater. Several other Guam bird species are close to extinction. Many of these birds are or were unique to Guam. Measures have been implemented to try to keep this destructive snake from invading other islands, including careful inspection of all cargo arriving from Guam. The removal of the brown tree snake in select habitat areas on Guam (which is a high-effort project, requiring the constant trapping of snakes) allowed the reintroduction of one bird, the flightless Guam rail, in 1998. The Guam rail had gone extinct in the wild, but a population is being maintained in captivity.

Other particularly destructive invasive species include several that are associated with humans, including cats, dogs, and rats, which often prey on birds and their eggs.

BACK FROM THE BRINK: SUCCESS STORIES

As shown in Table 2.11 in Chapter 2, nine bird species under ESA protection have recovered (i.e., been delisted). Four of the species—the Palau fantail flycatcher, the Palau ground dove, the Palau owl, and the Tinian (old world flycatcher) monarch—inhabit the small islands of Palau and Tinian, respectively, in the Pacific Ocean. All four species were listed in 1970. The Palau species were delisted in 1985 and the Tinian species in 2004.

Bald Eagles

The bald eagle is a raptor with special emphasis in the United States. (See Figure 8.12.) A symbol of honor, courage, nobility, and independence (eagles do not fly in flocks), the bald eagle is found only in North America, and its image is engraved on the official seal of the United States of America.

FIGURE 8.12

The bald eagle was once endangered because of habitat destruction and pollution by pesticides, such as DDT. Its populations have recovered with protection and a ban on DDT. ©nialat/Shutterstock.

Bald eagles came dangerously close to extinction during the 20th century, largely due to DDT, which was introduced in 1947. Two decades later the bird was listed as endangered in 1967. (See Table 2.1 in Chapter 2.) Populations started to recover with the banning of DDT in 1972. The species also benefited from habitat protection and attempts to clean up water pollution. In 1995 the bald eagle's status under the ESA was changed from endangered to threatened. In 1999 the species was proposed for delisting. A year later all delisting criteria contained in species recovery plans were achieved. However, the USFWS was slow to complete the delisting process. In June 2007 the bald eagle was finally delisted because of recovery. At that time the USFWS estimated there were 9,789 nesting pairs of the bird in the United States.

Peregrine Falcons

Many falcon species have declined with the spread of humans. Like other predatory species, falcons were often hunted, either for sport or because they were considered a threat to chickens or livestock. They also declined because of being exposed to DDT. In 1970 the American peregrine falcon (see Figure 8.13) and the arctic peregrine falcon were listed as endangered. Both subspecies ranged throughout the United States.

The recovery of the peregrine falcons was made possible by the banning of DDT and by the establishment of special captive breeding centers on several continents. The arctic peregrine falcon and the American peregrine falcon were delisted in 1994 and 1999, respectively.

Aleutian Canada Geese

Aleutian Canada geese inhabit the Aleutian Islands off the coast of Alaska and migrate back and forth to the Northern California and Oregon coasts. (See Figure 8.14.) The species was first listed as endangered in 1967. (See Table 2.1 in Chapter 2.) It was officially delisted in 2001. In the delisting notice the USFWS (March 20, 2001, http://www.fws.gov/policy/library/66fr15643.html) indicates that the population increased from less than 1,000 individuals during the 1960s to about 37,000 individuals between 1999 and 2000. The conservation efforts that led to recovery included captive breeding, removal of foxes that preyed on the birds, and relocation and reintroduction of geese to unoccupied islands.

Brown Pelicans

The brown pelican is a coastal bird found in the United States along the Atlantic coast from Virginia southward, along the Gulf coast in Alabama, Louisiana, and Texas, and along the Pacific coast. (See Figure 8.15.) Its brownish-gray feathers were highly sought after for women's hats during the late 1800s and early 1900s. As a result, the species underwent a dramatic decline. Its numbers were further decimated following World War I

FIGURE 8.13

FIGURE 8.14

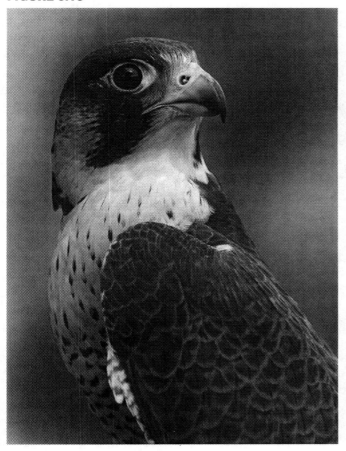

Peregrine falcon. ©*Cheryl Ann Quigley/Shutterstock.*

Aleutian Canada geese. ©*U.S. Fish and Wildlife Service.*

(1914–1918), when fishermen killed thousands of the birds, claiming they were competing for food fish. The use of DDT over the following decades took a huge toll on the birds by causing severe weakening of the shells of their eggs.

In 1970 the brown pelican was listed as endangered throughout its range. By the mid-1980s DDT restrictions and conservation efforts had allowed the Atlantic coast population of the species to rebound. In 1985 that population was delisted because of recovery. In 2009 the brown pelican throughout the remainder of the United States was also delisted.

FOREIGN SPECIES OF ENDANGERED AND THREATENED BIRDS

The IUCN indicates in *Red List of Threatened Species Version 2013.2* that in 2013 a total of 1,308 bird species were considered threatened out of 10,065 evaluated and known species.

As of November 2013, there were 227 totally foreign species of birds listed under the ESA. (See Table 8.3.) Categories include various species, such as cranes, eagles, owls, parakeets, parrots, pheasants, pigeons, and warblers.

FIGURE 8.15

Brown pelican

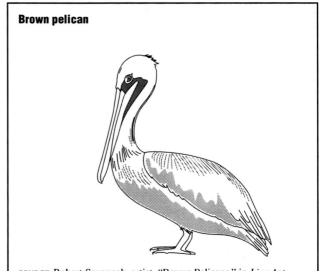

SOURCE: Robert Savannah, artist, "Brown Pelicans," in *Line Art (Drawings)*, U.S. Department of the Interior, U.S. Fish and Wildlife Service, undated, http://www.fws.gov/pictures/lineart/bobsavannah/brownpelicans.html (accessed November 12, 2013)

TABLE 8.3

Foreign endangered and threatened bird species, November 2013

Common name	Scientific name	Listing status*	Historic range
Abbott's booby	Papasula (=Sula) abbotti	E	Indian Ocean—Christmas Island
African penguin	Spheniscus demersus	E	Africa
Alaotra grebe	Tachybaptus rufolavatus	E	Madagascar
Aldabra warbler (old world warbler)	Nesillas aldabranus	E	Indian Ocean—Seychelles (Aldabra Island)
Algerian nuthatch	Sitta ledanti	E	Algeria
Amsterdam albatross	Diomedia amsterdamensis	E	Indian Ocean—Amsterdam Island
Andean condor	Vultur gryphus	E	Colombia to Chile and Argentina
Andean flamingo	Phoenicoparrus andinus	E	South America
Andrew's frigatebird	Fregata andrewsi	E	East Indian Ocean
Anjouan Island sparrowhawk	Accipiter francesii pusillus	E	Indian Ocean—Comoro Islands
Anjouan scops owl	Otus rutilus capnodes	E	Indian Ocean—Comoro Islands
Arabian ostrich	Struthio camelus syriacus	E	Jordan, Saudi Arabia
Atitlan grebe	Podilymbus gigas	E	Guatemala
Audouin's gull	Larus audouinii	E	Mediterranean Sea
Aukland Island rail	Rallus pectoralis muelleri	E	New Zealand
Azores wood pigeon	Columba palumbus azorica	E	East Atlantic Ocean—Azores
Bahaman or Cuban parrot	Amazona leucocephala	E	West Indies—Cuba, Bahamas, Caymans
Banded cotinga	Cotinga maculata	E	Brazil
Banded wattle-eye	Platysteira laticincta	E	Cameroon
Bannerman's turaco	Tauraco bannermani	E	Cameroon
Barbados yellow warbler (=wood)	Dendroica petechia petechia	E	West Indies—Barbados
Bar-tailed pheasant	Syrmaticus humiae	E	Burma, China
Bermuda petrel	Pterodroma cahow	E	Entire
Black-breasted puffleg	Eriocnemis nigrivestis	E	Ecuador
Black-fronted piping-guan	Pipile jacutinga	E	Argentina
Black hooded (black-headed) antwren	Formicivora erythronotos	E	Brazil
Black-necked crane	Grus nigricollis	E	China (Tibet)
Black stilt	Himantopus novaezelandiae	E	New Zealand
Blue-throated macaw	Ara glaucogularis	E	Bolivia
Blue-throated (=ochre-marked) parakeet	Pyrrhura cruentata	E	Brazil
Blyth's tragopan pheasant	Tragopan blythii	E	Burma, China, India
Brazillian merganser	Mergus octosetaceus	E	Brazil
Brown eared pheasant	Crossoptilon mantchuricum	E	China
Cabot's tragopan pheasant	Tragopan caboti	E	China
Caerulean paradise flycatcher	Eutrichomyias rowleyi	E	Indonesia
Campbell Island flightless teal	Anas aucklandica nesiotis	E	New Zealand (Campbell Island)
Canarian black oystercatcher	Haematopus meadewaldoi	E	Atlantic Ocean—Canary Islands
Cantabrian capercaillie	Tetrao urogallus cantabricus	E	Spain and Portugal
Cauca guan	Penelope perspicax	E	Columbia
Cebu black shama (thrush)	Copsychus niger cebuensis	E	Philippines
Chatham Island petrel	Pterodroma axillaris	E	Pacific Ocean—New Zealand (Chatham Island)
Chatham Island pigeon	Hemiphaga novaeseelandiae chathamensis	E	New Zealand
Chatham Island robin	Petroica traversi	E	New Zealand
Cheer pheasant	Catreus wallichii	E	India, Nepal, Pakistan
Cherry-throated tanager	Nemosia rourei	E	Brazil
Chilean woodstar	Eulidia yarrellii	E	Chile
Chinese egret	Egretta eulophotes	E	China, Korea
Chinese monal pheasant	Lophophorus lhuysii	E	China
Christmas Island goshawk	Accipiter fasciatus natalis	E	Indian Ocean—Christmas Island
Clarke's weaver	Ploceus golandi	E	Kenya
Cloven-feathered dove	Drepanoptila holosericea	E	Southwest Pacific Ocean—New Caledonia
Cuba hook-billed kite	Chondrohierax uncinatus wilsonii	E	West Indies—Cuba
Cuba sandhill crane	Grus canadensis nesiotes	E	West Indies—Cuba
Dappled mountain robin	Arcanator orostruthus	T	Mozambique, Tanzania
Djibouti francolin	Francolinus ochropectus	E	Djibouti
Edward's pheasant	Lophura edwardsi	E	Vietnam
Eiao Polynesian warbler	Acrocephalus percernis aquilonis	E	Eiao, Marqueses Islands, Polynesia
Elliot's pheasant	Syrmaticus ellioti	E	China
Erect-crested penguin	Eudyptes sclateri	T	New Zealand
Esmeraldas woodstar	Chaetocercus berlepschi	E	Colombia and Ecuador
Euler's flycatcher	Empidonax euleri johnstonei	E	West Indies—Grenada
Eurasian peregrine falcon	Falco peregrinus peregrinus	E	Europe, Eurasia south to Africa and Mideast
Eyrean grasswren (flycatcher)	Amytornis goyderi	E	Australia
Fiji petrel	Pseudobulweria macgillivrayi	E	Pacific Ocean, Fiji
Fiordland crested penguin	Eudyptes pachyrhynchus	T	New Zealand
Floreana tree-finch	Camarhynchus pauper	E	Ecuador
Forbes' parakeet	Cyanoramphus auriceps forbesi	E	New Zealand
Freira	Pterodroma madeira	E	Atlantic Ocean—Madeira Island
Fringe-backed fire-eye	Pyriglena atra	E	Brazil
Galapagos hawk	Buteo galapagoensis	E	Ecuador (Galapagos Islands)
Galapagos penguin	Spheniscus mendiculus	E	Ecuador (Galapagos Islands)
Galapagos petrel	Pterodroma phaeopygia	T	Pacific Ocean, Ecuador

TABLE 8.3

Foreign endangered and threatened bird species, November 2013 [CONTINUED]

Common name	Scientific name	Listing status*	Historic range
Giant ibis	Pseudibis gigantea	E	Cambodia, Lao People's Democratic Republic, and Vietnam
Giant scops owl	Mimizuku (=Otus) gurneyi	E	Philippines—Marinduque and Mindanao Island
Glaucous macaw	Anodorhynchus glaucus	E	Paraguay, Uruguay, Brazil
Golden parakeet	Aratinga guarouba	E	Brazil
Golden-shouldered parakeet	Psephotus chrysopterygius	E	Australia
Gorgeted wood-quail	Odontophorus strophium	E	Columbia
Greater adjutant	Leptoptilos dubius	E	Southeast Asia
Great Indian bustard	Ardeotis (=Choriotis) nigriceps	E	India, Pakistan
Greenland white-tailed eagle	Haliaeetus albicilla groenlandicus	E	Greenland and adjacent Atlantic islands
Grenada gray-fronted dove	Leptotila rufaxilla wellsi	E	West Indies—Grenada
Grenada hook-billed kite	Chondrohierax uncinatus mirus	E	West Indies—Grenada
Grey-necked rockfowl	Picathartes oreas	E	Cameroon, Gabon
Ground parrot	Pezoporus wallicus	E	Australia
Guadeloupe house wren	Troglodytes aedon guadeloupensis	E	West Indies—Guadeloupe
Gurney's pitta	Pitta gurneyi	E	Myanmar and Thailand
Harpy eagle	Harpia harpyja	E	Mexico south to Argentina
Helmeted honeyeater	Lichenostomus melanops cassidix (=Meliphaga c.)	E	Australia
Helmeted hornbill	Buceros (=Rhinoplax) vigil	E	Thailand, Malaysia
Hooded crane	Grus monacha	E	Japan, Russia
Hook-billed hermit (hummingbird)	Ramphodon (=Glaucis) dohrnii	E	Brazil
Horned guan	Oreophasis derbianus	E	Guatemala, Mexico
Humboldt penguin	Spheniscus humboldti	T	South America
Ibadan malimbe	Malimbus ibadanensis	E	Nigeria
Imperial parrot	Amazona imperialis	E	West Indies—Dominica
Imperial pheasant	Lophura imperialis	E	Vietnam
Imperial woodpecker	Campephilus imperialis	E	Mexico
Indigo macaw	Anodorhynchus leari	E	Brazil
Japanese crane	Grus japonensis	E	China, Japan, Korea, Russia
Japanese crested ibis	Nipponia nippon	E	China, Japan, Russia, Korea
Jerdon's courser	Rhinoptilus bitorquatus	E	India
Junin grebe	Podiceps taczanowskii	E	Peru
Junin rail	Laterallus tuerosi	E	Peru
Kaempfer's tody-tyrant	Hemitriccus kaempferi	E	Brazil
Kagu	Rhynochetos jubatus	E	South Pacific Ocean—New Caledonia
Kakapo	Strigops habroptilus	E	New Zealand
Koch's pitta	Pitta kochi	E	Philippines
Kokako (wattlebird)	Callaeas cinerea	E	New Zealand
Lesser rhea (incl. Darwin's)	Rhea (=Pterocnemia) pennata	E	Argentina, Bolivia, Peru, Uruguay
Little blue macaw	Cyanopsitta spixii	E	Brazil
Long-legged warbler	Trichocichla rufa	E	Fiji, south pacific
Long-tailed ground roller	Uratelornis chimaera	E	Malagasy Republic (=Madagascar)
Lord Howe wood rail	Gallirallus (=Tricholimnas) sylvestris	E	Australia (Lord Howe Island)
Madagascar pochard	Aythya innotata	E	Madagascar
Madagascar red owl	Tyto soumagnei	E	Madagascar
Madagascar sea eagle	Haliaeetus vociferoides	E	Madagascar
Madagascar serpent eagle	Eutriorchis astur	E	Madagascar
Magenta petrel	Pterodroma magentae	E	Pacific Ocean, New Zealand
Margaretta's hermit	Phaethornis malaris margarettae	E	Brazil
Marquesas pigeon	Ducula galeata	E	Polynesia, Marquesas Islands
Martinique trembler (thrasher)	Cinclocerthia ruficauda gutturalis	E	West Indies—Martinique
Marungu sunbird	Nectarinia prigoginei	E	Zaire
Mascarene black petrel	Pterodroma aterrima	E	Indian Ocean—Mauritius (Reunion Island)
Mauritius cuckoo-shrike	Coquus typicus	E	Indian Ocean—Mauritius
Mauritius fody	Foudia rubra	E	Indian Ocean—Mauritius
Mauritius kestrel	Falco punctatus	E	Indian Ocean—Mauritius
Mauritius olivaceous bulbul	Hypsipetes borbonicus olivaceus	E	Indian Ocean—Mauritius
Mauritius parakeet	Psittacula echo	E	Indian Ocean—Mauritius
Merriam's Montezuma quail	Cyrtonyx montezumae merriami	E	Mexico (Vera Cruz)
Mikado pheasant	Syrmaticus mikado	E	Taiwan
Mindoro imperial (=zone-tailed) pigeon	Ducula mindorensis	E	Philippines
Morden's owlet	Otus ireneae	E	Kenya
New Zealand bushwren	Xenicus longipes	E	New Zealand
New Zealand shore plover	Thinornis novaeseelandiae	E	New Zealand
New Zealand thrush (wattlebird)	Turnagra capensis	E	New Zealand
Night (=Australian) parrot	Geopsittacus occidentalis	E	Australia
Noisy scrub-bird	Atrichornis clamosus	E	Australia
Nordmann's greenshank	Tringa guttifer	E	Russia, Japan, south to Malaya, Borneo
Norfolk Island parakeet	Cyanoramphus cookii (=novaezelandiae c.)	E	Australia (Norfolk Island)
Norfolk Island white-eye	Zosterops albogularis	E	Indian Ocean—Norfolk Islands
Northern bald ibis	Geronticus eremita	E	Southern Europe, southwestern Asia, northern Africa
Orange-bellied parakeet	Neophema chrysogaster	E	Australia

TABLE 8.3

Common name	Scientific name	Listing status*	Historic range
Oriental white stork	Ciconia boyciana (=ciconia b.)	E	China, Japan, Korea, Russia
Palawan peacock pheasant	Polyplectron emphanum	E	Philippines
Paradise parakeet	Psephotus pulcherrimus	E	Australia
Peruvian plantcutter	Phytotoma raimondii	E	Peru
Philippine eagle	Pithecophaga jefferyi	E	Philippines
Pink-headed duck	Rhodonessa caryophyllacea	E	India
Pink pigeon	Columba mayeri	E	Indian Ocean—Mauritius
Plain wanderer (=collared-hemipode)	Pedionomus torquatus	E	Australia
Pollen's vanga	Xenopirostris polleni	T	Madagascar
Ponape greater white-eye	Rukia longirostra	E	West Pacific Ocean—Federated States of Micronesia
Ponape mountain starling	Aplonis pelzelni	E	West Pacific Ocean—Federated States of Micronesia
Queen Charlotte goshawk	Accipiter gentilis laingi	T	Canada
Raso lark	Alauda razae	E	Atlantic Ocean—Raso Island (Cape Verde)
Razor-billed curassow	Mitu mitu mitu	E	Brazil (Eastern)
Red-billed curassow	Crax blumenbachii	E	Brazil
Red-browed parrot	Amazona rhodocorytha	E	Brazil
Red-capped parrot	Pionopsitta pileata	E	Brazil
Red-faced malkoha (cuckoo)	Phaenicophaeus pyrrhocephalus	E	Sri Lanka (=Ceylon)
Red-necked parrot	Amazona arausiaca	E	West Indies—Dominica
Red siskin	Carduelis cucullata	E	South America
Red-spectacled parrot	Amazona pretrei pretrei	E	Brazil, Argentina
Red-tailed parrot	Amazona brasiliensis	E	Brazil
Relict gull	Larus relictus	E	India, China
Resplendent quetzel	Pharomachrus mocinno	E	Mexico to Panama
Reunion cuckoo-shrike	Coquus newtoni	E	Indian Ocean—Reunion
Rodrigues fody	Foudia flavicans	E	Indian Ocean—Rodrigues Island (Mauritius)
Rodrigues warbler (old world warbler)	Bebrornis rodericanus	E	Mauritius (Rodrigues Islands)
Rothschild's starling (myna)	Leucopsar rothschildi	E	Indonesia (Bali)
Royal cinclodes	Cinclodes aricomae	E	Peru
Salmon-crested cockatoo	Cacatua moluccensis	T	Indonesia
Sao Miguel bullfinch (finch)	Pyrrhula pyrrhula murina	E	Eastern Atlantic Ocean—Azores
Scarlet-breasted robin (flycatcher)	Petroica multicolor multicolor	E	Australia (Norfolk Island)
Scarlet-chested parakeet	Neophema splendida	E	Australia
Sclater's monal pheasant	Lophophorus sclateri	E	Burma, China, India
Semper's warbler (=wood)	Leucopeza semperi	E	West Indies—St. Lucia
Seychelles fody (weaver-finch)	Foudia sechellarum	E	Indian Ocean—Seychelles
Seychelles kestrel	Falco araea	E	Indian Ocean—Seychelles Islands
Seychelles lesser vasa parrot	Coracopsis nigra barklyi	E	Indian Ocean—Seychelles (Praslin Island)
Seychelles magpie-robin (thrush)	Copsychus sechellarum	E	Indian Ocean—Seychelles Islands
Seychelles paradise flycatcher	Terpsiphone corvina	E	Indian Ocean—Seychelles
Seychelles scops owl	Otus magicus (=insularis) insularis	E	Indian Ocean—Seychelles Islands
Seychelles turtle dove	Streptopelia picturata rostrata	E	Indian Ocean—Seychelles
Seychelles warbler (old world warbler)	Bebrornis sechellensis	E	Indian Ocean—Seychelles Islands
Seychelles white-eye	Zosterops modesta	E	Indian Ocean—Seychelles
Siberian white crane	Grus leucogeranus	E	C.I.S. (Siberia) to India, including Iran and China
Slender-billed curlew	Numenius tenuirostris	E	Algeria, Bulgaria, China, Greece, Hungary, Italy, Kazakstan, Morocco, Romania, Russia, Slovenia, Tunisia, Turkey, Turkmenistan, Ukraine, Uzbekistan, Yugoslavia
Slender-billed grackle	Quisicalus palustris	E	Mexico
Socorro mockingbird	Mimus graysoni	E	Mexico
Solitary tinamou	Tinamus solitarius	E	Brazil, Paraguay, Argentina
Southeastern rufous-vented ground cuckoo	Neomorphus geoffroyi dulcis	E	Brazil
southern rockhopper penguin	Eudyptes chrysocome	T	New Zealand—Campbell Plateau
Spanish imperial eagle	Aquila heliaca adalberti	E	Spain, Morocco, Algeria
St. Lucia Forest thrush	Cichlherminia iherminieri santaeluciae	E	St. Lucia, WestIndies
St. Lucia house wren	Troglodytes aedon mesoleucus	E	West Indies—St. Lucia
St. Lucia parrot	Amazona versicolor	E	West Indies—St. Lucia
St. Vincent parrot	Amazona guildingii	E	West Indies—St. Vincent
Swinhoe's pheasant	Lophura swinhoii	E	Taiwan
Tahiti flycatcher	Pomarea nigra	E	South Pacific Ocean—Tahiti
Taita thrush	Turdus olivaceus helleri	E	Kenya
Thyolo alethe	Alethe choloensis	E	Malawi, Mozambique
Trinidad white-headed curassow	Pipile pipile pipile	E	West Indies—Trinidad
Tristam's woodpecker	Dryocopus javensis richardsi	E	Korea
Turquoise parakeet	Neophema pulchella	E	Australia
Ulugura bush-shrike	Malaconotus alius	T	Tanzania
Van Dam's vanga	Xenopirostris damii	T	Madagascar
Vinaceous-breasted parrot	Amazona vinacea	E	Brazil
West African ostrich	Struthio camelus spatzi	E	Spanish Sahara
Western bristlebird	Dasyornis longirostris (=brachypterus l.)	E	Australia

TABLE 8.3

Common name	Scientific name	Listing status*	Historic range
Western rufous bristlebird	Dasyornis broadbenti littoralis	E	Australia
Western tragopan pheasant	Tragopan melanocephalus	E	India, Pakistan
Western whipbird	Psophodes nigrogularis	E	Australia
White-breasted guineafowl	Agelastes meleagrides	T	West Africa
White-breasted thrasher	Ramphocinclus brachyurus	E	West Indies—St. Lucia, Martinique
White-browed tit-spinetail	Leptasthenura xenothorax	E	Peru
White eared pheasant	Crossoptilon crossoptilon	E	China (Tibet), India
White-flippered penguin	Eudyptula albosignata	T	New Zealand
White-naped crane	Grus vipio	E	Mongolia
White-necked rockfowl	Picathartes gymnocephalus	E	Africa—Togo to Sierra Leone
White-tailed laurel Pigeon	Columba junoniae	T	Atlantic Ocean—Canary Islands
White-winged cotinga	Xipholena atropurpurea	E	Brazil
White-winged guan	Penelope albipennis	E	Peru
White-winged wood duck	Cairina scutulata	E	India, Malaysia, Indonesia, Thailand
Yellow-billed parrot	Amazona collaria	T	Jamaica
Yellow-eyed penguin	Megadyptes antipodes	T	New Zealand

*E = Endangered; T = Threatened.

SOURCE: Adapted from "Generate Species List," in *Species Reports*, U.S. Department of the Interior, U.S. Fish and Wildlife Service, November 2013, http://ecos .fws.gov/tess_public/pub/adHocSpeciesForm.jsp (accessed November 7, 2013)

CHAPTER 9
INSECTS AND SPIDERS

Insects are members of the Animalia kingdom and belong to the phylum Arthropoda, along with crustaceans. There are many classes of arthropods, including insects and arachnids. Both are invertebrates, but insects have six legs, whereas arachnids have eight legs. The arachnids include spiders, mites, ticks, scorpions, and harvestmen.

Insects are the most diverse group in the animal kingdom. Scientists are not certain of the total number of insect species; estimates range as high as 30 million species. The International Union for Conservation of Nature (IUCN) indicates in *Red List of Threatened Species Version 2013.2* (November 2013, http://www.iucn redlist.org/about/summary-statistics) that 1 million of the species have been described. Insects have not been as thoroughly studied as the vertebrate groups, so there are likely to be many endangered insects whose state is unknown.

With the exception of butterflies, which are esteemed for their beauty, many insects and arachnids are not appreciated by humans. However, the creatures play important roles in nature, and their extinction would have negative impacts on many ecosystems and society in general. One of the most beneficial activities is pollination. Bees, wasps, flies, butterflies, moths, and beetles help plants reproduce. In "A Class of Distinction" (2007, http://www.cals.ncsu.edu/course/ent425/text01/impact1 .html), John R. Meyer calls insects "allies" to humans noting "we depend on them to keep the natural environment clean and productive." He goes on to state, "They have shaped human cultures and civilizations in countless ways, they supply unique natural products, they regulate the population densities of many potential pest species, they dispose of our wastes, bury the dead, and recycle organic nutrients. Indeed, we seldom stop to consider what life would be like without insects and how much we depend on them for our very survival."

Insects and arachnids, like many other species, suffer from diminished habitat as a result of encroaching development, industrialization, changing land use patterns, and invasive species.

THREATENED AND ENDANGERED INSECT SPECIES IN THE UNITED STATES

As of November 2013, there were 71 U.S. insect species listed under the Endangered Species Act (ESA). (See Table 9.1.) The predominant species types include beetles, butterflies, and pomace flies. Other listed insects include damselflies, flies, moths, skippers, a dragonfly, a grasshopper, and a naucorid. (See Figure 9.1.) Most of the listed insects are endangered, and nearly all have recovery plans in place.

According to the U.S. Fish and Wildlife Service (USFWS), most of the imperiled insects are found exclusively in either California, Hawaii, or Texas.

Table 9.2 shows the 10 insect species with the highest expenditures under the ESA during fiscal year (FY) 2012. Nearly $13.3 million was spent on these species.

Notably absent from the list of endangered and threatened species shown in Table 9.1 are any bee species. During the late 20th century, reports of mass deaths of honeybees began rising in the United States. This is concerning because bees are the major pollinators of the nation's agricultural crops. In "Hive and Seek: Domestic Honeybees Keep Disappearing, but Are Their Wild Cousins in Trouble, Too?" (ScientificAmerican.com, May 8, 2012), Sarah Fecht notes that bees are estimated to pollinate approximately one-third of the food that Americans eat "at a value of about $15 billion per year." However, much of this work is accomplished by honeybees, which are not native to the United States. In fact, North America has no native honeybee species. Honeybees were imported to the colonies from Europe during

TABLE 9.1

Endangered and threatened insect species, November 2013

Common name	Scientific name	Listing status[a]	U.S. or U.S./foreign listed	Recovery plan date	Recovery plan stage[b]
American burying beetle	Nicrophorus americanus	E; EXPN	US/foreign	9/27/1991	F
Ash Meadows naucorid	Ambrysus amargosus	T	US	9/28/1990	F
Bay checkerspot butterfly	Euphydryas editha bayensis	T	US	9/30/1998	F
Behren's silverspot butterfly	Speyeria zerene behrensii	E	US	1/20/2004	D
Blackburn's sphinx moth	Manduca blackburni	E	US	9/28/2005	F
Blackline Hawaiian damselfly	Megalagrion nigrohamatum nigrolineatum	E	US	None	—
Callippe silverspot butterfly	Speyeria callippe callippe	E	US	None	—
Carson wandering skipper	Pseudocopaeodes eunus obscurus	E	US	9/13/2007	F
Casey's June beetle	Dinacoma caseyi	E	US	4/1/2013	O
Cassius blue butterfly	Leptotes cassius theonus	SAT	US	None	—
Ceraunus blue butterfly	Hemiargus ceraunus antibubastus	SAT	US	None	—
Coffin Cave mold beetle	Batrisodes texanus	E	US	8/25/1994	F
Comal Springs dryopid beetle	Stygoparnus comalensis	E	US	2/14/1996	RF(1)
Comal Springs riffle beetle	Heterelmis comalensis	E	US	2/14/1996	RF(1)
Crimson Hawaiian damselfly	Megalagrion leptodemas	E	US	None	—
Delhi Sands flower-loving fly	Rhaphiomidas terminatus abdominalis	E	US	9/14/1997	F
Delta green ground beetle	Elaphrus viridis	T	US	3/7/2006	F
El Segundo blue butterfly	Euphilotes battoides allyni	E	US	9/28/1998	F
Fender's blue butterfly	Icaricia icarioides fenderi	E	US	6/29/2010	F
Flying earwig Hawaiian damselfly	Megalagrion nesiotes	E	US	None	—
Hawaiian picture-wing fly	Drosophila sharpi	E	US	None	—
Hawaiian picture-wing fly	Drosophila digressa	E	US	None	—
Helotes mold beetle	Batrisodes venyivi	E	US	10/4/2011	F
Hine's emerald dragonfly	Somatochlora hineana	E	US	9/27/2001	F
Hungerford's crawling water beetle	Brychius hungerfordi	E	US/foreign	9/28/2006	F
Karner blue butterfly	Lycaeides melissa samuelis	E	US/foreign	9/19/2003	F
Kern primrose sphinx moth	Euproserpinus euterpe	T	US	2/8/1984	F
Kretschmarr Cave mold beetle	Texamaurops reddelli	E	US	8/25/1994	F
Laguna Mountains skipper	Pyrgus ruralis lagunae	E	US	None	—
Lange's metalmark butterfly	Apodemia mormo langei	E	US	4/25/1984	RF(1)
Lotis blue butterfly	Lycaeides argyrognomon lotis	E	US	12/26/1985	F
Miami blue butterfly	Cyclargus (=Hemiargus) thomasi bethunebakeri	E	US	None	—
Mission blue butterfly	Icaricia icarioides missionensis	E	US	10/10/1984	F
Mitchell's satyr butterfly	Neonympha mitchellii mitchellii	E	US	4/2/1998	F
Mount Charleston blue butterfly	Plebejus shasta charlestonensis	E	US	None	—
Mount Hermon June beetle	Polyphylla barbata	E	US	9/28/1998	F
Myrtle's silverspot butterfly	Speyeria zerene myrtleae	E	US	9/29/1998	F
Nickerbean blue butterfly	Cyclargus ammon	SAT	US	None	—
Northeastern beach tiger beetle	Cicindela dorsalis dorsalis	T	US	9/29/1994	F
Oceanic Hawaiian damselfly	Megalagrion oceanicum	E	US	None	—
Ohlone tiger beetle	Cicindela ohlone	E	US	9/28/1998	F
Oregon silverspot butterfly	Speyeria zerene hippolyta	T	US	8/22/2001	RF(1)
Pacific Hawaiian damselfly	Megalagrion pacificum	E	US	None	—
Palos Verdes blue butterfly	Glaucopsyche lygdamus palosverdesensis	E	US	1/19/1984	F
Pawnee montane skipper	Hesperia leonardus montana	T	US	9/21/1998	F
Puritan tiger beetle	Cicindela puritana	T	US	9/29/1993	F
Quino checkerspot butterfly	Euphydryas editha quino (=E. e. wrighti)	E	US/foreign	9/17/2003	F
Saint Francis' satyr butterfly	Neonympha mitchellii francisci	E	US	4/23/1996	F
Salt Creek tiger beetle	Cicindela nevadica lincolniana	E	US	2/20/2009	O
San Bruno elfin butterfly	Callophrys mossii bayensis	E	US	10/10/1984	F
Schaus swallowtail butterfly	Heraclides aristodemus ponceanus	E	US	5/18/1999	F
Smith's blue butterfly	Euphilotes enoptes smithi	E	US	11/9/1984	F
Taylor's (=whulge) checkerspot	Euphydryas editha taylori	E	US	6/29/2010	F
Tooth Cave ground beetle	Rhadine persephone	E	US	8/25/1994	F
Uncompahgre fritillary butterfly	Boloria acrocnema	E	US	3/17/1994	F
[Unnamed] ground beetle	Rhadine infernalis	E	US	10/4/2011	F
[Unnamed] ground beetle	Rhadine exilis	E	US	10/4/2011	F
[Unnamed] pomace fly	Drosophila aglaia	E	US	None	—
[Unnamed] pomace fly	Drosophila heteroneura	E	US	None	—
[Unnamed] pomace fly	Drosophila montgomeryi	E	US	None	—
[Unnamed] pomace fly	Drosophila mulli	T	US	None	—
[Unnamed] pomace fly	Drosophila musaphilia	E	US	None	—
[Unnamed] pomace fly	Drosophila neoclavisetae	E	US	None	—
[Unnamed] pomace fly	Drosophila obatai	E	US	None	—
[Unnamed] pomace fly	Drosophila substenoptera	E	US	None	—
[Unnamed] pomace fly	Drosophila tarphytrichia	E	US	None	—
[Unnamed] pomace fly	Drosophila hemipeza	E	US	None	—
[Unnamed] pomace fly	Drosophila ochrobasis	E	US	None	—
[Unnamed] pomace fly	Drosophila differens	E	US	None	—

TABLE 9.1

Endangered and threatened insect species, November 2013 [CONTINUED]

Common name	Scientific name	Listing status[a]	U.S. or U.S./foreign listed	Recovery plan date	Recovery plan stage[b]
Valley elderberry longhorn beetle	*Desmocerus californicus dimorphus*	T	US	6/28/1984	F
Zayante band-winged grasshopper	*Trimerotropis infantilis*	E	US	9/28/1998	F

[a]E = Endangered; T = Threatened; SAT = Threatened due to similarity of appearance; EXPN = Experimental population, non-essential.
[b]F = Final; D = Draft; RF = Final revision; O = Other.

SOURCE: Adapted from "Generate Species List," in *Species Reports*, U.S. Department of the Interior, U.S. Fish and Wildlife Service, November 2013, http://ecos.fws.gov/tess_public/pub/adHocSpeciesForm.jsp (accessed November 7, 2013), and "Listed FWS/Joint FWS and NMFS Species and Populations with Recovery Plans (Sorted by Listed Entity)," in *Recovery Plans Search*, U.S. Department of the Interior, U.S. Fish and Wildlife Service, November 2013, http://ecos.fws.gov/tess_public/pub/speciesRecovery.jsp?sort=1 (accessed November 7, 2013)

FIGURE 9.1

Ash Meadows naucorid

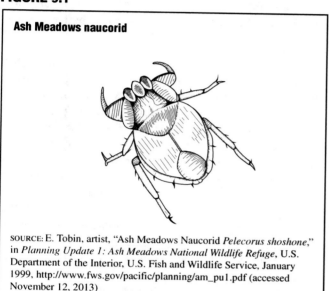

SOURCE: E. Tobin, artist, "Ash Meadows Naucorid *Pelecorus shoshone*," in *Planning Update 1: Ash Meadows National Wildlife Refuge*, U.S. Department of the Interior, U.S. Fish and Wildlife Service, January 1999, http://www.fws.gov/pacific/planning/am_pu1.pdf (accessed November 12, 2013)

TABLE 9.2

Insect species with the highest expenditures under the Endangered Species Act, fiscal year 2012

Ranking	Species	Expenditure
1	Beetle, valley elderberry longhorn (*Desmocerus californicus dimorphus*)	$4,830,808
2	Butterfly, Quino checkerspot (*Euphydryas editha quino* (= E. e. wrighti))	$2,117,111
3	Beetle, American burying (*Nicrophorus americanus*)	$2,012,757
4	Butterfly, Karner blue (*Lycaeides melissa samuelis*)	$1,298,182
5	Butterfly, Fender's blue (*Icaricia icarioides fenderi*)	$1,160,894
6	Butterfly, Oregon silverspot (*Speyeria zerene hippolyta*)	$683,195
7	Butterfly, Palos Verdes blue (*Glaucopsyche lygdamus palosverdesensis*)	$375,745
8	Skipper, Laguna Mountains (*Pyrgus ruralis lagunae*)	$297,695
9	Dragonfly, Hine's emerald (*Somatochlora hineana*)	$248,068
10	Butterfly, Miami blue (*Cyclargus* (=Hemiargus) *thomasi bethunebakeri*)	$227,369

SOURCE: Adapted from "Table 2. Species Ranked in Descending Order of Total FY2012 Reported Expenditures, Not Including Land Acquisition Costs," in *Federal and State Endangered and Threatened Species Expenditures: Fiscal Year 2012*, U.S. Department of the Interior, U.S. Fish and Wildlife Service, 2012, http://www.fws.gov/endangered/esa-library/pdf/2012.EXP.FINAL.pdf (accessed November 4, 2013)

the 1600s and over the centuries have become "farmed" animals that live in human-made and monitored hives. Honeybees are extensively bred and sold as commercial products. As such, they do not qualify for protection under the ESA.

Beetles

According to the San Diego Zoo (2014, http://animals.sandiegozoo.org/animals/beetle) beetles comprise the largest group within the animal kingdom with about 350,000 known species. They vary widely in size and color, but all have antler-like antennae on their heads. Most live on land. Beetles are beneficial members of their ecosystems. The San Diego Zoo notes, "Beetles create usable soil for vegetation by eating animal waste, rotten wood, and animal carcasses. They pollinate flowers and keep other insect populations in balance through predation."

As shown in Table 9.1 there were dozens of beetle species listed under the ESA as of November 2013. Like many other imperiled animals they face threats from habitat loss and alteration, particularly urban and agricultural development.

VALLEY ELDERBERRY LONGHORN BEETLES. As shown in Table 9.2, in 2012 more than $4.8 million was devoted to the valley elderberry longhorn beetle, a species found only in California. It is a stout-bodied beetle nearly 1 inch (2.5 cm) long when fully grown. (See Figure 9.2.) The species overwhelmingly prefers only one type of host plant: elderberry shrubs along creeks and rivers in California's Central Valley. This is an area that experienced extensive agricultural and urban development during the 20th century. Long-term destruction and fragmentation of riparian (river and stream) ecosystems imperiled the beetle population. It was first listed under the ESA in 1980 as a threatened species. Two areas in Sacramento County were designated critical habitat. A recovery plan was finalized in 1984.

FIGURE 9.2

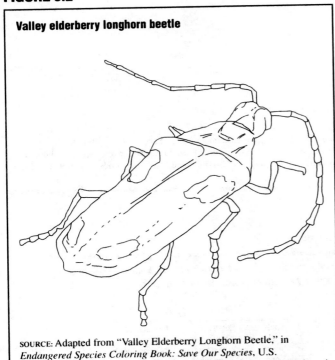

Valley elderberry longhorn beetle

SOURCE: Adapted from "Valley Elderberry Longhorn Beetle," in *Endangered Species Coloring Book: Save Our Species*, U.S. Environmental Protection Agency, May 2008, http://www.epa.gov/espp/coloring/cbook.pdf (accessed November 12, 2013)

In September 2006 the USFWS published *Valley Elderberry Longhorn Beetle (Desmocerus californicus dimorphus): 5-Year Review—Summary and Evaluation* (http://ecos.fws.gov/docs/five_year_review/doc779.pdf) and recommended that the species be delisted. The agency noted that 50,000 acres (20,200 hectares [ha]) of the riparian habitat preferred by the beetle had been given protected status and that over 5,000 acres (2,020 ha) had been restored.

In September 2010 the Pacific Legal Foundation (PLF), a private organization that typically litigates against the ESA, petitioned the USFWS to conduct the delisting based on the information contained in the five-year review. In "The Elderberry Longhorn Beetle Doesn't Belong on Any ESA List" (2012, http://www.pacificlegal.org/page.aspx?pid=1136), the PLF complains about the agency's failure to act on its own delisting recommendation, noting that "landowners, flood control districts, and others must still devote their limited resources to protect a beetle that in reality no longer requires federal protection." As described in Chapter 2, the agency must determine within 90 days whether a delisting petition contains "substantial information" suggesting that a species may require delisting under the ESA. When the agency failed to meet this deadline, the PLF sued the USFWS. In January 2011 the agency (http://www.gpo.gov/fdsys/search/citation.result.FR.action?federalRegister.volume=2011&federalRegister.page=3069&publication=FR) published its petition find-

ing that delisting was warranted. This triggered a mandatory status review which the law requires be completed in 12 months. When the agency missed that deadline the PLF sued it again. In October 2012 the agency (https://www.federalregister.gov/articles/2012/10/02/2012-23843/endangered-and-threatened-wildlife-and-plants-removal-of-the-valley-elderberry-longhorn-beetle-from#h-14) officially proposed to delist the beetle because of recovery. As of February 2014, the proposal had not been finalized.

Butterflies, Moths, and Skippers

Butterflies, moths, and skippers are flying insects that belong to the order Lepidoptera. Scientists believe there could be several hundred thousand species in this order. Skippers have stockier bodies than butterflies and are structurally different from moths. As such, they are considered to be an intermediate between butterflies and moths.

Like amphibians, many butterflies and moths are considered to be indicator species (meaning that their well-being gives scientists a good indication of the general health of their habitat) because they are particularly sensitive to environmental degradation. The decline of these species serves as a warning to humans about the condition of the environment. For example, certain moth species feed on lichen, a fungus-based organism that grows on trees, rocks, and other solid surfaces. Lichen are very susceptible to air pollutants. Reductions in the number of lichen-feeding moths can indicate the presence of harmful air pollution in an area. Part of the reason butterflies are sensitive to many aspects of the environment is that these species undergo a drastic metamorphosis, or change, from larva to adult as a natural part of their life cycle. Butterfly larvae are generally crawling, herbivorous (plant-eating) caterpillars, whereas butterfly adults fly and eat nectar. Butterflies can thrive only when intact habitats are available for both caterpillars and adults. Consequently, healthy butterfly populations tend to occur in areas with healthy ecosystems. Because many species are extremely sensitive to changing environmental conditions, butterflies and moths are carefully monitored by scientists and conservationists around the world.

The major threats to butterflies include:

- Habitat destruction
- Mowing of pastures, ditches, and highway rights-of-way
- Collisions with moving automobiles
- Insecticides

QUINO CHECKERSPOT BUTTERFLIES. As shown in Table 9.2, more than $2.1 million was spent under the ESA during 2012 on the Quino checkerspot butterfly. (See Figure 9.3.) Once populous throughout Southern

FIGURE 9.3

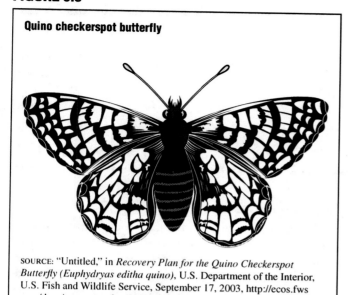

Quino checkerspot butterfly

SOURCE: "Untitled," in *Recovery Plan for the Quino Checkerspot Butterfly (Euphydryas editha quino)*, U.S. Department of the Interior, U.S. Fish and Wildlife Service, September 17, 2003, http://ecos.fws.gov/docs/recovery_plan/030917.pdf (accessed November 12, 2013)

FIGURE 9.4

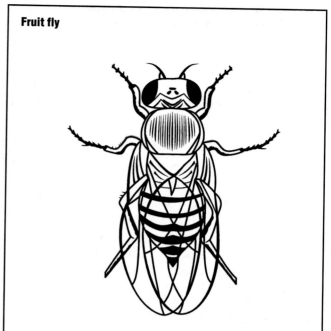

Fruit fly

SOURCE: Paul Preuss, "Drosophila," in *Fruit Fly Sequencing Stands as Genetic Research Milestone*, U.S. Department of Energy, Lawrence Berkeley National Laboratory, March 23, 2000, http://www.lbl.gov/Science-Articles/Archive/drosophila-sequenced.html (accessed November 12, 2013)

California, it has largely disappeared except for a few small populations in the southern part of the state and in northern Mexico. It was first listed under the ESA as endangered in 1997. In 2009 the USFWS (http://ecos.fws.gov/docs/five_year_review/doc2515.pdf) published the results of a five-year status review for the butterfly. It notes the butterfly's preferred habitat includes patchy shrub landscapes and scrublands, which are patches of shrubs alternating with open ditches or swales. At the time of the review the species was found only in Riverside and San Diego Counties in California and some northern areas of Baja California Norte in Mexico. The Agency recommended maintaining the butterfly's listing as endangered noting that it continues to face threats including habitat loss, habitat alterations due to climate change, and invasive species.

Hawaiian Insects

As of November 2013, there were 16 Hawaiian insects listed under the ESA: 12 subspecies of the pomace fly, two damselflies, a Hawaiian picture-wing fly, and the Blackburn's sphinx moth. (See Table 9.1.)

POMACE FLIES. Pomace flies (also known as Hawaiian picture-wing flies) belong to the genus *Drosophila*, a group commonly called fruit flies. (See Figure 9.4.) There are more than 100 species of *Drosophila*. They are relatively large flies with elaborate markings on their wings. The Hawaiian subspecies are renowned for their colorful wing patterns. They prefer mostly mesic (adequately moist) forest and wet forest habitats. Each fly is dependent on one or more specific host plants. This dependence is one of the factors that has imperiled the flies. All the host plants face threats to their survival because of competition with nonnative plants and trampling and ingestion by livestock and wild animals.

In 2006 all 12 subspecies were listed under the ESA. All but one were designated as endangered. (See Table 9.1.) *Drosophila mulli* was designated as threatened. As of February 2014, a recovery plan had not been issued for the Hawaiian pomace flies.

In 2010 the USFWS (http://www.gpo.gov/fdsys/pkg/FR-2010-04-08/pdf/2010-7915.pdf#page=1) initiated a five-year review for the pomace flies and dozens of other listed species found in Hawaii, Idaho, Washington, Guam, and the Commonwealth of the Northern Mariana Islands. As of February 2014, the results of the review had not been published.

THREATENED AND ENDANGERED FOREIGN SPECIES OF INSECTS

In *Red List of Threatened Species Version 2013.2*, the IUCN indicates that in 2013, 896 species of insects were threatened. This number accounted for 19% of the 4,610 evaluated species and less than 0.1% of the 1 million described species.

As of November 2013, there were four totally foreign insects listed under the ESA. (See Table 9.3.) All four were butterfly species and were listed as endangered.

TABLE 9.3

Foreign endangered and threatened insect species, November 2013

Common name	Scientific name	Listing status*	Historic range
Corsican swallowtail butterfly	Papilio hospiton	E	Corsica, Sardinia
Homerus swallowtail butterfly	Papilio homerus	E	Jamaica
Luzon peacock swallowtail butterfly	Papilio chikae	E	Philippines
Queen Alexandra's birdwing butterfly	Troides alexandrae	E	Papua New Guinea

*E = Endangered.

SOURCE: Adapted from "Generate Species List," in *Species Reports*, U.S. Department of the Interior, U.S. Fish and Wildlife Service, November 2013, http://ecos
.fws.gov/tess_public/pub/adHocSpeciesForm.jsp (accessed November 7, 2013)

THREATENED AND ENDANGERED ARACHNID SPECIES IN THE UNITED STATES

Arachnids are invertebrates with eight legs. They include spiders, mites, ticks, scorpions, and harvestmen. As of November 2013, there were 12 U.S. species of arachnids listed under the ESA. (See Table 9.4.) All the arachnids had endangered status, and all had recovery plans in place. The imperiled arachnids fall into four species types:

- Harvestmen—three species

- Meshweaver—four species

- Pseudoscorpion—one species

- Spider—four species

Ten of the arachnids are cave-dwelling species found only in Texas. The only imperiled arachnids outside of Texas are the Kauai Cave wolf spider, which inhabits Hawaii, and the spruce-fir moss spider, which is found in North Carolina and Tennessee.

Table 9.5 shows the 10 arachnid species with the highest expenditures under the ESA during FY 2012. Nearly $300,000 was spent conserving these species.

Texas Cave Arachnids

Ten of the listed arachnids are found only in underground karst caves in three counties in Texas. (See Figure 9.5.) Karst is a geological term referring to a type of underground terrain resulting when limestone bedrock is exposed to mildly acidic groundwater over a long period. Eventually, the bedrock becomes a honeycomb of cracks, fissures, holes, and other openings. There are dozens of these karst caves located in Bexar, Travis, and Williamson Counties in Texas. In recent decades scientists have discovered unusual invertebrate species living in these caves. The tiny cave dwellers are eyeless and have no pigment (color) to their bodies. Ten of the creatures have been added to the endangered species list. They include four meshweavers (tiny web-making arachnids), three harvestmen (commonly known as daddy longlegs or granddaddy longlegs), two true spiders, and one pseudoscorpion.

The species were listed under the ESA after a collection of conservation groups petitioned the USFWS in 1992. The creatures were listed as endangered in 2000. In 2003 approximately 1,000 acres (405 ha) were designated

TABLE 9.4

Endangered arachnid species, November 2013

Common name	Scientific name	Listing status[a]	U.S. or U.S./foreign listed	Recovery plan date	Recovery plan stage[b]
Bee Creek Cave harvestman	Texella reddelli	E	US	08/25/1994	F
Bone Cave harvestman	Texella reyesi	E	US	08/25/1994	F
Braken Bat Cave meshweaver	Cicurina venii	E	US	10/04/2011	F
Cokendolpher Cave harvestman	Texella cokendolpheri	E	US	10/04/2011	F
Government Canyon Bat Cave meshweaver	Cicurina vespera	E	US	10/04/2011	F
Government Canyon Bat Cave spider	Neoleptoneta microps	E	US	10/04/2011	F
Kauai cave wolf or pe`e pe`e maka `ole spider	Adelocosa anops	E	US	07/19/2006	F
Madla's Cave meshweaver	Cicurina madla	E	US	10/04/2011	F
Robber Baron Cave meshweaver	Cicurina baronia	E	US	10/04/2011	F
Spruce-fir moss spider	Microhexura montivaga	E	US	09/11/1998	F
Tooth Cave pseudoscorpion	Tartarocreagris texana	E	US	08/25/1994	F
Tooth Cave spider	Leptoneta myopica	E	US	08/25/1994	F

[a]E = Endangered.
[b]F = Final.

SOURCE: Adapted from "Generate Species List," in *Species Reports*, U.S. Department of the Interior, U.S. Fish and Wildlife Service, November 2013, http://ecos
.fws.gov/tess_public/pub/adHocSpeciesForm.jsp (accessed November 7, 2013), and "Listed FWS/Joint FWS and NMFS Species and Populations with Recovery Plans (Sorted by Listed Entity)," in *Recovery Plans Search*, U.S. Department of the Interior, U.S. Fish and Wildlife Service, November 2013, http://ecos.fws
.gov/tess_public/pub/speciesRecovery.jsp?sort=1 (accessed November 7, 2013)

TABLE 9.5

Arachnid species with the highest expenditures under the Endangered Species Act, fiscal year 2012

Ranking	Species	Expenditure
1	Meshweaver, Braken Bat Cave (Cicurina venii)	$150,500
2	Spider, spruce-fir moss (Microhexura montivaga)	$29,290
3	Spider, Kauai cave wolf or pe`e pe`e maka `ole (Adelocosa anops)	$25,923
4	Meshweaver, Government Canyon Bat Cave (Cicurina vespera)	$21,590
5	Spider, Government Canyon Bat Cave (Neoleptoneta microps)	$21,300
6	Meshweaver, Robber Baron Cave (Cicurina baronia)	$20,900
7	Meshweaver, Madla's Cave (Cicurina madla)	$20,200
8	Harvestman, Bone Cave (Texella reyesi)	$1,750
9	Spider, Tooth Cave (Leptoneta myopica)	$1,500
10	Harvestman, Bee Creek Cave (Texella reddelli)	$1,150

SOURCE: Adapted from "Table 2. Species Ranked in Descending Order of Total FY2012 Reported Expenditures, Not Including Land Acquisition Costs," in *Federal and State Endangered and Threatened Species Expenditures: Fiscal Year 2012*, U.S. Department of the Interior, U.S. Fish and Wildlife Service, 2012, http://www.fws.gov/endangered/esa-library/pdf/2012.EXP.FINAL.pdf (accessed November 4, 2013)

as critical habitat for six of the arachnids. In addition, four of the species are included in the USFWS's *Recovery Plan for Endangered Karst Invertebrates in Travis and Williamson Counties, Texas* (August 1994, http://ecos.fws.gov/docs/recovery_plan/940825.pdf), which also covers other imperiled invertebrate species living in the caves. The other six arachnids are included in *Bexar County Karst Invertebrates Recovery Plan* (August 2011, http://ecos.fws.gov/docs/recovery_plan/Final%202001%20Bexar%20Co%20Invertebrates%20Rec%20Plan_1.pdf).

In December 2009 the USFWS published five-year reviews for four of the arachnids: Bee Creek Cave harvestman, Bone Cave harvestman, Tooth Cave pseudoscorpion, and Tooth Cave spider. The agency recommended maintaining the endangered listings for all of the species, noting that no significant steps had been taken toward protecting the caves in which the spiders occur.

FIGURE 9.5

A karst cave provides habitat for endangered invertebrates

SOURCE: Lisa O'Donnell, William R. Elliott, and Ruth A. Stanford, "Front Cover," in *Recovery Plan for Endangered Karst Invertebrates in Travis and Williamson Counties, Texas*, U.S. Department of the Interior, U.S. Fish and Wildlife Service, 1994, http://ecos.fws.gov/docs/recovery_plans/1994/940825.pdf (accessed November 12, 2013)

Kauai Cave Wolf Spiders

The Kauai Cave wolf spider, which ranges from about 0.5 to 0.75 of an inch (1.3 to 1.9 centimeters [cm]) in length, is a blind species found only in special caves on the southern part of the island of Kauai in Hawaii. (See Figure 9.6.) These caves were formed by young lava flows. Unlike most other spiders, which trap their prey in webs, the Kauai Cave wolf spider hunts its prey directly. Its prey includes the Kauai Cave amphipod, a species that is also highly endangered. The USFWS originally listed both species as endangered in January 2000. Female Kauai Cave wolf spiders lay 15 to 30 eggs per clutch and carry the young on their back after hatching. Cave species are extremely sensitive to changes in temperature and light. In April 2006 the USFWS published *Recovery Plan for the Kauai Cave Arthropods: The Kauai Cave Wolf Spider (*Adelocosa anops*) and the Kauai Cave Amphipod (*Spelaeorchestia koloana*)* (http://ecos.fws.gov/docs/recovery_plan/060719.pdf). At that time fewer than 28 individual wolf spiders were known to exist. The critical habitat established for the species in 2003 includes 14 units totaling 272 acres (110 ha) in the southern part of the island.

FIGURE 9.6

Kauai Island cave location

■ Presumed and known distribution cave wolf spider and amphipod   ⋯⋯ Elevation (500 ft. contours)   — Primanry roads

Kauai

Main Hawaiian Islands

Island of Kauai

5 2.5 0   5 Kilometers

5 2.5 0   5 Miles

SOURCE: "Figure 1. Island of Kauai," in *Recovery Plan for the Kauai Cave Arthropods: The Kauai Cave Wolf Spider (Adelocosa anops) and the Kauai Cave Amphipod (Spelaeorchestia koloana)*, U.S. Department of the Interior, U.S. Fish and Wildlife Service, 2006, http://ecos.fws.gov/docs/recovery_plan/060719.pdf (accessed November 12, 2013)

Spruce-Fir Moss Spiders

The spruce-fir moss spider is a member of the tarantula family, but is very tiny, measuring only 0.1 to 0.15 of an inch (0.3 to 0.4 cm) in length when fully grown. (See Figure 9.7.) According to the USFWS in "Spruce-Fir Moss Spider" (August 2000, http://www.fws.gov/asheville/pdfs/Spruce%20Fir%20Moss%20Spider.pdf), the spider is found only in the highest mountain forests of western North Carolina and eastern Tennessee. These forests contain Fraser fir and red spruce trees. The spider lives in damp moss mats that grow on rocks sheltered beneath the trees.

The spider was placed on the list of endangered species in 1995. Its populations have declined largely due to the introduction of an invasive European insect species: the balsam-woolly adelgid. The balsam-woolly adelgid infests Fraser fir trees, causing them to die within two to seven years. The death and subsequent toppling of many fir trees thins the forest, allowing winds to blow over other types of trees. The resulting increase in light level and temperature causes the moss mats on the forest floor to dry up.

In July 2001 the USFWS designated critical habitat for the species, including areas in the Great Smoky Mountains National Park and the Pisgah and Cherokee National Forests, as well as a preserve managed by the Nature Conservancy. This designation of critical habitat was prompted by a lawsuit against the USFWS, which had previously deemed designating critical habitat "not prudent" because it believed the spider would be more vulnerable to collectors.

In July 2008 the USFWS initiated a five-year status review of 20 southeastern species, including the spruce-fir moss spider. As of February 2014, the results of the review had not been published.

THREATENED AND ENDANGERED FOREIGN SPECIES OF SPIDERS

The IUCN notes in *Red List of Threatened Species Version 2013.2* that 21 species of arachnids were threatened in 2013. This number accounted for 60% of the 35 evaluated species, but less than 0.1% of the more than 102,000 described arachnid species.

As of February 2014, there were no foreign spiders listed under the ESA.

FIGURE 9.7

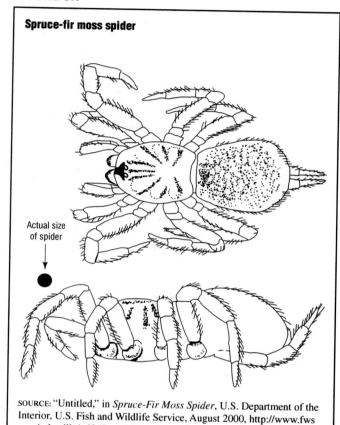

Spruce-fir moss spider

Actual size of spider

SOURCE: "Untitled," in *Spruce-Fir Moss Spider*, U.S. Department of the Interior, U.S. Fish and Wildlife Service, August 2000, http://www.fws.gov/asheville/pdfs/Spruce%20Fir%20Moss%20Spider.pdf (accessed November 12, 2013)

CHAPTER 10
PLANTS

Plants belong to the Plantae kingdom. In general, there are two types of land-growing plants: vascular and nonvascular. Vascular plants have specially developed organs similar to veins that move liquids through their system. This category includes trees, shrubs, flowers, and grasses. Nonvascular plants are mosses, liverworts, and hornworts. The vast majority of plant species on the earth are vascular plants that reproduce through their flowers.

In science, plants are more often identified by their scientific name than are animals. Plant species are so abundant and diverse that many plants have multiple common names. However, there are plants that have no common names because they are rare or are geographically remote. To avoid confusion, this chapter will include the scientific name for any specific common name given.

Several factors contribute to the endangerment of plant species. Many species are the victims of habitat loss because of land and agricultural development. Others have declined because of pollution or habitat damage, or as a result of competition with invasive species. Still other imperiled plants have succumbed to introduced or unknown plant diseases. Finally, collectors or dealers often illegally seek rare, showy, or unusual plants and have depleted populations through overcollection.

The preservation of plant species is important for many reasons. Not only are plants of aesthetic value but also they are crucial components of every ecosystem on the earth. Furthermore, plants serve several functions that are directly beneficial to humans. First, they provide genetic variation that is used in the breeding of new crop varieties—native plants provide genes that allow for adaptation to local environments and resistance to pests, disease, or drought. In addition, plants are the source of many human medicines.

AMERICAN CHESTNUT TREE: MAKING A COMEBACK?

During the 1800s the American chestnut (*Castanea dentata*) was the predominant tree of many forests in the eastern United States. Its range extended from Maine to Mississippi. (See Figure 10.1.) In *American Chestnut ... an American Wood* (February 1973, http://www.fpl.fs.fed.us/documnts/usda/amwood/230chest.pdf), the U.S. Forest Service indicates that the heaviest concentrations were in the southern Appalachian Mountains, where the tree made up more than one-third of the overstory trees (the topmost layer of foliage in a forest). Mature trees reached 3 to 5 feet (0.9 to 1.5 meters [m]) in diameter and rose to 90 feet (27 m) in height with a huge canopy. The species was fast growing and produced a light, durable wood that was extremely popular for firewood and for making furniture, shingles, caskets, telephone poles, railroad ties, and other products. The trees were also valued for their chestnuts and tannin content. Tannin is an extract used in the leather industry.

In 1904 observers in New York City reported that an unknown blight (disease) was killing American chestnut trees at the Bronx Zoo. By 1940 the blight had spread through the entire range of the species, leaving all the trees dead or dying. The tree structure was not damaged by the disease, so the harvesting of dead trees continued for several more decades. Even though sprouts would grow from the stumps that were left behind, they eventually succumbed to the blight. By the 1970s the American chestnut had been virtually eliminated. Approximately 3 billion to 4 billion trees had been killed. The culprit was a fungus originally called *Endothia parasitica*, but later renamed *Cryphonectria parasitica*. Scientists believe the disease came into the United States with ornamental chestnut trees that were imported from Japan or China. Oriental trees could carry the disease, but not succumb to it, because they had a natural immunity to it.

FIGURE 10.1

Historical distribution of the American chestnut

SOURCE: Joseph R. Saucier, "Figure 1. Natural Range of American Chestnut," in *American Chestnut (Castanea dentata). An American Wood*, U.S. Department of Agriculture, U.S. Forest Service, February 1973, http://www.fpl.fs.fed.us/documnts/usda/amwood/230chest.pdf (accessed November 12, 2013)

During the 1920s scientists began crossing the remaining American chestnut trees with the oriental species. Even though the hybrid trees resulted with some resistance to the blight, they were inferior in quality to the original American species. Advances in genetic research and forestry techniques have gradually led to better hybrids. Three organizations have played a key role in the research: the American Chestnut Foundation (TACF), the American Chestnut Research and Restoration Center (ACRRC) at the State University of New York, and the American Chestnut Cooperators' Foundation (ACCF) at Virginia Tech University. The TACF and the ACRRC focus on crossing naturally blight-resistant Asiatic species with American species, whereas the ACCF produces crosses between American chestnut trees that are found to have some resistance to the blight in hopes of eventually producing offspring with higher resistance. All three organizations are confident that vigorous blight-resistant American chestnut trees can be developed during the 21st century.

PROTECTION OF PLANTS UNDER THE ENDANGERED SPECIES ACT

The Endangered Species Act (ESA) of 1973 protects listed plants from deliberate destruction or vandalism. Plants also receive protection under the consultation requirements of the act; that is, all federal agencies must consult with the U.S. Fish and Wildlife Service (USFWS) to determine how best to conserve species and to ensure that no issued permits will jeopardize listed species or harm their habitat.

Regardless, many conservationists believe plants receive less protection than animals under the ESA. First, the ESA only protects plants that are found on federal lands. It imposes no restrictions on private landowners whose property is home to endangered plants. Critics also complain that the USFWS has been slow to list plant species and that damage to plant habitats is not addressed with the same seriousness as for animal species. However, the USFWS points out that the number of plants listed under the ESA has risen dramatically over the past three decades. As of November 2013, this number was nearly 900. In fact, plants (and lichens) accounted for 57% of all species listed under the ESA at that time. (See Figure 10.2.)

In 2000, in an effort to bolster conservation efforts for plants, the USFWS formed an agreement with the Center for Plant Conservation (CPC), a national association of botanical gardens and arboreta. The two organizations are cooperating in developing conservation measures to help save North American plant species, particularly those that are listed as threatened or endangered. Central to the effort is the creation of educational programs that are aimed at informing the public about the importance of plant species for aesthetic, economic, bio-

FIGURE 10.2

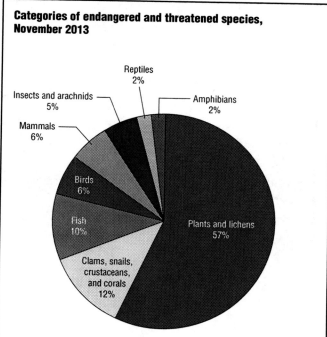

Categories of endangered and threatened species, November 2013

SOURCE: Adapted from "Summary of Listed Species Listed Populations and Recovery Plans as of Fri, 01 Nov 2013 16:05:31 GMT," in *Species Reports*, U.S. Department of the Interior, U.S. Fish and Wildlife Service, November 1, 2013, http://ecos.fws.gov/tess_public/pub/Boxscore.do (accessed November 1, 2013)

logical, and medical reasons. The CPC also aids in developing recovery plans for listed plant species and collects listed species for preservation. As of February 2014, the CPC's (http://www.centerforplantconservation.org/) collection included over 750 "of America's most imperiled native plants."

THREATENED AND ENDANGERED U.S. PLANT SPECIES

As of November 2013, there were 866 U.S. plant species listed under the ESA. (See Table 10.1.) Nearly all the plants had recovery plans in place. Because several species of imperiled plants are often found in the same ecosystem, many recovery plans cover multiple plant species.

The status of most plant species has not been studied in detail. Thus, many more plants are probably in danger of extinction than are listed under the ESA.

The 10 plants with the highest expenditures under the ESA during fiscal year (FY) 2012 are listed in Table 10.2. The golden paintbrush (*Castilleja levisecta*) dominated the list with more than $900,000 in spending. It is a rare flowering herb found only in parts of Oregon and Washington. Almost $800,000 was spent on Johnson's seagrass (*Halophila johnsonii*), a plant that lives underwater in salty lagoons in southeastern Florida. (See Figure 10.3.)

TABLE 10.1

Endangered and threatened plant species, November 2013

Common name	Scientific name	Species group	Listing status[a]	U.S. or U.S./foreign listed	Recovery plan date	Recovery plan stage[b]
Aboriginal prickly-apple	Harrisia (=Cereus) aboriginum (=gracilis)	Flowering plants	E	US	None	—
Acuna cactus	Echinomastus erectocentrus var. acunensis	Flowering plants	E	US/foreign	None	—
A`e	Zanthoxylum hawaiiense	Flowering plants	E	US	5/11/1998	F
A`e	Zanthoxylum dipetalum var. tomentosum	Flowering plants	E	US	5/11/1998	F
A`e	Zanthoxylum oahuense	Flowering plants	E	US	None	—
`Ahinahina	Argyroxiphium sandwicense ssp. macrocephalum	Flowering plants	T	US	7/29/1997	F
`Ahinahina	Argyroxiphium sandwicense ssp. sandwicense	Flowering plants	E	US	9/30/1993	F
Aiakeakua, popolo	Solanum sandwicense	Flowering plants	E	US	8/23/1998	F
`Aiea	Nothocestrum breviflorum	Flowering plants	E	US	5/11/1998	F
`Aiea	Nothocestrum peltatum	Flowering plants	E	US	8/23/1998	F
`Akoko	Euphorbia haeleeleana	Flowering plants	E	US	7/10/1999	F
`Akoko	Chamaesyce celastroides var. kaenana	Flowering plants	E	US	8/10/1998	F
`Akoko	Chamaesyce deppeana	Flowering plants	E	US	8/10/1998	F
`Akoko	Chamaesyce remyi var. kauaiensis	Flowering plants	E	US	6/17/2010	O
`Akoko	Chamaesyce remyi var. remyi	Flowering plants	E	US	6/17/2010	O
`Akoko	Chamaesyce kuwaleana	Flowering plants	E	US	8/10/1998	F
`Akoko	Chamaesyce herbstii	Flowering plants	E	US	8/10/1998	F
`Akoko	Chamaesyce rockii	Flowering plants	E	US	8/10/1998	F
`Akoko	Chamaesyce eleanoriae	Flowering plants	E	US	6/17/2010	O
`aku	Cyanea tritomantha	Flowering plants	E	US	None	—
`Ala `ala wai nui	Peperomia subpetiolata	Flowering plants	E	US	None	—
Alabama canebrake pitcher-plant	Sarracenia rubra ssp. alabamensis	Flowering plants	E	US	10/8/1992	F
Alabama leather flower	Clematis socialis	Flowering plants	E	US	12/27/1989	F
Alabama streak-sorus fern	Thelypteris pilosa var. alabamensis	Ferns and allies	T	US	10/25/1996	F
Alani	Melicope saint-johnii	Flowering plants	E	US	8/10/1998	F
Alani	Melicope balloui	Flowering plants	E	US	7/29/1997	F
Alani	Melicope christophersenii	Flowering plants	E	US	None	—
Alani	Melicope degeneri	Flowering plants	E	US	6/17/2010	O
Alani	Melicope haupuensis	Flowering plants	E	US	9/20/1995	F
Alani	Melicope knudsenii	Flowering plants	E	US	9/20/1995	F
Alani	Melicope lydgatei	Flowering plants	E	US	8/10/1998	F
Alani	Melicope makahae	Flowering plants	E	US	None	—
Alani	Melicope mucronulata	Flowering plants	E	US	7/29/1997	F
Alani	Melicope munroi	Flowering plants	E	US	7/10/1999	F
Alani	Melicope ovalis	Flowering plants	E	US	7/29/1997	F
Alani	Melicope pallida	Flowering plants	E	US	9/20/1995	F
Alani	Melicope paniculata	Flowering plants	E	US	6/17/2010	O
Alani	Melicope quadrangularis	Flowering plants	E	US	8/23/1998	F
Alani	Melicope reflexa	Flowering plants	E	US	8/28/2013	F
Alani	Melicope zahlbruckneri	Flowering plants	E	US	9/26/1996	F
Alani	Melicope hiiakae	Flowering plants	E	US	None	—
Alani	Melicope adscendens	Flowering plants	E	US	7/29/1997	F
Alani	Melicope puberula	Flowering plants	E	US	6/17/2010	O
Aleutian shield fern	Polystichum aleuticum	Ferns and allies	E	US	9/30/1992	F
Amargosa niterwort	Nitrophila mohavensis	Flowering plants	E	US	9/28/1990	F
American chaffseed	Schwalbea americana	Flowering plants	E	US	9/29/1995	F
American hart's-tongue fern	Asplenium scolopendrium var. americanum	Ferns and allies	T	US/foreign	9/15/1993	F
`Anaunau	Lepidium arbuscula	Flowering plants	E	US	8/10/1998	F
Antioch Dunes evening-primrose	Oenothera deltoides ssp. howellii	Flowering plants	E	US	4/25/1984	RF(1)
`Anunu	Sicyos alba	Flowering plants	E	US	9/26/1996	F
Apalachicola rosemary	Conradina glabra	Flowering plants	E	US	9/27/1994	F
Applegate's milk-vetch	Astragalus applegatei	Flowering plants	E	US	4/10/1998	F

TABLE 10.1

Endangered and threatened plant species, November 2013 [CONTINUED]

Common name	Scientific name	Species group	Listing status[a]	U.S. or U.S./foreign listed	Recovery plan date	Recovery plan stage[b]
Arizona cliff-rose	Purshia (=Cowania) subintegra	Flowering plants	E	US	6/16/1995	F
Arizona hedgehog cactus	Echinocereus triglochidiatus var. arizonicus	Flowering plants	E	US	9/30/1984	D
Ash-grey paintbrush	Castilleja cinerea	Flowering plants	T	US	None	—
Ash Meadows blazingstar	Mentzelia leucophylla	Flowering plants	T	US	9/28/1990	F
Ash Meadows gumplant	Grindelia fraxinipratensis	Flowering plants	T	US	9/28/1990	F
Ash Meadows ivesia	Ivesia kingii var. eremica	Flowering plants	T	US	9/28/1990	F
Ash Meadows milk-vetch	Astragalus phoenix	Flowering plants	T	US	9/28/1990	F
Ash Meadows sunray	Enceliopsis nudicaulis var. corrugata	Flowering plants	T	US	9/28/1990	F
Ashy dogweed	Thymophylla tephroleuca	Flowering plants	E	US	7/29/1988	F
Asplenium-leaved diellia	Diellia erecta	Ferns and allies	E	US	12/10/2002	F
Aupaka	Isodendrion laurifolium	Flowering plants	E	US	7/10/1999	F
Aupaka	Isodendrion longifolium	Flowering plants	T	US	12/10/2002	F
Aupaka	Isodendrion hosakae	Flowering plants	E	US	5/23/1994	F
Autumn buttercup	Ranunculus aestivalis (=acriformis)	Flowering plants	E	US	9/16/1991	F
Avon Park harebells	Crotalaria avonensis	Flowering plants	E	US	5/18/1999	—
`Awikiwiki	Canavalia pubescens	Flowering plants	E	US	None	—
`Awikiwiki	Canavalia molokaiensis	Flowering plants	E	US	8/28/2013	F
`Awikiwiki	Canavalia napaliensis	Flowering plants	E	US	6/17/2010	O
Awiwi	Hedyotis cookiana	Flowering plants	E	US	9/20/1995	F
Awiwi	Centaurium sebaeoides	Flowering plants	E	US	7/10/1999	F
Bakersfield cactus	Opuntia treleasei	Flowering plants	E	US	9/30/1998	F
Baker's larkspur	Delphinium bakeri	Flowering plants	E	US	None	—
Bariaco	Trichilia triacantha	Flowering plants	E	US	8/20/1991	F
Barneby reed-mustard	Schoenocrambe barnebyi	Flowering plants	E	US	9/14/1994	F
Barneby ridge-cress	Lepidium barnebyanum	Flowering plants	E	US	7/23/1993	F
Beach jacquemontia	Jacquemontia reclinata	Flowering plants	E	US	5/18/1999	F
Beach layia	Layia carnosa	Flowering plants	E	US	9/29/1998	F
Bear Valley sandwort	Arenaria ursina	Flowering plants	T	US	None	—
Beautiful goetzea	Goetzea elegans	Flowering plants	E	US	4/28/1987	F
Beautiful pawpaw	Deeringothamnus pulchellus	Flowering plants	E	US	5/18/1999	F
Ben Lomond spineflower	Chorizanthe pungens var. hartwegiana	Flowering plants	E	US	9/28/1998	F
Ben Lomond wallflower	Erysimum teretifolium	Flowering plants	E	US	9/28/1998	F
Big-leaved crownbeard	Verbesina dissita	Flowering plants	T	US/foreign	None	—
Black lace cactus	Echinocereus reichenbachii var. albertii	Flowering plants	E	US	3/18/1987	F
Black spored quillwort	Isoetes melanospora	Ferns and allies	E	US	7/7/1993	F
Blowout penstemon	Penstemon haydenii	Flowering plants	E	US	7/17/1992	F
Blue Ridge goldenrod	Solidago spithamaea	Flowering plants	T	US	10/28/1987	F
Bradshaw's desert-parsley	Lomatium bradshawii	Flowering plants	E	US	6/29/2010	F
Brady pincushion cactus	Pediocactus bradyi	Flowering plants	E	US	3/28/1985	F
Braun's rock-cress	Arabis perstellata	Flowering plants	E	US	7/22/1997	F
Braunton's milk-vetch	Astragalus brauntonii	Flowering plants	E	US	9/30/1999	F
Britton's beargrass	Nolina brittoniana	Flowering plants	E	US	6/20/1996	RF(1)
Brooksville bellflower	Campanula robinsiae	Flowering plants	E	US	6/20/1994	F
Bunched arrowhead	Sagittaria fasciculata	Flowering plants	E	US	9/8/1983	F
Bunched cory cactus	Coryphantha ramillosa	Flowering plants	T	US/foreign	4/13/1990	F
Burke's goldfields	Lasthenia burkei	Flowering plants	E	US	None	—
Butte County meadowfoam	Limnanthes floccosa ssp. californica	Flowering plants	E	US	3/7/2006	F
California jewelflower	Caulanthus californicus	Flowering plants	E	US	9/30/1998	F
California Orcutt grass	Orcuttia californica	Flowering plants	E	US	9/3/1998	F
California seablite	Suaeda californica	Flowering plants	E	US	2/10/2010	D
California taraxacum	Taraxacum californicum	Flowering plants	E	US	None	—
Calistoga allocarya	Plagiobothrys strictus	Flowering plants	E	US	None	—

TABLE 10.1

Endangered and threatened plant species, November 2013 [CONTINUED]

Common name	Scientific name	Species group	Listing status[a]	U.S. or U.S./foreign listed	Recovery plan date	Recovery plan stage[b]
Canby's dropwort	Oxypolis canbyi	Flowering plants	E	US	4/10/1990	F
Canelo Hills ladies'-tresses	Spiranthes delitescens	Flowering plants	E	US	None	—
Capa rosa	Callicarpa ampla	Flowering plants	E	US	7/31/1995	F
Cape Sable thoroughwort	Chromolaena frustrata	Flowering plants	E	US	None	—
Carter's mustard	Warea carteri	Flowering plants	E	US	5/18/1999	F
Carter's panicgrass	Panicum fauriei var. carteri	Flowering plants	E	US	12/9/1993	D
Catalina Island mountain-mahogany	Cercocarpus traskiae	Flowering plants	E	US	None	—
Chapman rhododendron	Rhododendron chapmanii	Flowering plants	E	US	9/8/1983	F
Chinese camp brodiaea	Brodiaea pallida	Flowering plants	T	US	None	—
Chisos Mountain hedgehog cactus	Echinocereus chisoensis var. chisoensis	Flowering plants	T	US	12/8/1993	F
Chorro Creek bog thistle	Cirsium fontinale var. obispoense	Flowering plants	E	US	9/28/1998	F
Chupacallos	Pleodendron macranthum	Flowering plants	E	US	9/11/1998	F
Clara Hunt's milk-vetch	Astragalus clarianus	Flowering plants	E	US	None	—
Clay-loving wild buckwheat	Eriogonum pelinophilum	Flowering plants	E	US	11/10/1988	F
Clay phacelia	Phacelia argillacea	Flowering plants	E	US	4/12/1982	F
Clay reed-mustard	Schoenocrambe argillacea	Flowering plants	T	US	9/14/1994	F
Clay's hibiscus	Hibiscus clayi	Flowering plants	E	US	9/20/1995	F
Clover lupine	Lupinus tidestromii	Flowering plants	E	US	9/29/1998	F
Coachella Valley milk-vetch	Astragalus lentiginosus var. coachellae	Flowering plants	E	US	None	—
Coastal dunes milk-vetch	Astragalus tener var. titi	Flowering plants	E	US	6/17/2005	F
Cobana negra	Stahlia monosperma	Flowering plants	T	US/foreign	11/1/1996	F
Cochise pincushion cactus	Coryphantha robbinsiorum	Flowering plants	T	US/foreign	9/27/1993	F
Colorado butterfly plant	Gaura neomexicana var. coloradensis	Flowering plants	T	US	5/25/2010	O
Colorado hookless cactus	Sclerocactus glaucus	Flowering plants	T	US	4/14/2010	O
Colusa grass	Neostapfia colusana	Flowering plants	T	US	3/7/2006	F
Conejo dudleya	Dudleya abramsii ssp. parva	Flowering plants	T	US	9/30/1999	F
Contra Costa goldfields	Lasthenia conjugens	Flowering plants	E	US	3/7/2006	F
Contra Costa wallflower	Erysimum capitatum var. angustatum	Flowering plants	E	US	4/25/1984	RF(1)
Cooke's koki`o	Kokia cookei	Flowering plants	E	US	5/27/1998	F
Cook's holly	Ilex cookii	Flowering plants	E	US	1/31/1991	F
Cook's lomatium	Lomatium cookii	Flowering plants	E	US	3/22/2013	F
Cooley's meadowrue	Thalictrum cooleyi	Flowering plants	E	US	4/21/1994	F
Cooley's water-willow	Justicia cooleyi	Flowering plants	E	US	6/20/1994	F
Coyote ceanothus	Ceanothus ferrisae	Flowering plants	E	US	9/30/1998	F
Crenulate lead-plant	Amorpha crenulata	Flowering plants	E	US	5/18/1999	F
Cumberland rosemary	Conradina verticillata	Flowering plants	T	US	7/12/1996	F
Cumberland sandwort	Arenaria cumberlandensis	Flowering plants	E	US	6/20/1996	F
Cushenbury buckwheat	Eriogonum ovalifolium var. vineum	Flowering plants	E	US	9/30/1997	D
Cushenbury milk-vetch	Astragalus albens	Flowering plants	E	US	9/30/1997	D
Cushenbury oxytheca	Oxytheca parishii var. goodmaniana	Flowering plants	E	US	9/30/1997	D
Davis' green pitaya	Echinocereus viridiflorus var. davisii	Flowering plants	E	US	9/20/1984	F
DeBeque phacelia	Phacelia submutica	Flowering plants	T	US	1/23/2013	O
Decurrent false aster	Boltonia decurrens	Flowering plants	T	US	9/28/1990	F
Del Mar manzanita	Arctostaphylos glandulosa ssp. crassifolia	Flowering plants	E	US/foreign	None	—
Deltoid spurge	Chamaesyce deltoidea ssp. deltoidea	Flowering plants	E	US	5/18/1999	F
Deseret milk-vetch	Astragalus desereticus	Flowering plants	T	US	None	—
Desert yellowhead	Yermo xanthocephalus	Flowering plants	T	US	2/22/2010	O
Diamond Head schiedea	Schiedea adamantis	Flowering plants	E	US	2/2/1994	F
Dudley Bluffs bladderpod	Lesquerella congesta	Flowering plants	T	US	8/13/1993	F
Dudley Bluffs twinpod	Physaria obcordata	Flowering plants	T	US	8/13/1993	F
Dwarf bear-poppy	Arctomecon humilis	Flowering plants	E	US	12/31/1985	F
Dwarf-flowered heartleaf	Hexastylis naniflora	Flowering plants	T	US	None	—

TABLE 10.1

Endangered and threatened plant species, November 2013 [CONTINUED]

Common name	Scientific name	Species group	Listing status[a]	U.S. or U.S./foreign listed	Recovery plan date	Recovery plan stage[b]
Haha	Cyanea mceldowneyi	Flowering plants	E	US	7/29/1997	F
Haha	Cyanea shipmanii	Flowering plants	E	US	5/11/1998	F
Haha	Cyanea st.-johnii	Flowering plants	E	US	8/10/1998	F
Haha	Cyanea superba	Flowering plants	E	US	8/10/1998	F
Haha	Cyanea pinnatifida	Flowering plants	E	US	8/10/1998	F
Haha	Cyanea platyphylla	Flowering plants	E	US	5/11/1998	F
Haha	Cyanea stictophylla	Flowering plants	E	US	5/11/1998	F
Haha	Cyanea grimesiana ssp. obatae	Flowering plants	E	US	8/10/1998	F
Haha	Cyanea hamatiflora ssp. carlsonii	Flowering plants	E	US	9/26/1996	F
Haha	Cyanea lobata	Flowering plants	E	US	7/29/1997	F
Haha	Cyanea macrostegia ssp. gibsonii	Flowering plants	E	US	9/29/1995	F
Haha	Cyanea asarifolia	Flowering plants	E	US	8/23/1998	F
Haha	Cyanea copelandii ssp. copelandii	Flowering plants	E	US	5/11/1998	F
Haha	Cyanea dunbarii	Flowering plants	E	US	None	—
Haha	Cyanea glabra	Flowering plants	E	US	12/10/2002	F
Haha	Cyanea mannii	Flowering plants	E	US	5/20/1998	F
Haha	Cyanea obtusa	Flowering plants	E	US	None	—
Haha	Cyanea procera	Flowering plants	E	US	9/26/1996	F
Haha	Cyanea recta	Flowering plants	T	US	9/20/1995	F
Haha	Cyanea truncata	Flowering plants	E	US	8/10/1998	F
Haha	Cyanea undulata	Flowering plants	E	US	5/31/1994	F
Haha	Cyanea acuminata	Flowering plants	E	US	8/10/1998	F
Haha	Cyanea remyi	Flowering plants	E	US	8/23/1998	F
Haha	Cyanea koolauensis	Flowering plants	E	US	8/10/1998	F
Haha	Cyanea longiflora	Flowering plants	E	US	8/10/1998	F
Haha	Cyanea copelandii ssp. haleakalaensis	Flowering plants	E	US	7/10/1999	F
Haha	Cyanea hamatiflora ssp. hamatiflora	Flowering plants	E	US	7/10/1999	F
Haha	Cyanea kuhihewa	Flowering plants	E	US	6/17/2010	O
Haha	Cyanea eleeleensis	Flowering plants	E	US	6/17/2010	O
Haha	Cyanea dolichopoda	Flowering plants	E	US	6/17/2010	O
Haha	Cyanea kolekoleensis	Flowering plants	E	US	6/17/2010	O
Haha	Cyanea duvalliorum	Flowering plants	E	US	None	—
Haha	Cyanea magnicalyx	Flowering plants	E	US	None	—
Haha	Cyanea maritae	Flowering plants	E	US	None	—
Haha	Cyanea mauiensis	Flowering plants	E	US	None	—
Haha	Cyanea munroi	Flowering plants	E	US	None	—
Haha nui	Cyanea horrida	Flowering plants	E	US	3/7/2006	F
Hairy Orcutt grass	Orcuttia pilosa	Flowering plants	E	US	3/19/1984	F
Hairy rattleweed	Baptisia arachnifera	Flowering plants	E	US	6/17/2010	O
Haiwale	Cyrtandra paliku	Flowering plants	E	US	None	—
Haiwale	Cyrtandra ferripilosa	Flowering plants	E	US	8/10/1998	F
Ha'iwale	Cyrtandra dentata	Flowering plants	E	US	None	—
Ha'iwale	Cyrtandra kaulantha	Flowering plants	E	US	6/17/2010	O
Ha'iwale	Cyrtandra oenobarba	Flowering plants	E	US	8/10/1998	F
Ha'iwale	Cyrtandra polyantha	Flowering plants	E	US	8/10/1998	F
Ha'iwale	Cyrtandra subumbellata	Flowering plants	E	US	8/10/1998	F
Ha'iwale	Cyrtandra crenata	Flowering plants	E	US	8/10/1998	F
Ha'iwale	Cyrtandra giffardii	Flowering plants	E	US	9/26/1996	F
Ha'iwale	Cyrtandra munroi	Flowering plants	E	US	9/29/1995	F
Ha'iwale	Cyrtandra filipes	Flowering plants	T	US	None	—
Ha'iwale	Cyrtandra limahuliensis	Flowering plants	E	US	9/20/1995	F
Ha'iwale	Cyrtandra oxybapha	Flowering plants	E	US	None	—

TABLE 10.1

Endangered and threatened plant species, November 2013 [CONTINUED]

Common name	Scientific name	Species group	Listing status[a]	U.S. or U.S./foreign listed	Recovery plan date	Recovery plan stage[b]
Haha	Cyanea mceldowneyi	Flowering plants	E	US	7/29/1997	F
Haha	Cyanea shipmanii	Flowering plants	E	US	5/11/1998	F
Haha	Cyanea st.-johnii	Flowering plants	E	US	8/10/1998	F
Haha	Cyanea superba	Flowering plants	E	US	8/10/1998	F
Haha	Cyanea pinnatifida	Flowering plants	E	US	8/10/1998	F
Haha	Cyanea platyphylla	Flowering plants	E	US	5/11/1998	F
Haha	Cyanea stictophylla	Flowering plants	E	US	5/11/1998	F
Haha	Cyanea grimesiana ssp. obatae	Flowering plants	E	US	8/10/1998	F
Haha	Cyanea hamatiflora ssp. carlsonii	Flowering plants	E	US	9/26/1996	F
Haha	Cyanea lobata	Flowering plants	E	US	7/29/1997	F
Haha	Cyanea macrostegia ssp. gibsonii	Flowering plants	E	US	9/29/1995	F
Haha	Cyanea asarifolia	Flowering plants	E	US	8/23/1998	F
Haha	Cyanea copelandii ssp. copelandii	Flowering plants	E	US	5/11/1998	F
Haha	Cyanea dunbarii	Flowering plants	E	US	None	
Haha	Cyanea glabra	Flowering plants	E	US	12/10/2002	F
Haha	Cyanea mannii	Flowering plants	E	US	5/20/1998	F
Haha	Cyanea obtusa	Flowering plants	E	US	None	
Haha	Cyanea procera	Flowering plants	E	US	9/26/1996	F
Haha	Cyanea recta	Flowering plants	T	US	9/20/1995	F
Haha	Cyanea truncata	Flowering plants	E	US	8/10/1998	F
Haha	Cyanea undulata	Flowering plants	E	US	5/31/1994	F
Haha	Cyanea acuminata	Flowering plants	E	US	8/10/1998	F
Haha	Cyanea remyi	Flowering plants	E	US	8/23/1998	F
Haha	Cyanea koolauensis	Flowering plants	E	US	8/10/1998	F
Haha	Cyanea longiflora	Flowering plants	E	US	8/10/1998	F
Haha	Cyanea copelandii ssp. haleakalaensis	Flowering plants	E	US	7/10/1999	F
Haha	Cyanea hamatiflora ssp. hamatiflora	Flowering plants	E	US	7/10/1999	F
Haha	Cyanea kuhihewa	Flowering plants	E	US	6/17/2010	O
Haha	Cyanea eleeleensis	Flowering plants	E	US	6/17/2010	O
Haha	Cyanea dolichopoda	Flowering plants	E	US	6/17/2010	O
Haha	Cyanea kolekoleensis	Flowering plants	E	US	6/17/2010	O
Haha	Cyanea duvalliorum	Flowering plants	E	US	None	
Haha	Cyanea magnicalyx	Flowering plants	E	US	None	
Haha	Cyanea maritae	Flowering plants	E	US	None	
Haha	Cyanea mauiensis	Flowering plants	E	US	None	
Haha	Cyanea munroi	Flowering plants	E	US	None	
Haha nui	Cyanea horrida	Flowering plants	E	US	3/7/2006	F
Hairy Orcutt grass	Orcuttia pilosa	Flowering plants	E	US	3/19/1984	F
Hairy rattleweed	Baptisia arachnifera	Flowering plants	E	US	6/17/2010	O
Haiwale	Cyrtandra paliku	Flowering plants	E	US	None	
Haiwale	Cyrtandra ferripilosa	Flowering plants	E	US	8/10/1998	F
Ha'iwale	Cyrtandra dentata	Flowering plants	E	US	None	
Ha'iwale	Cyrtandra kaulantha	Flowering plants	E	US	6/17/2010	O
Ha'iwale	Cyrtandra oenobarba	Flowering plants	E	US	6/17/2010	O
Ha'iwale	Cyrtandra polyantha	Flowering plants	E	US	8/10/1998	F
Ha'iwale	Cyrtandra subumbellata	Flowering plants	E	US	8/10/1998	F
Ha'iwale	Cyrtandra crenata	Flowering plants	E	US	9/26/1996	F
Ha'iwale	Cyrtandra giffardii	Flowering plants	E	US	9/29/1995	F
Ha'iwale	Cyrtandra munroi	Flowering plants	E	US	None	F
Ha'iwale	Cyrtandra filipes	Flowering plants	T	US	9/20/1995	F
Ha'iwale	Cyrtandra limahuliensis	Flowering plants	T	US	9/20/1995	F
Ha'iwale	Cyrtandra oxybapha	Flowering plants	E	US	None	

TABLE 10.1

Endangered and threatened plant species, November 2013 [CONTINUED]

Common name	Scientific name	Species group	Listing status[a]	U.S. or U.S./foreign listed	Recovery plan date	Recovery plan stage[b]
Ha'iwale	Cyrtandra sessilis	Flowering plants	E	US	None	—
Ha'iwale	Cyrtandra tintinnabula	Flowering plants	E	US	5/11/1998	F
Ha'iwale	Cyrtandra viridiflora	Flowering plants	E	US	8/10/1998	F
Hala pepe	Pleomele forbesii	Flowering plants	E	US	None	—
Hala pepe	Pleomele hawaiiensis	Flowering plants	E	US	9/26/1996	F
Hala pepe	Pleomele fernaldii	Flowering plants	E	US	None	—
Harperella	Ptilimnium nodosum	Flowering plants	E	US	3/5/1991	F
Harper's beauty	Harperocallis flava	Flowering plants	E	US	9/14/1983	F
Hartweg's golden sunburst	Pseudobahia bahiifolia	Flowering plants	E	US	None	—
Hau kuahiwi	Hibiscadelphus giffardianus	Flowering plants	E	US	5/11/1998	F
Hau kuahiwi	Hibiscadelphus hualalaiensis	Flowering plants	E	US	5/11/1998	F
Hau kuahiwi	Hibiscadelphus woodii	Flowering plants	E	US	8/23/1998	F
Hawaiian bluegrass	Poa sandvicensis	Flowering plants	E	US	8/23/1998	F
Hawaiian gardenia (=Na'u)	Gardenia brighamii	Flowering plants	E	US	9/30/1993	F
Hawaiian red-flowered geranium	Geranium arboreum	Flowering plants	E	US	7/29/1997	F
Hawaiian vetch	Vicia menziesii	Flowering plants	E	US	5/18/1984	F
Hayun lagu (=(Guam), Tronkon guafi (Rota))	Serianthes nelsonii	Flowering plants	E	US	2/2/1994	F
Heau	Exocarpos luteolus	Flowering plants	E	US	9/20/1995	F
Heliotrope milk-vetch	Astragalus montii	Flowering plants	T	US	9/27/1995	D
Heller's blazingstar	Liatris helleri	Flowering plants	T	US	1/28/2000	RF(1)
Hickman's potentilla	Potentilla hickmanii	Flowering plants	E	US	6/17/2005	F
Hidden Lake bluecurls	Trichostema austromontanum ssp. compactum	Flowering plants	T	US	None	—
Highlands scrub hypericum	Hypericum cumulicola	Flowering plants	E	US	5/18/1999	F
Higo chumbo	Harrisia portoricensis	Flowering plants	T	US	11/12/1996	F
Higuero de sierra	Crescentia portoricensis	Flowering plants	E	US	9/23/1991	F
Hillegrand's reedgrass	Calamagrostis hillebrandii	Flowering plants	E	US	None	—
Hilo ischaemum	Ischaemum byrone	Flowering plants	E	US	5/11/1998	F
Hinckley oak	Quercus hinckleyi	Flowering plants	T	US	9/30/1992	O
Ho'awa	Pittosporum napaliense	Flowering plants	E	US	6/17/2010	F
Hoffmann's rock-cress	Arabis hoffmannii	Flowering plants	E	US	9/26/2000	F
Hoffmann's slender-flowered gilia	Gilia tenuiflora ssp. hoffmannii	Flowering plants	E	US	9/26/2000	F
Holei	Ochrosia kilaueaensis	Flowering plants	E	US	9/26/1996	F
Holmgren milk-vetch	Astragalus holmgreniorum	Flowering plants	E	US	9/29/2006	F
Holy Ghost ipomopsis	Ipomopsis sancti-spiritus	Flowering plants	E	US	9/26/2002	F
Honohono	Haplostachys haplostachya	Flowering plants	E	US	9/20/1993	D
Hoover's spurge	Chamaesyce hooveri	Flowering plants	T	US	3/7/2006	F
Houghton's goldenrod	Solidago houghtonii	Flowering plants	T	US	9/17/1997	F
Howell's spectacular thelypody	Thelypodium howellii spectabilis	Flowering plants	T	US/foreign	6/3/2002	F
Howell's spineflower	Chorizanthe howellii	Flowering plants	E	US	9/29/1998	F
Huachuca water-umbel	Lilaeopsis schaffneriana var. recurva	Flowering plants	E	US/foreign	None	—
Hulumoa	Korthalsella degeneri	Flowering plants	E	US	None	—
Ihi'ihi	Marsilea villosa	Ferns and allies	E	US	4/18/1996	F
Indian Knob mountain balm	Eriodictyon altissimum	Flowering plants	E	US	9/28/1998	F
Ione (incl. Irish Hill) buckwheat	Eriogonum apricum (incl. var. prostratum)	Flowering plants	E	US	None	—
Ione manzanita	Arctostaphylos myrtifolia	Flowering plants	T	US	None	—
Island barberry	Berberis pinnata ssp. insularis	Flowering plants	E	US	9/26/2000	F
Island bedstraw	Galium buxifolium	Flowering plants	E	US	9/26/2000	F
Island malacothrix	Malacothrix squalida	Flowering plants	E	US	9/26/2000	F
Island phacelia	Phacelia insularis ssp. insularis	Flowering plants	E	US	9/26/2000	F
Island rush-rose	Helianthemum greenei	Flowering plants	T	US	9/26/2000	F
Jesup's milk-vetch	Astragalus robbinsii var. jesupi	Flowering plants	E	US	11/21/1989	F
Johnson's seagrass	Halophila johnsonii	Flowering plants	T	US	10/4/2002	F
Johnston's frankenia	Frankenia johnstonii	Flowering plants	E	US/foreign	5/24/1988	F

TABLE 10.1

Endangered and threatened plant species, November 2013 (CONTINUED)

Common name	Scientific name	Species group	Listing status[a]	U.S. or U.S./foreign listed	Recovery plan date	Recovery plan stage[b]
Jones cycladenia	Cycladenia humilis var. jonesii	Flowering plants	T	US	12/30/2008	O
Kamakahala	Labordia triflora	Flowering plants	E	US	7/10/1999	F
Kamakahala	Labordia cyrtandrae	Flowering plants	E	US	8/10/1998	F
Kamakahala	Labordia lydgatei	Flowering plants	E	US	5/31/1994	F
Kamakahala	Labordia tinifolia var. lanaiensis	Flowering plants	E	US	7/10/1999	F
Kamakahala	Labordia helleri	Flowering plants	E	US	6/17/2010	O
Kamakahala	Labordia pumila	Flowering plants	E	US	6/17/2010	O
Kamakahala	Labordia tinifolia var. wahiawaensis	Flowering plants	E	US	8/23/1998	F
Kamanomano	Cenchrus agrimonioides	Flowering plants	E	US	12/10/2002	F
Kauai hau kuahiwi	Hibiscadelphus distans	Flowering plants	E	US	6/5/1996	F
Kauila	Colubrina oppositifolia	Flowering plants	E	US	9/26/1996	F
Kaulu	Pteralyxia macrocarpa	Flowering plants	E	US	None	—
Kaulu	Pteralyxia kauaiensis	Flowering plants	E	US	9/20/1995	F
Kearney's blue-star	Amsonia kearneyana	Flowering plants	E	US	5/24/1993	F
Keck's checker-mallow	Sidalcea keckii	Flowering plants	E	US	None	—
Kenwood Marsh checker-mallow	Sidalcea oregana ssp. valida	Flowering plants	E	US	9/30/1998	F
Kern mallow	Eremalche kernensis	Flowering plants	E	US	None	F
Key tree cactus	Pilosocereus robinii	Flowering plants	E	US/foreign	5/18/1999	F
Kincaid's Lupine	Lupinus sulphureus ssp. kincaidii	Flowering plants	T	US	6/29/2010	F
Kio'ele	Kadua coriacea	Flowering plants	E	US	7/29/1997	F
Kiponapona	Phyllostegia racemosa	Flowering plants	E	US	9/26/1996	F
Kneeland Prairie penny-cress	Thlaspi californicum	Flowering plants	E	US	8/14/2003	F
Knieskern's beaked-rush	Rhynchospora knieskernii	Flowering plants	T	US	9/29/1993	F
Knowlton's cactus	Pediocactus knowltonii	Flowering plants	E	US	3/29/1985	F
Kodachrome bladderpod	Lesquerella tumulosa	Flowering plants	E	US	10/27/2009	O
Kohe malama malama o kanaloa	Kanaloa kahoolawensis	Flowering plants	E	US	7/10/1999	F
Koki'o	Kokia drynarioides	Flowering plants	E	US	5/6/1994	F
Koki'o	Kokia kauaiensis	Flowering plants	E	US	8/23/1998	F
Koki'o ke'oke'o	Hibiscus waimeae ssp. hannerae	Flowering plants	E	US	8/23/1998	F
Koki'o ke'oke'o	Hibiscus arnottianus ssp. immaculatus	Flowering plants	E	US	5/20/1998	F
Kolea	Myrsine linearifolia	Flowering plants	T	US	8/23/1998	F
Kolea	Myrsine mezii	Flowering plants	E	US	6/17/2010	O
Kolea	Myrsine juddii	Flowering plants	E	US	8/10/1998	F
Kolea	Myrsine vaccinioides	Flowering plants	E	US	None	—
Kolea	Myrsine knudsenii	Flowering plants	E	US	6/17/2010	O
Ko'oko'olau	Bidens conjuncta	Flowering plants	E	US	None	—
Ko'oko'olau	Bidens micrantha ssp. kalealaha	Flowering plants	E	US	7/29/1997	F
Ko'oko'olau	Bidens wiebkei	Flowering plants	E	US	8/28/2013	F
Ko'oko'olau	Bidens campylotheca waihoiensis	Flowering plants	E	US	None	—
Ko'oko'olau	Bidens campylotheca pentamera	Flowering plants	E	US	None	—
Ko'oko'olau	Bidens micrantha ctenophylla	Flowering plants	E	US	None	—
Ko'oko'olau	Bidens amplectens	Flowering plants	E	US	None	—
Ko'oloa'ula	Abutilon menziesii	Flowering plants	E	US	9/29/1995	F
Kopa	Hedyotis schlechtendahliana var. remyi	Flowering plants	E	US	7/10/1999	F
Kopiko	Psychotria grandiflora	Flowering plants	E	US	6/17/2010	O
Kopiko	Psychotria hobdyi	Flowering plants	E	US	6/17/2010	O
Kral's water-plantain	Sagittaria secundifolia	Flowering plants	T	US	8/12/1991	F
Kuahiwi laukahi	Plantago princeps	Flowering plants	E	US	7/10/1999	F
Kuahiwi laukahi	Plantago hawaiensis	Flowering plants	E	US	5/11/1998	F
Kuawawaenohu	Alsinidendron lychnoides	Flowering plants	E	US	9/20/1995	F
Kuenzler hedgehog cactus	Echinocereus fendleri var. kuenzleri	Flowering plants	E	US	3/28/1985	F
Kula wahine noho	Isodendrion pyrifolium	Flowering plants	E	US	5/11/1998	F

TABLE 10.1

Endangered and threatened plant species, November 2013 [CONTINUED]

Common name	Scientific name	Species group	Listing status[a]	U.S. or U.S./foreign listed	Recovery plan date	Recovery plan stage[b]
Kuluʻi	Nototrichium humile	Flowering plants	E	US	8/10/1998	F
La Graciosa thistle	Cirsium loncholepis	Flowering plants	E	US	None	—
Laguna Beach liveforever	Dudleya stolonifera	Flowering plants	T	US	None	—
Lake County stonecrop	Parvisedum leiocarpum	Flowering plants	E	US	3/7/2006	F
Lakela's mint	Dicerandra immaculata	Flowering plants	E	US	5/18/1999	F
Lakeside daisy	Hymenoxys herbacea	Flowering plants	T	US/foreign	9/19/1990	F
Lanai sandalwood (= ʻiliahi)	Santalum freycinetianum var. lanaiense	Flowering plants	E	US	9/29/1995	F
Lane Mountain milk-vetch	Astragalus jaegerianus	Flowering plants	E	US	None	—
Large-flowered fiddleneck	Amsinckia grandiflora	Flowering plants	E	US	9/29/1997	F
Large-flowered skullcap	Scutellaria montana	Flowering plants	T	US	5/15/1996	F
Large-flowered woolly meadowfoam	Limnanthes floccosa ssp. grandiflora	Flowering plants	E	US	3/22/2013	F
Large-fruited sand-verbena	Abronia macrocarpa	Flowering plants	E	US	9/30/1992	F
Last Chance townsendia	Townsendia aprica	Flowering plants	T	US	8/20/1993	F
Lauʻehu	Panicum niihauense	Flowering plants	E	US	7/10/1999	F
Laulihilihi	Schiedea stellarioides	Flowering plants	E	US	8/23/1998	F
Layne's butterweed	Senecio layneae	Flowering plants	T	US	12/11/2002	F
Leafy prairie-clover	Dalea foliosa	Flowering plants	E	US	9/30/1996	F
Leedy's roseroot	Rhodiola integrifolia ssp. leedyi	Flowering plants	T	US	9/25/1998	F
Lee pincushion cactus	Coryphantha sneedii var. leei	Flowering plants	T	US	3/21/1986	F
Lehua makanoe	Lysimachia daphnoides	Flowering plants	E	US	6/17/2010	O
Lewton's polygala	Polygala lewtonii	Flowering plants	E	US	5/18/1999	F
Liliwai	Acaena exigua	Flowering plants	E	US	7/29/1997	F
Little Aguja (= Creek) pondweed	Potamogeton clystocarpus	Flowering plants	E	US	6/20/1994	F
Little amphianthus	Amphianthus pusillus	Flowering plants	T	US	7/7/1993	F
Lloyd's Mariposa cactus	Echinomastus mariposensis	Flowering plants	T	US/foreign	4/13/1990	F
Loch Lomond coyote thistle	Eryngium constancei	Flowering plants	E	US	3/7/2006	F
Lompoc yerba santa	Eriodictyon capitatum	Flowering plants	E	US	None	—
Longspurred mint	Dicerandra cornutissima	Flowering plants	E	US	7/1/1987	F
Louisiana quillwort	Isoetes louisianensis	Ferns and allies	E	US	9/30/1996	F
Loʻulu	Pritchardia remota	Flowering plants	E	US	3/31/1998	F
Loʻulu	Pritchardia munroi	Flowering plants	E	US	9/26/1996	F
Loʻulu	Pritchardia kaalae	Flowering plants	E	US	8/10/1998	F
Loʻulu	Pritchardia schattaueri	Flowering plants	E	US	9/26/1996	F
Loʻulu	Pritchardia affinis	Flowering plants	E	US	9/26/1996	F
Loʻulu	Pritchardia napaliensis	Flowering plants	E	US	8/23/1998	F
Lyon's pentachaeta	Pentachaeta lyonii	Flowering plants	E	US	8/23/1998	F
Lyrate bladderpod	Lesquerella lyrata	Flowering plants	T	US	9/30/1999	F
MacFarlane's four-o'clock	Mirabilis macfarlanei	Flowering plants	T	US	10/17/1996	F
Maguire primrose	Primula maguirei	Flowering plants	T	US	6/30/2000	RF(1)
Mahoe	Alectryon macrococcus	Flowering plants	E	US	9/27/1990	F
Makou	Peucedanum sandwicense	Flowering plants	T	US	7/29/1997	F
Malheur wire-lettuce	Stephanomeria malheurensis	Flowering plants	E	US	8/23/1998	F
Mancos milk-vetch	Astragalus humillimus	Flowering plants	E	US	3/21/1991	F
Mann's bluegrass	Poa mannii	Flowering plants	E	US	12/20/1989	F
Many-flowered navarretia	Navarretia leucocephala ssp. plieantha	Flowering plants	E	US	9/20/1995	F
Maʻoliʻoli	Schiedea hawaiiensis	Flowering plants	E	US	3/7/2006	F
Maʻoliʻoli	Schiedea kealiae	Flowering plants	E	US	None	—
Maʻoliʻoli	Schiedea apokremnos	Flowering plants	E	US	8/10/1998	F
Mapele	Cyrtandra cyaneoides	Flowering plants	E	US	8/23/1998	F
Marcescent dudleya	Dudleya cymosa ssp. marcescens	Flowering plants	T	US	9/30/1999	F
Marin dwarf-flax	Hesperolinon congestum	Flowering plants	T	US	9/30/1998	F

Common name	Scientific name	Species group	Listing status[a]	U.S. or U.S./foreign listed	Recovery plan date	Recovery plan stage[b]
Mariposa pussypaws	Calyptridium pulchellum	Flowering plants	T	US	None	—
Marsh sandwort	Arenaria paludicola	Flowering plants	E	US	9/28/1998	F
Mat-forming quillwort	Isoetes tegetiformans	Ferns and allies	E	US	7/7/1993	F
Maui remya	Remya mauiensis	Flowering plants	E	US	7/29/1997	F
Mauna Loa (=Ka'u) silversword	Argyroxiphium kauense	Flowering plants	E	US	11/21/1995	F
McDonald's rock-cress	Arabis macdonaldiana	Flowering plants	E	US	2/28/1984	F
Mead's milkweed	Asclepias meadii	Flowering plants	T	US	9/22/2003	F
Mehamehame	Flueggea neowawraea	Flowering plants	E	US	12/10/2002	F
Menzies' wallflower	Erysimum menziesii	Flowering plants	E	US	9/29/1998	F
Mesa Verde cactus	Sclerocactus mesae-verdae	Flowering plants	T	US	3/30/1984	F
Metcalf Canyon jewelflower	Streptanthus albidus ssp. albidus	Flowering plants	E	US	9/30/1998	F
Mexican flannelbush	Fremontodendron mexicanum	Flowering plants	E	US/foreign	None	—
Miccosukee gooseberry	Ribes echinellum	Flowering plants	T	US	None	—
Michaux's sumac	Rhus michauxii	Flowering plants	E	US	4/30/1993	F
Michigan monkey-flower	Mimulus michiganensis	Flowering plants	E	US	9/17/1997	F
Minnesota dwarf trout lily	Erythronium propullans	Flowering plants	E	US	12/16/1987	F
Missouri bladderpod	Physaria filiformis	Flowering plants	T	US	4/7/1988	F
Mohr's Barbara button	Marshallia mohrii	Flowering plants	T	US	11/26/1991	F
Monterey clover	Trifolium trichocalyx	Flowering plants	E	US	6/17/2005	F
Monterey gilia	Gilia tenuiflora ssp. arenaria	Flowering plants	E	US	9/29/1998	F
Monterey spineflower	Chorizanthe pungens var. pungens	Flowering plants	T	US	9/29/1998	F
Morefield's leather flower	Clematis morefieldii	Flowering plants	E	US	5/3/1994	F
Morro manzanita	Arctostaphylos morroensis	Flowering plants	T	US	9/28/1998	F
Mountain golden heather	Hudsonia montana	Flowering plants	T	US	9/14/1983	F
Mountain sweet pitcher-plant	Sarracenia rubra ssp. jonesii	Flowering plants	E	US	8/13/1990	F
Munz's onion	Allium munzii	Flowering plants	E	US	None	—
Naenae	Dubautia kalalauensis	Flowering plants	E	US	6/17/2010	O
Naenae	Dubautia kenwoodii	Flowering plants	E	US	6/17/2010	O
Na`ena`e	Dubautia waialealae	Flowering plants	E	US	6/17/2010	O
Na`ena`e	Dubautia latifolia	Flowering plants	E	US	8/23/1998	F
Na`ena`e	Dubautia herbstobatae	Flowering plants	E	US	8/10/1998	F
Na`ena`e	Dubautia imbricata imbricata	Flowering plants	E	US	6/17/2010	O
Na`ena`e	Dubautia pauciflorula	Flowering plants	E	US	5/31/1994	F
Na`ena`e	Dubautia plantaginea ssp. humilis	Flowering plants	E	US	12/10/2002	F
Na`ena`e	Dubautia plantaginea magnifolia	Flowering plants	E	US	6/17/2010	O
(=Na`ena`e) lo`ulu	Pritchardia hardyi	Flowering plants	E	US	6/17/2010	O
Nani wai`ale`ale	Viola kauaiensis var. wahiawaensis	Flowering plants	E	US	9/20/1995	F
Nanu	Gardenia mannii	Flowering plants	E	US	8/10/1998	F
Napa bluegrass	Poa napensis	Flowering plants	E	US	None	—
Na Pali beach hedyotis	Hedyotis st.-johnii	Flowering plants	E	US	8/23/1998	F
(=Native yellow hibiscus) ma`o hau hele	Hibiscus brackenridgei	Flowering plants	E	US	12/10/2002	F
Navajo sedge	Carex specuicola	Flowering plants	T	US	9/24/1987	F
Neches River rose-mallow	Spiranthes parksii	Flowering plants	E	US	9/21/1984	F
Neches River rose-mallow	Hibiscus dasycalyx	Flowering plants	T	US	None	—
Nehe	Lipochaeta fauriei	Flowering plants	E	US	9/20/1995	F
Nehe	Lipochaeta lobata var. leptophylla	Flowering plants	E	US	8/10/1998	F
Nehe	Lipochaeta kamolensis	Flowering plants	E	US	7/29/1997	F
Nehe	Lipochaeta micrantha	Flowering plants	E	US	9/20/1995	F
Nehe	Melanthera tenuifolia	Flowering plants	E	US	8/10/1998	F
Nehe	Lipochaeta waimeaensis	Flowering plants	E	US	8/23/1998	F
Nellie cory cactus	Coryphantha minima	Flowering plants	E	US	9/20/1984	F
Nelson's checker-mallow	Sidalcea nelsoniana	Flowering plants	T	US	6/29/2010	F

TABLE 10.1

Endangered and threatened plant species, November 2013 [CONTINUED]

Common name	Scientific name	Species group	Listing status[a]	U.S. or U.S./foreign listed	Recovery plan date	Recovery plan stage[b]
Nevin's barberry	Berberis nevinii	Flowering plants	E	US	None	—
Nichol's Turk's head cactus	Echinocactus horizonthalonius var. nicholii	Flowering plants	E	US	4/14/1986	F
Nioi	Eugenia koolauensis	Flowering plants	E	US	8/10/1998	F
Nipomo Mesa lupine	Lupinus nipomensis	Flowering plants	E	US	None	—
No common name	Achyranthes mutica	Flowering plants	E	US	7/10/1999	F
No common name	Amaranthus brownii	Flowering plants	E	US	3/31/1998	F
No common name	Cyrtandra waiolani	Flowering plants	E	US	None	—
No common name	Delissea undulata	Flowering plants	E	US	9/26/1996	F
No common name	Lobelia gaudichaudii ssp. koolauensis	Flowering plants	E	US	8/10/1998	F
No common name	Neraudia ovata	Flowering plants	E	US	9/26/1996	F
No common name	Phyllostegia floribunda	Flowering plants	E	US	None	—
No common name	Phyllostegia hirsuta	Flowering plants	E	US	8/10/1998	F
No common name	Phyllostegia knudsenii	Flowering plants	E	US	9/20/1995	F
No common name	Phyllostegia parviflora	Flowering plants	E	US	7/10/1999	F
No common name	Platydesma remyi	Flowering plants	E	US	None	—
No common name	Cyanea purpurellifolia	Flowering plants	E	US	None	—
No common name	Sanicula purpurea	Flowering plants	E	US	7/10/1999	F
No common name	Schiedea hookeri	Flowering plants	E	US	7/10/1999	F
No common name	Schiedea membranacea	Flowering plants	E	US	9/20/1995	F
No common name	Schiedea sarmentosa	Flowering plants	E	US	None	—
No common name	Schiedea verticillata	Flowering plants	E	US	3/31/1998	F
No common name	Abutilon eremitopetalum	Flowering plants	E	US	9/29/1995	F
No common name	Abutilon sandwicense	Flowering plants	E	US	8/10/1998	F
No common name	Schiedea obovata	Flowering plants	E	US	8/10/1998	F
No common name	Schiedea trinervis	Flowering plants	E	US	8/10/1998	F
No common name	Bonamia menziesii	Flowering plants	E	US	7/10/1999	F
No common name	Chamaesyce halemanui	Flowering plants	E	US	9/20/1995	F
No common name	Cyanea (=Rollandia) crispa	Flowering plants	E	US	8/10/1998	F
No common name	Delissea rhytidosperma	Flowering plants	E	US	9/20/1995	F
No common name	Gahnia lanaiensis	Flowering plants	E	US	9/29/1995	F
No common name	Geocarpon minimum	Flowering plants	T	US	7/26/1993	F
No common name	Gouania hillebrandii	Flowering plants	E	US	7/16/1990	F
No common name	Gouania meyenii	Flowering plants	E	US	8/10/1998	F
No common name	Gouania vitifolia	Flowering plants	E	US	8/10/1998	F
No common name	Kadua degeneri	Flowering plants	E	US	8/10/1998	F
No common name	Kadua parvula	Flowering plants	E	US	8/10/1998	F
No common name	Hesperomannia arborescens	Flowering plants	E	US	8/10/1998	F
No common name	Hesperomannia arbuscula	Flowering plants	E	US	8/10/1998	F
No common name	Hesperomannia lydgatei	Flowering plants	E	US	8/10/1998	F
No common name	Lipochaeta venosa	Flowering plants	E	US	5/31/1994	F
No common name	Lobelia niihauensis	Flowering plants	E	US	5/23/1994	F
No common name	Lobelia oahuensis	Flowering plants	E	US	8/10/1998	F
No common name	Munroidendron racemosum	Flowering plants	E	US	8/10/1998	F
No common name	Neraudia angulata	Flowering plants	E	US	9/20/1995	F
No common name	Neraudia sericea	Flowering plants	E	US	8/10/1998	F
No common name	Phyllostegia glabra var. lanaiensis	Flowering plants	E	US	7/10/1999	F
No common name	Remya kauaiensis	Flowering plants	E	US	9/29/1995	F
No common name	Schiedea kaalae	Flowering plants	E	US	9/20/1995	F
No common name	Schiedea salicaria	Flowering plants	E	US	8/10/1998	F
No common name	Silene alexandri	Flowering plants	E	US	None	—
No common name	Silene lanceolata	Flowering plants	E	US	9/26/1996	F
No common name	Stenogyne angustifolia angustifolia	Flowering plants	E	US	9/20/1993	D

TABLE 10.1

Endangered and threatened plant species, November 2013 [CONTINUED]

Common name	Scientific name	Species group	Listing status[a]	U.S. or U.S./foreign listed	Recovery plan date	Recovery plan stage[b]
No common name	Stenogyne kanehoana	Flowering plants	E	US	8/10/1998	F
No common name	Tetramolopium arenarium	Flowering plants	E	US	9/26/1996	F
No common name	Tetramolopium filiforme	Flowering plants	E	US	8/10/1998	F
No common name	Tetramolopium lepidotum ssp. lepidotum	Flowering plants	E	US	8/10/1998	F
No common name	Tetramolopium remyi	Flowering plants	E	US	9/29/1995	F
No common name	Tetramolopium rockii	Flowering plants	T	US	9/26/1996	F
No common name	Tetraplasandra bisattenuata	Flowering plants	E	US	6/17/2010	O
No common name	Tetraplasandra lydgatei	Flowering plants	E	US	None	—
No common name	Vigna o-wahuensis	Flowering plants	E	US	7/10/1999	F
No common name	Viola helenae	Flowering plants	E	US	5/31/1994	F
No common name	Viola lanaiensis	Flowering plants	E	US	9/29/1995	F
No common name	Viola oahuensis	Flowering plants	E	US	8/10/1998	F
No common name	Wikstroemia villosa	Flowering plants	E	US	None	—
No common name	Calyptranthes thomasiana	Flowering plants	E	US/foreign	9/30/1997	F
No common name	Chamaecrista glandulosa var. mirabilis	Flowering plants	E	US	5/12/1994	F
No common name	Cordia bellonis	Flowering plants	E	US	10/1/1999	F
No common name	Cyrtandra gracilis	Flowering plants	E	US	None	—
No common name	Daphnopsis hellerana	Flowering plants	E	US	8/7/1992	F
No common name	Lepanthes eltoroensis	Flowering plants	E	US	7/15/1996	F
No common name	Lobelia monostachya	Flowering plants	E	US	8/10/1998	F
No common name	Lysimachia filifolia	Flowering plants	E	US	9/20/1995	F
No common name	Mitracarpus maxwelliae	Flowering plants	E	US	10/6/1998	F
No common name	Mitracarpus polycladus	Flowering plants	E	US/foreign	10/6/1998	F
No common name	Phyllostegia mollis	Flowering plants	E	US	8/10/1998	F
No common name	Pittosporum halophilum	Flowering plants	E	US	None	—
No common name	Pittosporum hawaiiense	Flowering plants	E	US	None	—
No common name	Platanthera holochila	Flowering plants	E	US	7/10/1999	F
No common name	Poa siphonoglossa	Flowering plants	E	US	9/20/1995	F
No common name	Silene hawaiiensis	Flowering plants	T	US	9/26/1996	F
No common name	Ternstroemia subsessilis	Flowering plants	E	US	7/31/1995	F
No common name	Xylosma crenatum	Flowering plants	E	US	9/20/1995	F
No common name	Cyperus pennatiformis	Flowering plants	E	US	7/10/1999	F
No common name	Myrcia paganii	Flowering plants	E	US	9/29/1997	F
No common name	Gesneria pauciflora	Flowering plants	T	US	10/6/1998	F
No common name	Schiedea haleakalensis	Flowering plants	E	US	7/29/1997	F
No common name	Schiedea helleri	Flowering plants	E	US	9/20/1995	F
No common name	Schiedea lydgatei	Flowering plants	E	US	9/26/1996	F
No common name	Schiedea spergulina var. leiopoda	Flowering plants	E	US	9/20/1995	F
No common name	Schiedea spergulina var. spergulina	Flowering plants	T	US	9/20/1995	F
No common name	Schoepfia arenaria	Flowering plants	T	US	1/10/1992	F
No common name	Alsinidendron viscosum	Flowering plants	E	US	9/20/1995	F
No common name	Remya montgomeryi	Flowering plants	E	US	9/20/1995	F
No common name	Aristida chaseae	Flowering plants	E	US	7/31/1995	F
No common name	Auerodendron pauciflorum	Flowering plants	E	US	9/29/1997	F
No common name	Catesbaea melanocarpa	Flowering plants	E	US	8/18/2005	F
No common name	Cyanea profuga	Flowering plants	E	US	None	—
No common name	Leptocereus grantianus	Flowering plants	E	US	7/26/1995	F
No common name	Lyonia truncata var. proctorii	Flowering plants	E	US	7/31/1995	F
No common name	Lysimachia lydgatei	Flowering plants	E	US	7/29/1997	F
No common name	Lysimachia maxima	Flowering plants	E	US	None	—
No common name	Mariscus fauriei	Flowering plants	E	US	9/26/1996	F
No common name	Phyllostegia waimeae	Flowering plants	E	US	9/20/1995	F

TABLE 10.1

Endangered and threatened plant species, November 2013 [CONTINUED]

Common name	Scientific name	Species group	Listing status[a]	U.S. or U.S./foreign listed	Recovery plan date	Recovery plan stage[b]
No common name	Phyllostegia velutina	Flowering plants	E	US	9/26/1996	F
No common name	Phyllostegia warshaueri	Flowering plants	E	US	9/26/1996	F
No common name	Phyllostegia wawrana	Flowering plants	E	US	9/20/1995	F
No common name	Phyllostegia bracteata	Flowering plants	E	US	None	—
No common name	Platydesma cornuta cornuta	Flowering plants	E	US	None	—
No common name	Platydesma cornuta decurrens	Flowering plants	E	US	None	—
No common name	Sanicula mariversa	Flowering plants	E	US	8/10/1998	F
No common name	Schiedea kauaiensis	Flowering plants	E	US	9/20/1995	F
No common name	Schiedea nuttallii	Flowering plants	E	US	7/10/1999	F
No common name	Silene perlmanii	Flowering plants	E	US	8/10/1998	F
No common name	Spermolepis hawaiiensis	Flowering plants	E	US	7/10/1999	F
No common name	Stenogyne bifida	Flowering plants	E	US	9/26/1996	F
No common name	Stenogyne campanulata	Flowering plants	E	US	9/20/1995	F
No common name	Stenogyne cranwelliae	Flowering plants	E	US	None	—
No common name	Trematolobelia singularis	Flowering plants	E	US	8/10/1998	F
No common name	Vernonia proctorii	Flowering plants	E	US	7/31/1995	F
No common name	Cranichis ricartii	Flowering plants	E	US	7/15/1996	F
No common name	Ilex sintenisii	Flowering plants	E	US	7/31/1995	F
No common name	Phyllostegia mannii	Flowering plants	E	US	9/26/1996	F
No common name	Eugenia woodburyana	Flowering plants	E	US	10/6/1998	F
No common name	Phyllostegia kaalaensis	Flowering plants	E	US	8/10/1998	F
No common name	Nesogenes rotensis	Flowering plants	E	US	5/3/2007	F
No common name	Osmoxylon mariannense	Flowering plants	E	US	5/3/2007	O
No common name	Lysimachia venosa	Flowering plants	E	US	6/17/2010	F
No common name	Phyllostegia hispida	Flowering plants	E	US	9/26/1996	O
No common name	Schiedea attenuata	Flowering plants	E	US	6/17/2010	O
No common name	Stenogyne kealiae	Flowering plants	E	US	6/17/2010	O
No common name	Keysseria (=Lagenifera) erici	Flowering plants	E	US	6/17/2010	O
No common name	Keysseria (=Lagenifera) helenae	Flowering plants	E	US	6/17/2010	O
No common name	Lysimachia iniki	Flowering plants	E	US	6/17/2010	O
No common name	Lysimachia pendens	Flowering plants	E	US	6/17/2010	O
No common name	Lysimachia scopulensis	Flowering plants	E	US	6/17/2010	O
No common name	Phyllostegia renovans	Flowering plants	E	US	6/17/2010	O
No common name	Tetraplasandra flynnii	Flowering plants	E	US	6/17/2010	O
No common name	Phyllostegia haliakalae	Flowering plants	E	US	6/17/2010	O
No common name	Phyllostegia pilosa	Flowering plants	E	US	None	—
No common name	Schiedea jacobii	Flowering plants	E	US	None	—
No common name	Schiedea laui	Flowering plants	E	US	None	—
No common name	Stenogyne kauaulaensis	Flowering plants	E	US	None	—
No common name	Festuca molokaiensis	Flowering plants	E	US	None	—
No common name	Diellia mannii	Ferns and allies	E	US	6/17/2010	O
No common name	Asplenium fragile insulare	Ferns and allies	E	US	4/10/1998	F
No common name	Diellia falcata	Ferns and allies	E	US	8/10/1998	F
No common name	Diplazium molokaiense	Ferns and allies	E	US	4/10/1998	F
No common name	Pteris lidgatei	Ferns and allies	E	US	4/10/1998	F
No common name	Adiantum vivesii	Ferns and allies	E	US	1/17/1995	F
No common name	Diellia unisora	Ferns and allies	E	US	8/10/1998	F
No common name	Elaphoglossum serpens	Ferns and allies	E	US	1/17/1995	F
No common name	Polystichum calderonense	Ferns and allies	E	US	1/17/1995	F
No common name	Tectaria estremerana	Ferns and allies	E	US	1/17/1995	F
No common name	Thelypteris inabonensis	Ferns and allies	E	US	1/17/1995	F
No common name	Thelypteris verecunda	Ferns and allies	E	US	1/17/1995	F

TABLE 10.1

Endangered and threatened plant species, November 2013 [CONTINUED]

Common name	Scientific name	Species group	Listing status[a]	U.S. or U.S./foreign listed	Recovery plan date	Recovery plan stage[b]
No common name	Thelypteris yaucoensis	Ferns and allies	E	US	1/17/1995	F
No common name	Diellia pallida	Ferns and allies	E	US	8/23/1998	F
No common name	Doryopteris takeuchii	Ferns and allies	E	US	None	—
No common name	Doryopteris angelica	Ferns and allies	E	US	6/17/2010	O
Nohoanu	Geranium multiflorum	Flowering plants	E	US	7/29/1997	F
Nohoanu	Geranium kauaiense	Flowering plants	E	US	6/17/2010	O
Nohoanu	Geranium hillebrandii	Flowering plants	E	US	None	—
Nohoanu	Geranium hanaense	Flowering plants	E	US	None	—
Northeastern bulrush	Scirpus ancistrochaetus	Flowering plants	E	US	8/25/1993	F
Northern wild monkshood	Aconitum noveboracense	Flowering plants	T	US	9/23/1983	F
North Park phacelia	Phacelia formosula	Flowering plants	E	US	3/21/1986	F
Oahu wild coffee (=kopiko)	Psychotria hexandra ssp. oahuensis	Flowering plants	E	US	None	—
Oha	Delissea rivularis	Flowering plants	E	US	9/20/1995	F
Oha	Delissea subcordata	Flowering plants	E	US	8/10/1998	F
Ohai	Sesbania tomentosa	Flowering plants	E	US	12/10/2002	F
ʻOha wai	Clermontia drepanomorpha	Flowering plants	E	US	5/11/1998	F
ʻOha wai	Clermontia lindseyana	Flowering plants	E	US	9/26/1996	F
ʻOha wai	Clermontia peleana	Flowering plants	E	US	9/26/1996	F
ʻOha wai	Clermontia pyrularia	Flowering plants	E	US	5/11/1998	F
ʻOha wai	Clermontia oblongifolia ssp. brevipes	Flowering plants	E	US	8/28/2013	F
ʻOha wai	Clermontia oblongifolia ssp. mauiensis	Flowering plants	E	US	7/29/1997	F
ʻOha wai	Clermontia samuelii	Flowering plants	E	US	7/10/1999	F
ʻOheʻohe	Tetraplasandra gymnocarpa	Flowering plants	E	US	8/10/1998	F
Okeechobee gourd	Cucurbita okeechobeensis ssp. okeechobeensis	Flowering plants	E	US	5/18/1999	F
Olulu	Brighamia insignis	Flowering plants	E	US	9/20/1995	F
Opuhe	Urera kaalae	Flowering plants	E	US	8/10/1998	F
Orcutt's spineflower	Chorizanthe orcuttiana	Flowering plants	E	US	None	—
Osterhout milkvetch	Astragalus osterhoutii	Flowering plants	E	US	9/30/1992	F
Otay mesa-mint	Pogogyne nudiuscula	Flowering plants	E	US/foreign	9/3/1998	F
Otay tarplant	Deinandra (=Hemizonia) conjugens	Flowering plants	T	US/foreign	12/28/2004	F
Pagosa skyrocket	Ipomopsis polyantha	Flowering plants	E	US	1/23/2013	O
Pāʻiniu	Astelia waialealae	Flowering plants	E	US	6/17/2010	O
Palapalai aumakua	Dryopteris crinalis var. podosorus	Ferns and allies	E	US	6/17/2010	O
Pallid manzanita	Arctostaphylos pallida	Flowering plants	T	US	4/7/2003	D
Palma de manaca	Calyptronoma rivalis	Flowering plants	T	US	6/25/1992	F
Palmate-bracted bird's beak	Cordylanthus palmatus	Flowering plants	E	US	9/30/1998	F
Palo colorado	Ternstroemia luquillensis	Flowering plants	E	US	7/31/1995	F
Palo de jazmin	Styrax portoricensis	Flowering plants	E	US	7/31/1995	F
Palo de nigua	Cornutia obovata	Flowering plants	E	US	8/7/1992	F
Palo de ramon	Banara vanderbiltii	Flowering plants	E	US	3/15/1991	F
Palo de rosa	Ottoschulzia rhodoxylon	Flowering plants	E	US	9/20/1994	F
Pamakani	Tetramolopium capillare	Flowering plants	E	US	7/29/1997	F
Pamakani	Viola chamissoniana ssp. chamissoniana	Flowering plants	E	US	8/10/1998	F
Papala	Charpentiera densiflora	Flowering plants	E	US	6/17/2010	O
Papery whitlow-wort	Paronychia chartacea	Flowering plants	T	US	5/18/1999	F
Parachute beardtongue	Penstemon debilis	Flowering plants	T	US	1/23/2013	O
Pariette cactus	Sclerocactus brevispinus	Flowering plants	T	US	4/14/2010	O
Parish's daisy	Erigeron parishii	Flowering plants	T	US	9/30/1997	D
Pauoa	Ctenitis squamigera	Ferns and allies	E	US	4/10/1998	F
Pecos (=puzzle, =paradox) sunflower	Helianthus paradoxus	Flowering plants	T	US	9/15/2005	F
Pedate checker-mallow	Sidalcea pedata	Flowering plants	E	US	7/31/1998	F
Peebles Navajo cactus	Pediocactus peeblesianus var. peeblesianus	Flowering plants	E	US	3/30/1984	F

TABLE 10.1

Endangered and threatened plant species, November 2013 [CONTINUED]

Common name	Scientific name	Species group	Listing status[a]	U.S. or U.S./foreign listed	Recovery plan date	Recovery plan stage[b]
Peirson's milk-vetch	Astragalus magdalenae var. peirsonii	Flowering plants	T	US	None	—
Pelos del diablo	Aristida portoricensis	Flowering plants	E	US	5/16/1994	F
Pendant kihi fern	Adenophorus periens	Ferns and allies	E	US	12/10/2002	F
Penland alpine fen mustard	Eutrema penlandii	Flowering plants	T	US	8/31/1993	O
Penland beardtongue	Penstemon penlandii	Flowering plants	E	US	9/30/1992	F
Pennell's bird's-beak	Cordylanthus tenuis ssp. capillaris	Flowering plants	E	US	9/30/1998	F
Persistent trillium	Trillium persistens	Flowering plants	E	US	3/27/1984	F
Peter's Mountain mallow	Iliamna corei	Flowering plants	E	US	9/28/1990	F
Pigeon wings	Clitoria fragrans	Flowering plants	T	US	5/18/1999	F
Pilo	Hedyotis mannii	Flowering plants	E	US	5/20/1998	F
Pilo kea lau li'i	Platydesma rostrata	Flowering plants	E	US	6/17/2010	O
Pima pineapple cactus	Coryphantha scheeri var. robustispina	Flowering plants	E	US/foreign	None	—
Pine Hill ceanothus	Ceanothus roderickii	Flowering plants	E	US	12/11/2002	F
Pine Hill flannelbush	Fremontodendron californicum ssp. decumbens	Flowering plants	E	US	12/11/2002	F
Pismo clarkia	Clarkia speciosa ssp. immaculata	Flowering plants	E	US	9/28/1998	F
Pitcher's thistle	Cirsium pitcheri	Flowering plants	T	US	9/20/2002	F
Pitkin Marsh lily	Lilium pardalinum ssp. pitkinense	Flowering plants	E	US/foreign	None	—
Po'e	Portulaca sclerocarpa	Flowering plants	E	US	9/26/1996	F
Pondberry	Lindera melissifolia	Flowering plants	E	US	9/23/1993	F
Popolo	Cyanea solanacea	Flowering plants	E	US	None	—
Popolo ku mai	Solanum incompletum	Flowering plants	E	US	12/10/2002	F
Prairie bush-clover	Lespedeza leptostachya	Flowering plants	T	US	10/6/1988	F
Presidio clarkia	Clarkia franciscana	Flowering plants	E	US	9/30/1998	F
Presidio manzanita	Arctostaphylos hookeri var. ravenii	Flowering plants	E	US	10/6/2003	F
Price's potato-bean	Apios priceana	Flowering plants	T	US	2/10/1993	F
Pua 'ala	Brighamia rockii	Flowering plants	E	US	9/26/1996	F
Purple amole	Chlorogalum purpureum	Flowering plants	T	US	None	—
Pu'uka'a	Cyperus trachysanthos	Flowering plants	E	US	12/10/2002	F
Pygmy fringe-tree	Chionanthus pygmaeus	Flowering plants	E	US	5/18/1999	F
Red Hills vervain	Verbena californica	Flowering plants	T	US	None	—
Relict trillium	Trillium reliquum	Flowering plants	E	US	1/31/1991	F
Roan Mountain bluet	Hedyotis purpurea var. montana	Flowering plants	E	US	5/13/1996	F
Robust spineflower	Chorizanthe robusta var. robusta	Flowering plants	E	US	12/20/2004	F
Rock gnome lichen	Gymnoderma lineare	Lichens	E	US	9/30/1997	F
Rough-leaved loosestrife	Lysimachia asperulaefolia	Flowering plants	E	US	4/19/1995	F
Rough popcornflower	Plagiobothrys hirtus	Flowering plants	E	US	9/25/2003	F
Round-leaved chaff-flower	Achyranthes splendens var. rotundata	Flowering plants	E	US	10/5/1993	F
Rugel's pawpaw	Deeringothamnus rugelii	Flowering plants	E	US	4/5/1988	D
Running buffalo clover	Trifolium stoloniferum	Flowering plants	E	US	6/27/2007	D
Ruth's golden aster	Pityopsis ruthii	Flowering plants	E	US	6/11/1992	RF(1)
Sacramento Mountains thistle	Cirsium vinaceum	Flowering plants	T	US	9/27/1993	F
Sacramento Orcutt grass	Orcuttia viscida	Flowering plants	E	US	3/7/2006	F
Sacramento prickly poppy	Argemone pleiacantha ssp. pinnatisecta	Flowering plants	E	US	8/31/1994	F
Salt marsh bird's-beak	Cordylanthus maritimus ssp. maritimus	Flowering plants	E	US/foreign	12/6/1985	F
San Benito evening-primrose	Camissonia benitensis	Flowering plants	T	US	9/21/2006	F
San Bernardino bluegrass	Poa atropurpurea	Flowering plants	E	US	None	—
San Bernardino Mountains bladderpod	Lesquerella kingii ssp. bernardina	Flowering plants	E	US	9/30/1997	D
San Clemente Island bush-mallow	Malacothamnus clementinus	Flowering plants	E	US	1/26/1984	F
San Clemente Island indian paintbrush	Castilleja grisea	Flowering plants	E	US	1/26/1984	F
San Clemente Island larkspur	Delphinium variegatum ssp. kinkiense	Flowering plants	T	US	1/26/1984	F
San Clemente Island lotus (=broom)	Acmispon dendroideus var. traskiae (=Lotus d. ssp. traskiae)	Flowering plants	T	US	1/26/1984	F
San Clemente Island woodland-star	Lithophragma maximum	Flowering plants	E	US	1/26/1984	F

TABLE 10.1

Endangered and threatened plant species, November 2013 [CONTINUED]

Common name	Scientific name	Species group	Listing status[a]	U.S. or U.S./foreign listed	Recovery plan date	Recovery plan stage[b]
San Diego ambrosia	Ambrosia pumila	Flowering plants	E	US/foreign	None	—
San Diego button-celery	Eryngium aristulatum var. parishii	Flowering plants	E	US	9/3/1998	F
San Diego mesa-mint	Pogogyne abramsii	Flowering plants	E	US	9/3/1998	F
San Diego thornmint	Acanthomintha ilicifolia	Flowering plants	T	US/foreign	None	—
Sandlace	Polygonella myriophylla	Flowering plants	E	US	5/18/1999	F
Sandplain gerardia	Agalinis acuta	Flowering plants	E	US	9/20/1989	F
San Francisco lessingia	Lessingia germanorum (=L.g. var. germanorum)	Flowering plants	E	US	10/6/2003	O
San Francisco manzanita	Arctostaphylos franciscana	Flowering plants	E	US	2/13/2013	O
San Francisco Peaks ragwort	Packera franciscana	Flowering plants	T	US	7/21/1987	F
San Jacinto Valley crownscale	Atriplex coronata var. notatior	Flowering plants	E	US	None	—
San Joaquin adobe sunburst	Pseudobahia peirsonii	Flowering plants	T	US	None	—
San Joaquin Orcutt grass	Orcuttia inaequalis	Flowering plants	T	US	3/7/2006	F
San Joaquin wooly-threads	Monolopia (=Lembertia) congdonii	Flowering plants	E	US	9/30/1998	F
San Mateo thornmint	Acanthomintha obovata ssp. duttonii	Flowering plants	E	US	9/30/1998	F
San Mateo woolly sunflower	Eriophyllum latilobum	Flowering plants	E	US	9/30/1998	F
San Rafael cactus	Pediocactus despainii	Flowering plants	E	US	12/6/2007	O
Santa Ana River woolly-star	Eriastrum densifolium ssp. sanctorum	Flowering plants	E	US	None	—
Santa Barbara Island liveforever	Dudleya traskiae	Flowering plants	E	US	6/27/1985	F
Santa Clara Valley dudleya	Dudleya setchellii	Flowering plants	E	US	9/30/1998	F
Santa Cruz cypress	Cupressus abramsiana	Conifers and cycads	E	US	9/26/1998	F
Santa Cruz Island bush-mallow	Malacothamnus fasciculatus var. nesioticus	Flowering plants	E	US	9/26/2000	F
Santa Cruz Island dudleya	Dudleya nesiotica	Flowering plants	T	US	9/26/2000	F
Santa Cruz Island fringepod	Thysanocarpus conchuliferus	Flowering plants	E	US	9/26/2000	F
Santa Cruz Island malacothrix	Malacothrix indecora	Flowering plants	E	US	9/26/2000	F
Santa Cruz Island rockcress	Sibara filifolia	Flowering plants	E	US	None	—
Santa Cruz tarplant	Holocarpha macradenia	Flowering plants	T	US	None	—
Santa Monica Mountains dudleya	Dudleya cymosa ssp. ovatifolia	Flowering plants	T	US	9/30/1999	F
Santa Rosa Island manzanita	Arctostaphylos confertiflora	Flowering plants	E	US	9/26/2000	F
Schweinitz's sunflower	Helianthus schweinitzii	Flowering plants	E	US	4/22/1994	F
Scotts Valley polygonum	Polygonum hickmanii	Flowering plants	E	US	9/28/1998	F
Scotts Valley spineflower	Chorizanthe robusta var. hartwegii	Flowering plants	E	US	9/28/1998	F
Scrub blazingstar	Liatris ohlingerae	Flowering plants	E	US	5/18/1999	F
Scrub buckwheat	Eriogonum longifolium var. gnaphalifolium	Flowering plants	T	US	6/20/1996	RF(1)
Scrub lupine	Lupinus aridorum	Flowering plants	E	US	6/20/1996	RF(1)
Scrub mint	Dicerandra frutescens	Flowering plants	E	US	5/18/1999	RF(1)
Scrub plum	Prunus geniculata	Flowering plants	E	US	6/20/1996	RF(1)
Seabeach amaranth	Amaranthus pumilus	Flowering plants	T	US	11/12/1996	F
Sea bean	Mucuna sloanei perseircea	Flowering plants	E	US	None	—
Sebastopol meadowfoam	Limnanthes vinculans	Flowering plants	E	US	9/29/1995	F
Sensitive joint-vetch	Aeschynomene virginica	Flowering plants	T	US	9/28/2006	F
Sentry milk-vetch	Astragalus cremnophylax var. cremnophylax	Flowering plants	E	US	8/15/1991	F
Shale barren rock cress	Arabis serotina	Flowering plants	E	US	9/29/2006	F
Shivwits milk-vetch	Astragalus ampullarioides	Flowering plants	E	US	5/18/1999	F
Short-leaved rosemary	Conradina brevifolia	Flowering plants	E	US	5/25/1988	F
Short's goldenrod	Solidago shortii	Flowering plants	E	US	None	—
Showy Indian clover	Trifolium amoenum	Flowering plants	E	US	12/12/2007	F
Showy stickseed	Hackelia venusta	Flowering plants	E	US	9/14/1994	F
Shrubby reed-mustard	Schoenocrambe suffrutescens	Flowering plants	E	US	4/14/1986	F
Siler pincushion cactus	Pediocactus (=Echinocactus, =Utahia) sileri	Flowering plants	T	US	None	—
Slender-horned spineflower	Dodecahema leptoceras	Flowering plants	E	US	3/7/2006	F
Slender Orcutt grass	Orcuttia tenuis	Flowering plants	T	US	7/31/1998	F
Slender-petaled mustard	Thelypodium stenopetalum	Flowering plants	E	US	7/31/1998	F

TABLE 10.1

Endangered and threatened plant species, November 2013 [CONTINUED]

Common name	Scientific name	Species group	Listing status[a]	U.S. or U.S./foreign listed	Recovery plan date	Recovery plan stage[b]
Slender rush-pea	Hoffmannseggia tenella	Flowering plants	E	US	9/13/1988	F
Small-anthered bittercress	Cardamine micranthera	Flowering plants	E	US	7/10/1991	F
Small's milkpea	Galactia smallii	Flowering plants	E	US	5/18/1999	F
Small whorled pogonia	Isotria medeoloides	Flowering plants	T	US/foreign	11/13/1992	RF(1)
Smooth coneflower	Echinacea laevigata	Flowering plants	E	US	4/18/1995	F
Snakeroot	Eryngium cuneifolium	Flowering plants	E	US	5/18/1999	F
Sneed pincushion cactus	Coryphantha sneedii var. sneedii	Flowering plants	E	US	3/21/1986	D
Soft bird's-beak	Cordylanthus mollis ssp. mollis	Flowering plants	E	US	2/10/2010	F
Soft-leaved paintbrush	Castilleja mollis	Flowering plants	E	US	9/26/2000	F
Solano grass	Tuctoria mucronata	Flowering plants	E	US	3/7/2006	F
Sonoma alopecurus	Alopecurus aequalis var. sonomensis	Flowering plants	E	US	None	—
Sonoma spineflower	Chorizanthe valida	Flowering plants	E	US	9/29/1998	F
Sonoma sunshine	Blennosperma bakeri	Flowering plants	E	US	None	—
Southern mountain wild-buckwheat	Eriogonum kennedyi var. austromontanum	Flowering plants	T	US	None	—
South Texas ambrosia	Ambrosia cheiranthifolia	Flowering plants	E	US	None	—
Spalding's catchfly	Silene spaldingii	Flowering plants	T	US	10/12/2007	F
Spreading avens	Geum radiatum	Flowering plants	E	US	4/28/1993	F
Spreading navarretia	Navarretia fossalis	Flowering plants	T	US/foreign	9/3/1998	F
Spring Creek bladderpod	Lesquerella perforata	Flowering plants	E	US	9/8/2006	F
Spring-loving centaury	Centaurium namophilum	Flowering plants	T	US	9/28/1990	F
Springville clarkia	Clarkia springvillensis	Flowering plants	T	US	None	—
Star cactus	Astrophytum asterias	Flowering plants	E	US/foreign	11/6/2003	F
Steamboat buckwheat	Eriogonum ovalifolium var. williamsiae	Flowering plants	E	US	9/20/1995	F
Stebbins' morning-glory	Calystegia stebbinsii	Flowering plants	E	US	12/11/2002	F
St. Thomas prickly-ash	Zanthoxylum thomasianum	Flowering plants	E	US	4/5/1988	F
Suisun thistle	Cirsium hydrophilum var. hydrophilum	Flowering plants	E	US	2/10/2010	D
Swamp pink	Helonias bullata	Flowering plants	T	US	9/30/1991	F
Telephus spurge	Euphorbia telephioides	Flowering plants	T	US	6/22/1994	F
Tennessee yellow-eyed grass	Xyris tennesseensis	Flowering plants	E	US	6/24/1994	F
Terlingua Creek cat's-eye	Cryptantha crassipes	Flowering plants	E	US	4/5/1994	F
Texas ayenia	Ayenia limitaris	Flowering plants	E	US/foreign	None	—
Texas golden gladecress	Leavenworthia texana	Flowering plants	E	US	None	—
Texas poppy-mallow	Callirhoe scabriuscula	Flowering plants	E	US	3/29/1985	F
Texas prairie dawn-flower	Hymenoxys texana	Flowering plants	E	US	4/13/1990	F
Texas snowbells	Styrax texanus	Flowering plants	E	US	7/31/1987	F
Texas trailing phlox	Phlox nivalis ssp. texensis	Flowering plants	E	US	3/28/1995	F
Texas wild-rice	Zizania texana	Flowering plants	E	US	2/14/1996	RF(1)
Thread-leaved brodiaea	Brodiaea filifolia	Flowering plants	T	US	None	—
Tiburon jewelflower	Streptanthus niger	Flowering plants	E	US	9/30/1998	F
Tiburon mariposa lily	Calochortus tiburonensis	Flowering plants	T	US	9/30/1998	F
Tiburon paintbrush	Castilleja affinis ssp. neglecta	Flowering plants	E	US	5/18/1999	F
Tiny polygala	Polygala smallii	Flowering plants	E	US	3/18/1987	F
Tobusch fishhook cactus	Sclerocactus brevihamatus ssp. tobuschii	Flowering plants	E	US	1/31/2001	RF(2)
Todsen's pennyroyal	Hedeoma todsenii	Flowering plants	E	US	None	—
Triple-ribbed milk-vetch	Astragalus tricarinatus	Flowering plants	E	US	5/6/1994	F
Uhiuhi	Caesalpinia kavaiense	Flowering plants	E	US	4/14/2010	O
Uinta Basin hookless cactus	Sclerocactus wetlandicus	Flowering plants	T	US	9/21/1995	D
Ute ladies'-tresses	Spiranthes diluvialis	Flowering plants	T	US	9/11/1998	F
Uvillo	Eugenia haematocarpa	Flowering plants	E	US	4/28/1987	F
Vahl's boxwood	Buxus vahlii	Flowering plants	E	US	None	—
Vail Lake ceanothus	Ceanothus ophiochilus	Flowering plants	T	US	None	—
Ventura Marsh milk-vetch	Astragalus pycnostachyus var. lanosissimus	Flowering plants	E	US	None	—

TABLE 10.1

Endangered and threatened plant species, November 2013 [CONTINUED]

Common name	Scientific name	Species group	Listing status[a]	U.S. or U.S./foreign listed	Recovery plan date	Recovery plan stage[b]
Verity's dudleya	Dudleya verityi	Flowering plants	T	US	9/30/1999	F
Vine Hill clarkia	Clarkia imbricata	Flowering plants	E	US	None	—
Virginia round-leaf birch	Betula uber	Flowering plants	T	US	9/24/1990	RF(2)
Virginia sneezeweed	Helenium virginicum	Flowering plants	T	US	10/2/2000	D
Virginia spiraea	Spiraea virginiana	Flowering plants	T	US	11/13/1992	F
Wahane	Pritchardia aylmer-robinsonii	Flowering plants	E	US	None	—
Walker's manioc	Manihot walkerae	Flowering plants	E	US/foreign	12/12/1993	F
Water howellia	Howellia aquatilis	Flowering plants	T	US	9/24/1996	D
Wawae iole	Huperzia mannii	Ferns and allies	E	US	7/29/1997	F
Wawae iole	Huperzia nutans	Ferns and allies	E	US	8/10/1998	F
Welsh's milkweed	Asclepias welshii	Flowering plants	T	US	9/30/1992	F
Wenatchee Mountains checkermallow	Sidalcea oregana var. calva	Flowering plants	E	US	9/30/2004	F
Western lily	Lilium occidentale	Flowering plants	E	US	3/31/1998	F
Western prairie fringed Orchid	Platanthera praeclara	Flowering plants	T	US/foreign	9/30/1996	F
West Indian walnut (=Nogal)	Juglans jamaicensis	Flowering plants	E	US/foreign	12/9/1999	F
Wheeler's peperomia	Peperomia wheeleri	Flowering plants	E	US	11/26/1990	F
White birds-in-a-nest	Macbridea alba	Flowering plants	T	US	6/22/1994	F
White bladderpod	Lesquerella pallida	Flowering plants	E	US	10/16/1992	F
White-haired goldenrod	Solidago albopilosa	Flowering plants	T	US	9/28/1993	F
White irisette	Sisyrinchium dichotomum	Flowering plants	E	US	4/10/1995	F
White-rayed pentachaeta	Pentachaeta bellidiflora	Flowering plants	E	US	9/30/1998	F
White sedge	Carex albida	Flowering plants	E	US	None	—
Wide-leaf warea	Warea amplexifolia	Flowering plants	E	US	2/17/1993	F
Willamette daisy	Erigeron decumbens var. decumbens	Flowering plants	E	US	6/29/2010	F
Willowy monardella	Monardella viminea	Flowering plants	E	US/foreign	None	—
Winkler cactus	Pediocactus winkleri	Flowering plants	T	US	10/2/1995	D
Wireweed	Polygonella basiramia	Flowering plants	E	US	5/18/1999	F
Wright fishhook cactus	Sclerocactus wrightiae	Flowering plants	E	US	12/24/1985	F
Yadon's piperia	Piperia yadonii	Flowering plants	E	US	6/17/2005	F
Yellow larkspur	Delphinium luteum	Flowering plants	E	US	None	—
Yreka phlox	Phlox hirsuta	Flowering plants	E	US	9/21/2006	F
Zapata bladderpod	Lesquerella thamnophila	Flowering plants	E	US	8/25/2004	F
Zuni fleabane	Erigeron rhizomatus	Flowering plants	T	US	9/30/1988	F

[a]E = Endangered; T = Threatened.

[b]F = Final; D = Draft; RD = Draft revision; RF = Final revision; O = Other.

SOURCE: Adapted from "Generate Species List," in *Species Reports*, U.S. Department of the Interior, U.S. Fish and Wildlife Service, November 2013, http://ecos.fws.gov/tess_public/pub/adHocSpeciesForm.jsp (accessed November 7, 2013), and "Listed FWS/Joint FWS and NMFS Species and Populations with Recovery Plans (Sorted by Listed Entity)," in *Recovery Plans Search*, U.S. Department of the Interior, U.S. Fish and Wildlife Service, November 2013, http://ecos.fws.gov/tess_public/pub/speciesRecovery.jsp?sort=1 (accessed November 7, 2013)

TABLE 10.2

Plant species with the highest expenditures under the Endangered Species Act, fiscal year 2012

Ranking	Species	Expenditure
1	Paintbrush, golden (Castilleja levisecta)	$913,747
2	Seagrass, Johnson's (Halophila johnsonii)	$782,255
3	Lupine, Kincaid's (Lupinus sulphureus ssp. kincaidii)	$761,052
4	Nehe (Lipochaeta kamolensis)	$728,469
5	Water-umbel, Huachuca (Lilaeopsis schaffneriana var. recurva)	$726,139
6	Peppergrass, Slickspot (Lepidium papilliferum)	$638,065
7	Daisy, Willamette (Erigeron decumbens var. decumbens)	$547,428
8	Howellia, water (Howellia aquatilis)	$539,612
9	Checker-mallow, Nelson's (Sidalcea nelsoniana)	$503,935
10	Sunshine, Sonoma (Blennosperma bakeri)	$494,726

SOURCE: Adapted from "Table 2. Species Ranked in Descending Order of Total FY2012 Reported Expenditures, Not Including Land Acquisition Costs," in *Federal and State Endangered and Threatened Species Expenditures: Fiscal Year 2012*, U.S. Department of the Interior, U.S. Fish and Wildlife Service, 2012, http://www.fws.gov/endangered/esa-library/pdf/2012.EXP.FINAL.pdf (accessed November 4, 2013)

FIGURE 10.3

Johnson's seagrass

SOURCE: "Johnson's Seagrass Sketches," in *Welcome to the Johnson's Seagrass Image Gallery*, U.S. Department of Commerce, National Oceanic and Atmospheric Administration, National Marine Fisheries Service, March 18, 2013, http://sero.nmfs.noaa.gov/pr/esa/JohnsonsSeagrassImageGallery.htm (accessed November 12, 2013)

Kincaid's lupine is a tall flowering plant found in western North America. (See Figure 10.4.) More than $750,000 was spent on the species under the ESA during FY 2012.

As of November 2013, there were recovery plans for several hundreds of listed plant species. (See Table 10.1.) Many of the plans cover multiple species. The USFWS provides links to the plans and details about them in "Listed FWS/Joint FWS and NMFS Species and Populations with Recovery Plans" (2014, http://ecos.fws.gov/tess_public/TESSWebpageRecovery?sort=1).

FIGURE 10.4

Kincaid's lupine and Fender's blue butterfly

SOURCE: Adapted from "Fender's Blue Butterfly; Kincaid's Lupine," in *Working Together: Partnerships for Endangered Species Recovery*, U.S. Department of the Interior, U.S. Fish and Wildlife Service, undated, http://www.fws.gov/endangered/esa-library/pdf/fullsize.pdf (accessed November 12, 2013)

PLANT TAXONOMY AND CATEGORIZATION

The taxonomy of plant species can be quite complicated and is plagued by disagreements among scientists. Historically, plants were categorized by morphology (physical characteristics, such as shape or color of their leaves, fruit, bark, and so on). During the 1960s a new classification scheme emerged that groups plants based on their evolutionary similarities, for example, their chemical properties and reproductive mechanisms. This taxonomy is part of the broader science known as phylogenetic systematics, which studies the evolutionary relationships between living organisms. In the future the systematics approach is expected to be used to classify all life forms.

In general, plants are assigned to the same taxonomic levels that are used to classify animals. This hierarchical structure includes kingdom, phylum, class, order, family, genus, and species. Beneath the species level, plants can be classified to subspecies, just as in animal taxonomy. There is an additional classification for plants at this level called variety (abbreviated as "var."). Varieties are subgroups with unique differences between them. For example, the invasive species known as kudzu has the scientific name *Pueraria montana*. There are two varieties: *Pueraria montana* var. *lobata* and *Pueraria montana* var. *montana*. The *lobata* variety is commonly found in the United States, whereas the *montana* variety is not.

Plant taxonomy also includes additional taxa (groups) between kingdom and phylum called subkingdom, superdivision, and division that distinguish between broad categories of plants. The subkingdom level distinguishes between vascular and nonvascular plants. Within vascular plants, there are two superdivisions: seed plants and seedless plants. Seed plants are divided into various divisions, the largest of which is flowering plants.

The USFWS uses four broad categories for plant types: conifers and cycads, ferns and allies, lichens, and flowering plants. These categories are division levels or similar groupings.

Conifers and Cycads

Conifers are cone-bearing, woody plants. Most are trees; only a few species are shrubs. Common tree types include cedar, cypress, fir, pine, redwood, and spruce. Cycads are unusual plants often mistaken for palms or ferns. They have thick, soft trunks and large, leaflike crowns. Cycads are found in tropical or semitropical regions. Their rarity makes them popular with collectors. As of November 2013, there were only three conifers or cycads listed under the ESA. (See Table 10.1.)

The Santa Cruz cypress (*Cupressus abramsiana*) and the gowen cypress (*Cupressus goveniana*) are conifers found only in Southern California. The Santa Cruz cypress was listed as endangered, and the gowen cypress was listed as threatened. Both species are imperiled because they have a limited range of distribution and are threatened by alteration and loss of habitat.

The Florida torreya (*Torreya taxifolia*) is a cycad. This scrubby tree is extremely rare and is found only on the bluffs along the Apalachicola River in the Florida Panhandle. An unknown disease virtually wiped out the species in the wild during the 1950s. Thus, it has been given an endangered listing.

Ferns and Allies

According to the International Union for Conservation of Nature (IUCN) in *Red List of Threatened Species Version 2013.2* (November 2013, http://www.iucnredlist.org/about/summary-statistics), there are approximately 12,000 described species considered to be ferns and allies. Ferns are an abundant and diverse plant group and are associated mostly with tropical and subtropical regions. In general, these plants are characterized by stems with long protruding leaves called fronds. Fern allies are plants with similar life cycles to ferns, but without their stem or leaf structure. Examples of fern allies include club mosses and horsetails.

As of November 2013, there were 30 fern and allied species listed under the ESA. (See Table 10.1.) Nearly all were endangered.

Lichens

Lichens are not truly plants. Scientists place them in the fungi kingdom, instead of the plant kingdom. Lichens are plantlike life forms composed of two separate organisms: a fungus and an alga. In *Red List of Threatened Species Version 2013.2*, the IUCN indicates that 17,000 described lichens are known to science. Biologists believe there are up to 4,000 lichen species in the United States. They are found in many different habitats and grow extremely slowly. Some lichens look like moss, whereas others appear more like traditional plants with a leafy or blade structure. Lichens do not have a "skin" to protect them from the atmosphere. As a result, they are highly sensitive to air contaminants and have disappeared from many urban areas, presumably because of air pollution. Lichens are most predominant in undisturbed forests, bogs, and wetlands, particularly in California, Florida, Hawaii, the Appalachians, and the Pacific Northwest. They are commonly found on rocky outcroppings. Lichens provide a foodstuff for some animals and are used by some bird species in nest building.

As of November 2013, there were two lichen species listed under the ESA: rock gnome lichen (*Gymnoderma lineare*) and Florida perforate cladonia (*Cladonia perforata*). (See Table 10.1.) Both were classified as endangered. During the 1970s rock gnome lichen was virtually wiped out in the Great Smoky Mountains National Park in Tennessee because of zealous collecting by scientists. Florida perforate cladonia is found only in rosemary scrub habitats in portions of Florida. It is endangered because of loss or degradation of those habitats.

Flowering Plants

Flowering plants are vascular plants with flowers—clusters of specialized leaves that participate in reproduction. The flowers of some species are large and colorful, whereas others are extremely small and barely noticeable to humans. In *Red List of Threatened Species Version 2013.2*, the IUCN indicates that there are 268,000 described flowering plants. Biologists estimate that 80% to 90% of all plants on the earth are flowering plants.

As of November 2013, there were 831 flowering plants listed as endangered or threatened under the ESA. (See Table 10.1.) They come from a wide variety of taxonomic groups and are found in many different habitats. Some of the largest families represented are:

- Asteraceae (asters, daisies, and sunflowers)
- Brassicaceae (mustard and cabbage)
- Campanulaceae (bellflowers)
- Fabaceae (legumes and pulses)
- Lamiaceae (mints)

GEOGRAPHICAL BREAKDOWN OF PLANTS

Most threatened and endangered plant species in the United States are concentrated in specific areas of the country. Hawaii, California, and the Southeast (particularly Florida) are home to the majority of listed plant species.

Hawaiian Plants

Figure 10.5 shows the eight major islands that make up the state of Hawaii. The island of Oahu is home to the state's capital Honolulu. Oahu, however, is not the largest of the islands. That distinction goes to the island labeled "Hawaii," which is commonly called "the Big Island." In the following discussion, the term *Hawaii* refers to the entire state.

According to the USFWS in "48 Kaua'i Species Protected under Endangered Species Act" (March 10, 2010, http://www.fws.gov/pacificislands/news%20releases/Kauai 48ListingNR031010.pdf), Hawaii has the most endangered and threatened species of any state in the country. Because of its isolation from continental land masses, many of the species found in Hawaii exist nowhere else in the world. In fact, an estimated 90% of Hawaiian plant species are endemic. Because of large-scale

deforestation and habitat destruction on the islands, Hawaii is home to more threatened and endangered plants than any other state in the nation. The USFWS (http://ecos.fws.gov/tess_public/pub/adHocSpeciesForm.jsp) reports that as of November 2013, there were more than 300 listed plant species in Hawaii. Nearly all are flowering plants and have an endangered listing.

Hawaiian plants have suffered from the introduction of invasive predators such as cows, pigs, and insects, as well as from the loss of critical pollinators with the decline of many species of native birds and insects. According to Marie M. Bruegemann in "A Plan for Hawaiian Plants and Their Ecosystems" (*Endangered Species Bulletin*, vol. 28, no. 4, July–December 2003), 100 of Hawaii's 1,500 known plant species are believed to have become extinct since the islands were colonized by humans.

The USFWS has developed more than a dozen recovery plans for imperiled Hawaiian plants. Many of the plans cover multiple species that are found in the same ecosystem or habitat type, such as:

- *Recovery Plan for the Big Island Plant Cluster* (September 1996, http://ecos.fws.gov/docs/recovery_plan/960926a.pdf)—22 species
- *Recovery Plan for the Oahu Plants* (August 1998, http://ecos.fws.gov/docs/recovery_plan/980810.pdf)—66 species
- *Recovery Plan for the Multi-island Plants* (July 1999, http://ecos.fws.gov/docs/recovery_plan/990710.pdf)—26 species
- *Recovery Outline for the Kauai Ecosystem* (June 2010, http://ecos.fws.gov/docs/recovery_plan/Recovery%20Outline%20Kauai%20Ecosystem.pdf)—45 plant species

Californian Plants

The USFWS (http://ecos.fws.gov/tess_public/pub/adHocSpeciesForm.jsp) reports that as of February 2014 California was home to 185 imperiled plants, including several types of checker-mallow, dudleya, evening primrose, grass, jewelflower, larkspur, manzanita, milk-vetch, paintbrush, rock-cress, spineflower, and thistle.

MILK-VETCH. Milk-vetch is an herbaceous perennial flowering plant that is found in various parts of the world. It received its common name during the 1500s because of a belief among European farmers that the plant increased the milk yield of goats. As of February 2014, there were 12 species of milk-vetch listed as threatened or endangered in California:

- Applegate's milk-vetch (*Astragalus applegatei*)
- Ash Meadows milk-vetch (*Astragalus phoenix*)

FIGURE 10.5

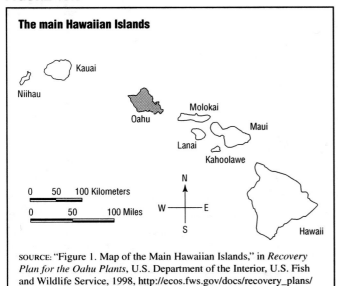

The main Hawaiian Islands

Kauai

Niihau

Oahu

Molokai

Maui

Lanai

Kahoolawe

0   50   100 Kilometers

0   50   100 Miles

N
W   E
S

Hawaii

SOURCE: "Figure 1. Map of the Main Hawaiian Islands," in *Recovery Plan for the Oahu Plants*, U.S. Department of the Interior, U.S. Fish and Wildlife Service, 1998, http://ecos.fws.gov/docs/recovery_plans/1998/980810.pdf (accessed November 12, 2013)

- Braunton's milk-vetch (*Astragalus brauntonii*)

- Clara Hunt's milk-vetch (*Astragalus clarianus*)

- Coachella Valley milk-vetch (*Astragalus lentiginosus* var. *coachellae*)

- Coastal dunes milk-vetch (*Astragalus tener* var. *titi*)

- Cushenbury milk-vetch (*Astragalus albens*)

- Fish Slough milk-vetch (*Astragalus lentiginosus* var. *piscinensis*)

- Lane Mountain milk-vetch (*Astragalus jaegerianus*)

- Peirson's milk-vetch (*Astragalus magdalenae* var. *peirsonii*)

- Triple-ribbed milk-vetch (*Astragalus tricarinatus*)

- Ventura Marsh milk-vetch (*Astragalus pycnostachyus* var. *lanosissimus*)

Peirson's milk-vetch is a plant with a long history of litigation and controversy in California. It is found in only one small area of Imperial County in the southern part of the state. This area is the Imperial Sand Dunes Recreation Area (ISDRA), which is managed by the U.S. Bureau of Land Management (BLM). ISDRA has a remote and barren landscape that is dominated by huge rolling sand dunes—the Algodones Dunes, the largest sand dune fields in North America. ISDRA covers 185,000 acres (75,000 hectares [ha]) and is a popular destination for off-highway vehicle (OHV) riders, receiving more than 1 million visitors annually.

In 1998 Peirson's milk-vetch was designated a threatened species by the USFWS because of the threat of destruction by OHVs and other recreational activities at ISDRA. The agency decided not to designate critical habitat at that time, fearing the remaining plants would be subject to deliberate vandalism. The BLM was sued by conservation groups and accused of not consulting with the USFWS about the threats to Peirson's milk-vetch before establishing a management plan for ISDRA. In 2000, in response to that lawsuit, the BLM closed more than a third of ISDRA to OHV use.

In October 2001 a petition to delist the species was submitted on behalf of the American Sand Association, the San Diego Off-Road Coalition, and the Off-Road Business Association. A month later two lawsuits were filed against the USFWS by conservation organizations challenging the agency's decision not to designate critical habitat for the species. Under court order, the USFWS proposed critical habitat in 2003.

In August 2004 the USFWS (http://www.fws.gov/policy/library/2004/04-17575.html) issued a final designation of critical habitat for Peirson's milk-vetch that encompassed 21,836 acres (8,837 ha) of ISDRA. This was less than half of the acreage originally proposed.

The reduction was made after an economic analysis revealed that closure of ISDRA areas to OHV use would have a negative impact on local businesses. In February 2008 the USFWS (http://edocket.access.gpo.gov/2008/pdf/08-545.pdf) issued a new final designation of critical habitat that included 12,105 acres (4,899 ha), substantially less area than was designated in 2004. (See Figure 10.6.) The new designation excluded acreage because of the "disproportionately high economic and social impacts" of including it in the critical habitat.

In June 2004 the USFWS completed a status review that was triggered by the 2001 delisting proposal and found that the species should remain listed as threatened. In 2005 the original petitioners and additional OHV and motorcycle associations submitted a new petition to delist Peirson's milk-vetch. In a 90-day finding the USFWS

FIGURE 10.6

Critical habitat for Peirson's milk-vetch

Note: BLM = Bureau of Land Management.

SOURCE: "Index Map of Critical Habitat for Astragalus magdalenae var. peirsonii (Peirson's Milk-Vetch)," in "Endangered and Threatened Wildlife and Plants; Revised Designation of Critical Habitat for Astragalus magdalenae var. peirsonii (Peirson's Milk-Vetch)," *Federal Register*, vol. 73, no. 31, February 14, 2008, http://www.gpo.gov/fdsys/pkg/FR-2008-02-14/pdf/08-545.pdf (accessed November 12, 2013) announced that the petition did present adequate information indicating that delisting might be warranted. However, in July 2008 the agency issued a 12-month finding that delisting was not warranted.

In September 2008 the USFWS (http://ecos.fws.gov/docs/five_year_review/doc1995.pdf) completed a five-year status review of Peirson's milk-vetch in which the agency recommended no changes to the species' threatened listing under the ESA. The USFWS noted that OHV activity remained the "primary threat" to the plant's survival.

In April 2012 the USFWS (http://www.gpo.gov/fdsys/pkg/FR-2012-04-27/pdf/2012-10212.pdf) provided notice that it was initiating a five-year review of dozens

of western species including the Peirson's milk-vetch. As of February 2014, the results of the review had not been released.

LOS ANGELES BASIN MOUNTAIN PLANTS. Many species of threatened and endangered plants have reached their precarious state because of urbanization and other human activity. Figure 10.7 shows the species distribution of six threatened and endangered plant species that are found in the mountains surrounding the Los Angeles basin:

- Braunton's milk-vetch (*Astragalus brauntonii*)
- Conejo dudleya (*Dudleya abramsii* ssp. *parva*)
- Lyon's pentachaeta (*Pentachaeta lyonii*)

FIGURE 10.7

Distribution of six endangered and threatened plant species in the mountains surrounding the Los Angeles basin

- ● *Astragalus brauntonii*
- ✚ *Dudleya cymosa* ssp. *marcescens*
- ▲ *Dudleya cymosa* ssp. *ovatifolia*
- ☐ *Dudleya abramsii* ssp. *parva*
- ■ *Dudleya verityi*
- ▨ *Pentachaeta lyonii*

SOURCE: "Figure 1. Distributions of the Six Plant Species," in *Recovery Plan for Six Plants from the Mountains Surrounding the Los Angeles Basin*, U.S. Fish and Wildlife Service, September 30, 1999, http://ecos.fws.gov/docs/recovery_plans/1999/990930a.pdf (accessed November 12, 2013)

- Marcescent dudleya (*Dudleya cymosa* ssp. *marcescens*)

- Santa Monica Mountains dudleya (*Dudleya cymosa* ssp. *ovatifolia*)

- Verity's dudleya (*Dudleya verityi*)

In September 1999 the USFWS published *Recovery Plan for Six Plants from the Mountains surrounding the Los Angeles Basin* (http://ecos.fws.gov/docs/recovery _plans/1999/990930a.pdf). The agency cited threats including "urban development, recreational activities, alteration of fire cycles, fire suppression and pre-suppression (fuel modification) activities, over collecting, habitat fragmentation and degradation, and competition from invasive weeds. Several of the plants are also threatened with extinction from random events because their numbers and ranges are so limited."

In April 2013 the USFWS (http://www.gpo.gov/ fdsys/pkg/FR-2013-04-01/pdf/2013-07495.pdf) published notice that it was initiating five-year status reviews for 18 animal and 38 plant species in California and Nevada, including dozens of California plants. As of February 2014, the results of the review had not been published.

Southeastern Plants

As of February 2014, the USFWS (http://ecos.fws.gov/ tess_public/pub/adHocSpeciesForm.jsp) indicated that the southeastern states contained more than 150 threatened and endangered plant species listed under the ESA. The most common families are the Asteraceae (asters, daisies, and sunflowers), Fabaceae (legumes and pulses), and Lamiaceae (mints).

FLORIDIAN PLANTS. Approximately 50 of the threatened and endangered plant species listed under the ESA are found only in Florida. They include multiple species of mint, pawpaw, rosemary, and spurge.

Many of Florida's imperiled plants are found in the southern part of the state—the only subtropical ecological habitat in the continental United States. The majority of native plant species located in the bottom half of the southern Florida ecosystem originated from the tropics.

In May 1999 the USFWS published *South Florida Multi-species Recovery Plan* (http://ecos.fws.gov/docs /recovery_plan/990518_1.pdf), which covered 68 species, including 35 plant species. In late 2006 an implementation schedule for many, but not all, of the species in the plan was issued. The *South Florida Multi-species Recovery Plan* is considered a landmark plan, because it was one of the first recovery plans to focus on an ecosystem approach to recovery, rather than on a species-by-species approach.

FIGURE 10.8

Pondberry

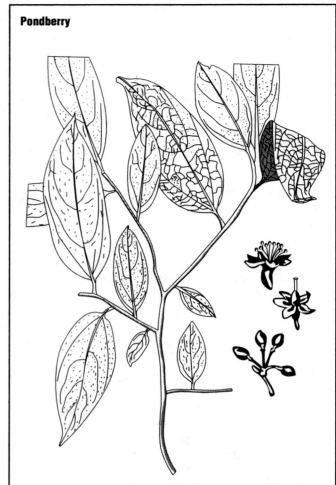

SOURCE: Linda DeLay et al., "Front Cover," in *Recovery Plan for Pondberry (Lindera melissifolia)*, U.S. Department of the Interior, U.S. Fish and Wildlife Service, 1993, http://ecos.fws.gov/docs/recovery_ plan/930923a.pdf (accessed November 12, 2013)

PONDBERRY. Another southeastern imperiled plant is the pondberry. (See Figure 10.8.) The plant is a member of the Lauraceae family, which includes dozens of trees and shrubs. The pondberry is a shrub that grows to be about 6 feet (1.8 m) tall. It is deciduous (meaning it loses its leaves during some part of the year) and produces tiny red berries during late summer or early fall. It prefers lowland habitats with moist soil. In "Pondberry" (February 26, 2013, http://www.dnr.sc.gov/ marine/mrri/acechar/specgal/berrypon.htm), the South Carolina Department of Natural Resources notes that "pondberry does not have any particular aesthetic value, nor are any horticultural, medicinal, or other economic uses known."

The pondberry has been listed under the ESA as endangered since 1986. A recovery plan for the species was issued in 1993. The elimination and development of lowland forests across the South contributed to its imperiled condition. According to Zoë Hoyle in "Pondberry:

TABLE 10.3

Foreign endangered and threatened plant species, November 2013

Common name	Scientific name	Listing status*	Historic range	Species group
Chilean false larch	Fitzroya cupressoides	T	Chile, Argentina	Conifers and cycads
Costa Rican jatropha	Jatropha costaricensis	E	Costa Rica	Flowering plants
Guatemalan fir (=pinabete)	Abies guatemalensis	T	Mexico, Guatemala, Honduras, El Salvador	Conifers and cycads

*E = Endangered; T = Threatened.

SOURCE: Adapted from "Generate Species List," in *Species Reports*, U.S. Department of the Interior, U.S. Fish and Wildlife Service, November 2013, http://ecos.fws.gov/tess_public/pub/adHocSpeciesForm.jsp (accessed November 7, 2013)

Modest but Mysterious" (*Compass*, no. 6, July 2006), scientists believe that the pondberry has always been rare. Approximately three dozen separate populations of the species are known to exist. They are so scattered that scientists believe the plant's seeds must have been spread by floods in the distant past. Extensive flood control measures implemented across the South in recent decades have likely limited the further spread of the species. Hoyle notes that approximately $5 million was spent by various federal agencies between 2002 and 2006 to study factors that affect the plant's survival. In April 2010 the USFWS (http://www.gpo.gov/fdsys/search/citation.result .FR.action?federalRegister.volume=2010&federalRegister .page=18233&publication=FR) initiated a five-year status review for 10 southeastern species, including the pondberry. As of February 2014, the results of that review had not been published.

THREATENED AND ENDANGERED FOREIGN SPECIES OF PLANTS

In *Red List of Threatened Species Version 2013.2*, the IUCN indicates that there were 10,065 species of threatened plants (including flowering plants, gymnosperms, ferns and allies, mosses, and green and red algae) and nine species of lichens, mushrooms, and brown algae in 2013. Habitat loss is the primary reason for the threatened status of the vast majority of IUCN-listed plants. The IUCN notes that 307,674 flowering plants, gymnosperms, ferns and allies, mosses, and green and red algae and 51,623 species of lichens, mushrooms, and brown algae are known and described around the world.

As of November 2013, the USFWS listed only three totally foreign species of plants as threatened or endangered under the ESA. (See Table 10.3.) All three are found in Mexico or in Central or South America.

IMPORTANT NAMES
AND ADDRESSES

Alaska Fisheries Science Center
National Oceanic and Atmospheric
Administration
U.S. Department of
Commerce
7600 Sand Point Way NE, Bldg. 4
Seattle, WA 98115
(206) 526-4000
FAX: (206) 526-4004
E-mail: afsc.webmaster@noaa.gov
URL: http://www.afsc.noaa.gov/

AmphibiaWeb
Museum of Vertebrate
Zoology
University of California
3101 Valley Life Sciences Bldg.
Berkeley, CA 94720-3160
(510) 642-3567
FAX: (510) 643-8238
E-mail: supportamphibiaweb@berkeley.edu
URL: http://amphibiaweb.org/

Bureau of Land Management
1849 C St. NW, Rm. 5665
Washington, DC 20240
(202) 208-3801
FAX: (202) 208-5242
URL: http://www.blm.gov/

Bureau of Reclamation
1849 C St. NW
Washington, DC 20240-0001
(202) 513-0501
FAX: (202) 513-0309
URL: http://www.usbr.gov/

Center for Biological Diversity
PO Box 710
Tucson, AZ 85702-0710
(520) 623-5252
1-866-357-3349
FAX: (520) 623-9797
E-mail: center@biologicaldiversity.org
URL: http://www.biologicaldiversity.org/

Center for Plant Conservation
PO Box 299
St. Louis, MO 63166-0299
(314) 577-9450
FAX: (314) 577-9456
E-mail: cpc@mobot.org
URL: http://www.centerforplant
conservation.org/

Congressional Research
Service
Library of Congress
101 Independence Ave. SE
Washington, DC 20540
(202) 707-5000
URL: http://www.loc.gov/crsinfo/

Convention on International
Trade in Endangered Species
of Wild Fauna and Flora
Secretariat
International Environment House
11 Chemin des Anémones
Geneva, CH-1219, Switzerland
(011-41-22) 917-81-39/40
FAX: (011-41-22) 797-34-17
E-mail: info@cites.org
URL: http://www.cites.org/

Defenders of Wildlife
1130 17th St. NW
Washington, DC 20036
(202) 682-9400
1-800-385-9712
E-mail: defenders@mail.defenders.org
URL: http://www.defenders.org/

Earth System Research
Laboratory
National Oceanic and Atmospheric
Administration
325 Broadway
Boulder, CO 80305-3337
URL: http://www.esrl.noaa
.gov/gmd/

Ecosystems—Wildlife: Terrestrial
and Endangered Resources Program
U.S. Geological Survey
12201 Sunrise Valley Dr.
Reston, VA 20192
(703) 648-4050
URL: http://www.usgs.gov/ecosystems/

Environmental Defense Fund
1875 Connecticut Ave. NW, Ste. 600
Washington, DC 20009
1-800-684-3322
URL: http://www.edf.org/

Goddard Institute for Space Studies
National Aeronautics and Space
Administration
2880 Broadway
New York, NY 10025
(212) 678-5500
URL: http://www.giss.nasa.gov/

Greenpeace U.S.A.
702 H St. NW, Ste. 300
Washington, DC 20001
(202) 462-1177
1-800-722-6995
FAX: (202) 462-4507
E-mail: info@wdc.greenpeace.org
URL: http://www.greenpeace.org/usa/

Heritage Foundation
214 Massachusetts Ave. NE
Washington, DC 20002-4999
(202) 546-4400
URL: http://www.heritage.org/

International Union for Conservation
of Nature
Rue Mauverney 28
Gland, 1196, Switzerland
(011-41-22) 999-0000
FAX: (011-41-22) 999-0002
E-mail: mail@iucn.org
URL: http://www.iucn.org/

International Whaling Commission
The Red House
135 Station Rd.
Impington, CB24 9NP, United Kingdom
(011-44-1223) 233-971
FAX: (011-44-1223) 232-876
E-mail: secretariat@iwcoffice.org
URL: http://iwc.int/home

Land Trust Alliance
1660 L St. NW, Ste. 1100
Washington, DC 20036
(202) 638-4725
FAX: (202) 638-4730
E-mail: info@lta.org
URL: http://www.lta.org/

National Association of Home Builders
1201 15th St. NW
Washington, DC 20005
(202) 266-8200
1-800-368-5242
FAX: (202) 266-8400
URL: http://www.nahb.com/

National Audubon Society
225 Varick St.
New York, NY 10014
(212) 979-3000
URL: http://www.audubon.org/

National Forest Service
U.S. Department of Agriculture
1400 Independence Ave. SW
Washington, DC 20250-0003
1-800-832-1355
E-mail: webmaster@fs.fed.us
URL: http://www.fs.fed.us

National Marine Fisheries Service
National Oceanic and Atmospheric Administration
1315 East-West Hwy.
Silver Spring, MD 20910
(301) 713-2379
FAX: (301) 713-2384
URL: http://www.nmfs.noaa.gov/

National Marine Mammal Laboratory
National Oceanic and Atmospheric Administration
7600 Sand Point Way NE, Bldg. 4
Seattle, WA 98115
(206) 526-4000
FAX: (206) 526-4004
E-mail: afsc.webmaster@noaa.gov
URL: http://www.afsc.noaa.gov/nmml/

National Ocean Service
National Oceanic and Atmospheric Administration
1305 East-West Hwy.
Silver Spring, MD 20910
(301) 713-3010
E-mail: nos.info@noaa.gov
URL: http://oceanservice.noaa.gov/

National Park Service
1849 C St. NW
Washington, DC 20240
(202) 208-3818
URL: http://www.nps.gov/

National Wildlife Federation
11100 Wildlife Center Dr.
Reston, VA 20190
(703) 438-6000
1-800-822-9919
URL: http://www.nwf.org/

National Wildlife Health Center
U.S. Geological Survey
6006 Schroeder Rd.
Madison, WI 53711-6223
(608) 270-2400
FAX: (608) 270-2415
URL: http://www.nwhc.usgs.gov/

National Wildlife Refuge System
U.S. Fish and Wildlife Service
1-800-344-9453
URL: http://www.fws.gov/refuges/

Natural Resources Defense Council
40 W. 20th St.
New York, NY 10011
(212) 727-2700
FAX: (212) 727-1773
E-mail: nrdcinfo@nrdc.org
URL: http://www.nrdc.org/

Nature Conservancy
4245 N. Fairfax Dr., Ste. 100
Arlington, VA 22203-1606
(703) 841-5300
1-800-628-6860
URL: http://nature.org/

Northeast Fisheries Science Center
National Oceanic and Atmospheric Administration
166 Water St.
Woods Hole, MA 02543-1026
(508) 495-2000
URL: http://www.nefsc.noaa.gov/

Northern Prairie Wildlife Research Center
U.S. Geological Survey
8711 37th St. SE
Jamestown, ND 58401
(701) 253-5500
FAX: (701) 253-5553
E-mail: npwrc@usgs.gov
URL: http://www.npwrc.usgs.gov/

Northwest Fisheries Science Center
National Oceanic and Atmospheric Administration
2725 Montlake Blvd. East
Seattle, WA 98112
(206) 860-3200
FAX: (206) 860-3217
URL: http://www.nwfsc.noaa.gov/

Pacific Legal Foundation
National Litigation Center
930 G St.
Sacramento, CA 95814
(916) 419-7111
FAX: (916) 419-7747
URL: http://www.pacificlegal.org/

Sierra Club
85 Second St., Second Floor
San Francisco, CA 94105
(415) 977-5500
FAX: (415) 977-5797
E-mail: information@sierraclub.org
URL: http://www.sierraclub.org/

TRAFFIC North America—Regional Office
1250 24th St. NW
Washington, DC 20037
(202) 293-4800
FAX: (202) 775-8287
E-mail: tna@wwfus.org
URL: http://www.traffic.org/

United Nations Environment Programme
United Nations Ave., Gigiri
PO Box 30552
Nairobi, 00100, Kenya
(011-254-20) 7621234
E-mail: unepinfo@unep.org
URL: http://www.unep.org/

U.S. Army Corps of Engineers
441 G St. NW
Washington, DC 20314-1000
(202) 761-0011
E-mail: hq-publicaffairs@usace.army.mil
URL: http://www.usace.army.mil/

U.S. Department of Justice
Environment and Natural Resources Division
Law and Policy Section
PO Box 7415
Ben Franklin Station
Washington, DC 20044
(202) 514-2701
E-mail: webcontentmgr.enrd@usdoj.gov
URL: http://www.justice.gov/enrd/

U.S. Fish and Wildlife Service
Endangered Species Program
4401 N. Fairfax Dr., Rm. 420
Arlington, VA 22203
URL: http://www.fws.gov/endangered/

U.S. Government Accountability Office
441 G St. NW
Washington, DC 20548
(202) 512-3000
E-mail: contact@gao.gov
URL: http://www.gao.gov/

Water Resource Center
U.S. Environmental Protection Agency
1200 Pennsylvania Ave. NW
Washington, DC 20460
URL: http://water.epa.gov/aboutow/
ownews/wrc/

Western Ecological Research Center
U.S. Geological Survey
3020 State University Dr. East
Modoc Hall, Rm. 3006
Sacramento, CA 95819

(916) 278-9485
FAX: (916) 278-9475
URL: http://www.werc.usgs.gov/

WildEarth Guardians
516 Alto St.
Santa Fe, NM 87501
(505) 988-9126
FAX: (505) 213-1895
E-mail: info@wildearthguardians.org
URL: http://www.wildearthguardians.org/
site/PageServer

Wilderness Society
1615 M St. NW
Washington, DC 20036
(202) 833-2300
1-800-843-9453
URL: http://www.wilderness.org/

World Wildlife Fund
1250 24th St. NW
Washington, DC 20037
(202) 293-4800
URL: http://www.worldwildlife.org/

RESOURCES

A leading source of information on endangered species is the U.S. Fish and Wildlife Service (USFWS), an agency of the U.S. Department of the Interior. The USFWS oversees the Endangered Species List. Its comprehensive website (http://www.fws.gov/endangered/) includes news stories on threatened and endangered species, information about laws protecting endangered species, regional contacts for endangered species programs, and a searchable database called the Threatened and Endangered Species System (http://ecos.fws.gov/tess_public/) with information on all listed species. Each listed species has an information page that provides details regarding the status of the species (whether it is listed as threatened or endangered and in what geographic area), *Federal Register* documents pertaining to listing, information on habitat conservation plans and national wildlife refuges pertinent to the species, and, for many species, links to descriptions of biology and natural history. Particularly informative are the recovery plans published for many listed species. These recovery plans detail the background research on the natural history of endangered species and list measures that should be adopted to aid in conservation.

The USFWS also maintains updated tables of the number of threatened and endangered species by taxonomic group, as well as lists of threatened and endangered U.S. species. The agency publishes the bimonthly *Endangered Species Bulletin*, which provides information on new listings, delistings, and reclassifications, besides news articles on endangered species. Finally, the USFWS prints an annual report on expenditures that have been made under the Endangered Species Act.

The National Marine Fisheries Service (NMFS) is responsible for the oversight of threatened and endangered marine animals and anadromous fish. The NMFS is a division of the National Oceanic and Atmospheric Administration (NOAA), which also operates the National Marine Mammal Laboratory, the Northeast Fisheries Science Center, and the Northwest Fisheries Science Center. NOAA's National Ocean Service is an excellent source of information about marine creatures.

The U.S. Geological Survey (USGS) performs research on many imperiled animal species. Data sheets on individual species are available from the USGS National Wildlife Health Center. Other important USGS centers include the Western Ecological Research Center, the Northern Prairie Wildlife Research Center, the Nonindigenous Aquatic Species information resource at the Center for Aquatic Resource Studies (http://nas.er.usgs.gov/), and the Ecosystems—Wildlife: Terrestrial and Endangered Resources Program.

Information on federal lands and endangered species management can be found via the National Wildlife Refuge System, the National Park Service, and the National Forest Service. Information on water quality in the United States is available via the U.S. Environmental Protection Agency (http://www.epa.gov/gateway/science/water.html). Information on wetlands can be found at the USFWS's National Wetlands Inventory (http://www.fws.gov/wetlands/).

Data and information related to global warming are available from the National Aeronautics and Space Administration's Goddard Institute for Space Studies and from NOAA's Earth System Research Laboratory, Global Monitoring Division.

Other federal agencies that proved useful for this book were the U.S. Department of Justice's Environment and Natural Resources Division, which defends the federal government in court cases involving environmental laws, such as the Endangered Species Act, and the U.S. Army Corps of Engineers, which maintains the National Inventory of Dams. The Department of the Interior operates the National Atlas of the United States (http://nationalatlas.gov/), an online mapping tool. The U.S. Government Accountability Office and the Congressional Research Service publish a number of reports that assess the policies and effectiveness of the Endangered Species Program.

The International Union for Conservation of Nature (IUCN) provides news articles on a wide array of worldwide conservation issues and maintains the *Red List of Threatened Species Version 2013.2* (http://www.iucnred list.org/about/summary-statistics). This site includes an extensive database of information on IUCN-listed threatened species. Species information that is available includes the Red List endangerment category, the year the species was assessed, the countries in which the species is found, a list of the habitat types the species occupies, major threats to continued existence, and current population trends. Brief descriptions of ecology and natural history and of conservation measures for protecting listed species are also available. Searches can also be performed by taxonomic group, Red List categories, country, region, or habitat.

The Convention on International Trade in Endangered Species of Wild Fauna and Flora (CITES) provides information on international trade in endangered species. It includes a species database of protected flora and fauna in the three CITES appendixes, as well as information on the history and aims of the convention and its current programs.

Many private organizations are dedicated to the conservation of listed species and their ecosystems. Readers with interest in a particular endangered species are advised to conduct Internet searches to locate these groups. The Save the Manatee Club, which focuses on West Indian manatees, and the Save Our Springs Alliance, which focuses on protection of the endangered Barton Springs salamander, are only two of many examples.

BirdLife International provides diverse resources on global bird conservation. It is an association of nongovernmental conservation organizations that has over 2.5 million members worldwide.

AmphibiaWeb (http://amphibiaweb.org/) provides detailed information on global amphibian declines. It maintains a watch list of recently extinct and declining species, discusses potential causes of amphibian declines and deformities, and provides detailed information on amphibian biology and conservation. AmphibiaWeb also sponsors a discussion board where readers can submit questions regarding amphibians.

TRAFFIC (http://www.traffic.org/) was originally founded to help implement the CITES treaty, but it now addresses diverse issues in the wildlife trade. It is a joint wildlife trade monitoring organization of the World Wildlife Fund and the IUCN. TRAFFIC publishes several periodicals and report series on the wildlife trade, including the *TRAFFIC Bulletin*, the TRAFFIC Online Report Series, and the *Species in Danger Series*.

The International Whaling Commission provides information on whaling regulations, whale sanctuaries, and other issues that are associated with whales and whaling. The Center for Biological Diversity plays a major role in the petition and listing process under the Endangered Species Act and conducts scientific investigations regarding imperiled species.

A useful historical resource was *The Endangered Species Act at Thirty: Renewing the Conservation Promise* (Dale D. Goble, J. Michael Scott, and Frank W. Davis, eds., 2006). The Gallup Organization provided information related to public polls that have been conducted in recent years concerning environmental issues.

Information Plus sincerely thanks all the previously mentioned organizations for the valuable information they provided.

INDEX

Page references in italics refer to photographs. References with the letter t following them indicate the presence of a table. The letter f indicates a figure. If more than one table or figure appears on a particular page, the exact item number for the table or figure being referenced is provided.

A

Acid deposition, 15
Africa, 117–118, 119
Agriculture, 55, 141, 143
Alaotra grebes, 3
Alaska
    Arctic National Wildlife Refuge, 11, 12f
    polar bears, 51–52
    sea otters, 45, 46(f3.7)
    subsistence taking, 24
    whaling, 41
Alaska National Interest Lands Conservation Act, 11
Aleutian Canada geese, 134, *135(f8.14)*
Alliance for the Wild Rockies, 60
Alligators, 95
American chestnut trees, 151, 152f, 153
American crocodile, 95, *96f*
American Farm Bureau Federation, 107
Amphibian Research and Monitoring Initiative, 84
Amphibians
    deformities, 87
    expenditures, 85(t6.2)
    foreign imperiled species, 87–88, 88t
    frogs and toads, 86–87
    salamanders, 84–86
    types, 83–84
Anadromous fish. *See* Marine and anadromous fish
ANWR (Arctic National Wildlife Refuge), 11, 12f
Arachnids, 146–149, 146(t9.4), 149f

Aransas National Wildlife Refuge, 131
Arctic National Wildlife Refuge (ANWR), 11, 12f
Arctic sea ice melt, 51–52
Ash Meadows naucorid, 143f
Asia, 113, 119
Atlantic Large Whale Entanglement Response Program, 39
Atlantic sturgeon, 62
Austin, TX, 85

B

Babbitt, Bruce, 33
Babbitt v. Sweet Home Chapter of Communities for a Better Oregon, 30
Bald eagles, 134, *134f*
Baleen whales, 37–38
Ballard, Save the Manatee Club v., 49
Barton Springs salamander, 85
Bats, 101, 103–104, 104f
Beach lighting, 94
Beach renourishment, 93–94
Bearded seals, 42, 43f
Bears, 50–52, 51f, 104–106
Beaufort Sea, 50
Bees, 141, 143
Beetles, 143–144, 144f
Benefits of savings species, 7–8
Bennett v. Spear, 30
Big cats, 113
Big game, 118
Bighorn sheep, 108
Biodiversity
    Convention on Biological Diversity, 4, 13
    ecosystems, 4–5
    mass extinctions, 3
Birds, 122t–123t
    Alaotra grebes, 3
    expenditures, 123(t8.2)

    foreign imperiled species, 135, 136t–139t
    passerines, 124–126
    raptors, 126–127
    success stories, 134–135
    threatened U.S. species, 121, 123
    threats to, 132–134, 133f
    water birds, 127, 129–132
    woodpeckers, 123–124, 124f
Bison, 4, *4f*, 108
Bitterroot ecosystem, 106
Black-footed ferrets, 109–111, *111f*
Bleaching, coral, 79–80
BLM (U.S. Bureau of Land Management), 30, 174
Boating, 47–49
BP oil spill, 132–133
Brown pelicans, 134–135, 135(f8.15)
Brown tree snakes, 133–134
Buena Vista Lake ornate shrew, 113
Bull trout, 60, 61f, 62
Bush, George W., 33
Butterflies, 144–145, 145(f9.3), 171(f10.4)
Bycatch
    dolphins, 42
    marine mammals, 35
    sea turtles, 93

C

Cabinet-Yaak ecosystem, 106
Caecilians, 83
California
    condors, 127, 129f
    giant garter snakes, 94
    Los Angeles basin, 175f
    plants, 173–176
    red-legged frogs, 86–87
    salamanders, 85–86
    sea otters, 45–47, 48f
    tiger salamanders, 85–86, *86f*

International Code of Botanical Nomenclature, 2
International Commission on Zoological Nomenclature, 2
International Convention for the Regulation of Whaling, 39
International issues
  amphibians, 87–88, 88*t*
  arachnids, 149
  birds, 135, 136*t*–139*t*
  clam, snail, crustacean, and corals, 78*t*
  conservation efforts, 13
  corals, 81, 81*t*
  dolphins and porpoises, 42
  fish, 68, 70*t*
  insects, 145, 146(*t*9.3)
  manatees and dugong, 49–50
  marine mammals, 37(*t*3.2)
  mollusks and crustaceans, 78
  number of imperiled species, 5, 6*t*
  plants, 177, 177*t*
  reptiles, 95
  sea otters, 47
  sea turtle protection, 93
  seals and sea lions, 44
  terrestrial mammals, 113, 114*t*–117*t*, 117–119
  whales, 41
International Union for Conservation of Nature (IUCN), 2
International Whaling Commission, 39
Introductions, California condor, 127
Invasive species
  birds, effects on, 133–134
  fish, 57
  threat of, 14–15
  zebra and quagga mussels, 74–75, 75*f*
IUCN (International Union for Conservation of Nature), 2
IUCN Red List Categories and Criteria, 3
Ivory trade, 117–118

J

Jackson County, MS, 132
Johnson's seagrass, 171(*f*10.3)

K

Karst caves, 146, 147*f*
Kauai Cave wolf spiders, 148
Kauai Island caves, 148*f*
Kemp's ridley sea turtles, 92
Keystone species, 5
Kincaid's lupine, 171(*f*10.4)
Klamath River basin, 66–68, 67*f*

L

Labeling, dolphin-safe tuna, 42
Land conservation, 9
Land Trust Alliance, 12

Land use, 14
Lawsuits
  bull trout, 60, 62
  ESA, 12–13
  gray wolves, 107
  Klamath River basin controversy, 66–68
  overprotection lawsuits, 29
  Peirson's milk-vetch, 174–175
  valley elderberry longhorn beetle, 144
Least terns, 129, 131(*f*8.7)
Leatherback sea turtles, 92
Legislation
  Equal Access to Judgment Act, 28–29
  Marine Turtle Protection Act (Florida), 93–94
  See also Endangered Species Act; Marine Mammal Protection Act
Lichens, 172
Lighting, beach, 94
Linnaeus, Carolus, 1
Listing process, Endangered Species Act, 12–13, 20–22, 20*f*
Little Tennessee River, 29–30, 54
Livestock losses, 107
Lizards, 94–95, 95*f*
Loggerhead sea turtles, 92
Logging, 30, 126
Los Angeles basin, CA, 175*f*
Lynxes, 109, 110*f*

M

Mammals. *See* Marine mammals; Terrestrial mammals
Manatees and dugongs, 47–50, *50*
Marbled murrelets, 129–130, *131*(*f*8.8)
Marine and anadromous fish, 62–68, 62*t*, 63*f*, 63*t*, 69*f*, 70*t*
Marine Mammal Health and Stranding Response Program, 39
Marine Mammal Protection Act
  manatee protection areas, 48–49
  polar bears, 50, 52
  provisions, 35–36
  Steller sea lions, 65
  subsistence taking, 24
Marine mammals, 36*t*
  apex predators, 35
  dolphins and porpoises, 41–42
  Endangered Species Act expenditures, 37(*t*3.3)
  foreign endangered and threatened species, 37(*t*3.2)
  manatees and dugongs, 47–50
  Marine Mammal Protection Act, 35–36
  polar bears, 50–52
  sea otters, 44–47
  seals and sea lions, 44
  sonar, 30
  subsistence taking, 24

whales, 37–41
Marine Turtle Protection Act (Florida), 93–94
Mass extinctions, 2–3
Migration, salmon, 63
Migratory shore birds, 127, 129
Migratory songbirds, 125–126
Migratory species convention, 13
Migratory whooping cranes, 131
Milk-vetch, 173–175
Minnesota, 107
Mississippi sandhill cranes, 132, 132*f*
Mobile, AL, 91
Monito geckos, 94–95, 95*f*
Montana, 105–106
Moths, 144
Mussels. *See* Clams and mussels

N

National Association of Home Builders v. Defenders of Wildlife, 30
National Inventory of Dams, 54
National Marine Fisheries Service (NMFS)
  Endangered Species Act expenditures, 30–31
  federal agency actions, 25
  Klamath River basin controversy, 67
  management of listed species, 5–6
  marine and anadromous fish, 62
  marine mammal protection, 36
  private-party petitions, 28
  recovery potential priority ranking system, 26*t*
  sea turtles, 93, 94
  whale recovery plans, 40–41
  white abalone, 77
National Oceanic and Atmospheric Administration (NOAA), 39–40, 80
National Park Service, 9, 11, 94
National Petroleum Reserve—Alaska (NPRA), 11, 12*f*
National Snow and Ice Data Center, 52
National Wilderness Preservation System, 9
National Wildlife Federation, 14
National Wildlife Refuge System, 9, 10*t*–11*t*
Natural Resources Defense Council, Winter v., 30
Natural stressors, 14
Nature Conservancy, 12
Nitrogen deposition, 15
Nixon, Richard M., 32
NMFS. *See* National Marine Fisheries Service
NOAA (National Oceanic and Atmospheric Administration), 39–40, 80
Nongovernmental organizations, 28–29
North Carolina, 149
North Cascades ecosystem, 106
North Continental Divide ecosystem, 105

U.S. Department of Justice, 29
U.S. Department of State, 93
U.S. Department of the Interior, 133
U.S. Fish and Wildlife Service (USFWS)
  amphibian deformities, 87
  arachnids, 147
  bats, 103–104
  black-footed ferrets, 111
  budget, 31*t*
  bull trout, 60, 62
  California red-legged frogs, 87
  California tiger salamander, 86
  candidate species backlog, 28
  Endangered Species Act expenditures, 30–31
  expenditures on steelhead, 68
  extinct species, 4
  federal agency actions, 25
  five-year status reviews, 23
  gopher tortoises, 91–92
  grizzly bears, 105–106
  Hawaiian forest birds, 125
  Hawaiian plants, 173
  Higgins eye pearlymussels, 72, 74
  land conservation, 9
  Los Angeles basin plants, 176
  management of listed species, 5–6
  manatee protection, 49
  marbled murrelets, 129–130
  marine mammal protection, 36
  Monito geckos, 94–95
  northern spotted owls, 126–127

oil field waste pits, 133
overprotection lawsuits, 29
pallid sturgeon, 59–60
Peirson's milk-vetch, 174–175
piping plovers, 129
plant categories, 172
plants, 153, 171
polar bears, 50–51
private-party petitions, 28
recovery plans, 25–26, 25*t*
red-cockaded woodpecker, 124
sea otters, 44–45
sea turtles, 94
South Florida Multi-species Recovery Plan, 176
Southwestern willow flycatchers, 124–125
Utah prairie dogs, 112
valley elderberry longhorn beetles, 144
vernal pool fairy shrimp, 78
Virginia northern flying squirrels, 112–113
wood storks, 131
U.S. Forest Service, 11
U.S. Geological Survey, 84
U.S. Navy, 30
USFWS. *See* U.S. Fish and Wildlife Service
Utah prairie dogs, 111–112

V

Valley elderberry longhorn beetles, 143–144, 144*f*

Vernal pool fairy shrimp, 77–78
Virginia northern flying squirrels, 112–113, 113*f*
Volunteers, 94

W

Wading birds, 130–131
Washington, 65, 66, 106
Water birds, 127, 129–132
West Indian manatees, 47–50, *50f*
West Virginia northern flying squirrels, 112–113, 113*f*
Western Great Lakes DPS, 107
Whales, 2*t*, 38–41, 38*f*, 40*t*, 41*t*
White abalone, 76–77
White rhinoceros, *120f*
White-nose syndrome, 103–104
Whooping cranes, *131*(*f*8.9)
Wildlife, benefits of, 7–8
Wildlife preserves, 9, 10*t*–11*t*, 11, 13
Winter v. Natural Resources Defense Council, 30
Wolves, 106–108, *107f*
Wood storks, 130–131
Woodpeckers, 124*f*
Woods Hole Oceanographic Institution, 39
World Commission on Protected Areas, 13
World Conservation Protection Centre, 13

Z

Zebra mussels, 74–75, 75*f*